BROOKINGS PAPERS ON EDUCATION POLICY

2000

Diane Ravitch
Editor

Sponsored by
the Brown Center on
Education Policy

Brookings Institution Press
Washington, D.C.

1775 Massachusetts Avenue, N.W., Washington, DC 20036

Library of Congress Catalog Card No. 98-664027
ISSN 1096-2719
ISBN 0-8157-7357-9

BROOKINGS PAPERS ON EDUCATION POLICY

2000

THE BROOKINGS INSTITUTION

The Brookings Institution is an independent organization devoted to nonpartisan research, education, and publication in economics, government, foreign policy, and the social sciences generally. Its principal purposes are to aid in the development of sound public policies and to promote public understanding of issues of national importance.

The Institution was founded on December 8, 1927, to merge the activities of the Institute for Government Research, founded in 1916, the Institute of Economics, founded in 1922, and the Robert Brookings Graduate School of Economics and Government, founded in 1924.

The general administration of the Institution is the responsibility of a Board of Trustees charged with safeguarding the independence of the staff and fostering the most favorable conditions for scientific research and publication. The immediate direction of the policies, program, and staff of the Institution is vested in the president, assisted by an advisory committee of the officers and staff.

In publishing a study, the Institution presents it as a competent treatment of a subject worthy of public consideration. The interpretations and conclusions in such publications are those of the author or authors and do not necessarily reflect the views of.the other staff members, officers, or trustees of the Brookings Institution.

BROOKINGS PAPERS ON EDUCATION POLICY contains the edited versions of the papers and comments that were presented at the third annual Brookings conference on education policy, held on May 17–18, 1999. The conference gives federal, state, and local policymakers an independent, nonpartisan forum to analyze policies intended to improve student performance. Each year Brookings convenes some of the best-informed analysts from various disciplines to review the current situation in education and to consider proposals for reform. This year's discussion focused on the Reauthorization of the Elementary and Secondary Education Act. The conference and journal were funded by the Herman and George R. Brown Chair in Educational Studies at Brookings. Additional support from the Miriam K. Carliner Endowment for Economic Studies and from the John M. Olin Foundation is gratefully acknowledged.

The papers in this volume have been modified to reflect some of the insights contributed by the discussions at the conference. In all cases the papers are the result of the authors' thinking and do not imply agreement by those attending the conference. Nor do the materials presented here necessarily represent the views of the staff members, officers, or trustees of the Brookings Institution.

2000 Subscription Rates

Individuals $19.95
Institutions $34.95

Standing order plans are available by calling 1-800/275-1447 or 202/797-6258
For foreign orders add $6.00 surface mail and $14.00 airmail

Send subscription orders to the Brookings Institution, Department 037, Washington, DC 20042-0037. Or call 202/797-6258 or toll free 1-800/275-1447. Or email bibooks@brook.edu.

Visit Brookings online at www.brookings.edu.

Beginning with the 1999 editions, all Brookings periodicals are available online through Online Computer Library Center. For details, contact the OCLC subscriptions department at 1-800/848-5878, ext. 6251.

Conference Participants

Charles Barone, *Office of Representative George Miller*
Eve Bither, *U.S. Department of Education*
Kristin Bunce, *U.S. Department of Education*
Sheila Byrd, *independent scholar*
Joseph Conaty, *U.S. Department of Education*
David Deschryver, *Center for Education Reform*
Emerson Elliott, *National Council for Accreditation of Teacher Education*
Robert Funk, *Center for Education Reform*
Mathew Gandal, *ACHIEVE*
Jane Hannaway, *Urban Institute*
Judith Johnson, *U.S. Department of Education*
Christina Jordan, *The Century Foundation*
Richard Kahlenberg, *The Century Foundation*
Marci Kanstoroom, *Thomas B. Fordham Foundation*
Helen Ladd, *Duke University*
Townsend Lange, *Office of Senator Judd Gregg*
Robert Maranto, *Federal Executive Institute*
Pamela Mendeles, *New York Times On-Line*
Denzel McGuire, *Senate Subcommittee on Children and Families*
Joyce Ladner, *Brookings Institution*
Ann O'Leary, *U.S. Department of Education*
Jennifer Olsen, *Heritage Foundation*
Michael Petrilli, *Thomas B. Fordham Foundation*
Heidi Ramirez, *U.S. Department of Education*
Nina Shokraii Rees, *Heritage Foundation*
Andrew Rotherham, *Progressive Policy Institute*
William L. Rukeyser, *Learning in the Real World*
Isabel Sawhill, *Brookings Institution*
Lisa Smith, *U.S. News and World Report*
William Testa, *Federal Reserve Bank of Chicago*
Roy Truby, *National Assessment Governing Board*
Wayne Upshaw, *Office of Management and Budget*
Janice Weinman, *U.S. Department of Education*
Susan Wilhelm, *U.S. Department of Education*

Introduction

DIANE RAVITCH

IN MAY 1999 the annual conference of the Brown Center on Education Policy of the Brookings Institution was devoted to a close examination of major components of the Elementary and Secondary Education Act (ESEA). The discussion was timely because the act was due to be reauthorized in 2000. This discussion, and the papers in this volume, provide a valuable opportunity to reflect on the evolving federal role in K-12 education. Until 1965, the federal government's involvement in elementary and secondary education was circumscribed and small; now, with the multiplication of federal programs and the demand for them, drawing the line between federal, state, and local roles in education has become increasingly difficult.

One of the enduring themes in the history of American education has been the effort by many educators and public officials to get the federal government to provide direct aid to public elementary and secondary schools. In the late nineteenth century, and then again in the early decades of the twentieth century, supporters of a substantial federal role in education attempted and failed to pass legislation. A modest federal role was established by passage of the Smith-Hughes Vocational Education Act in 1917. An even larger role was briefly assayed during the Great Depression of the 1930s, when the federal government created the Civilian Conservation Corps and the National Youth Administration, both of which were quietly eliminated during World War II at the urging of the leaders of public education, who wanted aid to public schools, not federal programs that were independent of the public system. Following the Soviet launch of *Sputnik* in 1957, Congress enacted the National Defense Education Act, which was intended to spur enrollments in science, mathematics, and foreign languages.

The general aid to education that educators sought remained elusive until 1965, when Congress passed the Elementary and Secondary Education Act in response to public concern about the schooling of disadvantaged children. This law, which represents the major federal commitment to the nation's elementary and secondary schools, has been reauthorized regularly since then, and it is up for reauthorization in 2000. No other single piece of federal legislation reveals so clearly the peculiar strengths and weaknesses of the federal role in education.

In higher education, the federal government has supported the expansion of educational opportunity by underwriting the cost of tuition for students who could not afford it. Beginning with the Servicemen's Readjustment Act of 1944 (known popularly as the "GI Bill of Rights"), the federal government assumed a clear responsibility for making higher education available to qualified students. Providing grants and loans to college students is no longer controversial, and policy debates are limited to deciding how much federal aid should be available for students at different income levels.

In precollegiate education, however, the uses of federal authority continue to stir heated controversy. In large part, this is because the federal role in the schools reaches far beyond questions of financing to unsettled issues of curriculum, method, and control. Although the federal government supplies less than 10 percent of the nation's K-12 education budget, federal legislation and regulations have a large impact on the cost and functioning of the public schools, in some instances (such as special education) mandating costly programs without supplying full funding for them. Unlike higher education, where federal aid goes to students in the form of scholarships, federal aid for K-12 education goes to states and school districts.

Historically, opponents of federal aid to the schools worried that the immense power of the federal government would be used to impose federal solutions on local schools and that children in Catholic schools would not receive a fair share of federal funds. Southern members of Congress opposed federal aid to the schools as well, fearing that the federal government would use its authority to end public school segregation. These fears were overcome by President Lyndon B. Johnson in 1965, who shepherded the ESEA legislation through a Congress with large Democratic majorities in both houses. President Johnson assuaged the concerns of urban representatives by insisting that the aid would benefit needy children, including those in Catholic schools; this key compromise was later voided by the U.S. Supreme Court.

The Elementary and Secondary Education Act has always been viewed as a vehicle for equal educational opportunity, funding programs and supplying revenues for disadvantaged students. It defines the role of the federal government as a guarantor of educational equality. The legislation promptly fulfilled the worst fears of segregationists. Soon after its passage, federal officials threatened to withhold ESEA funds from southern school districts until they dismantled the dual system of racially segregated schools. Working in tandem with enforcement of the Civil Rights Act by the federal judiciary, federal officials used the ESEA program as leverage to end state-imposed racial segregation.

Since 1965, ESEA has grown to encompass dozens of different programs. Altogether, the various programs authorized by ESEA receive appropriations of about $11 billion annually. The largest of these programs is Title I, which sends money to local school districts based on their enrollment of poor students and is especially popular because it allocates federal funds to almost every congressional district. Among the other programs in ESEA are bilingual education; the Eisenhower professional development program (teacher training); aid for technology programs; the Safe and Drug-Free Schools and Communities program; Goals 2000 (aid to states to strengthen their standards); and research, assessment, and statistics. In addition, there is a program called Impact Aid (for communities presumably burdened by their proximity to military bases or other federal facilities); a program to aid the development of charter schools; a program to advance "women's educational equity"; the Even Start family literacy program; and programs to support the education of Native Americans, Native Hawaiians, Native Alaskans, migrant children, homeless children, the gifted and talented, and migrant children, as well as civic education, arts education, and various forms of technical assistance. This list does not exhaust the full menu of programs encompassed in ESEA but suggests its wide reach and random nature.

Because it was not possible, and possibly not very useful, to examine all of these programs, some of which are small, this volume of *Brookings Papers on Education Policy* looks closely at those programs that appear to have the largest impact, both in terms of cost and in what they may suggest about the general principles that characterize the federal role in education. (Other major federal education programs, most notably special education and Head Start, are not part of ESEA.) The topics discussed in the papers are a reconsideration of the federal role in schools; the Title I program; the bilingual education program; the Safe and Drug-Free Schools and Community program; the Technology for Education program; professional development of teachers; Goals 2000; and federal support for education research. Each of these papers is followed by two commentaries.

Paul T. Hill's discussion of the federal role in education raises fundamental questions about how federal programs effect the schools. An analyst for many years at the Rand Corporation, Hill observes that the federal role as currently defined, with extensive reliance on categorical programs, each of which has separate funding streams and discrete personnel, has disrupted the coherence of schools. The multiplication of programs, which once seemed to be a good idea, has led to unforeseen and undesirable consequences. The more federally funded programs in a school, he argues, the weaker is the authority of the principal and the less able is the school to focus relentlessly on teaching and learning. Instead, the school becomes entangled in directives, regulations, and contradictory missions. Federal programs have also had the unintended consequence of "colonizing" state education departments, by placing a majority of the department's employees on federal payrolls. The negative consequences of the federal role in schooling are not, Hill suggests, what its earlier opponents feared; the federal government has not imposed nefarious schemes on local schools. Instead, the real burden of the federal role stems from its structural rigidity and its inflexibility. He proposes a way out of this dilemma, while recognizing that interest groups have been aligned to keep the status quo intact, regardless of its egregious effects on schools.

George Farkas and L. Shane Hall assess the Title I program. (Farkas developed and implemented a well-validated reading program for disadvantaged children.) They find that the Title I program has yet to produce consistent improvement in the reading and mathematics achievement of poor children. This stems in part, they note, from Title I being a funding stream, not a program with distinctive features. They point out that school districts regularly use these funds to pay for expenses that would otherwise come from district sources, despite clear congressional requirements that districts must maintain their own level of effort and must use the Title I funds to supplement, not supplant, their own funds. They pay particular attention to the 1994 reauthorization of Title I, which encouraged schools to adopt "whole school" reforms and allowed funding to cover children in all grades. Some in Congress and the Clinton administration have hailed the success of these changes, but Farkas and Hall report that their true effect was to reduce the money and attention devoted to the poorest and most disadvantaged children in the early elementary grades. They contend that the most effective use of federal funds would be to concentrate singularly on the children who have fallen far behind, and to do this in preschool or in the first three years of schooling. But this is precisely what Title I no longer does, according to their analysis. Their proposals for reform emphasize the importance of training tutors to use scientifically validated methods of teaching reading. Absent this training, they believe, Title I funds will continue to be diverted in ways that subsidize the whole school but fail to help the neediest children, who are on a dangerous downward trajectory unless they get direct, personal attention.

Lawrence W. Sherman subjects the Safe and Drug-Free Schools and Communities program to withering analysis and reveals the inherent flaws of what he calls "symbolic pork." The program is popular because it addresses subjects about which the public is deeply concerned: school safety and substance abuse. Yet Sherman shows that, despite public perceptions and despite several recent incidents of horrific gun violence, the schools are very safe. Violence in the schools, he finds, is not a widespread problem. The schools with the greatest number of violent events are those in the most dangerous communities, and their problems should be addressed in the streets, not in the schools. Furthermore, the most popular programs in the schools to promote safety or combat drug and alcohol use with the help of federal funds are ineffective. Most of the current appropriation of about $600 million, he holds, is wasted on activities that have no bearing on the problems. Nonetheless, Congress and the administration continue to support the program and to avoid responsibility for changing it. While acknowledging that a politically popular program is generally evidence-proof, Sherman nonetheless makes specific proposals to tie future funding to evidence of effectiveness. Sherman's paper suggests an important principle: Having a well-named program is more important than having an effective program. No member of Congress is likely to stand up and oppose a program that promises safe and drug-free schools.

Robert B. Schwartz and Marian A. Robinson evaluate the effects of the Goals 2000 program, which was first authorized in 1994. Although it is difficult to isolate the effects of this particular federal program from ongoing state activities, Schwartz and Robinson conclude that Goals 2000 has made a genuine contribution by encouraging states to set academic standards and by infusing the language of standards into other federal programs as well. They describe the continuity of purpose from the Bush administration's America 2000 program to the Clinton administration's Goals 2000 program but note the erosion of political support among members of both parties in Congress around these issues. Having stimulated the states to set standards, the federal effort appears to have reached a stalemate. In light of these political realities, Schwartz and Robinson predict that the responsibility will pass from the federal government to the states and the private sector. This may be an example of a successful federal policy whose longevity was limited by the fact that it had no interest groups, no constituency to fight for its survival.

Christine H. Rossell evaluates the federal bilingual education program. Based on her studies of the implementation of bilingual education in California, Massachusetts, and New York City, she concludes that the program is of dubious value. She finds that the means by which children are assigned to it are arbitrary and can be easily manipulated by states and districts to raise or lower the eligible population and that the definition of "bilingual education" varies widely from place to place. She concludes with specific ideas to make the program more valuable for the language minority children who are its intended beneficiaries by fundamentally transforming the program.

Julia E. Koppich examines the Dwight D. Eisenhower Professional Development Program, which is one of many teacher training programs funded by the federal government. She notes that its earlier emphasis on mathematics and science kept it admirably targeted to specific school subjects, making it a valuable resource for states and local school districts that wanted to strengthen teachers' knowledge of their subject. Since its last reauthorization, however, recipients were able to use the funds for other school subjects, thus diluting its focus. She urges a rededication of the program so that it specifically aims to improve teachers' subject matter knowledge.

Gary Chapman measures the impact of the federal investment in technology in the schools. Whether this is a worthwhile investment, he notes, depends on one's view of technology as a learning tool. After carefully considering the case for and against technology in the schools, Chapman comes out for a balanced approach; he recognizes the enormous importance of technology in the workplace of the future but raises serious questions about children's need for learning experiences that computers cannot provide.

Maris A. Vinovskis examines the disappointing history of the federal Office of Educational Research and Improvement (OERI). Vinovskis finds that OERI, originally known as the National Institute of Education, has never been able to attract a distingushed group of education researchers, nor has it ever been able to escape the suspicion on Capitol Hill that its research is affected by political considerations. This perception has been strengthened, he notes, by the lobbying activities of the federal regional education laboratories, as well as by the Clinton administration's surprise decision not to reappoint the well-regarded commissioner of education statistics in 1999. Vinovskis offers suggestions for strengthening the research agency and considers proposals for reconstituting it as a quasi-independent agency with its own bipartisan board but warns that the agency may not survive unless it can command broad respect for the quality of its research.

These papers raise fundamental questions about how to improve the federal role in education. A theme that runs through several of these papers is that powerful interest groups can protect an ineffective program, regardless of poor evaluations. This rigidity guarantees that federal programs cannot be changed unless those who receive dollars from them are protected in the future. Even if evaluations show that federal dollars have not made a difference, it does not matter when it comes time for reauthorization. The losers are the children who were supposed to be the beneficiaries of federal programs and, indirectly, the nation, which thought that it was investing in needy children, not the status quo. Once the federal dollars start to flow, the program is safe. No matter how ineffective the program, no matter how many evaluations document its failure, it gets reauthorized on the hope or claim that the next five years will be better than the last five. Particularly powerful is a program with a swell-sounding name such as Safe and Drug-Free Schools and Communities or the tiny Women's Educational Equity Program, which still provides funds for "gender-fair" materials more than twenty years after the nation's publishers began to scour their products for any evidence of gender bias. How many members of Congress will go on record against "women's educational equity" when only a few million dollars are involved? It seems that the way to achieve eternal life is to become a federal program with a name that states highly laudable purposes.

Certain questions must be asked again and again: What should the federal government do that only the federal government can do well? What is the federal government doing now that it should stop doing? What is the federal government doing now that it should do differently because what it is doing is not working?

Certainly, the federal government must be responsible for statistics and research, and it must continue its financial aid to disadvantaged youngsters, though the present formula for distributing that aid must be revised to make sure that it helps the children who need help, instead of adding to the bureaucracy and paperwork of state and local school districts. What is it doing that it should not be doing? It should certainly not sustain programs that waste money or that cannot show any measurable benefit for children. What is it doing now that should be done differently? Most of the essays in this volume propose concrete changes that could improve the way that the federal government dispenses financial aid to education.

These issues become urgent in the year 2000 because of the proliferation of proposals to expand the federal role in education. Should the federal government subsidize school construction (and relieve states of that burden)? Should it pay to add more teachers to the nation's schools? Should it pay for teacher training? Should it pay to put computers and Internet access in every classroom? Should it pay for after-school programs? What the nation seems to have lost is any sense of principle with which to answer such questions. If Americans say, "Yes, the federal government should pay for all this and more," then they must figure out how to avoid the inflexibility and ridigity of federal regulation, how to preserve local autonomy, how to make sure that public schools are something more than the sum of whatever federal programs have been passed. Ultimately, schools are not just a conglomeration of programs; they are institutions that are responsible for the most vulnerable members of society. The adults in schools must have the power and authority to make decisions on the spot, decisions that may differ from school to school, depending on the circumstances and the individual children involved. As the federal role in schooling continues to grow far beyond anyone's imaginings, the need to make sense of it grows, too. Federal education policy should be based on clear evidence of effectiveness, not on wishful thinking and the need to satisfy interest groups. Congress must be prepared to attend to rigorous evaluations of its programs and to eliminate those that fail. Until that happens, the role of the federal government in education is likely to remain disappointing.

The Federal Role in Education

PAUL T. HILL

THE ACTION IN Kurt Vonnegut's novel *Cat's Cradle* is driven by an effort to protect the world from ice nine, a form of water that is solid at high temperatures. Normal water is transformed into ice nine upon contact, so that a drop of it can freeze an ocean and an animal that drinks or breathes it is instantly frozen solid.

Has the federal government been the ice nine of K-12 education, inexorably transforming public schools from intimate community assets into complex, impersonal, rule-driven institutions? This paper will argue in the affirmative. Contact with the federal government has not transformed schools as absolutely or to as disastrous an extent as Vonnegut's book portrays contact with ice nine. But many of the weaknesses of today's public schools are caused by their forced adoption of attributes common to bureaucracies and regulated industries, and not previously common to schools.

The federal government can eliminate the aspects of its program that weaken schools without abandoning its commitment to equal educational opportunity for poor, minority, and handicapped children. Federal policy can be rebuilt on the premise that no program or rule must burden schools if any other way exists to reach a public objective.

Since enactment of the Elementary and Secondary Education Act (ESEA) in 1965, federal programs and related state and court actions have made schools more like standard government institutions in three ways, by forcing schools to (1) become operators of programs and appliers of rules, instead of intimate communities; (2) cope with a complex political environment engineered by courts, bureaucracies, and legislatures; and (3) operate under constraints imposed by flawed proxy measures of equity that facilitate government oversight but interfere with effective instruction.

These government-imposed preoccupations differ from schools' specific mission, which is to instruct, inspire, and nurture children. Are government and good schools completely incompatible? This paper will answer no, schools can be both public and good. However, American society has now gone too far in patterning schools on other government institutions and is paying the price, as public schools become more formal, politicized, and regulated as well as less effective.

The federal government had good reason to become engaged with the public schools when it did, in the aftermath of the *Brown* v. *Board of Education* decision in 1954, and not all the consequences of government involvement can or should be reversed. Before the federal government accepted a role in K-12 education, schools in white areas had no obligation to admit African American students or anyone else who was "different." Schools could readily give up on children who were slow to learn, and severely handicapped students could be excluded altogether. Federal intervention in K-12 education has made it illegal (if still not rare) for schools to discriminate on the basis of color and to exclude handicapped students. These gains are real, and no one suggests that America reverse them now.

But has federal policy made the schools better; that is, has it improved the average quality of schools available to the children that attend them? The answer is not a clear yes. Government has succeeded in what it can do best, which is to create broad movements, make investments, and redistribute opportunities. But it has not succeeded in doing what it cannot do, which is to create intimate, imaginative, and highly productive institutions.

Schools are places where teachers and others stand in for parents, and they have a responsibility to make sure children learn things they will need to function as adults. Schools have definite ideas about what students should learn at a particular time, and most assume that groups of children can learn together.

However, recognizing that every child develops at his or her own rate—and that a child who has mastered one set of skills can struggle with another—good schools leave room for individualization. Because neither teachers, administrators, nor parents can anticipate everything necessary to help a child or a group of children learn, good schools are flexible. Neither students nor schools can be programmed in advance. Schedules and job descriptions cannot prevent a school, or an individual teacher, from doing whatever is necessary at the time. Though no school can do everything, a good school deploys its staff members to the best advantage of students. To the degree possible, every child gets access to the teacher or instructional experience that he or she needs at a particular time.

No good school ignores a child because of race, gender, or physical abilities. However, no school is good just because it does not discriminate or promote invidious relationships among people. A school is good because it nurtures and guides all children and teaches effectively.

People who attended both public and Catholic parochial schools face two competing perceptions. First, on average, Catholic schools now have higher academic standards and are more communal, more focused on instruction, and more coherent than public schools. Second, Catholic schools are not much different now than they were thirty or forty years ago when most people considered them mediocre. How to reconcile these perceptions? The answer is that the Catholic schools have stayed roughly the same, or improved slightly, while public schools have declined.

Today's Catholic parochial schools and their neighboring public schools differ in a number of ways.[1]

—Catholic schools have missions stated in terms of the kinds of knowledge, skills, and values of the graduates they intend to produce. Public schools are organizations that run externally mandated programs.

—Catholic schools recognize the differences among children but regard these differences as at most temporary impediments to the student's learning the knowledge, skills, and habits that the school intends to impart to all students. In contrast, public schools classify students as handicapped, language minority, gifted, and so on and offer distinct programs of study for different categories of student.[2]

—Teachers and administrators in Catholic schools are jointly responsible for the school's results, while public school teachers and administrators are responsible for their specific personal tasks.

—Staff members in Catholic schools are school employees while staff members in public schools are civil servants who work under formally written job descriptions and collective bargaining agreements that spell out everything from hours of work to what students they can serve.

The point is not to praise Catholic schools but to trace the effects of federal government programs on public schools. Before federal elementary and secondary education programs were enacted, public schools had far fewer separate programs. Children were not classified according to guidelines set by regulators outside the school, and schools did not have to compete for teachers' allegiance with external funding sources, administrative units, or unions. This is not to say that federal programs are responsible for all the differences between Catholic and public schools. Since long before the enactment of federal elementary and secondary education programs, public schools were larger on average, and less unified by common beliefs, than Catholic schools. Starting in the early twentieth century, public school teachers were more likely than Catholic school teachers to complain about unnecessary paperwork.

Not all of the policies, programs, rules, and contractual provisions that have weakened schools were initiated by the federal government. Some come from litigation, some come from collective bargaining, and some come from state laws established in imitation of federal statutes. However, federal government programs and initiatives introduced the idea that government could act on some parts of schools and not others, introducing programs for some children and not others, different rules to control the work of different teachers, and central office coordinators who would choose and supervise some teachers.

All major federal initiatives in K-12 education stemmed from the *Brown* decision, which first construed school enrollments as state action and established that discrimination denies children their rights under the Fourteenth Amendment. Though many federal policymakers have understood that nondiscrimination does not in itself make a good school, most major federal programs started as antidiscrimination measures. The largest federal education program, Title I of the Elementary and Secondary Education Act, was meant to overcome school districts' perceived habit of neglecting the needs of low-income and minority students. Federal programs for the handicapped and limited-English-speaking students were patterned after court orders resulting from lawsuits that alleged denial of equal protection of the laws. Aside from the large funding programs, the most conspicuous federal activity on K-12 education has been the enforcement of antidiscrimination statutes by the Office for Civil Rights (OCR). Though the federal government has also mounted small programs intended to train teachers, conduct research, or develop new instructional methods, these programs have received minuscule amounts of funding and have had short, uncertain lives, as compared with the big group-oriented programs.

Can the national commitment to equal educational opportunity for all be sustained without weakening schools? This paper says yes and suggests principles for a new federal role. It shows how government policies have made schools more formal and complex; engineered political pressures that distorted schools' operations and priorities; and imposed requirements that facilitate oversight by legislatures, bureaucracies, and courts, yet impede effective instruction.

Formal, Complex Schools

The ice nine of government policy has made retaining the characteristics of good schools difficult for many schools. Public schools that receive federal funds are organized around programs, each designed for a given category of students; students are instructed accordingly. Teachers specialize, taking responsibility for particular instructional routines and for the students classified as needing or entitled to them. How did this happen?

Forcing Students and Teachers into Categories

Until the 1960s, elementary and secondary education policy was considered off-limits for the federal government. President John F. Kennedy strove to establish a program of general federal aid to education, but his effort foundered politically on the issue of whether Catholic schools would also benefit from federal funds. President Lyndon B. Johnson got around the church-state barriers via a new theory of federal aid, the child benefit theory. Under this theory, the federal government could pay for services to children without increasing funding for schools. Thus, federal funds could benefit children in Catholic schools without supporting religious education. Under the same theory, federal funding for public schools could be shaped in ways that encouraged educators to place greater priority on the education of children who, because of their poverty, racial minority status, or other characteristics, had not been the primary concern of local schools.[3]

Under the child benefit theory, Title I was not designed to improve schools as wholes. It supported only extra services, or the purchase of equipment, for special programs for specified populations.[4] Special staff members provided these services and used equipment paid for from federal program funds. Children for whom federal programs were not specifically intended were not supposed to benefit in any way from the goods and services thereby provided.

In the first decade of its existence, Title I was a clear political success, providing funds to every congressional district and the vast majority of school districts, dominating the time and attention of local administrators, and generating research and publicity.[5] Though the program's effectiveness in raising student achievement was not clear, its effects on changing patterns of service delivery were evident everywhere. Title I could not fund services for every disadvantaged child, and its services were normally focused on reading and arithmetic instruction in the lowest income schools.

Title I also demonstrated the federal government's power through threats to cancel grants that local schools had come to depend on, to force reallocation of state and local funds. School administrators who had resisted Title I as an unwarranted exercise of federal power were succeeded by people who bought into—and became expert at administering—federal programs.

Other federal programs have built on this politically successful model. ESEA in the late 1990s contained more than sixty programs in addition to Title I, funding services for students with limited-English proficiency, Native Americans, and migrants and supporting school safety, magnet schools, teacher training initiatives, and many other purposes. In the mid-1970s a major new program for the handicapped built on the Title I example, and the preexisting Vocational Education program came to imitate it. To varying degrees, these programs all required separate and distinct services for their beneficiaries and forced equal use of state and local funds.

Federal programs were not the only acts of government that transformed schools. States enacted additional programs modeled on Title I, each targeted to a category of student, teacher, or service. State-funded programs often supported similar services for disadvantaged children in elementary and high schools not covered by Title I. Litigation in federal courts led to decrees affecting how schools are organized, staffed, and operated.

At about the same time Title I and its imitators were changing the nature of schools, many local school boards found that they could no longer meet teacher unions' salary demands. They started to offer unions concessions over teacher work rules, policies on teacher assignment, limitations on teachers' responsibility outside their classrooms, and constraints on school principals' management discretion.[6]

Limiting Teacher Responsibility

Title I and subsequent federal programs introduced something that schools had never before encountered: programs and funds controlled outside the school, providing staff and equipment that are sent into the school to perform particular functions.

This arrangement ensured that federal program funds could be tracked to identifiable adults, whose activities could be readily described to federal program auditors and evaluators. The downside of this arrangement was that programs developed on a districtwide basis often did not consider the specific needs of individual schools. Specialized teachers might not use the same teaching methods and present material on the same schedule as regular classroom teachers. Principals and classroom teachers had no formal authority to demand that the specialists collaborate with them, though many did so successfully on their own.[7]

As the number of federal programs increased (and as state legislatures enacted additional programs patterned after Title I), schools (especially those in poverty areas eligible for several separate programs) were served by increasing numbers of specialist teachers who did not work for the principal and did not need to coordinate with regular classroom teachers.

Classroom teachers' responsibility for individual children's learning was diluted, as more and more of their students' instruction was provided outside the classroom and by others. A teacher who could not expect a child to attend his or her reading class every day—and whose students might be confused by things they were taught elsewhere—was not clearly accountable for what that student learned. Similarly, a principal who could not coordinate teachers' schedules and methods, and had little to say about who was assigned to teach in the school or whether teachers who had become school mainstays would be abruptly transferred out, could not be expected to run a coherent instructional program.

In light of consistent research findings that disadvantaged students learn more in schools that are unified around a clear instructional mission, pressure to reverse the fragmenting effects of federal programs has been strong.[8] Congress and federal Title I administrators recognized this as a problem as early as the late 1970s and progressively softened the requirement that program services be distinct and easily identifiable.[9] The current version of Title I encourages schools to adopt schoolwide programs, which make coordinated use of all the assets of a school, including teachers and equipment purchased by Title I.

However, the basic pattern was set. Deregulation of Title I and other program regulations (starting with the Educational Consolidation and Improvement Act in 1980) has continued to the present time. Efforts to strengthen schools, however, constantly struggle against the centrifugal tendencies created by federal and state program requirements and work rules established in union contracts. Some schools are wholeheartedly implementing schoolwide programs, but many are still finding it difficult to place all administrators and teachers into the same boat. Different adults owe loyalty to different program administrators in the central office; many have work rules that limit their obligation to invest time in overall school improvement; and, despite the heroic voluntary efforts of many individuals, many have job security that allows them to resist schoolwide improvement efforts that might require changes in their teaching practices.[10]

As schools are increasingly patterned by the ice nine of government, they progressively lose their integrity as organizations.[11] Assets (staff members, equipment) are added to or subtracted from schools. Constraints in the form of new goals, performance quotas, testing programs, and regulations governing treatment of students and teachers are imposed on schools by school boards, central office administrators, and state and federal funding agencies. Staff members and students are brought into the school or taken out of it in pursuit of districtwide priorities, such as fulfillment of union contracts and maintenance of racial balance. New curricula and staff training programs are selected for whole districts and then infused into schools. Budget shortfalls are met by mandated districtwide reductions in school staffing or services, and the use of budget increases is also determined at the district level, in negotiations between the school board and teachers unions.

People in schools still strive to make them caring and adaptive places that meet students' needs. However, teachers and principals must now negotiate their ways around rules, structures, and working conditions imposed by government. Whether or not government's initiatives were necessary at the time, they have certainly burdened schools.

Political Engineering

Federal programs have deliberately put schools under new political pressures. On the assumption that past neglect of disadvantaged students was caused by local politics, in which their parents had few allies and little influence, federal programs tried to change the balance of local political forces. All large federal programs were expressly organized around constituency groups, helped parent groups organize, and gave parents official roles in school decisionmaking. Some gave parents new access to judicial remedies, on the assumption that the ability to threaten litigation would increase their influence on schools. Most tried to colonize state and local education agencies with individuals paid to advocate for compliance with federal program rules. As a result teachers are sometimes forced to treat students differently, depending on their links to organized external groups that have been set up and empowered by government actions. Many school principals' jobs have been changed, from the managers of small productive organizations to brokers among well-established interest groups and coordinators of compliance processes.

Schools were never without their politics. Even in private schools where government has little influence, different parents sometimes make competing demands, and the way these are resolved can affect teacher actions and student opportunities. Donors have influence. Staff members can disagree, and even form competing factions, about the relative importance of arts and sciences or athletics versus academics. Individual staff members can also compete for approval, status, or good job opportunities.

However, in those situations, people's interests and their influence are defined within the school community. Federal programs, court orders, and regulations have deliberately sought to reengineer the politics of individual schools, increasing the leverage exercised by certain groups within the school and creating leverage for outside groups that previously had no standing in school decisionmaking. The consequence is that individual schools operate in a far more complex political environment now than before ESEA was enacted.

Federal Programs' Focus on Constituencies

Like other Great Society programs, Title I was founded on a political argument that state and local education politics favored the white middle class and excluded the poor and minorities. To help low-income and minority students, the federal government would have to override, and ultimately alter, the innate bias of state and local politics. Title I therefore required that federal funds be tied to easily identified objects or services and that those assets be used only for the benefit of individual children deemed eligible under federal rules.[12] In the face of evidence that some localities, especially in the South, resisted using federal funds in these ways, the U.S. Office of Education created increasingly stringent program rules. These required localities not only to use federal funds as intended, but also to show that as much state and local money was spent on disadvantaged students as on other pupils.[13]

This evolution of the federal role was strongly promoted by a coalition of Office of Education officials and newly burgeoning Washington, D.C.–based educational interest groups. As Samuel Halperin wrote approvingly in 1975:

> ESEA has become a rallying point for those concerned about achieving full educational opportunity for specific segments of the population [leading to] ... special programs for out of school youth[,] ... migrant workers[,] ... neglected youngsters and juvenile delinquents[,] ... handicapped children[,] ... children forced to speak one language at home and another in the schools[, and] ... preschool children.... Now the social movements which spawned ESEA are merging with those demanding greater child development and day-care services ... and have pushed through school lunch, breakfast, special milk, and related programs.[14]

Title I tried to create local bases of political and administrative support by building cadres of federally paid compliance officers in state education departments and local school districts and by creating low-income parent advisory councils that could veto school districts' plans for the use of federal funds. It also put pressure on state and local superintendents by requiring frequent public evaluations of program effectiveness. Pressure to demonstrate student learning gains led most states to focus their Title I money on children in early grades, where reading gains are easier to measure. Performance pressure also led the U.S. Department of Education to require concentration of Title I funds in local schools with the highest proportions of low-income children.

Politicization of Parent Involvement

Since the earliest days of Title I, federal officials have tried to stimulate creation of grass-roots support groups for it and other programs such as education of the handicapped and bilingual education. Influenced by War on Poverty empowerment strategies, federal regulation writers' preferred approach was to organize the parents of program recipients and give them veto power over local uses of program funds. This, it was believed, would ensure that funds were spent on the right children. Federal administrators also encouraged formation of local interest groups of citizens and educators dedicated to the schooling of specified groups of children. The Title I program pioneered these approaches, but federal administrators of programs for handicapped children raised the creation of local support groups to a high art.[15] Federal programs for the handicapped did more than organize parents; they also gave parents of handicapped children unique legal rights to oversee services proposed for their children and to bring lawsuits against school districts that did not offer what the parents thought their children needed.

Administrators of state programs followed suit. By the mid-1970s, the soft collaborative ideal of parental involvement in education had taken on a hard political edge. Localities where students were compelled to attend certain schools because of desegregation court orders tried to compensate by giving parents a chance to influence school programs. The idea of authoritative parent advisory councils influenced the site-based management movement that started in Miami and was quickly adopted throughout the country. Teacher groups also demanded decisionmaking power. The idea of shared parent-teacher governance of schools reached its apogee in the 1988 Illinois law on Chicago reform, which mandated elected local site councils to govern all Chicago schools.

Some schools improved under this new politicization of parent and teacher involvement, but many did not. Many Title I parent advisory councils were inactive, and others were controlled by activist factions that less combative parents could not challenge. Other groups (for example, parents of the gifted and talented) organized politically to protect their children's education in the face of the extraordinary legal leverage enjoyed by parents of the handicapped. As Anthony S. Bryk and others reported about the Chicago school reform, some schools changed dramatically for the better but the majority did not improve and many got dramatically worse as latent rivalries among parent and teacher factions came to the surface and dominated school life.[16]

Engineering New Leverage for Favored Groups

Until the mid-1970s, federal programs had generally paid for all the activities—services, purchasing, and administrative record-keeping—that they required states and localities to undertake. In the late 1970s, however, Congress and federal officials started exploiting all the leverage available to the donor of funds that the recipient had come to rely on. States and school districts that had become accustomed to receiving and using Title I funds found that new strings were attached. If they were to continue receiving Title I and other grant funds, they had to create new sports programs for women, make their buildings accessible to handicapped children, follow federal standards for equal employment opportunity, and so on.

The most important unfunded mandate, the federal program for handicapped children—the Individuals with Disabilities Education Act (IDEA)—created an entitlement requiring that some students receive all the services they need regardless of the effects on other school or district activities or the needs of other students.[17]

Unfunded entitlements strictly limit school leaders' ability to make judgments about services to children. The severity of the trade-off between fulfilling entitlements and serving other students depends on the numbers of entitlees and the cost of their services. The numbers of disabled children range from less than 10 percent to nearly 20 percent of the students in some districts. Though services for children with the most common forms of handicapping conditions typically cost only 20 to 50 percent more than local average per pupil expenditures, services to more profoundly disabled or disturbed students can cost five to ten times the district average.

In the early days of the federal program for handicapped children, how funding of special education services affected the regular school program was not clearly evident. Extremely expensive services were rare. In a school district serving five thousand students, a $50,000 placement for one student would require a transfer of at most $10 (and probably far less than that) from the average amount available for the education of any other child. This deduction was difficult to observe, because cross-subsidies among groups of students were (and still are) created in the school district central bureaucracy, where parents cannot easily see them. However, as special education has grown and the numbers of students and handicapping conditions have increased, regular classrooms increasingly bear—and show—the cost of accommodations made.[18]

Unfunded mandates are a form of political engineering. They use the federal government's leverage as a donor, based on the implied threat to remove a grant on which the recipient has come to depend, to give designated groups new claims on locally funded services.

The federal government in 1975 enacted the biggest unfunded mandate of all, the Education for All Handicapped Children Act. That statute established a new civil right that was limited to a particular class of citizens. It required all school districts to provide "appropriate" services to all handicapped children, as defined by an individualized education plan approved by parents and experts in education of the disabled. School districts were required to reconcile two different principles: to educate handicapped children in the "least restrictive environment" while providing any form of service considered necessary for the child's education. Parents who were not satisfied with a district's plans could seek redress in the courts, and school districts were required to pay for any service or placement required (including, in some cases, placement in private residential facilities), whatever the cost.

The Education for All Handicapped Children Act did not derive from Title I but was based on court orders that had established new rules for the education of severely handicapped children in Pennsylvania.[19] The act applied the principles established in one case in one federal judicial region to the whole country. It established the principle that the federal government could make certain children the beneficiaries of an absolute service entitlement—an entitlement that was established without reference to the needs of other students or the budget priorities and tax capacities of states and localities.[20]

Early supporters of the Education for All Handicapped Children Act claimed that the number of children requiring expensive special services was low and that the financial impact on regular education would be slight. Critics feared that the demands of parents with severely handicapped children would escalate; others predicted that the numbers of parents seeking special accommodations for their children would increase and an alliance between these parents and handicapped-education providers would lead to uncontrolled expansion of special education programs.

Special education grew rapidly in the late 1970s and 1980s. Real school spending increased by 61 percent from 1967 to 1991. However, only about one-fourth of the increase was directed at "regular education." The share of expenditures going to regular education dropped from 80 percent to 59 percent between 1967 and 1991, while the share going to special education climbed from 4 percent to 17 percent. Of the new net money spent on education, about 38 percent went to special education for severely handicapped and learning-disabled children.[21] Increasing numbers of parents sought individually tailored accommodations for their children, and the definitions of "handicapping conditions" proliferated. Virtually any child who had trouble learning to read or adjusting to the behavioral demands of schools could be considered handicapped and was therefore entitled to a special accommodation. Litigation on schools' obligations under the law also forced schools to accept responsibility for medical services (for example, catheterization) and limited schools' ability to deal aggressively with disruptive student behavior.[22]

Not every parent who wanted individualized treatment for his or her child was willing to accept the "handicapped" or "special education" label. Thus, many parents and advocacy groups organized to seek special treatment for other children under such labels as "gifted" or "bilingual." The high-water mark for such efforts was a proposal made by a Title I reauthorization commission in 1993, to give every child in the United States a judicially enforceable "opportunity to learn" guarantee. To date, no group other than the handicapped has been able to gain an absolute entitlement to services.[23] Once organized for action, however, many of these groups were able to win political concessions from districts and schools.

By establishing that some students have more claims on political and legal protection than others, programs for the handicapped helped foster a virtually universal feeling among public school teachers and parents that they are not being treated fairly and that they must, therefore, look out for themselves. As Alfie Kohn has shown, many advantaged parents act on this feeling by using their influence and access to obtain the best placements for their own children.[24]

For schools, as for communities, political engineering by outside parties can have disastrous consequences. Nobody knows what a group will do with new powers, or how groups will react to policies that afford advantages to their rivals. The local school or district is responsible for making realistic decisions about what can best benefit the most students and what accommodations for special needs are possible. However, if only one group has such an entitlement, district and school leaders face a different problem: They are obliged fully to satisfy the entitlements first and then fund the education of all other children out of what is left.

One thing is clear, however. Politicizing school life draws attention toward the agendas of organized adult groups and away from the more mundane concerns of teaching and learning.

Colonization of Local and State Agencies

Local school systems, especially in large urban districts, depend heavily on federal funding to staff their central offices. Federal funds pay for major shares of most school districts' testing and evaluation programs, teacher training programs, and purchases of equipment. Though they are generally not as dependent on federal funding as state departments of education, local districts are heavily influenced and constrained by federal programs and their resident managers. Federal program coordinators often resist local reform initiatives that increase individual schools' control of funds, citing possible disruption of relations with the federal government and possible job loss for specialists employed to deliver federal program services.

This situation is the result of a deliberate effort by federal program managers to colonize state and local education agencies. By offering to pay for staff members who would administer federal programs and manage federally mandated compliance processes, federal programs such as Title I and IDEA created new sources of leverage on schools' use of funds and distribution of services.

Ted Sanders's experience in Ohio shows how thoroughly colonized the states have become. When he became Ohio's superintendent of public instruction in 1991, Sanders intended to make the state education department a force for school improvement throughout the Buckeye State. He quickly discovered, however, that he had practically nothing to say about the responsibilities of the more than six hundred employees who nominally worked for him. The vast majority of them were funded by federal programs—Title I, programs for the handicapped, vocational education, and so on—and had demanding oversight and enforcement duties. Those people were often the best-educated and most experienced employees of the Ohio Department of Education; most of the remaining employees were administrators and financial specialists, not people who could contribute to a statewide school improvement program.[25]

Many state departments of education draw most of their funding from federal sources.[26] The federal share of state agency operating funds for all states in 1993 was 41 percent; for Michigan, 77 percent; Iowa, 71 percent; Alabama, 69 percent; South Dakota, 62 percent; Maryland, 61 percent; New Hampshire, 60 percent; North Dakota, 59 percent; and Utah, 59 percent. In many states, the only employees on the state payroll are those who work directly for the superintendent and those who collect funds from the legislature and write checks to localities. Though some states, notably Kentucky, have been able to steer their own courses independently of the federal government, many have no real agenda beyond keeping federal funds flowing.

Starting in the early 1990s, several states tried to reassert control of their departments of education, hoping to turn them into forces for general school improvement. Illinois, Kentucky, Ohio, Texas, and Virginia were among the first to try to rehabilitate these institutions. In the mid-1990s, states that were committed to standards-based reform also tried to make their education departments into instruments for general school improvement (for example, Maryland, Missouri, Oregon, and Washington). Though some are starting to make progress, the continuing presence of many paid "colonists" from federal programs remains an obstacle.

Today's chief state school officers are often experts in the administration of federal programs. Their delegate in Washington, the Council of Chief State School Officers (CCSSO), supports strong "categorical" regulations on the use of federal funds and opposes initiatives that would give individual schools greater discretion. This position confirms the status of the CCSSO as the point of contact between federal regulators and individual states as well as an advocate for federal regulation of states and local districts.

Local school districts are not as thoroughly colonized. The majority of central office staff members are still paid from state and local funds, and the superintendent is clearly more accountable to the local school board than to federal program managers in Washington and the state capitol.

However, colonization definitely limits the flexibility of local school districts. Many districts are unable to take full advantage of flexibility provisions recently written into Title I because their federal program coordinators insist on maintaining patterns of service that have withstood earlier compliance audits. Federal program coordinators also resist allowing schools to choose the teachers who will deliver federally paid instructional services, and they control much of the money available for teacher in-service training. Though superintendents are often able to negotiate successfully for cooperation, they must treat their own federal coordinators as representatives of an outside power.

Such constraints on superintendents impede certain kinds of local school improvement initiatives. Superintendents often find that they cannot deliver on promises to evaluate schools on the basis of productivity, not compliance. School leadership teams of teachers and administrators often find that promised "lump-sum school budgeting" is not real, because teachers hired with federal program dollars are still controlled by central office coordinators. Philanthropists often find that schools cannot implement privately funded reform initiatives because federal program operations cannot be changed to accommodate them.

Through these methods—creating new political leverage for selected parents, favoring certain groups in the competition for funds, helping potential interest groups to form and create agendas, and colonizing state and local education agencies—the federal government created new forces to influence schools. By the same methods, federal programs have helped turn public schools into inflexible government institutions, forced to respond as much or more to political forces as to the imperatives of teaching and learning.

Proxies for Equity

Forty-five years after *Brown* v. *Board of Education*, the Fourteenth Amendment remains the basis of the federal role in education. Virtually all federal programs and rules identify inequalities and attempt to remedy them.

Equity is the historic basis for federal initiatives in K-12 education. Before the *Brown* decision, many states and localities practiced discrimination and neglected the needs of minority students. Actions in federal courts, the enactment of Title I, and enforcement efforts by the U.S. Office of Education (predecessor to the Department of Education) turned American school districts around.

Despite these successes, equity has often proven to be a problematic basis for action. Equity in education is difficult to identify. Because different children need different instructional experiences, identical treatment, or identical levels of expenditure, is not always equitable. Teachers are not commodities, and a few minutes with one may benefit a child more than several hours with another. Some children learn a great deal from books, while others are inspired by contact with computers, and others respond best to a great deal of interpersonal "face time."

Even an "identical outcomes" standard is not unequivocally equitable. Some children find it easy to attain high levels of skill in some areas (for example, drawing, instrumental music, or dance) that others could never attain. Would it be equitable to require schools to teach all students to the same level of proficiency if that meant that the most gifted students would not fully develop their skills? Is it equitable to allow a student with low aptitudes in a given subject to neglect it to develop skills in an area where he or she has higher aptitude? Teachers and parents face such questions all the time and try to resolve them in the best interest of individual children. No single equity principle can apply: What is best—equitable—in one case might not be equitable in another.

Formulas that define equity as universal attainment of certain minimum outcomes offer only a temporary escape from this conundrum. Ultimately, one must determine whether it is equitable to accept a universal outcomes standard, no matter how high or low, if evidence exists that people who exceed the standard do better in jobs, further education, and so on.

Inequalities such as those recognized by *Brown*, for example, government policies expressly constructed to deny minority children access to publicly funded schools, allow unambiguous remedial action. However, not every need and deficiency of schools can be approached effectively from this perspective. Some differences in student outcomes are caused by factors other than discrimination. Some educational failures affect every student in a school, district, or state and cannot be addressed by interventions on behalf of a particular subset of students. Some educational problems require flexible and innovative solutions that must be crafted within the classroom or school.

Government does not fare well with such complexity. Needing to judge complex situations from a distance, government agencies and courts are forced to adopt relatively simple proxy measures for equity. Sometimes, as in the case of laws and regulations on the education of handicapped children, government intervenes simply by giving one group access to courts and quasi-judicial proceedings that other groups do not have. This tilts the allocation of school resources (dollars, teachers, equipment, time) in the direction of favored groups, but it does not ensure either that they will benefit or that other disadvantaged children will not be hurt by the results. Thus, it is often difficult for anyone to be sure that government has promoted a situation that is equitable from the perspective of one disadvantaged group without increasing inequity when viewed from the perspective of another. An activity can be considered equity-promoting whether or not it creates the greatest possible advantage per dollar spent, or benefits as many people as possible, or makes some people worse off in the course of making its direct beneficiaries better off.

Government programs and prescriptions can inhabit an unreal world in which contrary prescriptions can be smoothly integrated, adult tasks can be easily distinguished, and children can be easily classified. Teachers, students, and parents do not live in such a world.

Nothing about this analysis is news. Government programs in all fields are forced to adopt measurable bases for action and are liable to goal displacement if the proxies they use are bad. In education, consistent use of bad proxies for equity can thwart efforts to make sure disadvantaged students get effective instruction.[27] Federal programs can sometimes create equity, at least as measured by the government's chosen proxies, without creating all the intended benefits. For example:

—Title I requires school districts to concentrate funds on certain schools, so that a low-income child in one school may get services while an equally low-income child in another school with a smaller concentration of poor students does not.

—Programs for education of the handicapped allow parents of individual children to press their demands in the courts, whether or not the benefits they gain are paid for by reducing expenditures on school programs that benefit poor, minority, or disadvantaged students.[28]

—Students classified as "behavior disordered" can be removed from classrooms only if their Individualized Education Plan (IEP) is formally changed, regardless of whether they are learning in the class or of the consequences of their behavior for other students.[29]

—Government civil right agencies will act against a charter school that enrolls handicapped children and does not provide the services specified in those children's Individualized Education Plans. This can happen even if parents chose the school expressly because they thought their children were being harmed by the public school district's special education program.[30]

Another example of an equity definition that does not benefit the children it is intended to protect is that Title I and other federal programs require equalization of local spending per child before federal funds can be added on. But the proxies for equal spending they use do not challenge the biggest source of local spending inequalities, which is the distribution of high-salaried teachers. As a proxy for equity, federal programs count the numbers of teachers in schools, not their real-dollar cost, so that the schools in the lowest income neighborhoods, which attract the lowest paid and least-qualified teachers, get far less than their share of funds.[31]

By convention, if not in reality, all these procedures promote equity. But they may not do as much for those children as other arrangements that strengthen the schools they attend or create significant movement toward the undefined but intensely desired goal of educational equality.

Using such proxies for equity places great emphasis on the rituals of compliance, not on problem solving. It is better suited to the protection of existing programs and the stabilization of adult working environments than to finding solutions to the problem of how to improve education for the disadvantaged and handicapped.

An overheard dialogue illustrates how commitment to poor proxies for equity can act like ice nine in schools. Two academics, one who had devoted his career to studying school desegregation and another who had specialized in school effectiveness research, were asked to define a good school. The first academic replied, "A good school is one in which every person knows her rights and suffers no discrimination." The second academic replied, "A good school is a caring environment where the adults use all their knowledge and energy to find ways to help every student learn to high standards."

These definitions of a good school might be compatible, but their differences in emphasis are clear. Under the second definition, a school is a unique problem-solving organization unified by a commitment to helping all children meet a common standard. If it lives up to its commitments, it will not classify any child in an arbitrary way or give up on any student without first exhausting all the time, energy, and expertise available. Under the first definition, a good school is built around a set of rules intended to prevent discrimination. The question arises as to whether a school so constructed can teach any child to the limits of his or her ability.

Associating equity with specific regulations and processes makes federal programs difficult to assail, but it does not make them effective. It also impedes serious discussion about how best to use all the resources available for the education of disadvantaged children. From the standpoint of people who equate fairness with the proxies for it developed under federal programs, critics who propose changes in Title I targeting or decisionmaking processes, or current methods for determining handicapped children's placements, are by definition risking equity.

Government deals with large issues, mass programs, and gross-grained oversight. It cannot, and generally does not need to, exercise fine-grained judgment about the activities of unique, intimate local groups. In creating new equity claims for particular groups, government has entered into situations where doing good is very difficult. The methods of administration and oversight that come naturally to a government of continental scale require use of simplifications and proxy measures that match up poorly with the needs of individual children and schools. The results are all but inevitable: Government is forced to use measures of merit that are only loosely related to its goals, and schools are forced to do things that make them less effective.

The Effects of Federal Programs

Federal initiatives in K-12 education have succeeded in making disadvantaged children the top priority at the national, state, and local levels. However, though federal programs have caused changes that helped low-income and minority children, federal programs have often done harm to those same children's education—and everyone else's—by weakening the schools. They do so by diverting funds and energy away from regular instruction and toward special programs, much as the child benefit theory anticipated and even ordained.

Public discourse about education has changed since the 1960s. No one seriously questions the importance and moral rightness of providing disadvantaged children with a fair opportunity to gain skills, stay in school, attend college, and achieve advanced training. School systems are now staffed almost entirely by people whose training is deeply influenced by values about education of the disadvantaged.

Changes in legal doctrines (for example, the 1954 *Brown* decision and subsequent Supreme Court actions), and demographic changes that make business more dependent than ever on immigrants and native-born minority workers, have also transformed national priorities.

However, the federal government has not been able to follow up its success in setting new priorities with effective action. Many of its programs and rules have weakened schools by putting process before results, caused displacement of goals from serving students to guaranteeing administrative compliance, and weakened schools' ability to pursue effective instructional programs and solve the problems presented by their students.

No one intended these outcomes. The people who write and advocate for federal program regulations can often demonstrate that local educators do not recognize or use all the options they have and that the negative outcomes of federal programs result from choices that state and local educators make.[32]

Federal programs have provided needed funds for many cash-strapped school systems, but they have also set off chains of events that have weakened the very institutions on which all children depend for their education. Federal programs did not directly cause the current unrest about public education. But they have contributed greatly to schools' loss of institutional coherence and educators' eroding sense of personal responsibility, which in turn led to pressure for new schools operated under new rules, the campaign for parental control via school choice, not political involvement, and the belief that public schools are not safe and caring enough.

The flight of middle- and working-class parents of all races from city schools and African American parents' growing demand for new options and the opportunity to send their children to private schools when nearby public schools are failing have many sources.[33] But it is hard to see how they would have happened to the current degree without the negative aspects of federal programs.

There are no villains here. One might blame the people who, in the 1960s and 1970s, were confident that the new federal initiatives would help the poor without harming anyone else (and would provide new advantages for poor children without simultaneously creating new obstacles to their education). While my work on the 1977 Title I reauthorization made a significant contribution to the regulatory structure of Title I, I do not berate myself now for actions taken then, nor should anyone else accept blame for acting in good faith in the context of those times. Yet, refraining from judging past actions does not justify persisting in the face of current knowledge about the harm done by many federal programs and policies. No one can claim that the current chaotic system of laws, regulations, constraints, and preferences is the best one that Americans could design for their children.

How can the federal government maintain its commitment to improving education for the disadvantaged, while promoting, rather than interfering with, the improvement of schools? Though many localities would probably retain their current commitment to improving education for poor and minority children even if all federal programs were eliminated, some might not. Moreover, some localities, particularly the poorest rural areas and biggest cities, would have difficulty maintaining even the marginal quality of their instructional programs without continued federal aid.

Toward a More Positive Federal Role

The federal government can be both a force for general school improvement and a source of initiative on behalf of the poor and disadvantaged. Accomplishing those goals, while helping schools become less governmental and more communal, requires fundamental changes at three levels: Federal programs must be funded and operated differently; the Department of Education must be organized differently, to become a national resource, not a captive of constituency-based interests; and Congress must oversee the department and its programs differently, focusing on its contributions to schools rather than its operation of separate categorical programs.

Can these things be done within the foreseeable future? Of course they can, if Congress decides to do so. Though the infrastructure built up to administer existing federal programs is large and powerful, it is not significantly larger or more powerful than the county-based welfare apparatus that Congress disassembled a few years ago. Similarly, though the constituencies that support the existing programs are large, they are not strongly united. Beneficiary groups, especially low-income and minority parents whose children benefit from Title I, are far more interested in better schools than in continuation of a particular federal program.

The foregoing statements come easily to a person who, like me, lives a continent away from Washington and spends much more time in the halls of schools than in Congress or the Department of Education. Schools and local education agencies would suffer if federal funds were withdrawn, and they would benefit if funding were, as it should be, increased. But most schools and districts could readily adapt to drastic revisions in federal program structure and administration. The barriers to change are not in the schools, states, or localities, but in Washington, in the form of congressional committee structures that make certain programs the property of powerful subcommittees, providers' lobbies, and other adult groups who gain from the ways the programs are now run. Necessary change will be politically difficult. But the needs of children and schools must not take a back seat to the self-protection interests of politicians.

Nothing about K-12 education, or the federal system, makes the current set of federal programs and regulatory structures inevitable. The federal government, if it chose, could construct a new role for itself, based on its unique perspectives and powers and its freedom of action. The federal government's perspective is national: The president and secretary of education are positioned to see emerging national needs that are less visible from within a state or region and to broker collaborations among states and regional organizations. The federal government's powers are also unique. Only it can spend the money raised by the Internal Revenue Service and redistribute funds from rich to poor states. The federal government's freedom of action is almost total because, unlike the state and local governments, it does not have to operate schools on a day-to-day basis.

Programs that commit all federal funds to set programs, and that consistently align federal officials with particular interest groups and government bureaucracies, limit the federal government's ability to use its unique perspectives and powers. Categorical programs such as Title I commit virtually all federal K-12 funds to a particular set of services and create a definite entitlement mentality among state and local administrators. Entitlement programs such as IDEA permanently enlist the federal government on one side in localities' struggle to stretch limited resources to meet diverse and ever-changing needs. The regulatory aspects of programs such as Title I, IDEA, and bilingual education also commit the federal government to a specific set of bureaucracies and decisionmaking processes.

If the federal program commits itself permanently to a set of beneficiaries, bureaucracies, and procedures, it fritters away its unique assets. The federal government can use its assets and make a continuing contribution to the quality of education for all American children, particularly the poor and disadvantaged, if it rebuilds its role according to these principles:[34]

—Subsidize children, not jurisdictions.

—Strengthen schools, not cross- or sub-school programs.

—Define results in terms of student and school performance.

—Attack emergent problems with short-term special-purpose grants.

—Make the Department of Education a national resource, not a federal ministry.

Subsidize Children, Not Jurisdictions

The federal government should support the education of disadvantaged children directly by funding the schools that educate these children, not government administrative structures. Congress should consolidate all federal grant programs into one funding mechanism, with procedures for identifying individual beneficiaries, providing funds directly to the schools those children attend, and ensuring that schools attended by beneficiaries get the same amounts of local and state dollars per pupil as other schools in the same district.[35]

Federal laws and regulations should not require that money be traceable to particular programs, services, or students. No federal program should require localities to treat identical children differently, depending on what school they attend.

Federal funding should not remove responsibility for judgments and trade-offs about a child's education from the only people who can make them well, teachers and parents. Congress might establish especially high weighting factors for severely disabled children or children in extremely high-cost areas. But laws that create absolute entitlements to specific services or permit court orders requiring optimal services for some children regardless of the consequences for other children's education must be amended. This implies avoiding federal prescriptions about who must sign off on decisions, what sorts of planning processes states and localities must follow, and who, if aggrieved, has a private right of legal action.

Congress might allow localities to set age-level priorities (for example, provide twice as much federal money per beneficiary pupil in grades six to eight as in grades nine to twelve). But it should not allow localities to create horizontal inequities among beneficiary children of a particular age, no matter where they go to school. Children's beneficiary status should depend on their demographic characteristics, not on their test scores or other school performance. Funding should not be reduced for disadvantaged students who perform at high levels.

This proposal will almost certainly strengthen demands for increased federal funding. The 30–40 percent of disadvantaged children who do not now receive Title I services would finally get them, and the need to spread federal funds among a larger number of students will generate demands to increase funding to match current per child amounts.[36] Because the money and its uses would be visible at the school level, the case for increased funding should also be easy to make. A school could add another teacher for every fifty or sixty disadvantaged students, thus creating many new opportunities for instructional improvement.

Because some of the data required to identify individual children can be collected only at the local level, federal grants would have to follow the general procedures used by Title I: Use census data (poverty counts) to allocate funds to the county level and use locally collected data (for example, free lunch counts, surveys of family language backgrounds, school surveys of handicapped children) to identify beneficiaries. These assessments might best be done at the county level, rather than by individual school districts. Government agencies that distribute funds should be paid administrative fees for their services, but these should not lead to establishment of permanent federally funded monitoring staffs.

The first step toward redefining the federal role would be to consolidate all federal grant programs into one statute and create clear definitions of beneficiaries. A reform of this scope would require scrutiny of some programs that do not normally come up for reauthorization at the same time as ESEA, for example, Vocational Education, IDEA, and the Department of Education's research structure. There is, however, no reason that those programs cannot be considered for reauthorization on the ESEA timetable. Including such programs in a review of ESEA is a necessary precondition for creating a rationalized and effective federal role in education.

Strengthen Schools

Federal policy must work with, not against, the reality that the only people who can help a student are that child's teachers, parents, and neighbors. Washington should avoid buttressing any particular administrative regime or creating permanent groups of federally paid state or local employees. It should, similarly, avoid mandating any particular orthodoxy in educational organization, whether that is systemic reform that aligns standards, tests, curriculum, teaching, charter schools, educational contracting, home schooling, cyber schooling, or anything else. Schools should be free to use federal money for teacher training, new instructional materials, or outside assistance that can improve teaching, but districts should not be free to use money for programs that put central office priorities before the needs of individual schools.

Other than eliminating earmarks that require states and localities to fund program-specific compliance monitors and coordinators, the federal government should neither solidify nor disassemble current state and local administrative structures. It should take a permissive but neutral stance toward such innovations in education provision as lump-sum budgeting of schools, private provision of school space and staffing, investment and school management by nongovernmental entities, and voucher plans that expand educational options for the disadvantaged.

Aside from eliminating funding earmarked for administration, the federal government should do nothing to encourage states or localities to disassemble the apparatus they have built for special education. Schools and communities must struggle with the question of what is to be done for children who cannot learn in normal classroom environments. Powerful interest groups and legal advocacy organizations, many created by federal subsidies, will continue to have great influence. But the federal government should not prevent schools from experimenting with different ideas about how best to serve the handicapped or from considering the effectiveness of alternative services and the needs of other children.

In general, the federal government should not encourage any changes in state special education laws or sponsor litigation to change extant court orders on education of the handicapped. It should, however, leave the writing of laws and regulations on special education to the states and allow issues on the rights of special education students to be resolved in courts and legislatures. It should also let rights-based litigation in other areas (for example, bilingual education, sex equity) proceed and Constitutional interpretations that establish individual students' rights to services evolve. The federal government should swear off the practice of picking out the one court ruling most favorable to a particular group's interests and erecting it into a national program.

Define Results in Terms of Student and School Performance

The federal government should measure the effects of its programs in terms of overall improvement in the educational outcomes of children, both disadvantaged and advantaged, not on maintenance of a particular administrative or service scheme. Accountability based on detailed fiscal reporting and regulatory compliance does not lead to good instruction.

To assess results of its subsidies for students and schools, the federal government could conduct special analyses of the results of new statewide standards-based tests. These tests, now either in place or under construction in a majority of states, are designed to produce school-by-school comparisons in students' average test scores and growth rates. States could be required to analyze these data, comparing student growth rates in all schools in which federal funds are used versus all other schools. States could then be required to create new schooling options for students in low-growth-rate schools. These options could be provided via state intervention, reconstitution, or creation of new schooling options (including use of districtwide choice plans, vouchers, or charters).

The Department of Education could also periodically commission national sample-based studies of localities and schools and provide information to governors, mayors, and the public.

Attack Emergent Problems with Short-Term Special-Purpose Grants

States and localities will continue to need help solving short-term problems such as teacher shortages, facilities decay, lack of technology, and overcrowding. However, the federal government should avoid creating expectations that particular jurisdictions will receive permanent federal support. It should not fund any state or local government entity for more than three years without at least a one-year hiatus. Further, these short-term interventions should be limited to a fixed percentage (for example, 10 percent) of all federal spending on K-12 education.

The secretary of education could then control a substantial fund for investment in and response to emergent problems of states and localities. The secretary, in consultation with a board representing Congress, presidential appointees, governors, and local educators and school providers, could devote as much as $1.5 billion per year to specific problem-solving activities. Because this fund could not become an entitlement for any locality or function, and no one program could continue for more than three years, the use of this fund could be disciplined by becoming a significant issue in presidential campaigns.

Make the Education Department a National Resource, Not a Federal Ministry

The Education Department should be re-missioned to emphasize national issues over the use of federal regulatory power. Its current organization, which fosters close alliances between particular constituency groups and the bureaus that run programs, should be changed.[37] All the separate categorical program offices could be replaced by a unified division that writes checks and ensures that funds go to the schools and children for whom they are designated.

A second major Investments Division would sponsor research, development, statistics, and emergency investments. No matter how states and localities seek to improve their schools, they will depend on the availability, both in their regions and nationally, of well-trained teachers, sound techniques for student assessment, new technologies and ideas about instruction and school management, and evidence of the effectiveness of particular instructional methods. Through its Investments Division, the Department of Education could invest in new ideas and fund rigorous clinical trials and demonstrations. Consistent with the principle that the department should be a source of ideas and not a regulator, these results would be disseminated via the marketplace of ideas, not translated into laws, regulations, or incentives.

Taken together, these principles could create a new federal role in education.

Conclusion

Would initiatives based on these principles thaw out all of the ice nine created by today's federal programs and regulations and establish a perfect federal role? The answer is no. Just as today's problems could not be anticipated in the 1960s, the challenges facing America's schools in the year 2010 cannot all be foreseen now. Future Congresses will need to reconsider and amend actions taken in 1999 and 2000.

Groups of providers and beneficiaries will always try to use federal power and dollars to create and solidify advantages for themselves. Professors and business leaders will be tempted to write their own ideas—about use of technology, adoption of whole school designs, the best teaching methods, the correct class size, or the perfect way to select and train teachers—into federal law.[38] Interest group representatives will draft laws and regulations that favor their constituencies; some will try to inflate court orders that apply only to specific cases into regulations that affect all schools.

The structure of the new federal role must be simple enough, and grounded on sufficiently clear principles, to withstand the inevitable processes of advocacy and advantage-taking. The foregoing suggestions lay a good foundation. But a more constructive federal role will need tending and defending. Creating a new and more constructive federal role is one thing; keeping it is another.

Comment by Christopher T. Cross

Paul T. Hill's paper sparks many thoughts, ideas, and recollections about the last thirty-five years of intensive federal activity in education. However, many questions arise from the paper and many issues need further examination. Hill's use of ice nine as a metaphor for federal involvement is colorful and effective, but it presents a picture that may be unnecessarily negative and one that fails to acknowledge the positive aspects of what does take place with federal aid. Ice nine has no benevolent uses. Once touched, disaster occurs. While some might argue that point, I suspect that even they would acknowledge that federal aid has made positive contributions in elementary and secondary education and in higher education. Hill's paper, while having a title related to federal aid, is essentially about the U.S. Department of Education and does not touch upon programs run in such disparate agencies as the National Endowment for the Humanities, the National Science Foundation (NSF), the Department of Defense, and the National Aeronautics and Space Administration. All of this is to say that the frame of reference must be clearly defined.

Now that nearly two generations have passed since enactment of the Elementary and Secondary Education Act (ESEA), a review would be useful of some of the reasons that gave birth to the programs that, for the most part, still exist today. A child born in 1960 who might have entered school when the program first took effect in 1965 is on the verge of turning forty and likely has children of his own in school. In Washington during that same time, a half-dozen or more changes in congressional leadership have occurred and, with the exception of Representative Patsy Mink (D-Hawaii), probably not a soul is around who was present at the creation and is still active in the policy arena. With turnover at the state and local level, more cycles have been completed than most can remember.

The situation that existed in the mid-1960s compelled the enactment of federal education programs. School integration was a central focus as was the recognition that many schools that had served African American children were destitute and often received an inferior allocation of funds. When Title I was created, it was aimed at righting some of those wrongs by providing financial aid. Enactment of ESEA came only seven years after President Dwight D. Eisenhower sent troops into Little Rock, Arkansas, and when other open acts of civil and criminal disobedience had taken place to prevent school desegregation. Defiance of court decisions led to court orders and federal action. While many of those cases were about federal education programs, most were (and are) about either constitutional issues or civil rights laws that often get played out in the schools. Keeping all of this in mind is important when examining the current situation.

In the past thirty-five years, states have become much more professional and less openly political in the Tammany Hall sense of graft and corruption. They have also built professional staffs, embraced inclusive social issues, and become rivals of the federal government for power and even moral authority. The problem is that the structure in place for the delivery of federal education programs was created in response to the problems of the 1950s and 1960s. Similar issues face society in other fields, such as health, welfare, transportation, and housing, where the issues have emerged and present different challenges but the structure has not evolved to meet them. What seemed to work no longer does.

Other Issues

One issue not addressed by Hill relates to the ways in which the federal government has chosen to organize education programs and the impact of that at the state and local level. For example, the old Office of Education and the existing U.S. Department of Education treat schools as silos—a silo for special education, for vocational education, for the education of disadvantaged children, and for children with a primary language other than English. Unfortunately, that has led to mimicry. States almost immediately organized their education agencies around these areas, as did most school districts of a reasonable size.

This simple act led to much of the program isolation evident today. In what has become a virtual chain-of-command structure, state and local officials usually have only minor influence over these programs and functions. Even in 1999, five years after enactment of major policy changes in Title I meant to eliminate this isolation, it still exists.

Unfortunately, Congress has exacerbated this problem by enacting laws calling for additional bureaucracies and protecting those already operating in the belief that doing so will help children. But that is not the case, and structural rigidity often works against good service. This approach is not limited to the political left or right, and the ultimate irony would be the legislatively mandated creation of offices to serve charter school or voucher programs. In discussing colonization of state agencies, Hill gives recognition to the problem, but without explaining the entire context at the federal level. A provocative question is what would change if the federal programs were reorganized into a single organization that served all schools and states? Would that change things or has the silo structure become so institutionalized that it is beyond change?

I agree with Hill's assertion that federal programs did not directly lead to the current unrest about public schools. I do believe, however, that he gives scant attention to the role of the federal judiciary in undermining the authority of the schools. It has become a cliché to say that the United States is a litigious society, but consideration must be given to how, as a result, the possibility of establishing a coherent school culture has been severely eroded. While separate programs contribute to the problem, the courts have had the greatest impact in rulings that limit authority over dress, publications, speech, discipline, and more. Teachers also erode the culture of a school by dressing and acting more inappropriately than many students. The function of adults as role models is too rare.

A More Positive Federal Role

In his paper, Hill posits what he terms a new, more positive, federal role. Much of it I can easily agree with, for it represents the wisdom of careful reviews of the past. However, some major questions arise, some of which point out both the ironies of any change and the difficulties of not doing some things.

Hill proposes that children, not jurisdictions, should be subsidized. On its face that is a compelling idea. However, saying that all schools should get the same amount of state and local aid, the question immediately arises of how that would be enforced. Would there be regulations? How would they be enforced? By whom? And a law of this nature would bring with it enormous potential for lawsuits, some of which might be brought by teacher unions to challenge the potential abrogation of contracts that often permit senior teachers to move to schools of their choosing, few of which are schools that need the most help. New policy invites legal challenges. Children attending school in areas with high concentrations of poverty represent the most difficult challenge. Any proposal that has money following the child needs to take that factor into account. I do not know how that can be done in a way that does not invite greater federal involvement or that does not do something extra for those schools where concentrations of poor children are highest.

Under the constitutional system of separation of powers, judicial review cannot be prevented. The best hope is that the courts will come to understand their role in undermining certain aspects of society and restore to schools some ability to make and enforce reasonable regulations.

Hill does not want to reduce federal funding for students who perform at high levels. While I believe that his motivation is to ensure that students who have come from behind are not allowed to slip back, are there any limits to this policy? To take a case that may appear extreme, what about a poor child who starts out needing help in the early grades and then by middle school is doing just fine? How can continuing extra help to that child be justified when his younger sister may need it, and he is doing well?

The notion of short-term, special-purpose grants is another major issue. One need look only at the all-too-frequent use by Congress of hold-harmless provisions in annual appropriations bills or the inability to close obsolete military bases to understand how difficult this concept would be to sustain. Once federal aid begins to flow, the natural political forces keep it coming. It becomes very hard to cut off. How long did it take to make even the smallest changes in impact aid?

Hill calls for the creation of a board to consult with the secretary of education on spending these special-purpose grants. Having congressional appointees on such a board would raise separation of powers issues, as that is an inherently administrative function.

Hill wants to make the U.S. Department of Education a resource and not a ministry. While the imagery of that is great, I have a hard time envisioning a cabinet position called the secretary of national educational resources.

While I believe his major proposal is an excellent idea, I cannot imagine Congress, and particularly the Senate, consolidating all legislation affecting elementary and secondary education into one bill. While I have long advocated this approach, it will never happen. The pressures of interest groups in keeping their own programs separate, combined with congressional work schedules, serve to make this impossible. If that does not occur, it is hard to see how much of the rest of what Hill calls for would, or could, emerge. In the absence of this one bill, it might be worth thinking about what could be done within the context of legislation that is pending in the 106th Congress to bring about some reforms.

One immediate action would be to streamline the technical assistance and dissemination activities that are contained within the ESEA and Office of Educational Research and Improvement laws. Currently, there are a host of organizations, ranging from regional labs to comprehensive centers. Their roles and the connection among them are unclear. Few have any relationship to the national research centers, and fewer still are informed about or informed by the work being done in agencies such as the National Institute of Child Health and Human Development and NSF.

The Department of Education has not given much thought to getting information directly into the hands of consumers (teachers) via the use of new forms of technology such as the Internet and CD-ROMs. Nor has any action been taken to teach teachers how to be informed consumers of research and evaluation information. The recent publication on comprehensive school reform by the American Institutes for Research, sponsored by several national education organizations, that takes a consumers' report approach is a good first step. These actions represent an extension of Hill's views on the creation of an Investments Division that would sponsor research, development, and statistics. Hill calls for dissemination, but a system that will serve the consumer must be carefully planned and implemented if it is to affect teaching and learning and result in improved student achievement.

While Hill recommends this Investments Division as a part of the Department of Education to handle these areas, I believe that the research function should be removed from the department and placed in an independent agency that I call the Agency for Learning. This agency would also serve to link together the research being done in all federal agencies that is relevant to education. By removing it from the department, and creating a policy board comprised of public officials and educators, it would be removed from the politics of the Department of Education.

While I agree with Hill that results should be defined in terms of student and school performance, the practical problems of doing that on a basis that is equitable across states are significant. Given the National Research Council report on the equating of state tests, the use of a national test seems to be the only reasonable approach. Without that or some similar mechanism, proxy measures, such as census poverty data, that are unfair, outdated, and irrelevant will have to be used.

Any attempt to look at a new and better way to structure federal aid and support for education must pay careful attention to special interest groups. While federal assistance and support programs can take on many different configurations, any proposal to advance in the legislative arena must factor in consultation with powerful lobby groups, such as the Council for Exceptional Children, the American Vocational Association, the Title I parents' organizations, and bilingual education organizations. I believe that each of these groups is ready to consider new approaches to federal aid, but none will accept a plan without consultation and the willingness of the architect to accept modifications. Clearly, doing consultation is a dangerous game because one can easily lose control of both the issue and the idea. The alternative is yet another dead-on-arrival idea that will sink below the waves after a few days of fame.

Comment by Sally Kilgore

Paul T. Hill has an intimate acquaintance with federal legislation in education—both as a policymaker and as an evaluator. In his paper, he makes masterful use of that knowledge in providing a lively and penetrating analysis of the effects of federal educational legislation.

Hill recounts that federal funding in education was justified, or otherwise rendered constitutional, using the child benefit theory. Federal funds, the theory argues, provide support services to children in a school setting in ways that do not intrude upon a state's rights (or responsibility) to control the shape and mission of schools within its boundaries. The federal legislative initiatives in education sought to remedy inequalities that existed within schools and school districts for certain identifiable classes of students—the economically disadvantaged, those lacking English language skills, those with identifiable physical or mental disabilities, and girls who had been denied the same opportunities as boys, particularly in sports.

Such legislation initially provided funding to identifiable classes of children experiencing inequities in the existing system. In reauthorizations, additional inequities were addressed by new conditions of eligibility for those federal funds. The efforts to equalize opportunities for women, for instance, were achieved almost exclusively through establishing such new eligibility criteria for federal funds. With the passing of the Education for All Handicapped Children Act, localities were required to reallocate local and state (not federal) money to address the inequities in educational opportunities for students requiring special services.

As Hill notes, in the early period (1960s and 1970s) legislators and bureaucrats intentionally designed legislation to challenge or redistribute political power within local districts, establishing parent advisory counsels and new channels for grievances. Parents made new claims and exerted new pressures upon schools and district administrators. Less consciously, federal legislation reconfigured power within district offices with the introduction of what Hill refers to as the "colonialists"; that is, the local and state enforcers of the federal will.

Hill recognizes the profoundly important role played by federal legislation in addressing inequalities of opportunities but claims, appropriately, that the long-term—and unanticipated—consequences for children and schools have been detrimental. Hill provides vivid accounts of colonialists penetrating district offices, schools frozen by the constraints of the colonialists, interest groups clamoring for equity, state education departments living off the dole, and the federal government engineering yet another shift in power within communities.

Lessons learned from these thirty years lead Hill to recommend that future legislation in education should balance the traditional, and rightful, concern for poor and disadvantaged children with an effort to effect general school improvement. Legislation that meets these conditions, Hill suggests, should be built upon these principles:

—Subsidize children, not jurisdictions.

—Attack emergent problems with short-term solutions.

—Make the Department of Education a national resource, not a federal ministry.

—Become school-friendly.

—Define results in terms of student and school performance.

Recent Effects of Federal Legislation

Hill's historical account, in my estimation, understates the effects of shifts in power that emerged with each reauthorization of federal programs in education. Similarly, he fails to emphasize the more perverse incentive systems inherent in federal legislation.

SHIFTING POWER STRUCTURES. The fragmentation of school authority and mission so aptly described by Hill dissipated as increasing numbers of schools were eligible to adopt a schoolwide program and as federal offices permitted the commingling of funds across programs. Commendably, legislators sought to integrate the findings of extensive research into the 1994 reauthorization of the Elementary and Secondary Education Act (ESEA), all but eliminating a number of the procedural constraints that had created ineffectual and even detrimental instructional practices such as pullout programs. Broad categories of expenditures were mandated; for example, at least 10 percent of the revenue must be spent on professional development.

Unanticipated by this recent legislation and not addressed by Hill, though, was the substantial shift in the distribution of power within school districts. Eliminating many regulations on the use of federal funds led, I argue, to shifts in power and authority among central office administrators. Superintendents in urban districts have been provided unprecedented opportunities to deploy large sums of federal money to effect changes in classroom practices. Superintendents can and do mobilize millions of federal dollars allotted for professional development to implement priorities formulated in the superintendent's office. On the surface, such empowerment should be a welcomed relief from the reign of colonialists. Under these new conditions the potential for a coherent mission is greater. Long-term stability, however, is compromised, and the adaptability of these initiatives to local school needs is questionable.

School improvement plans required for Title I schoolwide projects must be made at the school level. Yet few school staff can deploy substantial resources in ways that reflect their understanding of the needs of students. Instead, district administrators usually control the particulars in classroom practice: the amount of time teachers devote to certain subjects, the instructional strategies used for certain subjects, which classrooms receive computers, and the specific software used for math and reading tutorials. Such district-level control in urban areas is often broad in scope and detailed in practice. Again, these actions are not inconsistent with research on effective instructional practices showing that, for instance, elementary teachers do not devote much time to mathematics and that they utilize ineffective instructional strategies in science and mathematics. These district actions are, however, inconsistent with research on effective strategies for change in organizational practices.

District officials who exercise such control claim that teachers and principals are unwilling to devote sufficient time to mathematics, are not equipped with the skills and knowledge to improve instructional strategies, and are not, for example, able to make sound decisions about software acquisitions for student learning. Certainly evidence can be marshaled to support their claim.

Research evidence, however, suggests that enduring change in practice originates from those persons required to carry out the change. Even if that evidence were not available, the folly remains. Increased district control leads to greater instability and insensitivity to varying needs across schools.

Increasing the authority with the most vulnerable part of any urban school system, its superintendent, leads to abandoned projects, cynical teachers, and weary administrators. The average shelf life of an urban school superintendent is 2.5 years. As is the way with transitions in bureaucratic or political leadership, new superintendents announce their presence by moving the organization in a new direction; if it was headed south, it must now go north. With such a short shelf life, teachers can (and perhaps should) ignore the new priorities and practices whenever possible. Changes in school practice implemented in one regime seldom endure, if they ever were practiced.

Certainly the experience in one urban school district illustrates this process. An innovative, committed, and intelligent school superintendent brought to a sleepy and lackluster district the press to be the best—to improve achievement levels of students, not within the decade, but within a year. The district adopted one of the most rigorous math programs available and required teachers to pursue lengthy training, at considerable expenditure of Title I funds. Elementary teachers were expected to devote ninety minutes a day to mathematics lessons, and pacing charts kept teachers moving from one topic to another.

Such fast-paced and relatively chaotic change was not well received. The school board bought out the superintendent's contract two years after the mathematics program had been adopted. Within four months of the departure of the superintendent, the mathematics program, its textbooks, and supporting materials were officially abandoned. No doubt some teachers acquired some skills and understandings as a result of that initiative, but in great measure, the effort—well intentioned as it was—sent millions of dollars down the proverbial drain.

The inability of district-level mandates to be equally relevant or useful to all schools is easily evident. For instance, instituting rules about mathematics instruction assumes that each school has the same instructional weaknesses. Such commonality is rarely accurate. Some schools, some grade levels, may have much greater need for improved reading instructional practices than for a new mathematics program. Well-intentioned superintendents have been known to mandate counselors for every elementary school, even when one or more schools have such services provided by a community agency housed within a school. Such mismatches are inevitable when strategies for change rely upon uniform mandates. Teacher cynicism and frustration inevitably emerge.

Earlier legislation, then, that concentrated authority with local and state colonialists had a long shelf life; practices endured in schools and classrooms well beyond legislation requiring them. The problem was that the endorsed practices did little to enhance achievement. Now, new conditions exist: Federal funds vacillate from one inspired vision to another with little possibility of penetrating the daily practices within the classroom and often failing to address a school's specific needs.

INCENTIVE SYSTEMS. Hill notes, but fails to develop, an argument about the perverse incentive structures that are inherent in much of the federal legislation. For districts, the amount of federal funds available varies directly with the proportion of students who possess some condition—economically disadvantaged, lacking proficiency in English, and so forth. Rationally, any savvy administrator would seek to maximize the number of students who meet such criteria.

Parents, too, have perverse incentives. Students with certain disabilities are entitled to more advantageous testing conditions (no time limits) and special tutors or services. As Hill notes, several investigations have uncovered the growing number of children with disabilities in upper-class suburban areas. Again, rational parents who seek to maximize the opportunities and advantages available to their children would (and should) seek to have them classified in ways that afford their children these special opportunities. The question for legislators, then, is how they can frame legislation that secures remedies but does not generate perverse incentives.

Some remedies can be achieved through changes in local practice. Others require reconstructing the particulars in legislation. For district-level incentives, the remedies seem fairly obvious: When districts are able to manipulate the amount of money flowing to them, the opportunity to undermine the original intent is great. Contrast Title I funds with bilingual education funding. Title I funds are distributed among districts according to census data collected by the Department of Commerce. The district has little capacity to manipulate the outcome. However, classifying children as lacking proficiency in English is almost exclusively within the purview of school officials. Thus, the regulatory structure of funding for bilingual programs creates more perverse incentives than that of Title I.

Remedies for undesirable incentives for students can, in part, be managed at the school or classroom level. For example, lifting time constraints for all students in state assessments, as well as classroom exams, eliminates one of the advantages associated with certain disabilities without curtailing the rights associated with that condition. Administratively, the change has some complications. Different types of assessments should be used under these conditions. Allocation of school time must be done differently under these conditions.

Misplaced Optimism?

It would be a mistake to take Hill's work as an exhaustive account of federal actions that impinged upon the school life of children and teachers in the last thirty years. Hill's scope appropriately focuses on the effects of legislation. That said, excluding the activities of state and federal courts overlooks the extraordinary confluence of events—both legislative initiatives and judicial decisions—that reconstituted the relations schools could and did have with students and their parents. Both branches established new avenues for conflict and grievances. Legislative actions also realigned local power structures, and judicial decisions introduced new procedural requirements that had, de facto, the same impact.

Identifying this confluence of legislative and judicial action is important for this discussion only if the judicial requirements undermine the anticipated effects of legislative changes. Thus, the ability of future legislation to mend the fractured relations between parents and schools is limited given all the judicial decisions that established due process for students, and so on. However, one can maintain optimism that legislative actions can affect the coherence of instruction experienced by children.

Guiding Principles for Future Legislation

If one takes these caveats and adjustments to Hill's account as valid, what are the ramifications for Hill's proposed principles to guide future legislation? The adjusted account requires that these principles acquire greater specificity to reduce the probability that unstable leadership or perverse incentives undermine the federal intent.

SUBSIDIZE CHILDREN, NOT JURISDICTIONS. Does the proposal to subsidize children, not jurisdictions, address the power or incentive problems with current practice? Only if the revenue transfers to parents instead of states. Cash does not have to move through a parent's bank account; a redeemable coupon or its equivalent could be used.

If new federal legislation subsidizes children and uses a public entity (even the school instead of the district and state offices), the likelihood is that federal auditors will require yet another trail of evidence linking each child with the expenditure of federal funds. A coupon transaction between the parent and school mitigates the need for such practices.

Suppose schools were eligible to receive coupons from parents if their practices and mission (1) accommodate the specified special needs within their regular program, (2) provide supplementary services before or after school that meet those needs, or (3) provide alternative services at the school site for those students requiring a separate program.

Other organizations could be certified to provide supplementary services with the understanding that they are sufficient accommodation and support for the student. Such a system would ensure that auditors would lack an oversight role on the procedural aspects of education and provide parents with meaningful options to meet their child's special needs. All changes introduce new problems. This change would be no exception. The new problem is: What institution, following what procedures, will determine which children are eligible to receive such coupons? Working through existing institutions—federal or state—would appear to provide the most cost-effective strategy.

ATTACK EMERGENT PROBLEMS WITH SHORT-TERM SOLUTIONS. Does this principle address the problems identified above? Relying more on short-term solutions can limit the likelihood that perverse incentives will be created with new streams of federal funding. But this principle is not sufficient to reduce the likelihood that local districts will exploit funding opportunities. To the degree feasible, identifying categories of children eligible to receive funding should be done by government agencies indifferent to the outcome, such as the Bureau of the Census. The greatest challenge to this principle will be bilingual funding, where many of the potential beneficiaries do everything they can to obscure their presence to government agencies.

STRENGTHEN SCHOOLS OVER PROGRAMS. Hill's emphasis on strengthening schools over programs is perhaps the most important principle for, in part, strategies that realize it will, of necessity, accord greater discretion at the school level and allow (but not ensure) more coherent and stable school policies to emerge.

With authority accorded to schools, a course of action could be sustained that is adapted to the specific needs of students at that school and to the particular resources in that neighborhood. However, some school systems in urban areas, for example, within New York and New Jersey, experience as much instability in school leadership as they do in district-level leadership.

In a sense then, this principle meets the Hippocratic test: Honoring it likely will move the federal role in education from harmful to not harmful. But taken by itself, devolving authority to schools will not lead to school improvement.

For school improvement to become more likely, building the capacity of principals and teachers should be part of the federal initiative. The current Title I funds set aside for professional development could serve as a model.

SERVICE, NOT A MINISTRY. Building the capacity of principals and teachers should be the first task, if the federal role in education is to become one more of service than of ministry—through research, support for discipline-based institutes, and long-term professional development programs at schools. Information, though, of another sort is needed by schools. Regarding any legislative or judicial action, who knows what the document says or means in practice? Part of the colonialists' power arose from their ability to be the sole interpreter of federal regulatory requirements. School lawyers presumably provide competing or alternative interpretations. But large pockets of relevant folks, especially principals, were unable to challenge the interpretations imposed by the colonialists.

As a secondary challenge, then, to becoming a resource instead of a ministry, federal offices must aggressively seek out ways to ensure that all parties have equal access to regulatory information in intelligible form. Democratizing access to such information should be an integral component of the role of a national resource.

What is evident from this evaluation of Hill's guiding principles for new legislation is that legislators who pick and choose among these principles, as if to suggest that Hill has offered them a buffet of policy options, will not get the federal role out of the box. Choosing to subsidize children, but disregarding the need to become school-friendly, could create more adverse circumstances for children than those they currently encounter.

DEFINE RESULTS IN TERMS OF STUDENT AND SCHOOL PERFORMANCE. Focusing on results when evaluating the effects of federal programs is essential—even fundamental. Lurking in the shadows, though, is the use of student or school performance as a condition of eligibility.

Legislators have been wise to avoid such criteria. The proposal, however, to require states to provide for reconstituting a school with persistently low performance is sound. Current Title I legislation requires that the effects of program initiatives be evaluated using the same assessment as that used for other students or schools. In the long run, this requirement may be the most positive change in the last reauthorization. Perverse incentives would inevitably arise with more intrusive directives than those exercised to date.

One best solution does not exist, but one best priority does: Maximize the likelihood that legislation encourages (or does not undermine) the development of coherent and effective instruction.

Notes

1. See, for example, James S. Coleman and Thomas Hoffer, *Public and Private High Schools: The Impact of Communities* (Basic Books, 1987); Anthony S. Bryk and others, *Catholic Schools and the Common Good* (Harvard University Press, 1993); Paul T. Hill, Gail E. Foster, and Tamar Gendler, *High Schools with Character* (Santa Monica, Calif.: RAND, 1990); Robert L. Crain, *The Effectiveness of New York City's Career Magnet Schools* (Columbia University, Institute on Education and the Economy, 1992); Adam Gamoran, "Do Magnet Schools Boost Achievement?," *Educational Leadership*, vol. 54, no. 2 (1996), pp. 42–46; and Paul T. Hill and others, *Schools' Integrative Capital* (University of Washington, Center on Re-Inventing Public Education, 1998).

2. Even today private schools use the concept of "disabilities" sparingly because no government fiscal or regulatory structure exists to push them into classifying students. Nobody denies that some children have special needs and that they appear in all schools, including private schools. But the label "special education" has become so elastic that it now includes children who would, in the absence of a federal program, be assisted by their regular classroom teachers and never considered "different."

3. See, for example, John F. Hughes and Anne O. Hughes, *Equal Education: A National Strategy* (Indiana University Press, 1972), chapter 2.

4. There were small federal programs intended to help schools and districts improve classrooms and teaching methods, and, for a time, the federal government subsidized the training of teachers no matter where they chose to teach. But such initiatives lacked the political appeal of intervention on behalf of children who had suffered neglect or discrimination, and they were not nearly as stable or as well funded as the Title I–style programs.

5. See, for example, Jane Hannaway, "Administrative Costs and Administrative Behavior Associated with Categorical Programs," *Educational Evaluation and Policy Analysis*, vol. 7, no. 1 (Spring 1985), pp. 57–64; and Jane Hannaway and Lee S. Sproull, "Who's Running the Show?: Coordination and Control in Educational Organizations," *Administrator's Notebook*, vol. 27, no. 9 (1978–79), pp. 1–4.

6. See Lorraine McDonnell and Anthony Pascal, *Teacher Unions and Educational Reform* (Santa Monica, Calif.: RAND, 1988). See also Lorraine McDonnell and Anthony Pascal, *Organized Teachers in American Schools* (Santa Monica, Calif.: RAND, 1979).

7. For a detailed account of these problems and schools' responses, see Jackie Kimbrough and Paul T. Hill, *Problems of Implementing Multiple Categorical Education Programs* (Santa Monica, Calif.: RAND, 1983).

8. See, for example, Fred M. Newmann and others, *Authentic Achievement: Restructuring Schools for Intellectual Quality* (San Francisco, Calif.: Jossey-Bass, 1996); Coleman and Hoffer, *Public and Private High Schools*; Bryk and others, *Catholic Schools and the Common Good*; Hill, Foster, and Gendler, *High Schools with Character*; Crain, *The Effectiveness of New York City's Career Magnet Schools*; Gamoran, "Do Magnet Schools Boost Achievement?"; and Hill and others, *Schools' Integrative Capital.*

9. Mary Jean Le Tendre, "Title I Schoolwide Programs: Improving Schools for All Children," *Journal of Education for Students Placed at Risk*, vol. 1, no. 2 (1996), pp. 109–11.

10. See, for example, Donna Muncey and Patrick McQuillan, *Reform and Resistance in Schools and Classrooms: An Ethnographic View of the Coalition of Essential Schools* (Yale University Press, 1996). See also Bruce A. Bimber, *The Decentralization Mirage: Comparing Decisionmaking Arrangements in Four High Schools* (Santa Monica, Calif.: RAND, 1994).

11. For an account of the effects of these programs, see Jackie Kimbrough and Paul T. Hill, *The Aggregate Effects of Federal Education Programs* (Santa Monica, Calif.: RAND, 1980).

12. Federal policy in this regard was influenced strongly by University of Chicago professor Benjamin Bloom's research showing that disadvantaged children could benefit by "compensatory" (for example, additional) instruction. On the influence of Bloom's work, see Hughes and Hughes, *Equal Education*, p. 43.

13. Washington Research Project, *Title I of ESEA: Is It Helping Poor Children?* (New York: NAACP Legal Defense and Education Fund, 1969). See also Hughes and Hughes, *Equal Education*, chapter 2.

14. Samuel Halperin, "Decennial Views of the Revolution: The Positive Side," *Phi Delta Kappan*, vol. 57, no. 3 (November 1975), pp. 147–51, quoted matter on p. 149.

15. See Paul T. Hill and Ellen L. Marks, *Federal Influence over State and Local Government: The Case of Nondiscrimination in Education* (Santa Monica, Calif.: RAND, 1982).

16. Anthony S. Bryk, *Democratic Localism: A Lever for Institutional Renewal* (Los Angeles, Calif.: Westview Press, 1997).

17. Patricia Morrissey, "The Individuals with Disabilities Education Act of 1997: Selected Observations," *National Association of Secondary School Principals' Bulletin*, vol. 82, no. 594 (January 1998), pp. 5–11.

18. As one superintendent said in an interview conducted for this paper, "If people knew how much special education drives a school system's budget, there would be a revolution."

19. See *Pennsylvania Association for Retarded Children* v. *Pennsylvania*, 343 Supp. 279, 307 (D.D. Pa. 1972).

20. See David Neal and David L. Kirp, *The Allure of Legalization Reconsidered: The Case of Special Education* (Stanford University, California Institute for Research on Educational Finance and Governance, 1983). See also Paul T. Hill and Doren Madey, *Education Policymaking through the Civil Justice System* (Santa Monica, Calif.: RAND, 1982).

21. See Richard Rothstein and Karen Hawley Miles, *Where's the Money Gone?: Changes in the Level and Composition of Education Spending* (Washington: Economic Policy Institute, 1995).

22. On rules for dealing with student behavior, see Jackson Toby, "Getting Serious about School Discipline," *Public Interest*, vol. 133 (Fall 1998), pp. 68–83.

23. The Department of Health, Education, and Welfare (HEW) Office of Civil Rights did succeed for a while in creating an administratively enforced entitlement to bilingual education, based on the principles established in *Lau* v. *Nichols*, 414 U.S. 563 (1974). *Lau* had the force of law only in the defendant's school district, San Francisco, but HEW applied the terms of the court order to school districts throughout the country.

24. Alfie Kohn, "Only for My Kid: How Privileged Parents Undermine School Reform," *Phi Delta Kappan* (April 1998), pp. 569–77.

25. Governor's Task Force on Education, *Model for the Future: An Organization Study of the Ohio Department of Education* (Columbus, Ohio: State of Ohio, 1991).

26. Data in the text are drawn from Department of Education, *The Use of Federal Administrative Funds for Administrative Costs* (Department of Education, Planning and Evaluation Service, 1998).

27. State-level litigation about whether different groups were getting equitable shares of federal and state program funds also led to rigid court-imposed funding categories, so that districts and schools are forced to spend fixed sums for items such as student transportation, even when they would prefer to use additional funds for teachers, instructional materials, and so on. See, for example, *Washington State Special Education Coalition* v. *State of Washington et al.* (known as the Doran Decision III), Thurston County Superior Court (WA), 1988.

28. See Kimbrough and Hill, *Problems of Implementing Multiple Categorical Education Programs*, for evidence that some services for handicapped children are paid for by reducing what is provided to Title I–eligible students who are not also handicapped.

29. For a discussion of the consequences of these requirements for handicapped children as well as for others, see Toby, "Getting Serious about School Discipline."

30. These results will be reported in a forthcoming University of Washington book on the results of a national study of charter school accountability.

31. Kati Haycock, "Eliminate Gross Disparities under Your Control," *School Administrator* (May 1997), pp. 30–31.

32. See, for example, Jackie Kimbrough, *The Aggregate Effects of Federal Education Programs* (Santa Monica, Calif.: RAND, 1981).

33. Denis P. Doyle, *Where the Connoisseurs Send Their Children to School* (Indianapolis, Ind.: Hudson Institute, 1995); Sari Horowitz, "Poll Finds Backing for D.C. School Vouchers: Blacks Support Idea More Than Whites," *Washington Post*, May 23, 1998; and Jean Johnson and John Immerwahr, "First Things First: What Americans Expect from the Public Schools," *American Educator*, vol. 18, no. 4 (1995), pp. 4–6, 8, 11–13, 44–45.

34. For a compatible, but different, set of principles, see Chester E. Finn and Michael J. Petrilli, "Washington versus School Reform," *Public Interest*, vol. 133 (Fall 1998), pp. 55–64.

35. Diane Ravitch named this idea a "portable entitlement." See Diane Ravitch, "Student Performance: The National Agenda in Education," in Marci Kanstoroom and Chester E. Finn Jr., eds., *New Directions: Federal Education Policy in the Twenty-First Century* (Washington: Thomas B. Fordham Foundation, 1999), pp. 139–46.

36. Unpublished estimates of the added cost of a "portable entitlement" range from $4 billion to $20 billion annually. The size of the estimate appears to depend on the analyst's view of the desirability of such a change in federal program strategy.

37. For more fully developed suggestions along the same line, see Christopher T. Cross, *The Federal Role in R, D, & D: A Vision of the Future* (Washington: Council on Basic Education, 1999).

38. For lists of such proposals, see Stanley Pogrow, "Title I: Wrong Help at the Wrong Time," in Marci Kanstoroom and Chester E. Finn Jr., eds., *New Directions: Federal Education Policy in the Twenty-First Century* (Washington: Thomas B. Fordham Foundation, 1999); and Tyce Palmaffy, "Title I: Despite the Best of Intentions," in Marci Kanstoroom and Chester E. Finn Jr., eds., *New Directions: Federal Education Policy in the Twenty-First Century* (Washington: Thomas B. Fordham Foundation, 1999).

Can Title I Attain Its Goal?

GEORGE FARKAS *and*
L. SHANE HALL

IN A STATEMENT released on April 1, 1965, President Lyndon B. Johnson used the following words to argue for passage of the Elementary and Secondary Education Act (ESEA) of 1965:

> This bill has a simple purpose: To improve the education of young Americans.... How many young lives have been wasted; how many families now live in misery; how much talent has the Nation lost; because we have failed to give all our people a chance to learn.... This bill represents a national determination that this shall no longer be true. Poverty will no longer be a bar to learning, and learning shall offer an escape from poverty.... For this truly is the key which can unlock the door to a great society.

More than thirty years and $118 billion later, two national evaluation studies have concluded that these goals have not been met.[1] The skill gap in reading, writing, and mathematics has not been closed between, on the one hand, children from low-income households—often African American or Hispanic and attending central city or rural school systems—and, on the other hand, middle-class children—often Anglo and attending suburban school systems.

This comes as no surprise. The federal government's more than thirty-year attempt to solve the problems of poverty—in particular, the diminished life chances of children from low-income households—has been largely unsuccessful. Title I of the ESEA is, and has been, the most heavily funded program in this area. At $8.3 billion for 1999 alone, this program is funded at approximately twice the level of the better-known Head Start program. The failure to win the War on Poverty is largely attributable to the failure of these two programs to achieve their goals: the school success of low-income children.

Our focus here is Title I—federal aid to schools with large numbers or percentages of poor children, historically targeted on boosting the performance of these children in grades one through three and usually working most intensely on reading. The ineffectiveness of this program occurs for many of the same reasons that cause the more general ineffectiveness of low-income schools and districts. The funding creates a separate bureaucracy within the larger central district bureaucracy, and the education officials do not have the same focus on getting the children reading at grade level as do the teachers in the schools.

The teachers themselves are poorly supported. Colleges of education teach them little of relevance to assisting low-income students to read. Once they begin teaching, they are typically isolated with a classroom of children who are cognitively and behaviorally unprepared to do the work prescribed by the curriculum. Training and supervision from administrators are often minimal.

Title I has functioned as a small add-on to this general situation. Deeply embedded in the existing culture of schools, it has funded additional teachers and aides who work with the lowest performing children in small groups or one-to-one. These teachers and aides often have little special training, or when they do have such training, it is based on the whole language model, which has been popular in education schools for many years. Thus, they are typically untrained in those research-based (phonics) models that are most effective, particularly for low-income children.

Unfortunately, the 1994 reauthorization of the ESEA introduced new problems and exacerbated old ones. It diluted what was already a weak intervention for the lowest performing, low-income children. What was once a program directed almost exclusively toward grades one through three, when it is still possible to successfully assist low performers, was expanded to cover grades four through twelve, so that now only 37 percent of participants are in grades one through three. What was once a program providing personalized, add-on services to the lowest performers in low-income schools was altered to enormously increase the number of schoolwide programs. The result has been to decrease add-on services provided to the lowest performers and to encourage school administrators to use the funds to displace local funds; that is, to spend the Title I money on goods and services (computers, copying machines, furniture, classroom teacher salaries) that would have been paid for with local funds.

As a result, the population of Title I participants has shifted, from an almost exclusive focus on students receiving additional, personalized assistance to include every student enrolled in more than sixteen thousand schools with schoolwide Title I programs. Consequently, the Department of Education in 1999 counts 11 million program participants, where before reauthorization in 1994 there were only 6 million. And a program that for many years has been criticized as being merely a funding stream, with too little impact on the neediest children, has become even more incoherent and minimal in impact.

This is a dire situation. To even begin to correct it, the damage done by the 1994 reauthorization must be undone, while the more long-standing problems that have plagued the program for the past thirty-three years must be corrected. Accordingly, we have adopted the following strategies: First, see the problem in its most fundamental terms. That is, begin with the nature and determinants of the cognitive skill gap between low- and middle-income children as they enter and age through their schooling years. Next, focus on the most cost-effective practices for bringing these children up to a middle-class performance level. Be fearless in describing the current state of instruction under Title I and the extent to which it differs from these practices. Finally, be bold in suggesting how the program might be improved.

The Problem of School Achievement for Low-Income Children

In all societies at all times, the children of lower class parents (parents with the lowest levels of education and income) have begun life at a disadvantage. Central to this is their home experience during the preschool years: imitation of nonstandard speech patterns, too little conversation with adults, weak vocabulary development, too little experience with books, too little practice using language to express complex ideas, little or no instruction and practice with phonological awareness and other prereading skills such as learning the names of the letters and the sounds they make. Perhaps most damaging is the immaturity that many low-income children bring to first grade. They often come to school unready to sit still, pay attention to the teacher and the lesson, and do their own work. A first-grade teacher with a class of twenty or more low-income children, more than half of whom are at this level of immaturity, typically finds it difficult-to-impossible to get them to concentrate on the assigned work and put forth the effort and time-on-task necessary to master the curriculum. This difficulty is further compounded by two instructional problems. First, the children are already behind in their skills. And second, the teacher is not typically using the most effective, research-based curriculum and instructional techniques.

As a consequence, children from low-income households reach the end of the first grade seriously behind in their schoolwork and already well into a cycle of failure in which their skills are below the level demanded by the curriculum, and their self-esteem, willingness to try, and time-on-task are inadequate to succeed at the assigned tasks.[2] They then fall even further behind during the summer.[3]

By the beginning of second grade, the situation of children who are receiving negative feedback from this process, and are not progressing at grade level, worsens dramatically. The second-grade curriculum assumes that students can read acceptably, and the reading level expected increases substantially during this year. The teacher has little choice in moving the class on to higher reading levels, because many other and related skills must be mastered: spelling and capitalization, punctuation, composing and writing essays and stories, and (sometimes) cursive writing. In addition, the students must be moving forward in their mathematics, social studies, science, music, art, and other subject matter instruction. All of these require substantial time-on-task, and many are themselves dependent upon the student's ability to read and write. Inevitably, children who begin second grade below the level expected by the curriculum, who are already discouraged about their inability to master the required material, and who receive less assistance from their parents than do middle-class children fall further behind during second grade. And then, low-income children fall even further behind middle-class children during the summer break.

The pattern repeats again in third grade. And the third-grade curriculum is the last to include substantial amounts of basic skills instruction. By now, the assigned reading is demanding in terms of sophisticated vocabulary and reading comprehension. Reading is not to be done simply line by line. Instead, students are expected to keep the main theme of the piece in mind while observing the development of subthemes. Reading must be fluent, as must the student's ability to compose and write essays and stories. Cursive writing must also be mastered. As noted by Nancy Madden and others, "Disadvantaged third graders who have failed a grade or who are reading significantly below grade level are very unlikely to graduate from high school . . . and will experience difficulties throughout their school careers."[4]

By fourth grade, the curriculum and teacher focus are no longer on basic skills, such as learning to read. Instead, students are expected to be reading to learn detailed subject matter in science, social studies, and so forth. Language arts and mathematics assume the more basic skills and advance rapidly through more sophisticated material. Yet, the majority of low-income fourth graders read below grade level.[5] At this point basic skills instruction is reduced, yet the curricular shift to higher order skills is a further obstacle for low-income children whose home life and school experience have provided weak vocabulary development and little experience in extended conversations using abstract concepts.[6] As a consequence, these students become essentially lost to the system. Whether or not they are placed in special education or other remedial programs, they never catch up.

To summarize this process, low-income and minority-group children begin first grade approximately one instructional year below middle-class children. As measured by instructional time (the time required to teach the curricular material that must be made up), the distribution of low-income childrens' skills shifts leftward relative to the national norms, so that by twelfth grade it is at the eighth-grade level.[7] Narrowing and ultimately eliminating this gap has long been the Title I goal.

What Could Be Done under Ideal Circumstances?

At least half the twelfth-grade gap could be eliminated if the first-grade gap were eliminated.[8] Thus a natural demarcation seems to exist between actions for children up to kindergarten versus those for first through twelfth grade.

Preschool through Kindergarten

Because too many low-income children enter first grade lacking the cognitive and behavioral skills and habits to do the assigned work, this problem must be attacked directly in the preschool and kindergarten years.

First, the oral English language skills and early alphabetic and phonemic awareness skills of these children must be increased during their preschool years. Perhaps most easily implemented and most valuable would be to improve the instruction provided by Head Start and similar programs. At present, Head Start has no curriculum whatever. Meanwhile, this federal program—with no issues of local control—is nonetheless totally decentralized and sets no standards for learning. Preschool and Head Start staff too often use the excuse that the children are not developmentally ready to avoid teaching them the very skills that middle-class parents provide as a matter of course. Yet research shows that children aged three to six are able to learn these skills and must be taught these skills if they are to succeed in school later.[9] Appropriately providing this instruction to low-income children requires strong skills on the instructor's part and is absolutely essential if these children are to be ready for elementary school.

Other desirable interventions include programmatic efforts to assist parents to provide more learning experiences for their preschoolers. Low-income parents should be taught to converse more with their children, to read to them, to work with them on phonemic awareness, and to teach them their letters and sounds.[10] Such instruction would be enormously valuable but has rarely been successfully implemented on a large scale.

Second, it is crucial that all children attend a full-day kindergarten, that kindergarten teachers work hard to get their students ready to read by the beginning of first grade, and that they use research-based instruction as the basis for their efforts. Far too often the attitude is, "It's only kindergarten, we can't expect teacher and student to get that much done." Yet, as noted by Grover Whitehurst, "For low income children, first grade is bearing down on them like a freight train."[11] And children who are unused to sitting still and doing academic work, who are without practice in phonemic awareness (particularly if they speak a language other than English, black English, or another strong dialect), and who do not know their letters and sounds by the beginning of first grade are unlikely to end the year reading at grade level. First-grade teachers in low-income schools often complain that kindergarten teachers send them children who are not ready to learn to read. The low-income schools that have solved this problem typically have a strong phonics-based instructional program operating in kindergarten.

Finally, a strong, skills-based program during the summer between kindergarten and first grade could provide low-income children a crucial head start toward successful reading in first grade. But this will be the case only if the program focuses on those skills—phonemic awareness, letter and sound correspondences, sounding out skills with decodable text, concentration in class, and good work habits—that research has shown to translate directly into reading success in first grade.

First through Twelfth Grade

Test-score data, classroom observation, and conversations with teachers lead to the same conclusion: Teachers in grades one through twelve in low-income schools are daily failing to adequately educate hundreds of thousands of children. The reality in each such classroom is a teacher with too little appropriate training and too little administrative support, attempting to work with twenty to thirty children, many of whom are unready to concentrate on schoolwork, unsupported at home, and unprepared intellectually to learn the assigned curriculum. If teachers were doctors and this many children had physical injuries that were not being successfully treated, the situation would be considered a national scandal, and aggressive efforts would be made to set matters right. And yet this instructional situation is even more damaging to these children because they are blamed for their failure. What can be done?

First, adopt a medical model. That is, allow zero tolerance for losing children instructionally. Every child could be approached on an individual basis with the goal of doing whatever is necessary to have that child performing at the level demanded by the curriculum. This would include assessment of phonemic awareness, letter and sound knowledge, word decoding skill, and the ability to sit still and concentrate at the beginning of first grade. Something like the case-management file maintained on the child's physical health by the child's doctor would be kept for each child in school. This file would focus on the child's healthy cognitive development and would be monitored to ensure that the child was progressing adequately through the curriculum.

Second, institute a schoolwide behavioral management system to assist teachers in gaining and retaining the discipline and order necessary for effective instruction.[12] This may be the most important prerequisite to the effective instruction of low-income children. Because these children have been inadequately socialized to the classroom and are cognitively unprepared for the curriculum, their teacher often spends so much time and effort maintaining order that time and effort on instruction are significantly reduced. The best of these teachers develop their own techniques for maintaining classroom discipline. Most involve some sort of public record of the number of each child's good and bad behaviors for that day ("smily" and "frowny" faces on the corner of the blackboard next to each child's name, for example), combined with rewards and punishments at the end of the day. Nevertheless, even the most effective use of these classroom systems is enormously enhanced by a schoolwide program in which appropriate student behavior within a positive learning environment is promoted by such devices as a creed recited by the children each day; daily assemblies with a positive message; administrators who are constantly present, are supportive, and know all children by name; and a disciplinary system that directly links the classroom with the front office. Further, the absence of this schoolwide support makes it much more difficult, if not impossible, for teachers to maintain effective behavioral management within their classrooms.

Third, teacher training and the classroom curriculum must be built around research-based instructional methods. This includes the use of decodable text for beginning readers and an early instructional focus on the most effective techniques, including phonemic awareness and explicit phonics instruction.[13]

Finally, appropriate and powerful interventions should be used early to bring low-performing children up to grade level. For children who are unable to concentrate, a medical workup and both behavioral and chemical therapy may be indicated.[14] For children who are falling behind the classroom instructional pace, and thus cannot participate successfully, intensive tutoring should be introduced to bring them back up to the classroom instructional level. This tutoring should use the most effective possible curriculum.[15] It should occur during the school year to catch children up to grade level, and during the summer to keep them from falling behind. It must then be available in future grades as an added boost for those who are once again beginning to fall behind. (Unfortunately, because low-income children benefit from weaker home inputs than do middle-class children, such falling behind by low-income children in higher grades is inevitable, given a national standard of curricular pace geared to middle-class student support levels.)

Why Has This Agenda Not Been Implemented?

This agenda would go a long way toward solving the schooling problems of low-income children. Certainly any serious attempt to solve these problems must include many of these elements. Why, then, has this agenda not been implemented? Answering this question will provide two benefits to our analysis of Title I policies. First, the culture and institutions of schooling that have made Title I what it is will be explained. Second, the likely system responses to change in Title I policies will be discussed. Such understanding is a necessary basis for meaningful strategizing about the likely benefits and costs of alternative policy changes.

Schools Have Weak Technical Environments

Organizational theorists John W. Meyer, W. Richard Scott, and their associates characterized the public schools as operating within strong institutional but weak technical environments. Consequently, according to these researchers, "organizational attention is directed toward maintaining conformity with the socially standardized categories of the educational system, while little effort is expended in the control and coordination of instructional activities."[16] Specifically regarding curriculum and the delivery of instruction, detailed standards of instructional content or procedures are lacking; instructional innovations are poorly supported and come and go unsystematically, whereas innovations in noninstructional areas such as school health and cafeteria services are better supported and are more stable; teachers receive little useful training or colleague support to assist them with their instructional duties; and little attention is paid to coordinating instruction, so that, for example, individual teachers and classes are permitted and even encouraged to pursue unrelated or contradictory programs and students are often promoted to the next grade without having mastered the present grade's material. As for monitoring the results of instruction, the job performance of teachers and principals is rarely observed systematically or monitored in a meaningful way, and although teachers constantly test their students, opposition exists within districts to using standardized test data to evaluate the performance of individual teachers, schools, or districts.[17]

Control by School District Administrative Elites

Analyzing the same behaviors from a rational choice perspective, Terry M. Moe agreed that the schools are too little concerned with the control and coordination of instructional activities but ascribed this to interest group politics within and beyond school districts. He stated, "The structure of education . . . has to do with who has power, with what their interests are, and with what kinds of structures they demand, design, and impose to see those interests pursued."[18] As presented in a longer work by John E. Chubb and Terry M. Moe, this rational choice and interest group politics view sees individual school actors pursuing power, self-interest, and rents via all the available techniques of interest group politics.[19]

Institutionalist researchers in the same tradition as Meyer and Scott have begun to adopt a similar perspective on organizational environments that fail to adequately control and coordinate their technical functions. As stated by Walter W. Powell, "How are practices and structures perpetuated over time, particularly in circumstances where utilitarian calculations would suggest they are dysfunctional? Why are practices reproduced when superior options are available? Why are less-than-optimal arrangements sustained, even in the face of opposition?" The answer, he said, lies in the exercise of power. "Practices and structures often endure through the active efforts of those who benefit from them. . . . It is clear that elite intervention may play a critical role in institutional formation. And once established and in place, practices and programs are supported and promulgated by those organizations that benefit from prevailing conventions. In this way, elites may be both the architects and products of the rules and expectations they have helped devise."[20]

This emphasis upon school district and education school elites and their use of power in the pursuit of self-interest via all means available, including "preservation of patterns of values[,] . . . the selection of new recruits, the socialization of successors, and control over the conditions of incumbency," provides a necessary background for understanding the implementation of Title I in the nation's school districts.[21] The districts we have observed display intensely networked management structures, supporting almost constant strategic behavior by individuals and groups. Classroom teacher is the lowest status among professional staff. Advancement out of this status typically requires the support of the school's principal and assistant principal, but professional specialty groups (for example, the group of reading curriculum specialists, Title I teachers, special education teachers, bilingual education teachers, and so on) and ethnic or other affiliation groups (for example, the Hispanic Teachers Association, the African-American Teachers Association, and their community affiliates) are also a resource.[22] The higher one seeks to rise, the more important are network connections. Every principal other's assistant principal. And the real jump in power, pres pensation is out of the schools and into the central adminis requiring patronage by individuals already there.

In addition to this vertical hierarchical structure is a horizontal structure of functional specialization, typically tied to funding streams. Not only does, say, the Curriculum Division have its own budget and management structure, but compensatory programs such as Title I, special education, and bilingual education account for even larger budgets, whose source is outside the district but whose expenditure is controlled by divisional managers within the district. When these vertical, horizontal, and other (such as ethnic group) structures are overlaid, the resulting grid provides almost unlimited potential for networked alliances and conflicts. For example, an assistant principal may be tapped for promotion into the central administration Reading Division, where his or her activities involve programs paid for with Title I funds but deployed and implemented by the staff of individual schools. Success requires the acquiescence and support of a wide variety of power centers. And each of these power centers has its own beliefs and culture, sustained by a network of personal affiliations, both within and outside the district. Only by understanding these can the deployment of resources and instructional practices for low-income children in the schools make sense.

The Reading Wars

In our visits to schools and districts over the past ten years, we have found the same conditions reported by Meyer and Scott at the beginning of the 1980s.[23] In particular, with regard to curriculum and instruction issues for low-income children, we have seen few serious and even fewer successful attempts to cope with the fact that low-income children enter school with nonstandard speech patterns, less mature behavior, and weaker oral vocabularies and knowledge of letters and sounds than do the middle-class children at whom the curriculum and teacher training are aimed.

Do most school districts begin working more intensively in kindergarten to help these students make up their deficits? No. Kindergarten is often optional or only half-day. And despite research to the contrary, many kindergarten teachers and district instructional specialists believe that the children are "not developmentally ready."[24] In this case, do districts modify at least their first-grade curriculum to be less demanding, so as to better match the skills brought to school by these students? No. As one administrator said, "It is politically impossible to officially 'dumb-down' the curriculum for inner-city children." Instead, low-income children are presented with a curriculum they are unprepared for, taught by teachers who are untrained to cope with the students' lack of preparation.

Are the most effective instructional methods being used? No. In spring 1997 one of us attended a meeting at which the reading director of one of the nation's largest school districts told some two hundred of the district's elementary school principals that "because whole language instruction has won out over phonics in the education schools for the past 10 years, few to none of your teachers know how to properly teach reading." The principals nodded their agreement. This raises the question: Where are the schools today in the phonics versus whole language reading war?

Efforts have been made to impose a truce, based on a National Research Council (NRC) report arguing for "a balanced approach."[25] In practice, this means implementing the results of research demonstrating that explicit phonemic awareness and word decoding skill training are the most effective instructional techniques for beginning readers. The strength of these findings is overwhelming.[26] This research also demonstrates that, while some children do pick up the necessary skills without explicit phonics instruction, those suffering most from the absence of this instruction are low-income, second-language, and ethnic minority children. And yet, the NRC recommendation for explicit (not "embedded") phonics instruction for beginning readers is far from being fully implemented.

A networked group of researchers has sought to solidify and disseminate the findings in support of phonics instruction. Reid Lyon, the chief of reading research at the National Institute of Child Health and Human Development (NICHD) and a reading disabilities specialist, has led this effort. Coordinating work by more than one hundred researchers across fourteen research centers, he verified the results and then undertook a public campaign of dissemination.[27] At first, the greatest success occurred among the top administrators of a few state education systems. Bill Honig, the California superintendent of instruction from 1983 to 1993 who presided over the takeover of the state's reading instruction by whole language, noted that since then state reading scores on the National Assessment of Educational Progress (NAEP) declined to next-to-last in the country. Honig thus declared himself a convert to phonics instruction for beginning readers. The California Department of Education moved to reduce whole language instruction and reintroduce phonics. Similar actions were taken by the Texas Department of Education, beginning in 1996.

Each side in the war has a social-movement-like commitment to a set of values and practices. On the phonics instruction side typically are scientifically oriented reading researchers—often with doctorates in cognitive psychology and appointments in psychology departments or medical schools and often affiliated with the NICHD research group—joined by some practitioners, including decisionmakers in some state education offices and local school districts, particularly in those states such as California and Texas that have had Republican governors.[28]

On the whole language side are advocates more typically based in the teacher training and community outreach departments of education schools, as well as in administrative positions within the instructional and compensatory education program divisions of local school districts. Title I funds controlled by these district administrators and shared with their allies in local university-based schools of education have played a central role as the funding base for the dissemination and maintenance of whole language instruction in a great many school districts.

Whole language is a rhetorical stance that resonates deeply with the core values of many education professionals. That is, it assists them in finding a sense of human agency and meaning in their professional work.[29] Building on these feelings, much of the organizational and political work of disseminating the whole language approach has been undertaken by a compensatory education program called Reading Recovery. Invented in New Zealand and first disseminated in the United States via the Ohio State University School of Education, Reading Recovery advocates have aggressively promoted their program and whole language philosophy to the point where both flourish in thousands of school districts nationwide. To take one example, in 1993–94 Reading Recovery operated in more than five hundred districts in California alone.[30] Its success at least partially stems from its structure as a networked interest group with a social-movement-like mentality.[31]

Reading Recovery is a compensatory education program that trains teachers to tutor at-risk first graders, one-to-one. It is based on a whole language philosophy that has traditionally resisted explicit instruction in phonemic awareness and sounding-out skills, preferring instead to teach a set of word guessing strategies (based on pictures in the text and the initial consonant of words) that research has shown to be used only by the weakest readers.[32] Despite these counterproductive instructional strategies, the program has an elite reputation in school districts and completely controls reading curriculum, teacher training in reading, and the expenditure of Title I funds in thousands of school districts. How has this occurred?

The answer lies in a remarkable example of grass-roots organizational growth across the national field of school districts, utilizing Title I funds to build mutually advantageous ties between education school faculty and school district administrators. Each district selects teachers to be trained at the university, on a fee-for-service basis. Typically the recruits are among the best teachers, which maintains the program's elite status and inclines it toward success (to the extent that these teachers are not rendered less effective by the whole language practices they are taught). After their university training in Reading Recovery, the teachers return to the district as reading specialists, receive higher salaries, are removed from the classroom to work with low-performing children one-to-one, and many rise to become district administrators with responsibility for reading curriculum and compensatory education programs. Other teachers, after receiving advanced degrees, stay on the education school faculty to administer the program there. These transactions are typically paid for by Title I program funds under the control of district administrators. Because these administrators have often themselves been trained in Reading Recovery and have close personal ties to other district staff who were so trained, they typically ignore the high unit costs of the program and the questionable validity of its research results.[33]

Despite research findings in opposition to its claims, whole language has come to dominate many districts' reading curricula. This has occurred partly because education school faculty who train reading teachers have become enamored of the whole language philosophy. But it has also been materially advanced by the financial base provided by Title I funds under the control of Reading Recovery–trained administrators and their allies. Even when phonics supporters in state education offices have moved to force local school districts to support "research-based instructional techniques," district administrators have used every trick, from simple lying to refusing to apply for earmarked funds, to resist.[34] This attitude is typified by what one superintendent said while refusing to continue funding the much lower (less than one-tenth) cost, paraprofessional (trained, managed, and compensated college student) tutoring program we had successfully demonstrated in her district: "We have $1.5 million of Title I funds, and they will always be completely dedicated to funding our Reading Recovery teachers."[35]

The Teaching Profession: A Comparison with Medicine

Because the daily implementation of Title I is strongly driven by the culture and structure of the teaching profession, any meaningful discussion of program reform requires an understanding of the profession itself. Using the comparative method, we contrast the structure and culture of teaching with that of medicine—the preeminent profession, which has demonstrated the ability to deliver high-quality services to the low-income community.

Superficially, at least, many similarities exist between school teaching and medicine. Both professions have government agencies and government funding directed toward them. Both have national lobbying organizations representing their interests. Each has its own professional school within many universities, where a faculty of experts conducts research to advance knowledge while training the next generation of researchers and practitioners. These faculty members belong to professional associations and contribute to a professional literature. Beginning doctors and teachers learn their trade by practicing it within the bureaucratic service delivery structures of hospitals and school districts, respectively, often in low-income areas. Both sets of practitioners must perform under difficult circumstances within these bureaucracies. As they establish themselves within their profession, each set of practitioners often migrates from low-income urban service delivery to a higher income clientele in the suburbs.

Given these structural similarities, what is it about these professions that leads to such dissimilar outcomes for the low-income individuals who are the recipients of their services? In particular, why is it that gunshot-wound victims receive excellent medical care at inner-city hospitals, while children with reading difficulties rarely show improvement in inner-city schools?

At least part of the answer lies in the dissimilar culture of the two professions. Medicine is grounded in an outcomes-oriented, scientific worldview, where evidence of effectiveness is central. Its practitioners are trained to use state-of-the-art techniques to achieve the best possible result for each patient. Doctors-in-training are constantly presented with specific cases and asked what they would do. Best practice is demonstrated, and beginning doctors' efforts are critiqued. An unexpected negative outcome for any patient—whatever the experience level of the doctor in charge—is the immediate subject of discussion at a weekly meeting attended by practitioners.

By contrast, the education profession is not solidly based on a scientific outlook. Regular reading of the *Educational Researcher* (published by the American Educational Research Association) demonstrates that many education school faculty believe that the field, by its intrinsic nature, cannot and should not attempt to be built on a scientific basis.

Thus, most teachers, not surprisingly, report that their education school training taught them little that usefully applies to classroom teaching. As noted by Lyon: "Most report that they received little formal instruction in reading development and disorders during either undergraduate and/or graduate studies, with the average teacher completing only two reading courses. Surveys of teachers taking these courses indicate: (A) teachers rarely have the opportunity to observe professors demonstrate instructional reading methods with children; (B) coursework is superficial and typically unrelated to teaching practice; and (C) the supervision of student teaching and practicum experiences is fragmentary and inconsistent."[36]

When a student completes medical school, he or she undertakes a closely monitored internship and residency. At each stage the focus is on optimum outcomes for the patient. But a beginning teacher in a low-income school district is typically placed in the classroom and left to fend for himself or herself. He or she receives little or no assistance or monitoring. It is expected that, like the experienced teachers, he or she will concentrate on controlling the behavior of a class where most of the children begin and end the year well below grade-level performance.

Title I Implementation

A great deal is known about the actions that should be taken to bring low-income children up to grade level. Also clear is the structure and culture of the education profession, and the reasons that these actions have not been implemented. What sort of program has Title I legislation aimed to produce?

A Coherent Program or Merely a Funding Stream?

Title I has always been about money—the desire to provide extra financial assistance to schools and school districts with high concentrations of low-income children. However, as critics have noted, a revenue-sharing funding stream does not necessarily constitute a coherent program. The question arises: Has it been the intent of the legislation to create a coherent program?

A reading of the legislation shows that, from the beginning, the focus has been on providing a funding stream rather than a coherent program. Thus the original 1965 legislation provided funds to local educational agencies (LEAs) to hire staff, build facilities, purchase equipment, and cover "all appropriate costs" for any and all programs with the broad purpose of meeting the educational needs of disadvantaged children. In particular, the Senate report on the bill states that it is not the legislation's intention to prescribe specific programs or projects, believing that such decisions are better made at the local level. This has been the case for much of Title I's history, leading to comments such as those by James Berke and Michael Kirst, calling Title I an enormous success "as a fiscal device."[37] That is, for most of its history Title I has been a revenue-sharing program, in which the federal government passes funds to local school districts to spend on assisting the education of low-income children. This spending must occur within federal guidelines, which are loose enough to permit wide variation in program implementation. The result has been a program shaped, not by designers in Washington, but by the practices and culture of the education profession as it exists at the grass roots. Further, even though nationwide Title I expenditures are large in absolute terms, they constitute less than 10 percent of the expenditures of local school districts. Accordingly, districts have treated these funds as little more than a small add-on to whatever they were doing already.

Which Children Have Been Served?

Title I funds are allocated by formula grants through state education agencies to local education agencies. At least some funding has typically been provided to almost all counties, to more than 90 percent of school districts, and to more than 70 percent of public elementary schools in the nation.[38] The U.S. Department of Education allocates funds to the county level, based primarily on census statistics regarding the numbers of poor children aged five to seventeen in those areas. State education agencies then suballocate the funds to school districts based on the number of children from low-income families in each district. More than 90 percent of the funds are allocated through basic grants (funds in proportion to the county's share of the nation's children in poverty), with approximately 10 percent coming through concentration grants focused on counties and school districts with either sixty-five hundred or more students from low-income households, or more than 15 percent of students from low-income households.

Each school district then allocates funds to individual schools based on the number of low-income students in each school. Districts may rank schools separately by grade span (there is a long tradition of targeting elementary schools), but they must serve schools with poverty rates of 75 percent or more before serving lower poverty schools, regardless of grade span.

Schools with very high poverty rates may also qualify for the status of "schoolwide program," which permits wide latitude regarding how the funds are spent. In particular, schoolwide programs are released from the requirement of providing add-on (usually pullout) services to the lowest performing children and are instead able to serve all children by using Title I funds to pay for teacher salaries or to purchase computers, books, copying machines, furniture—whatever will benefit the school as a whole. This raises the possibility of displacement; that is, using Title I funds to pay for goods and services that the district would have paid for with its own funds in the absence of Title I, thereby decreasing the add-on services provided by Title I to the lowest performing children. This is one reason that, before the 1994 reauthorization, the threshold for attaining this status was set high—a school had to have 75 percent or more of its students in poverty (on free or reduced-price lunch)—and there were consequently very few schoolwide programs in the nation.

However, using the logic that pullout programs are bad because they are stigmatizing and the student misses regular classroom instruction while they are out of the classroom, the 1994 reauthorization changed the regulations so as to facilitate and encourage the use of schoolwide programs. For the 1995–96 school year, the threshold to qualify to be a schoolwide program decreased to 60 percent of students in poverty, and for the 1996–97 and subsequent school years the threshold decreased further to only 50 percent in poverty. The response has been dramatic. In 1988–89 only two hundred schools were in schoolwide status. By 1995 approximately five thousand were in this status, and by 1999 the number has risen to approximately sixteen thousand.[39] All other Title I schools are designated "targeted assistance" and must direct their Title I activities to the lowest performing children, who are provided add-on (typically pull-out) services. Priority for service is usually determined by testing the students and giving highest priority to those with the lowest scores.

The 1994 reauthorization instituted a second dramatic shift in the program's target population. Districts were encouraged to direct their funding beyond its usual focus on grades one through three, so as to also serve grades four through twelve. The impact of this policy is indicated by the fact that a program that once served children in grades one through three almost exclusively now has only 37 percent of its participants in these grades.[40]

What was for more than twenty-five years a program providing personal add-on instructional assistance to the lowest performing first to third graders in low-income schools has, in the past five years, dramatically reduced its services to these children. Further, these changes have made problematic the meaning of the term "program participant." This is because, with few schoolwide programs before the 1994 reauthorization, Title I program participation for most children referred to the actual receipt of personalized, small group or one-to-one, add-on instruction. Now, however, with the proliferation of schoolwide programs as well as extensive expenditures in grades above grade three, "program participants" include all students in schools with the schoolwide program designation. That is, the definition of a Title I program participant as a student receiving personal, customized add-on instructional assistance has effectively been eliminated. This is why the Department of Education reported annual program participation of 6 million students in the early 1990s, but 11 million students in 1999.[41] If the funds were spread thinly before, imagine the present situation.

Before reauthorization of Title I in 1994, most participants received personal add-on services. It is therefore this definition of program participation that applies to the data presented below from that time period.

Detailed information for subsequent time periods is not yet fully available. However, where more recent information is available (such as the Department of Education report *Promising Results, Continuing Challenges*, released in March 1999), we report that information also. However, note that for the post-reauthorization time period, the definition of "program participant" has become increasingly problematic.

Using NAEP data from 1994, we have calculated the effect of students' demographic characteristics on their rates of Title I program participation. The results are shown in table 1. Males participate at a slightly higher rate than females. Participation rates are highest in the West and lowest in the Northeast. Both African Americans and Hispanics participate at more than three times the rate of whites. The children of poorly educated parents have the highest participation rates. And rates are highest both in the central city and in rural areas. Despite the growth of schoolwide programs and the expansion of Title I to grades four through twelve, these participation rate patterns across demographic groups are similar to those reported for 1998 by the U.S. Department of Education.[42]

Table 2 shows the distribution of Title I participation across schools in 1996, by type of school. Participation rates are highest among elementary schools; schools in a city, town, or rural area; and schools with a high percentage of poor children. Among elementary schools with 75 percent or more on free or reduced-price lunch, the program participation rate is 98 percent. Once again, these patterns are similar to those reported by the department for 1998.

Table 3 displays the NAEP reading and mathematics skill levels of participating and nonparticipating students. Available data permit us to calculate these for reading scores in 1994 and for mathematics scores in 1996.

The second column of table 3 reports program participation rates. Combining the mathematics data, which are for 1996, with the reading data for 1994 shows a significantly increased rate of participation by fourth graders during this two-year period, from 13.6 percent to 22.0 percent. For eighth graders the participation rate almost doubled during this period, from 6.5 percent to 11.7 percent.

The percentage distributions of these students across skill levels demonstrates what has long been known and was emphasized in the *Prospects* study, the largest and most definitive evaluation of Title I ever undertaken. Title I students are very low performing, and the program has

Table 1. Title I Participation Rates in 1994 by Background Characteristics

Background characteristic	*Percent*
Gender	
Male	14.8
Female	12.3
Region	
Northeast	10.0
Southeast	14.5
Central	11.9
West	17.0
Race/ethnicity	
White	7.7
African American	28.2
Hispanic	30.2
Asian	5.0
Pacific Islander	6.3
American Indian	21.2
Parents' education	
Less than high school	21.7
Graduated high school	16.7
Education after high school	9.2
Graduated college	9.8
Type of location	
Large city	17.0
Fringe/large town	9.3
Rural/small town	16.5

Source: National Assessment of Educational Progress reading assessment data.
Note: Sample = 7,382.

generally been unable to narrow the gap between their performance and that of nonparticipants.[43] Thus, among fourth graders, 80.4 percent of participants scored below basic in reading, while this was the case for only 33.1 percent of nonparticipants. Similarly in math, 69.2 percent of participants scored below basic, whereas only 26.4 percent of nonparticipants scored this low.

Consistent with the move toward schoolwide programs, the department's recent report compares NAEP average scores over time, separately for low- and high-poverty schools, instead of for individual participating and nonparticipating students. In reading, the primary focus of Title I, high-poverty schools averaged 190 in 1988, 184 in 1994, and 188 in 1996. Low-poverty schools averaged 217 in 1988, 220 in 1994, and 225 in 1996. If anything can be concluded from this, it is that the large perfor-

Table 2. Public Schools Participating in the Title I Program, 1996

Characteristic of public schools	*Percent*
All public schools	66
Instructional level	
Elementary school	75
Middle school	53
High school	50
Locale	
City	64
Urban fringe	48
Town	66
Rural	82
Percent of students eligible for free or reduced-price lunch	
Less than 35	45
35–49	75
50–74	86
75 or more	93
Elementary schools by the percent of students eligible for free or reduced-price lunch	
Less than 35	49
35–49	83
50–74	94
75 or more	98

Source: Carin Celebuslei and Elizabeth Farris, *Status of Education Reform in Public Elementary and Secondary Schools: Principals' Perspectives*, NCES 98–025 (Department of Education, National Center for Education Statistics, 1998).

mance gap between low- and high-poverty schools widened significantly between 1988 and 1996, from 27 points to 37 points.

How Have the Funds Been Spent?

Table 4 shows the distribution of Title I funds across expenditure categories during 1990–91.[44] Although the specific distribution of funds has changed from year to year, it remains the case that the great majority of Title I funds are spent on the salaries of classroom teachers, Title I specialists, and instructional aides.

Specialists and teachers are at the top of the salary scale, with annual compensation (including fringes) often reaching $40,000 or more. Aides are at the bottom, typically paid on the order of $8–11 per hour. Thus, each Title I dollar buys significantly more aide than teacher instructional hours. Title I currently employs approximately fifty thousand aides and more than eighty thousand teachers and specialists, working in approximately forty-five thousand schools.[45] The remainder of Title I funds are

Table 3. Title I Participants and Nonparticipants at Each Achievement Level, Fourth, Eighth, and Twelfth Graders

Title I participation	*Number*	*Weighted percent*	*Below basic*	*Basic*	*Proficient*	*Advanced*
		Reading				
Fourth grade						
Participated	1,099	13.6	80.4	16.2	3.3	0.1
Did not participate	6,283	86.4	33.1	24.6	33.8	8.5
Eighth grade						
Participated	653	6.5	64.6	30.2	5.2	0.0
Did not participate	9,482	93.5	28.1	40.7	28.2	3.0
Twelfth grade						
Participated	280	2.3	59.1	30.4	10.0	0.5
Did not participate	9,655	97.7	24.7	34.1	36.9	4.3
		Mathematics				
Fourth grade						
Participated	1,458	22.0	69.2	27.3	3.5	0.0
Did not participate	5,169	78.0	26.4	44.3	26.4	2.9
Eighth grade						
Participated	792	11.7	71.4	22.7	5.7	0.2
Did not participate	6,354	88.3	33.2	36.3	26.2	4.3
Twelfth grade						
Participated	167	2.0	75.5	23.2	1.3	0.0
Did not participate	6,737	98.0	29.9	51.5	16.6	2.0

Note: National Assessment of Educational Progress, 1994 reading and 1996 mathematics data.

spent on program administration, counselors and other personnel, materials, and funding for specialized training and intervention programs.

Table 5 shows the instructional activities paid for by Title I funds during 1985–86 and 1990–91. These are the most recent detailed breakdowns available, and the distribution of activities likely has changed in recent years. In particular, since the 1994 reauthorization, pullout programs have been significantly reduced, and schoolwide programs have been enormously increased. However, our recent observations across a variety of schools and districts indicate that the instructional activities listed here continue to be the principal mechanisms by which Title I instruction is delivered. When it comes to working with students, not much is new under the sun.

What do these activities represent in practice? To the extent that they depart from ordinary classroom instruction, they involve small group and one-to-one instruction, as well as assistance in maintaining order

Table 4. Distribution of Title I Funds across Expenditure Categories, 1990–91

Expenditure category	*Percent*
Salaries for classroom teachers and specialists (benefits included)	55
Salaries for instructional aides	17
Salaries for administrators	4
Salaries for counselors and other certified personnel	3
Salaries for noncertified personnel	2
Other salaries	2
Materials	8
All other (fixed charges, indirect costs)	9

Source: Mary Ann Millsap and others, *The Chapter 1 Implementation Study*, interim report, prepared by Abt Associates (Department of Education, 1992).

within a larger classroom. The greatest amount of this work occurs in elementary schools and focuses on reading instruction, although other grade levels and other subjects (particularly mathematics) are also covered. As for instructional techniques, they tend to be whatever is current practice in the particular district or school. Unfortunately, in recent years this has typically been whole language instruction, and our recent observations suggest that this continues to be the case. Thus, we are not surprised to learn that Title I instruction has been unable to narrow the performance gap for the children it serves. But does this mean that program services have been of no value whatsoever?

The Effectiveness of Title I Service

Certainly evaluation studies have reliably determined that Title I has failed to accomplish its mission of closing the achievement gap between

Table 5. Districts Offering Different Types of Chapter 1 Projects
Percent

Chapter 1 project	*1985–86*	*1990–91*
Limited pullout	89	82
In-class	37	62
Extended pullout	12	24
Replacement	7	12
Summer add-on	6	11
Preschool or kindergarten	n.a.	10
Add-on projects (before and after school)	6	9
Schoolwide	1	4

Source: Mary Ann Millsap and others, *The Chapter 1 Implementation Study*, interim report, prepared by Abt Associates (Department of Education, 1992).
n.a. = Not available.

low- and middle-income students. As reported by authors of the most recent and best available evaluation: "After controlling for student, family, and school differences between Chapter 1 participants and nonparticipants, we still find that participants score lower than nonparticipants and that this gap in achievement is *not* closed over time."[46]

But does this imply that Title I services have been completely ineffective, a total waste of more than $100 billion? It does not. As also noted by these authors: "This inability to find a compensatory effect of Chapter 1 does not mean the program was a failure. Limitations of this study do not allow us to determine whether Chapter 1 students would have been academically worse off without the assistance they received."[47]

The problem is methodological. No one has undertaken a random assignment study, in which eligible students are randomly assigned to Title I or no Title I services. Instead, evaluation designs have been based on comparing outcomes for Title I students with outcomes for students who did not receive these services. At least the time period under study, 1991–93, was before the 1994 reauthorization, so most Title I students received personalized, add-on services. But at this time, Title I regulations required that the lowest performing students receive services. So the two groups—Title I participants and nonparticipants—are not comparable, and the Title I participants could have performed even lower in the absence of services. That is, the evaluation design was biased against finding an effect of the program.

Does this mean that Title I may be having a large positive effect on the students served? This is unlikely, for then the effect would have overwhelmed the bias and been visible in this and previous studies. But it is possible, perhaps even likely, that, under some circumstances, Title I has had a modest positive effect on the students served. Given that more than 100,000 teachers and aides, many of them people of good will and at least some skill, have worked in Title I for many years, it is difficult to imagine that their efforts have not brought some positive results for low-income children.

Displacement of Local Funds

Federal revenue sharing is typically accompanied by the displacement of local funds. Federal funds are used to pay for goods and services that would have been paid for by local funds, so that the local governmental unit can save its own funds (for example, by avoiding a local tax increase). In the evaluation of manpower and training programs, the magnitude of such displacement has been one of the central empirical issues.[48] The substitution of federal funds for local funds that would otherwise have been spent occurs at a rate of about 50 percent. That is, only about half of federal monies granted to local government agencies are used to provide goods and services that would not have been provided anyway.

What about the displacement of local funds by Title I funds? In the legislation's earliest years, the issue went completely unaddressed. The 1965 ESEA included no provision to prohibit the use of federal funds to supplant state and local funds. This was soon understood to be a problem, however, as a 1969 Senate report on that year's amendments to ESEA stated that evidence indicated that Title I funds were not being properly used. An inquiry at the time by the federal Office of Education found cases of supplanting, excessive use of Title I funds for capital outlays, use of Title I funds to maintain segregated school systems, and use of the funds for general school needs. To address this problem, the 1969 amendments prohibited supplanting state and local funds with federal ones and stated that the intention was for Title I funds to be supplementary, allowing local school districts to provide goods and services that they would not otherwise be able to afford.

This prohibition of supplanting was reemphasized in the 1974 amendments, as was the statement that Title I funds are to be used solely for "excess costs," defined in the legislation as costs "directly attributable" to programs assisted under Title I that exceed average per pupil expenditures of a local school district (expenditures for any state and local services for special programs to serve the educationally disadvantaged, for bilingual education, or for special education for the disabled are excluded from the average).

More recently, the language of "no supplanting" has given way to "maintenance of effort." Thus, the 1978 amendments to the ESEA included a provision in which an LEA can receive Title I funds only if the state authority finds that the combined fiscal effort per student or aggregate expenditures are not less than the expenditures of the previous year. If they are, Title I funds are to be proportionally reduced. A waiver provision for "unforeseen circumstances" is included. In 1981 this maintenance of effort provision was made more specific by requiring that the year's expenditures must be no less than 90 percent of those expenditures the previous year. This requirement has remained in place through the 1994 amendments to the ESEA.

The intent of the legislation has been to provide add-on services that would not be provided otherwise. Yet our observations in local school districts suggest that, as with other federal revenue-sharing programs, Title I displacement is a significant problem, appreciably reducing the add-on benefits received by the lowest performing children.

Schoolwide programs are particularly worrisome, because one of their main effects is to make it easier for administrators to spend Title I funds in this manner. Yet the use of these programs has exploded since they were targeted for increase in the 1994 ESEA reauthorization.

It is easy to see how Title I reformers believed that giving such flexibility to the schools most affected by neighborhood poverty would be a positive step, empowering principals to use the money to improve schools as a whole. Unfortunately, the reformers ignored the possibility that central administrators would direct, or otherwise induce, individual school administrators to spend the funds on goods and services that the district would otherwise have paid for out of its own funds, reducing or eliminating the add-on instructional services (particularly aides and tutors) that had previously been provided to the lowest performing children. But this is occurring. Substitution of federal for local funds should be expected to occur in school districts under constant financial pressure, where fungibility is the first instinct of many central administrators.

Such displacement has significantly reduced the impact of the program on low-income children. Even before the 1994 reauthorization dramatically increased schoolwide programs, the authors of the *Prospects* evaluation concluded as follows: "We cannot assume that funds or services labeled 'Chapter 1' represented additional resources, or even different services, from those schools or districts would have undertaken without Chapter 1 funds. . . . Chapter 1 funding was so long established, and so endemic to the U.S. public school system, that the *allocation* of Chapter 1 funds to a school district or school may not have necessarily meant that the resources for that district or school were increased on net."[49]

And this was for the time period before the 1994 reauthorization enormously expanded displacement-prone schoolwide programs. Clearly the displacement issue has been given far too little consideration in recent discussions of Title I.

The 1994 Reauthorization and Its Consequences

Since its inception in 1966, Title I has had a number of major flaws. It has not been a coherent program, but a funding stream that local districts have spent on whatever activities they were already engaged in. The additional services provided to each student have typically been so modest that the chances of significantly assisting that student to reach grade-level performance have been low.[50] Teachers and aides have been inadequately trained in research-based instructional methods, in particular, phonics-based reading instruction. The tendency toward displacement of funds has always been present.

The Department of Education's 1999 report *Promising Results, Continuing Challenges* provided an opportunity to see the results of the 1994 reauthorization. The good news is that a continuing emphasis has been placed on standards and accountability. When this is combined with the NRC report on reading instruction and the department's efforts to reference that report in its implementation of the Reading Excellence Act, a continued push is evident toward the use of research-based instructional techniques.

Unfortunately, much of the remaining news is bad. What was never a coherent program is even less coherent now. What were once minimal services delivered to each eligible student have been watered down even further. What was once a focus on grades one through three—the time when low-income children can still be saved from falling hopelessly behind grade level—has been decreased. What was once a mild temptation toward displacement of Title I funds has become an open invitation to use them in this manner.

Each of these outcomes resulted from policies deliberately pursued in the 1994 reauthorization. Policy analysts seemed to have had an inadequate understanding of how the program operates on the ground and of the most important issues to be addressed for the program to succeed.

National politics also played a role. Politics may have been, and continues to be, decisive in driving the program toward its current unfortunate state. Both Democrats and Republicans have seen political gains in expanding the program to serve more grades in more schools with more flexibility for districts and principals to spend the funds as they see fit. The inevitable result has been that the neediest children with the most to gain from an intensive treatment—very low income first through third graders who are already falling behind—are having less and less of the funds directed toward them.

In particular, currently about one-third of the program participants are in grades one through three; the program used to focus almost exclusively on those grades. Furthermore, the program's budget now must serve almost twice as many participants. Why so many, each receiving so little? With the fiscal 1999 Title I appropriation at $8.3 billion, 11 million participants average $755 each.[51] But 6 million would average $1,383 each. And more to the point, if the bottom one-fifth of students in grades one through three were targeted, 2.1 million children would be served (assuming 3.5 million total at each grade level), which would allow $3,952 per child. If per child resources of this magnitude were spent effectively to provide add-on services to these children, the original goal of bringing these children up to grade level might be achieved.

But these services are reduced, dollar for dollar, when the funds are used to displace local district funds. Yet such actions are invited in schoolwide programs. And, between 1988 and 1998, schoolwide programs increased from two hundred to sixteen thousand. And in schoolwide programs, goods and services do not have to be targeted at add-on services for the lowest performers. Instead, furniture for the entire school, computers for the entire school, copiers for the entire school, books for the entire school, and so on can be purchased. What school district could resist such an opportunity to conserve its own funds?[52] Yet the department does almost nothing to police this issue, and no evaluation studies have attempted to estimate the magnitude of the increases in displacement, which have likely accompanied this recent increase in schoolwide Title I programs.[53]

Why did the 1994 reauthorization take this direction, which has led to such a sharp discontinuity with the previous twenty-eight years of program implementation? The answer, we believe, is that Title I's failure to close the cognitive skill gap led to a desire for strong action and a mistaken analysis of the problem led to the wrong policies being pursued.

What was this mistaken analysis? It was based on two principles. First, pullout should be reduced or eliminated, because it is stigmatizing and the pulled-out student misses in-class instruction. Instead, inclusion is to be fostered. Second, the flexibility of district administrators to spend Title I funds, by increasing schoolwide programs and extending Title I to grades four through twelve, should be increased. Flexibility seems to have been promoted because these analysts did not know how to improve the program after its admitted failure for so many years; they chose to "let all flowers bloom" by delegating responsibility to the district level. Such flexibility is so politically popular that it has become the mantra of both political parties. It is also beloved by the many entrepreneurs in the enormous grants economy of the education field, because each of these hopes to thereby increase their share of the pie. As noted by Stanley Pogrow, "Creating local standards in medicine is a form of malpractice."[54]

Yet both pillars of the 1994 reauthorization are built on misunderstandings. Pullout is necessary for one-to-one instruction, and such instruction is the most effective way to raise the performance of low-performing students.[55] This is why the first thing middle-class parents do when their child is having difficulty in school is to hire a one-to-one tutor. Only with one-to-one tutoring can three vital instructional conditions be achieved: individual assessment followed by instruction on the student's current performance level (instead of teaching to a small group or class average); complete privacy within which to risk failure, combined with no other child being present to give the answer; and the presence of a caring and encouraging adult, able to detect and immediately correct the student's difficulties, whatever their source.

The reason Title I was ineffective in the past is that it involved pulling out groups of children, each with a different performance level and central instructional problem. These students were taught by teachers and aides using relatively ineffective, whole language techniques. Because the program was kept separate from the rest of the school, the children pulled out were the lowest performers, and Title I staff were unable to succeed with them, morale was low, and the children and program were stigmatized. The call for inclusion thus understandably arose. Yet a better plan would have been to employ a research-based (phonics) curriculum, provide Title I staff with adequate training and supervision, and have them apply this curriculum one-to-one. Only under these conditions might low-income, low-performing students be brought up to grade level.

As for stigmatization and missed class time, neither is a problem when the program is properly implemented. For example, the Reading One-to-

One program, the Howard Street program, the Book Buddies program, and others have demonstrated that when tutoring is one-to-one, using an effective curriculum and adequate training and management, students look forward to tutoring, and nontutored students beg to be included.[56] At program start-up, teachers are often concerned that pulled-out students will miss class time. But this concern is met in several ways. First, the teacher chooses when during the day he or she would like the student pulled out. Thus, scheduling can minimize the loss of instructional time. Second, the students tutored are typically the lowest performing in what is already a low-performing class. These students are far behind the demands of the curriculum, are often immature, and have attention deficit problems. They are unable to concentrate in a class of twenty to thirty students, and their presence greatly increases the teacher's difficulty in working with the other students. But if five tutors come to the classroom door and take out the five lowest performers for one-to-one instruction, the teacher is better able to succeed with the remaining students, and the pulled-out students receive intensive, one-to-one instruction designed to focus on what they need to help them regain full participation in the class.[57]

The movement toward flexibility and the resulting increases in funds allocated to schoolwide programs and to grades four through twelve have done great damage to the chances of Title I achieving its goal. There are four reasons for this. First, these older children are typically so far behind grade level that it is almost impossible to catch up. Second, even less is known about successful intervention in grades four through twelve than about grades one through three.

Third, the institution of a schoolwide program almost guarantees a reduction in add-on services to the lowest performing children. The purpose of schoolwide programs is to free administrators from the demand to target add-on services to the lowest performing students. This is based on the idea that, in very low income schools, all students need help. Yet this is false. As noted by the authors of the *Prospects* study, "Differences in academic achievement within schools are far greater than average differences between schools. . . . Poor schools are not filled solely with low-achieving students. . . . There are good students in all schools, even in the most troubled places."[58] The lowest performing students in these schools need help, and what would help them the most is intensive personal attention, not a nebulous schoolwide program that involves spending Title I money on computers, furniture, or even additional classroom teachers.

Fourth, middle and high school principals have little or no knowledge of effective compensatory programs on which to spend their newly acquired Title I funds. The obstacles to the creation of such programs are overwhelming. The difficulties of bringing low-performing elementary school children up to grade level are vastly greater for middle and high school students. They are now very far behind and have had six or more years of daily school failure. Their social-psychological defenses against trying hard at schoolwork are well developed. And their primary focus is elsewhere—on adult activities, which hold much more attractiveness than schoolwork. Little wonder that these principals either spend their Title I funds on completely ineffective programs or simply use the funds to purchase goods and services they would have purchased anyway with local funds.[59]

The Department of Education's Direction for Title I

Promising Results, Continuing Challenges indicates the direction the Department of Education has charted for Title I. The continued emphasis on high standards and accountability is welcome. But the goal that "*all* children reach challenging standards" and the specific policies to achieve this are sadly out of touch with the reality of the children's current performance level and the extent to which the current pattern of Title I expenditure is significantly assisting them.

The reality is a Title I program in which, in 1994, 80 percent of all participating fourth graders had reading skills below the basic level. This massive level of failure continues to be widespread among children in high-poverty schools. Even this department report, with its claim of "promising results," acknowledges that, in 1998, 68 percent of all fourth graders in high-poverty schools have reading skills below the basic level. (Note that the department's 1998 figures are based on all students in high-poverty schools, even though the *Prospects* study reported that these schools have children who are doing fine. The department is including high performers in high-poverty schools, who have received no personally targeted services, among program participants.)

Beyond a general focus on "standards and accountability," the department's recommendations come down to two. First, a general emphasis is placed on "staying the course" with the changes brought by the 1994 reauthorization. Second, a plan is put forth to reduce the number of Title I aides, so as to increase the number of Title I teachers. The reason given is that these aides "lacked educational credentials required to deliver high-quality instruction."[60] However, the issue is not credentials, it is skills and training. Having failed, over a thirty-year period, to put a serious training program in place for the aides, the department now wishes to fire them because they "lack credentials."

Most of the reading curriculum experts in this program were trained in, and still practice, whole language instructional techniques. Program funds also pay for equipment and materials, few of which are of much assistance to the lowest performing children. (Despite exaggerated claims, most low-performing elementary school children placed in front of computers play with them for a while and then lose interest. And like so much else in low-income schools, computer-assisted learning tends to be inadequately implemented.) Finally, some of the funds pay for special programs. But many of these are not effectively targeted on the lowest performing children and do not have the personnel, curriculum, training, and administrative support to be successfully implemented for these children. And, with the move to schoolwide programs, add-on direct services to the lowest performing children have decreased.

The department wants to stay the course with this program. Instead of training both teachers and aides in effective practices, the department plans to simply scapegoat the aides.

We have observed many Title I aides and teachers at work in the schools. In addition, one of us has provided in-service reading instruction training for all the Title I teachers and aides in one of the nation's larger cities. We have observed these teachers and aides to be heterogeneous in their skills and abilities. Certainly the teachers operate at higher skill levels than the aides, but they frequently cost three to four times as much. And when one of us trained both teachers and aides, he found that their knowledge of reading instruction was not all that dissimilar. In particular, the teachers knew almost nothing about such research-based phonics techniques as the use of decodable text and explicit instruction in phonological processing, blending and segmenting, and other word-attack skills. In our opinion, an aide who had been trained in these matters would be a better reading instructor than a teacher who had not been so trained.

Further, the department's latest recommendation—to fire the aides—reflects the general lack of attention to costs in educational cost-benefit calculations. As with the proliferation of high-cost programs such as Reading Recovery, where a $50,000 per year teacher is tutoring at most eight children one-to-one, the department is ignoring the possibility that this $50,000 could pay for three aides and even more tutors, who could serve three or more times as many students on a personal basis. Because of the instructional advantages inherent in the one-to-one setting, less credentialled but properly trained and supervised aides or tutors can be effective in this setting.[61]

Proposals for Structural Reform

Frustration with the cognitive performance being achieved by low-income children is widespread. As charter schools, voucher experiments, and city and state takeover of urban districts become commonplace, similar proposals have been suggested for the reform of Title I. The most dramatic of these goes to the heart of the issue of how effectively the funds are being spent by changing the recipients of the funds.

Change the Recipients of the Funds

Many of the central determinants of poor Title I performance—a focus on politics rather than performance; too little attention to skills, training, and management; the use of whole language instead of research-based methods; and a tendency to displacement of funds and other sorts of mismanagement—are directly traceable to the control of these funds by a separate bureaucracy within the central administration of local school districts. A tempting solution is to bypass this bureaucracy, sending the funds directly to the principals and teachers of eligible children, allowing the children's parents to decide how the funds should be spent, or sending the funds as a block grant to state education agencies.

A PORTABLE ENTITLEMENT. Perhaps the most radical suggestion is to fully fund Title I (increase the funding so that every low-income child receives a grant) and tie the money directly to each child, with parents having authority over how it is spent. As described by Chester Finn, Marci Kanstoroom, and Michael J. Petrilli:

> How to empower these parents? By insisting that Title I funds follow children to the school or education provider of their choice—be it the neighborhood school, a public school across town, a private school, a tutoring company, an after-school program, or a summer program. Instead of funding school districts, the federal government would fund children, much as Pell grants do for higher education. All poor kids would have funds "strapped to their backs." And we say ALL poor kids, because we favor the idea of expanding Title I funding to serve all eligible youngsters so long as the aid is truly portable, child by child and school by school.[62]

Similarly, Diane Ravitch wrote, "Turn the key federal program for poor kids—Title I—into a portable entitlement, so that the money follows the child, like a college scholarship. Presently, federal money goes to the school district, where bureaucrats watch it, dispense it and find manifold ways to multiply their tasks and add to their staffs. As a portable entitlement, Title I's $8 billion would allow poor children to attend the school of their choice instead of being stuck in low-performing schools."[63]

What would this mean in practice? Finn explains it as follows.[64] The idea is to change Title I from a district-based program to a child-based program, with each eligible child entitled to a certain amount of Title I aid no matter where he or she goes to school. The states would manage this program, and it would be their job to get the appropriate amount of Title I money into each school's bank account based on how many Title I students enrolled in the school.

The states would also set the limits for just how portable the funds would be. In particular, each state would decide whether the funds could go only to public schools or whether they could also go to private schools. Each state would decide whether the parents would be able to direct any portion of the funds to a nonschool provider. (An example would be a tutor or tutoring program, operating in an after-school program or in the evening. The Reading Excellence Act already provides funding for Tutorial Assistance Grants in which, in sufficiently low-income schools, parents have a choice of the after-school tutoring program—one provided by the school, and another by an outside vendor—they wish to instruct their child.)

This plan has a number of positive features. Even if a state does not permit parents to direct funds to a nonschool provider, local Title I bureaucracies would be reduced in size, perhaps even eliminated. Displacement might also be reduced, as district administrators would have less opportunity to make Title I dollars fungible against goods and services they would otherwise have provided.[65] Overall, it would be an evolutionary step, in which principals and teachers in low-income schools would be empowered to make their own best choices as is now the case in charter schools.

FULL PARENTAL EMPOWERMENT. A more revolutionary change would follow if a state allows parents to direct funds to a nonschool provider. Imagine that each low-income parent has a "Title I expenditure account" for each of his or her children, from which approved expenditures can be allocated at will. These might include school-provided services during the school day or in an after-school program, as well as tutorial services provided in the home or neighborhood after school and during the summer. If this were combined with a program in which local high school students with good grades were trained as tutors to be certified and hired by the parents with Title I funds, perhaps under the supervision of the eligible student's school in an after-school program, benefits might be provided both to the high school and elementary school student. Furthermore, the funds would be kept in the neighborhood, without the overhead and profit charged by private sector tutoring firms. (Sylvan Learning Systems routinely pays its tutors $10 per hour while charging parents $30 per hour.)

Such a program would have multiple benefits. The high school students would be able to earn money to pay for college. Tutor training and the experience of tutoring would strengthen the tutor's reading skills, and assisting an elementary school student would enhance the tutor's self-esteem and perhaps even inspire the tutor to eventually enter the teaching profession.

The student being tutored would have a high school student to bond with and look up to. In neighborhoods where English is a second language, the tutors would be bilingual, so they would be ideally suited to assist elementary school students with the transition to English. These tutoring jobs could serve as an incentive and reward for high school students to work hard at their studies. The efforts of these tutors would go where they are needed the most—to increase the reading and homework assistance for low-income students in elementary school. And the funding would go where it is needed the most and where it can do the most good for the future—to high school students striving to escape the traps present in low-income neighborhoods and better their future by attending college.

One danger in such a plan is that parents would use their control over Title I funds to defund the Title I programs in their local schools, or to escape these schools altogether. This possibility could be eliminated by sending the majority of each child's grant directly to the child's school, leaving only a modest sum of money under the parent's discretion. School-based efforts to involve low-income parents in their child's education, which are rarely successful under current conditions, might be undertaken much more energetically and successfully if these schools had a financial incentive to be in contact with the parents and to respond to their children's needs.

Perhaps a greater danger would be fraud and misuse by parents of their Title I account. Checks and balances would have to be installed. For these reasons, a plan based on (even partial) parental decisionmaking should be first tried as a limited experiment, accompanied by a rigorous evaluation.

Would such a plan immediately allow low-income schools to bring their students up to the performance level of middle-income children? Not if the families of low-income children still provide them with less prereading and other developmental skills during the preschool years and less home instruction and homework assistance during the school years. And not if the teachers of low-income students are still using less than fully effective instructional and classroom management techniques. But it would do something very important. By putting Title I funds in the hands of parents, whose motivation is solely to provide add-on services for their own child, this plan would completely eliminate the rampant displacement and reduction in personalized, add-on services to low-income, low-performing children that currently plagues Title I. For this reason alone, this is an attractive policy alternative.

BLOCK GRANTS TO STATES. An alternative method for disbursing Title I funds is as block grants to states. As with vouchers for parents, this has been suggested by those analysts—Chester E. Finn Jr. and Paul T. Hill, in particular—who wish to keep the funds away from district bureaucrats and who see the many different federal funding programs as distractions that have kept the schools from focusing on their main job.

Where, as in California and Texas, state-level education departments have, at least recently, promoted research-based instructional methods, this might be a positive step, which would give state-level bureaucrats further leverage in their efforts to improve the instructional practices of local school districts. Many local school districts will, as they have done in California and Texas, promise to change their instructional methods to receive the money and then do nothing. Further, a single consolidated state grant of revenue sharing from the federal government would likely encourage the displacement of local funds at rates even higher than is currently the case. Nor will such a plan do anything to improve the home situations of low-income children. A possible result of consolidating federal education aid as a block grant to states would be to reduce targeted aid to low-income schools, at least in some states that are financially hard-pressed.

Schoolwide Reforms

Much attention is currently being given to schoolwide reform models. Many of these programs are organized around positive practices. Some of them, although far too few, have evidence of effectiveness.[66] But these programs are often expensive to implement and too often are not effective. Learning to implement successfully what is already known appears to offer a higher cost-benefit ratio than further invention and testing of new programs. An additional disturbing aspect exists to these schoolwide programs. Typical of the field of education, bringing in outside staff and spending a great deal of money seem to be necessary simply to induce schools to undertake management, training, and curriculum implementation that use common sense and best practices. Surely this mechanism is too inefficient to rely on for the reform of all the schools in the nation.

Reform the Profession

Finally, an overarching problem must be confronted: an education profession with too little focus on effective school management, a nonscientific culture, and entrenched elites wielding power under a system of perverse incentives, where true expertise is minimal, management and training are poor, and the most desirable promotion is the one out of the classroom. Successfully raising the achievement of low-income children cannot be done without significantly altering at least some of these conditions.

The 1960s, 1970s, and 1980s saw relatively little progress in these matters. But when the Bush administration began, and the Clinton administration continued, a focus on national standards and accountability in education, some progress began to appear. As the Department of Education has sought to faithfully implement the Reading Excellence Act, with its focus on research-based methods of instruction, more progress has been made. This momentum of reform must continue and be extended to the schools of education as well as the state and local education agencies. This effort to change the culture of the education profession may ultimately yield the greatest gains in improving student achievement.

Some will say that such a cultural change is unlikely in the near future. Yet the volatility of the education profession—always swinging from one new reform to another, always pursuing the latest funding opportunity—indicates that change is possible. Now what is needed is the firm hand of scientific practice to stabilize the process with a focus on effective outcomes.

Paul Hill said, "It is now clear that every aspect of public K-12 education, from financing, school staffing, use of time, the authority of principals, instructional methods, and school accountability are all profoundly influenced by federal priorities."[67] If this is so, why not use this power to change the culture of the profession?

Current Department of Education staff are enforcing the provisions of the Reading Excellence Act to disseminate scientifically validated instructional techniques. The method is identical to that used by the National Science Foundation—empanel appropriate groups of scientific experts to be the judges for grant competitions. The department should audit Title I schools for effective training and management practices. New teachers should have an expert teacher in the classroom with them to provide hands-on training in effective practices. A minimum number of in-service training hours from appropriate experts should be required. A behavioral management program must be functioning in the school. It would not be difficult to train auditors who could assess Title I schools for the presence of these activities.

What Should Be Done?

Several policies would improve the effectiveness of Title I. These include reducing the displacement of local funds by federal funds, redirecting services toward the lowest performing students, and building a more coherent program.

Reduce Displacement and Redirect Services to the Lowest Performers

First, reduce displacement, and redirect services to the lowest performing students. Children who are significantly behind the rest of the class in first grade, and who are completely lost to the system by third grade, require the most powerful possible intervention, including personalized instructional attention over an extended period, if they are to catch up to the rest of the class. The growth of schoolwide programs that displaced Title I funds away from add-on services to these children has been a disaster. Title I must be rededicated to provide add-on services to the lowest performing children in low-income schools. This could be accomplished by a simple mandate in the regulations or by changing the regulations back to once again reduce the number of schoolwide programs. This, however, does nothing to address the after-school and summer assistance needs of these children. Accordingly, some version of parental empowerment would allow the parent to contract with a tutor or other provider for such additional assistance for their child.

The reduction of services to the neediest by schoolwide programs has been widely observed by teachers in the schools. For example, consider this statement from the International Reading Association's recommendations for Title I reauthorization:

> At its core, the idea of schoolwide programs was to offer increased instructional time for students who need it most. Unfortunately, in most cases this has not happened. Resources are often diverted from the core mission of enhancing the basic instructional program to other projects.... Schools receiving schoolwide funding should be required to demonstrate a commitment to seeing that the neediest students are provided instructional time and materials on appropriate levels, aligned with but *above and beyond their regular classroom reading and/or math instruction.*[68]

Redirect the Program to Grades One through Three

The expansion of Title I to grades four through twelve has gone against everything that is known about the development of reading skill and cost-effective interventions to improve it. It has also, no doubt, greatly increased the displacement of Title I funds. That only 37 percent of Title I participants are in grades one through three is unconscionable. This effect of the 1994 reauthorization must be rolled back, and the program retargeted on grades one through three.

Build a Coherent Program

Both Democrats and Republicans have pushed Title I toward decentralization and revenue sharing. The result has been enormous variability in instructional techniques, with little focus on the most effective practices.

The Department of Education should work directly to implement what is already known about best practices in curriculum, training, and management. Because in many cases what should be done is already known, the focus should be on making sure it is implemented. Such actions would surely have the highest cost-benefit ratio of any that could be taken. Unfortunately, the decentralized education system, and the small share of local educational costs contributed by the federal government, makes this difficult to achieve.

CURRICULUM. Two recent events have significantly altered the state of the reading wars. First, the NRC report sought to end the conflict by noting the advantages of both phonics instruction (particularly for beginning readers) and of whole language instruction (particularly for more advanced readers), arguing for a "balanced approach" using the best of each method. Second, Congress passed the Reading Excellence Act, which included language mandating the use of "scientifically validated" instructional techniques. The Department of Education has followed this up by stressing that scientifically validated methods will be a key criterion in judging the interstate competition for the approximately $240 million available under the act during fiscal 1999. This is one example of how the department can utilize revenue sharing to nudge the states and localities toward best curriculum practices.

How successful is such nudging likely to be, and would the curriculum be better off without it? The answer is that success rates are likely to be mixed. Trickle-down has a long way to go from the department to individual classrooms, and along the way are many stops, some manned by curriculum experts with a long-standing antipathy to phonics. However, the very existence of large numbers of such individuals, heavily entrenched in school districts and education schools, suggests the department must continue waving the NRC report and arguing for the use of scientifically based instructional methods. Absent this, a push back toward whole language instruction may be inevitable.

TRAINING. The problem with teacher training is that it is not very good and there is too little of it. Teachers report that their education school training provided relatively little of value in the classroom. Following this training, they are typically placed into classrooms (often the least desirable ones—those with low-income children) and left on their own. Useful and extensive in-service training and in-class modeling of instruction by an experienced teacher are rare. Instead, beginning teaching is too often a sink-or-swim experience, and when the class is composed of low-income children, far too many new teachers find themselves sinking.

A portion of the Title I money should be targeted on training and should be spent on hands-on instruction in scientifically validated methods. Even better would be to require that the principal or other instructional leader spend at least a portion of each new teacher's first few months with him or her in the classroom, modeling effective classroom management and instructional technique. (This is common practice in the more effective schools serving low-income children.)

MANAGEMENT. Authors such as Chubb and Moe have argued that what is needed is to "get the incentives right," perhaps by moving toward privatizing the schools, for good management to follow as it does in the private sector—via survival of the fittest. However, the public schools are not likely to be privatized any time soon. Yet many schools serving low-income children are inadequately managed and operate within a district culture and structure that do relatively little to improve this situation.

What can be done to improve these conditions? Individual public schools can be provided with more control over their own resources and greater decisionmaking power in general. What the NRC report and the Department of Education's emphasis on this report did for reading can be done for school management. A few basic, desirable management actions should be identified and advertised widely. Then, Title I schools should be monitored to see that they are implemented. Because learning occurs in the classroom, these actions should be classroom-based and apply to all classes in the school. In each case an administrator or trainer and the teacher should be jointly responsible for the outcomes. These might include (1) training on, and rating of, classroom management techniques that are effective in creating and maintaining the order and discipline necessary for learning, (2) provision of sufficient time-on-task and steady coverage of an appropriate curriculum in core subjects such as reading and mathematics, and (3) use of effective instructional techniques to get this curriculum across to the students. Each administrator and teacher pair should rate itself and be rated by the principal on each of these items, and Title I audits should focus on these instructional delivery issues instead of solely on financial accounting matters.

Further, effective schooling for low-income children requires starting them early and providing them with skilled teachers. Title I principals should be rated on their ability to provide effective reading and mathematics instruction in kindergarten and their ability to recruit, train, and retain good teachers, while dismissing poor ones.

PAID AND VOLUNTEER TUTORS. The Clinton administration's America Reads initiative has demonstrated that relatively large numbers of college students and community residents can be fielded at low unit cost to work on reading with low-income students, one-to-one. At least some research has shown that when these tutors are properly trained and managed, utilizing a serious instructional curriculum and decodable text books with beginning readers, significant gains can be attained.[69] Local high school students could also be used extensively as tutors for elementary school students in low-income neighborhoods. Ideally, these high school students could provide the home assistance that low-income parents are unable to provide.

RESEARCH AND DEVELOPMENT. Much of the culture and practice in the education field stands on a shaky scientific basis. Furthermore, scientific research played a key role in recent successful attempts to re-insert phonics into the practice of beginning reading instruction. Doesn't this argue for increased emphasis and expenditures on research and development if the field of education is to attain the capabilities and success rate of, for example, medicine?

The answer is yes and no. On the one hand, scientific knowledge is the basis of all technical progress, and too little such knowledge exists in the education field. On the other hand, instead of looking for even more new programs, perhaps those proven elements of programs should be implemented. For example, direct instruction's effectiveness was demonstrated thirty years ago and continues to this day. But teachers were discouraged by what they perceived to be its rigid implementation style and took to whole language instead.[70] More generally, few disagree that effective schools would embody the curriculum, training, and management elements listed above.

Continued scientific research, particularly testing the effectiveness of alternative management strategies, would be valuable for effective program implementation. Such research should certainly be undertaken in a much more far-reaching and rigorous fashion than has been the case heretofore. But cognitive gains for low-income children are more likely to come from successfully implementing what is already known, than from the invention and testing of entirely new programs. This is much more a matter of engineering application than of basic research.

THE VIEW FROM THE CLASSROOM. A great many creative proposals have been suggested for reforming Title I. Their sometimes radical nature is an appropriate response to more than thirty years of failed efforts. Yet all this creativity must be held to the highest and most difficult standard: What will be the effect on the classroom and the students? The school system and the education profession function relatively poorly for low-income children. Changes could be instituted that make low-income children, their teachers, and their families even worse off than they are now. As Chester Finn warned, "First, do no harm."[71]

To help low-income children succeed, their teachers must be engaged. It is therefore useful to ask, what is the view from the classroom? Given the opportunity, how would the teachers currently on the front line, in the low-income classrooms, like to see the Title I money spent?

The teachers we have spoken with might respond as follows. Yes, show me the most effective instructional techniques. Yes, assist me to implement a behavioral management program that works. Yes, start the children off earlier and provide them better preschool instruction, so that they come to my class better prepared to do the work. Yes, provide the students with a tutor at home if their parents cannot help with the homework. Yes, provide me with the assistance (aides or tutors, both in the class and pull-out) to help the lowest performing children catch up while allowing me to work more intensively with a smaller group of children who are ready to learn the assigned curriculum.

THE VIEW FROM THE LOW-INCOME HOUSEHOLD. As the preponderance of research has shown, the learning deficits of low-income children begin and end in the household. Shoring up this household by providing parents with vouchers that they can spend on after-school, evening, and summer tutoring for their children is the strongest action that could be taken to improve this situation. Is there any doubt about how these parents would respond if they were asked whether they wanted this opportunity?

Conclusion

The many difficulties standing in the way of increased school achievement by low-income children suggest the necessity of undertaking mixed strategies. In particular, Title I reauthorization should include the following: (1) a plan to reduce displacement and to retarget Title I funds on providing add-on services to the lowest performers in grades one through three; (2) at least some funds sent directly to principals and teachers in low-income schools, to be used at their discretion to assist the education of at-risk students; (3) at least some funds sent as a Title I account to the parents of low-income students, so that they can hire tutors to assist students after school and during the summer (this should perhaps first be tried as a carefully evaluated experiment); (4) serious attempts to tie funding to demonstrable and audited improvements in the use of scientifically validated curriculum, training, and management; and (5) a continued and serious effort to improve the scientific basis and outcomes-orientation of schools of education, in particular, and the profession, in general.

Realistically, the chances that this particular turn in the five-year ESEA reauthorization cycle will single-handedly and forever fix the Title I program are slim to none. Instead, a commitment should be made to the long haul and to detailed implementation efforts to shore up the classrooms and homes in low-income neighborhoods to the greatest extent possible. Embarking on a serious and dramatic reform of Title I resembles the attempt to reform the Russian economy. It must be undertaken as a long-term process, with the expectation that there will be many twists and turns along the way. This undertaking must be accompanied by a serious effort to provide effective, personalized add-on services to the lowest performing low-income children, whose cognitive skill improvement is the reason for the program.

Comment by Chester E. Finn Jr.

The fine paper by George Farkas and L. Shane Hall makes me angry. Not, let me hasten to add, at the writers, for I have only the smallest quibbles with what they have done. No, I am angry at the mounting signs that the 1999–2000 federal legislative cycle will, once again, make Title I worse, or at least not better, despite tons of evidence—much of it recapitulated in Farkas and Hall's paper—that the program is failing and needs a top-to-bottom overhaul that probably is not going to happen. Much the same can be said of the entire Elementary and Secondary Education Act (ESEA) in which it is embedded.

The central problem is that, after three and a half decades, this largest of all federal K-12 education programs is encrusted with vested interests, hoary assumptions, and lots of inertia. The efficacy of the activities that it pays for, and the educational well-being of the disadvantaged youngsters who are its putative focus, seem substantially less important than the maintenance of the program's vast apparatus and the flow of its dollars.

As of mid-summer 1999, the White House view is clear. Its mantra is "Stay the course." Senior officials contend that Title I was properly redirected in 1994 and now needs only minor tweaking. They have no doubt that the five-year-old press for "schoolwide" programs is well warranted and that the complex, top-down, command-and-control accountability structures enacted in 1994 are the proper framework for program success. The pending White House ESEA proposal would double and redouble the amount and intrusiveness of top-down control. It reminds me of the old merchant's joke line: "We lose money on every item we sell, so we're planning to make it up in volume."

Congress is at sixes and sevens, lacking significant ideas of its own except for a general sense that the program's accountability features ought to be strengthened in some nebulous way so that it will work better. Members and staff seem unwilling or unable to imagine anything different from Title I's current, basic assumptions, and they act as if they are terrified lest the money go anywhere different from where it has always gone.

Two proposals for change are worth considering. Each would make significant changes in ESEA, though only for states that opt to embrace them. The Academic Achievement for All ("Straight A's") proposal would treat states much like giant charter schools, allowing them great freedom from ESEA's regulatory regime in return for markedly improved academic results, including those of their disadvantaged youngsters. And Senator Judd Gregg (R-N.H.) has suggested a "child-centered" funding option for Title I under which the dollars (in participating states) would accompany eligible children to the school of their choice.

Each proposal signals a radical shift. The first would replace Title I's historic emphasis on inputs and regulations with a sharp focus on academic results. The second would shift the basic funding strategy away from aiding districts and instead make the federal dollars assist individual children. Radical, but optional. Neither proposal would alter the underlying program for the rest of the country, nor is either assured of enactment.

Staying the present course would be okay if Title I were a successful program that was accomplishing its historic mission of narrowing the achievement gap between disadvantaged and middle-class kids. But everyone knows by now that, thirty-five years after President Lyndon B. Johnson persuaded Congress to enact it, this is not happening, the evidence of gap narrowing is trivial or transitory, and millions of poor children are not learning basic skills in school. Yet in response to all the evaluations and evidence that Title I is failing, one of three things is typically heard:

First, it is not a real program anyway, it is more like a funding stream. It has long since proven its ability to move federal money into nearly every school district and congressional district. That is all that should be expected from it.

Second, it is beginning to succeed—anecdotes are popular in this connection—but unfortunately the evaluations are too slow to capture that truth satisfactorily. In other words, its imminent success is masked by sluggish analysis. (Never mind that this has been said during every previous reauthorization cycle.)

Third, it may not be working well now, but it would if it had more money, more accountability mechanisms, more this, or more that. In this view, nothing is wrong with the program's theory or structure. Instead, its implementation is stingy or cowardly.

Those are the most common rejoinders to allegations of program failure. As for alternatives—radical overhauls—they are making little headway against the combination of inertia, Panglossian rhetoric, and entrenched interests. I detect no passion for trying to re-create this important program along fundamentally different lines.

That is why I am angry. This huge program essentially wastes $8 billion a year and fails to keep its promise to America's neediest girls and boys. The reasons for its failure have been identified. No dearth of promising ideas exists for how to fix it. But none is expected to be embraced by the 106th Congress, by the executive branch, or by the major education interest groups. As for other influential groups that might offset the establishment's wimpishness, business, governors, civil rights organizations, editorial writers, and the Christian right have all been relatively quiet. Everyone seems to be saying "I don't have a dog in that fight."

The Farkas and Hall paper does a superb job of summarizing the shortcomings of the present Title I program, the basic errors built into the 1994 amendments, and some of the most promising ideas for fundamental reform. Their analysis does not rely on theory, opinion, or ideology. It is grounded in wide-ranging experience, observation, and research. And it leads to a handful of strong, coherent recommendations for change. Allow me to restate their five chief proposals and add a few comments:

1. Reduce dollar displacement—which means make Title I funds available for supplemental services instead of ordinary school operations—and focus those services on the lowest performing youngsters in the earliest grades. In other words, pour extra instruction into the youngest children with the widest learning gaps and at least get them literate. This seems to me indisputable good sense, but it would undo key provisions of the 1994 amendments, which neither the Clinton administration nor the public school establishment wants to do. It would undermine the schoolwide approach, which does not seem to be working for the neediest kids anyway. It would reestablish some version of add-on programs for seriously disadvantaged youngsters, which goes against the grain of contemporary education sensibilities. (It sounds too much like tracking.) It would shift money from middle and high schools into the primary grades. But these changes must be made to help the children who need it most.

2. Send some of the money into low-income schools for principals and teachers to use at their discretion to assist their at-risk pupils. I wish the authors had said more about how this would work, particularly when they also argue that there is need for a coherent nationwide Title I strategy. Either I am missing a crucial conceptual link or an internal contradiction exists between site-based decisions and nationwide uniformity. I suspect they are offering a financial cookie to those who cherish schoolwide programs and decentralized decisionmaking while also trying to

get teachers and principals to buy into the other program changes they are proposing.

3. Use some of the money to create a "Title I account" to be drawn upon by the parents of low-income students, particularly for after-school tutoring and summer programs. This is a good start toward parent empowerment, which Title I has never done. My own instinct is to go considerably further to place decisions in the hands of parents by insisting that the full per pupil Title I payment be made portable so that all the money accompanies the child to the school (or other education provider) of the family's choice, albeit within boundaries set by the state. The basic Title I funding stream should be redirected from school systems to individual children, much as happened with federal higher education aid in the early 1970s. But this smells like vouchers and is therefore deeply controversial. (That does not make it wrong.)

4. Tie funding to demonstrable and audited improvements in the use of scientifically validated curricula, training, and management. This is key to the authors' notion of a coherent national program strategy. It tends to fly in the face of the idea of empowering parents and giving teachers and principals discretionary funds, but this program is big enough—and sick enough—that several cures can be tried at once. The likeliest way to do this is to allow states to structure their Title I programs differently from one another. Simply requiring federal Title I dollars to be spent for scientifically validated curricula and methods would work a revolution in the program.

5. Engage in a serious effort to improve the scientific basis and outcomes orientation of the education profession in general and ed schools in particular. This one made me grin. Nobody would term the authors naïve, but this recommendation has a pie-in-the-sky quality to it. Today's education profession has lamentably little respect for science when it clashes with ideology and is palpably leery of heavy emphasis on outcomes.

Taken as a whole, the recommendations proffered by Farkas and Hall are bold and worthy. They are also complicated and, perhaps, a bit inconsistent. My own diagnosis of Title I is a little simpler. From where I sit, Title I has three central failings:

First, as noted by these authors and many other analysts, it is not producing the desired results in terms of student achievement.

Second, it does not begin to serve all needy children. Close to half of America's low-income kids receive no Title I services because of intricate formulas, federally imposed spending priorities, and the fact that the basic program was designed to support school systems instead of kids.

Third, Title I funds today do not accompany eligible children to the schools of their choice. Youngsters who get Title I services in one public school cannot count on getting them in another public school. This leaves parents powerless to improve bad situations for their daughters and sons, places a major federal impediment in the path to school choice, and holds school systems harmless from their own failures by assuring them a continued flow of federal dollars based on demographic formulas, not program effectiveness or customer satisfaction.

The single most important reform that could be made in Title I would be to turn the program into a portable entitlement, one that serves all poor children, at least in the early grades, and whose dollars accompany them to the school or other education provider of their parents' choice, with the range of those choices delimited by state law. If Congress does not have the stomach to impose so sweeping a change on the whole country, it should at least allow states that are so inclined to restructure and operate their Title I programs this way.

And if that is too much to swallow, then Congress should, at the very least, allow kids trapped in failed Title I programs—the country has hundreds of schools like that—to take their money to other providers. Florida recently has agreed (amid much controversy) to let children leave failing public schools for other schools (including private schools), yet the federal Title I funds will not move with them. The federal dollars will stay in the failed public schools until and unless the district chooses to move them. Worse, if a youngster goes from a mostly poor public school to a middle-class public school in search of a better education, in most circumstances the district is barred by federal law from moving those dollars. Although this is meant to keep Title I dollars targeted on the "highest need" schools, what it often does is keep those dollars subsidizing the payrolls of failed schools. This cannot be good policy. At the very least, a student's right to select another school should be part of the Title I accountability apparatus. Federal policy should be neutral with respect to school choice. Washington should not force states or communities to go farther in that direction than they are inclined to, but it should not get in their way. Federal dollars should be as portable as a state is willing to let its own dollars be.

Comment by Douglas Carnine and Hans Meeder

George Farkas and L. Shane Hall provide an excellent historical analysis of Title I, identify many important variables such as added time for instruction, express the need to use research-based practices, and make three pointed recommendations: (1) reduce displacement and redirect services to the lowest performers, (2) redirect the programs to grades one to three, and (3) build a coherent program. Their paper also captures the greatest challenge to their recommendations and others: "The problem with teacher training is that it is not very good and there is too little of it." The dilemma is in recommending that more or less of things be done that may or may not be working in the first place. Consequently, a good starting point might be to know what is being done and what effects it might have, as difficult, complicated, and expensive as it might be.

Accountability is needed in education funding to ensure that federal dollars contribute to student learning and are not wasted or, worse yet, used to fund practices that hinder children's learning. For example, a robust accountability system would allow for a comparison of the relative merits of schoolwide programs versus concentrated grants on pullouts.

But lessons learned from good management practice reveal that setting up the right accountability system is difficult. If accountability is to be productive, it must measure the right things, report accurate results, and create consequences that reward or discourage certain educational behaviors. Finally, for accountability to be fair, it must be linked with tangible reforms that give greater control and flexibility to those who are being held accountable. For example, a sound accountability system could give information about the success of targeting resources in kindergarten or grades one through three, allowing local districts to make better decisions about allocations of resources.

Children need to master subject content and skills to apply their knowledge. Teachers need to master content and effective pedagogy. However, it is not particularly useful or realistic to envision federal officials establishing academic achievement benchmarks or goals for children within a particular state or overtly controlling teacher professional development.

Not only would that raise serious objections about federal intrusion, but based on evidence, it is not necessary. States such as North Carolina and Texas are seeing achievement gains among their students because they are building an education accountability system that is understandable and engendering public pressure for high achievement for all children. It is a work in progress. For example, Texas has decided to align teacher professional development for early reading instruction with its content standards and is beginning to address the knowledge and pedagogy gaps that have been identified in the teaching work force.

The question is whether federal legislation is going to move to an accountability-based model where districts and schools have the authority and the responsibility to meet state and local accountability goals. This fundamental question hearkens to Paul T. Hill's comments about how much policymakers should tweak federal legislation. Should policymakers advocate for their preferred practice (for example, ranging from contracting out for services to adding new categorical programs) or should they support strong accountability legislation that allows states, districts, and schools the flexibility to select practices on their own?

The way to change the culture of education is to make accountability work. Spasmodic tweaks will not be effective. For example, research-based practices are of little interest outside of the context of accountability. If a culture is built around process and bureaucracy, no need exists to go through the pain of change entailed in adopting unfamiliar, research-based practices.

Accountability for Student Learning

The content of what children should learn (for example, reading, math, social studies, and science) is appropriately defined by the individual states. Effective state assessments are aligned to these content standards and measure student achievement against these standards. The current Title I already requires participating states to establish such content standards and assessment systems.

But for creating effective educational accountability, deciding on good content standards and assessing students by those standards is not enough. The reporting system must create local understanding and local pressure for real improvement, which requires testing every grade, every year. How can all the teachers in an elementary school be held accountable if testing occurs only for fourth or fifth graders?

Creating an effective school report card is an important foundation for the accountability structure. The following components of an effective school report card should be explicitly required of states as part of Elementary and Secondary Education Act (ESEA) participation.

An effective school report card must report student achievement data that are disaggregated by gender, race, and ethnicity; English proficiency; migrant status; disability; and economic disadvantage. If data are averaged for all students within a school, accountability for all students from all backgrounds is compromised. The only way to make progress in closing the achievement gap between disadvantaged and nondisadvantaged students is to know what the gap looks like.

The school report card should also provide information about the "value-added" by the school. That is, what is the average gain that students make, and how large were the gains of students with various demographic characteristics? This value-added factor (or gain score) gets at the fundamental question about a school's effectiveness: How much did the school add to a child's education, and how much is simply attributable to family background and other environmental factors?

The school report card system should provide comparative information about school performance among all schools in the state. The system should associate schools that have similar student populations and allow citizens to know how well students in these similar schools performed.

And most important, the report should make explicit the achievement level of the best of the similar schools. Having access to this information helps all parents and students from all types of schools. It helps students and parents in low-income schools know how well the best-achieving similar schools are performing. For example, a parent looking at such a report card might ask, "If students at the Wesley Elementary School in Houston are 98 percent school-lunch eligible and are achieving a pass rate of over 80 percent on the Texas reading and math assessments, why are students in my child's similar school only passing at a 50 percent level?" This type of reporting also holds affluent schools to the same kind of accountability, as they are compared with the highest achieving schools in their peer group.

To further safeguard the accountability for the federal dollars spent by the states, the state tests given to students must meet commonly accepted scientific standards:

—Be fair.
—Be valid.
—Be reliable.
—Be aligned with the specific content of the state standards.
—Be administered to all students, even if that requires a version in Spanish or another language. (Federal law already calls for including students with Individualized Education Plans (IEPs) in special education in the testing unless the IEP specifically excludes the students. Many students with IEPs who take the state test are eligible for accommodations.)

Within twelve months of the enactment of the new ESEA, each state should have its assessments technically reviewed by an external team of experts, identified in consultation with national professional organizations for assessment. The state would respond to this review and plan actions (if any) that will be taken to strengthen the state assessment.

Accountability for Quality Teaching

To ensure quality teaching, teachers should master their subject matter and keep abreast of changes in pedagogy.

Current requirements under the Eisenhower professional development program eloquently describe what sustained, intensive professional development should look like. The problem is that little professional development at the local level looks like what is described in the law, and almost no one knows what the law says.

To promote professional development that will reach the Eisenhower ideals, an accountability system needs to be established. Federal professional development funds should be tied to improving teacher knowledge in content areas—so teachers are assessed as to how well they know the content that they will be required to teach their students. These content tests should be developed by each state, specifically aligned to the state's learning standards, reported to the public, and meet the commonly accepted scientific standards, which would be a formal review for technical quality.

Education faces a difficult challenge in the area of pedagogy because of a lack of rigorous research and a lack of attention to research findings. The only pedagogy area in which the research has been synthesized in a systematic fashion is beginning reading (for example, the National Research Council's report *Preventing Reading Difficulty in Young Chil-*

dren). For three years, federal professional development should be limited to pedagogy training for research-based reading instruction. As pedagogy for other academic disciplines is synthesized, federal professional development funds could be applied to those disciplines as well.

Any noncertified teacher who is seeking to gain a credential must now take courses in pedagogy. In cases where school employees are using federal professional development funds to earn credit toward a full certification, this limitation on pedagogy training should not apply. Furthermore, this limitation on pedagogy should not apply to state or local funds for teacher professional development.

Federal professional development funds could still be available for improving the content expertise of teachers in important subjects such as math, science, and social studies. Teachers must be experts in the subjects that they teach. But professional development in pedagogy should be limited to the subject areas in which reliable research has been effectively synthesized and distributed within the field.

Accountability—The Federal Role

Can federal policy be crafted so it encourages or rewards states that are making significant progress in raising student achievement? Relying on state assessments in isolation is not sufficient. At least one common measure must exist to determine if disadvantaged students in different states are making reasonable gains with the use of federal dollars.

To safeguard against differences among state tests, all states should be encouraged to participate in the National Assessment of Educational Progress (NAEP). This test samples a broad cross-section of students within a state so not every student would need to take the test. The NAEP scores would provide a crude metric by which citizens, educators, and leaders could judge the relative achievement of the students in their state.

An incentive system could be developed for states that participate in NAEP. The incentive system would reward states that achieve high levels of progress according to their relative NAEP scores. For example, 50 percent of new program funding increases (for Title I, Education Technology, Title VI block grant, and so on) would be allocated according to current rules for student population and poverty data. The remaining 50 percent of new dollars would be allocated to states on a ranking system that weighs each state's relative progress in raising achievement of each group of students in the state on the NAEP assessments.

States making high rates of progress on NAEP would receive a significantly larger portion of these incentive funds. States making no progress or with dropping scores would receive no incentive funds. Every state would be guaranteed to continue receiving its current allocation of funds, even if it does not participate in NAEP.

More specifically, incentive funding for Title I would go to states based only on the rate of progress disadvantaged students in the state are making. Incentive funds linked to other programs could be based on a mix of progress for all students and for disadvantaged students, depending on how funding is already targeted. Teacher professional development funds could likewise be allocated to states based on their relative rates of student achievement gains. Teacher quality is clearly linked to student achievement. This initiative would support that linkage and reward effective professional development.

States that are already reaching high levels of achievement will eventually begin to top out at a high level. For these states, additional options besides their share of the incentive funds must be offered. This is where the concept of "Straight A's" or super-flexibility has merit. If a state shows consistently high rates of achievement and rates of growth in achievement, especially for children from disadvantaged backgrounds, why not allow those states to negotiate a flexible, data-driven arrangement whereby it receives all of its share of K-12 education funding in a flexible grant? If the state makes continued gains for all students, based on objective NAEP data, the negotiated arrangement would continue. If student achievement slips significantly, the state would be required to return to the typical arrangement for receiving ESEA funding.

Local Capacity for Research-Based Decisionmaking

A final issue that must be addressed is the role of local decisionmaking. For historical and political reasons, Americans have chosen not to pursue the option of establishing a centralized, national curriculum for learning. They have depended on local decisionmaking. Unfortunately, the quality of decisionmaking has been lacking in many places.

It is lacking for two primary reasons. First, no uniform market demand or public accountability exists for good decisionmaking and high student achievement. Until recent decades, the economy did not demand high levels of education for all students, and education systems were designed to give only a basic education to all students. Only students who were clearly "college material" needed to learn at higher levels, and such students usually self-selected into the college prep track. Because the economy did not demand high achievement for a large majority of students, the public system responded in kind.

As market demands have shifted for more highly educated students, public systems have not been particularly responsive. In part, they have been isolated from direct accountability for results. Indications that education is substandard usually do not appear until the student has been out of school for a few years.

But to simply assume that free-market forces will improve education is not supported by observing the existing private education marketplace. Many profitable yet low-achieving private schools have adopted the same whole language approach to reading that is widely criticized in public schools. The market has not weeded out these schools, because many parents find the "child-centered, discovery learning" philosophy that they offer appealing. It may be disastrous for children from disadvantaged backgrounds, but in today's private education marketplace, it fares well. Similarly, in higher education, private and public colleges of education seem to have been equal in their support of whole language.

Second, quality research to inform educational decisions is lacking. Because there has not been a high economic or public demand for effective education, a dearth of federal investment has been made in high-quality research on teaching and learning that can give local decisionmakers reliable knowledge. Educators are receptive to change, because they generally want the best for children; but because of a serious knowledge gap and a romanticized tradition of learning coming from colleges of education, schools are regularly swayed by the promises of the newest reform movement.

Some policymakers say confidently, "We've always known what works, but educators just don't care because there are no market forces in education." That is not entirely true. Until the recent investment in research by the National Institute of Child Health and Human Development (NICHD), it was not known why many children could not grasp phonics instruction. The research also determined that some children need explicit instruction in how to break apart the sounds of words before they receive instruction in the sounds and blending of letters. This research knowledge gap and observed failure of some students to grasp phonics was part of the reason that the whole language movement was an attractive option to many teachers.

Now more sophisticated research provides the knowledge to help children learn to read who were falling through the gaps of traditional phonics. In addition, research funded by the U.S. Office of Special Education programs has found that many children who had been thought to be incapable of learning to read could in fact learn to read. The weight of research on reading is forcing all educators to pay attention and question their leanings toward the constructivist, discovery learning philosophy of education. Research does matter.

To implement accountability and responsibility throughout public education, the need to build capacity for high-quality decisionmaking at every level must be taken seriously. Access to research-based information and implementation assistance must be readily available to parents, classroom teachers, building principals, citizen school boards and district leaders, and state officials.

Reforms of ESEA and the Office of Educational Research and Improvement must:

—Engage federal panels (supervised by NICHD and the Department of Education) in ongoing reviews and syntheses of high-quality research on teaching and learning. These reviews must give higher weight to scientifically rigorous research, and the findings must be compiled in language that is usable by classroom teachers and school leaders. The National Reading Panel has already established clear rules of evidence and is an extraordinary model for how this review process can work across a variety of academic disciplines.

—Invest in high-quality research on teaching and learning, with a strong emphasis on large-scale testing and evaluation about math, science, instruction for non-English speakers, and classroom management. This research should be regularly reviewed and synthesized.

—Expand and improve the Comprehensive School Reform Demonstration (CSRD) program, which helps schools purchase implementation assistance for whole school reforms from organizations that have expertise in reaching high levels of student achievement.

—Create a program, similar to the CSRD, that provides funding to school districts to purchase implementation assistance to help institutionalize effective decisionmaking practices and methods for moving research into practice.

Conclusion

Accountability does need to be strengthened in this authorization of the ESEA. But an important choice must be made about how to strengthen that accountability. Federal control could be increased through more directives and funding penalties for poor performance. That sounds appealing in the short term, given the lackadaisical progress that many schools and districts are making. But, based on experience, this approach has very little prospect for long-term gains. Federal requirements are effective at ensuring minimum compliance, not at energizing high-quality results.

Instead, states and localities could establish effective accountability systems that will energize local understanding and demand for high achievement. Federal resources could be used to strengthen the capacity for local decisionmaking using high-quality research findings. States that help students, particularly those from disadvantaged backgrounds, make significant achievement gains could be rewarded. And greater flexibility and autonomy could be made available for states and districts that prove their ability to raise student achievement.

This flexible mix of local accountability and federal incentives provides the greatest promise for helping all America's children experience educational excellence.

Notes

1. Michael J. Puma and others, *Prospects: Final Report on Student Outcomes* (Department of Education, Planning and Evaluation Service, Office of the Undersecretary, April 1997); and L. F. Carter, *A Study of Compensatory and Elementary Education: The Sustaining Effects Study* (Department of Education, Office of Program Evaluation, 1983).

2. Connie Juel, "Learning to Read and Write: A Longitudinal Study of Fifty-Four Children from First through Fourth Grade," *Journal of Educational Psychology*, vol. 80 (1988), pp. 437–47; Robert E. Slavin, Nancy L. Karweit, and Nancy A. Madden, *Effective Programs for Students at Risk* (Boston: Allyn and Bacon, 1989); Connie Juel, *Learning to Read in One Elementary School* (New York: Springer-Verlag, 1994); and George Farkas, *Human Capital or Cultural Capital?: Ethnicity and Poverty Groups in an Urban School District* (New York: Aldine de Gruyter, 1996).

3. Barbara Heyns, *Summer Learning and the Effects of Schooling* (New York: Academic Press, 1978); Doris R. Entwisle and Karl L. Alexander, "Winter Setback: The Racial Composition of Schools and Learning to Read," *American Sociological Review*, vol. 59 (June 1994), pp. 446–60; Doris R. Entwisle and Karl L. Alexander, "Summer Setback: Race, Poverty, School Composition, and Mathematics Achievement in the First Two Years of School," *American Sociological Review*, vol. 57 (February 1992), pp. 72–84; and Daniel M. O'Brien, "Family and School Effects on the Cognitive Growth of Minority and Disadvantaged Elementary School Students," paper presented at the Twentieth Annual Research Conference of the Association for Public Policy Analysis and Management, New York, November 8–10, 1998.

4. See Nancy Madden and others, "Success for All: Longitudinal Effects of a Restructuring Program for Inner-City Elementary Schools," *American Educational Research Journal,* vol. 30 (1993), pp. 123–48, especially p. 125.

5. Farkas, *Human Capital or Cultural Capital?*; and Christopher Jencks and Meredith Phillips, eds., *The Black-White Test Score Gap* (Brookings, 1998).

6. Stanley Pogrow, "Title I: Wrong Help at the Wrong Time," in M. Kanstoroom and C. Finn, eds., *New Directions: Federal Education Policy in the Twenty-First Century* (Washington: Thomas B. Fordham Foundation, March 1999), pp. 41–60.

7. Farkas, *Human Capital or Cultural Capital?*; Jencks and Phillips, *The Black-White Test Score Gap*; and Lawrence C. Stedman, "An Assessment of the Contemporary Debate over U.S. Achievement," in Diane Ravitch, ed., *Brookings Papers on Education Policy 1998* (Brookings, 1998), pp. 53–85.

8. Jencks and Phillips, *The Black-White Test Score Gap.*

9. See Grover Whitehurst and C. J. Lonigan, "Child Development and Emergent Literacy," *Child Development*, vol. 68 (1998), pp. 848–72; Grover Whitehurst, "Getting Ready to Read: Family Influences in Context," paper presented at the Green Center Conference on Attaining Universal Literacy, University of Texas at Dallas, May 1998; and Barbara Foorman and others, "The Case for Early Reading Intervention," in Benita A. Blachman, ed., *Foundations of Reading Acquisition and Dyslexia: Implications for Early Intervention* (Mahwah, N.J.: Lawrence Erlbaum Associates, 1997), pp. 243–64.

10. Phonemic awareness is the ability to hear and manipulate the distinct sounds in spoken language. Skills include identifying beginning and ending sounds, blending and segmenting sounds in spoken words, dropping sounds and pronouncing the remaining sounds, swapping sounds, and rhyming.

11. Whitehurst, "Getting Ready to Read."

12. Anthony S. Bryk, Valerie E. Lee, and Peter B. Holland, *Catholic Schools and the Common Good* (Harvard University Press, 1993); and Mary Zahn, "Head of the Class: Inside the Back-to-Basics World of the Marva Collins School," *Milwaukee Journal Sentinel*, February 21, 1999.

13. Marilyn Adams, *Beginning to Read: Thinking and Learning about Print* (MIT Press, 1990); and Bill Honig, *Teaching Our Children to Read: The Role of Skills in a Comprehensive Reading Program* (Thousand Oaks, Calif.: Corwin Press, 1996). See also Benita A. Blachman, ed., *Foundations of Reading Acquisition and Dyslexia: Implications for Early Intervention,* part IV*: Implications for Intervention* (Mahwah, N.J.: Lawrence Erlbaum Associates, 1997).

14. Russell A. Berkley and Joseph Biederman, "Toward a Broader Definition of the Age-of-Onset Criterion for Attention-Deficit Hyperactivity Disorder," *Journal of the American Academy of Child and Adolescent Psychiatry,* vol. 36 (1997), pp. 1204–10; and Joseph Biederman, "Are Stimulants Overprescribed for Children with Behavioral Problems?," *Pediatrics News* (August 1996).

15. For a presentation of the Reading One-to-One curriculum we have developed, see George Farkas, "Reading One-to-One: A Program Serving Large Numbers of Students While Still Achieving Strong Effects," in J. Crane, ed., *Social Programs That Work* (New York: Russell Sage Foundation Press, 1998), chapter 2; and George Farkas, *Reading One-to-One Tutor's Manual* (University of Texas at Dallas, Center for Education and Social Policy, 1998).

16. John W. Meyer, W. Richard Scott, and Terrence E. Deal, "Institutional and Technical Sources of Organizational Structure: Explaining the Structure of Educational Organizations," in John W. Meyer and W. Richard Scott, eds., *Organizational Environments: Ritual and Rationality* (Beverly Hills, Calif.: Sage Publications, 1983), pp. 45–70.

17. John W. Meyer and Brian Rowan, "The Structure of Educational Organizations," in John W. Meyer and W. Richard Scott, eds., *Organizational Environments: Ritual and Rationality* (Beverly Hills, Calif.: Sage Publications, 1983), pp. 71–98, quoted matter on p. 75; and Meyer, Scott, and Deal, "Institutional and Technical Sources of Organizational Structure," pp. 58–60.

18. Terry M. Moe, "Politics and the Theory of Organization," *Journal of Law, Economics, and Organization,* special issue, vol. 7 (1991), pp. 106–29.

19. John E. Chubb and Terry M. Moe, *Politics, Markets, and America's Schools* (Brookings, 1990).

20. Walter W. Powell, "Expanding the Scope of Institutional Analysis," in W. Powell and P. DiMaggio, eds., *The New Institutionalism in Organizational Analysis* (University of Chicago Press, 1991), pp. 190–91.

21. Powell, "Expanding the Scope of Institutional Analysis," p. 191.

22. Consider the following interchange when the Dallas school board was appointing an interim superintendent to take the place of a superintendent who had been sent to prison (*Dallas Morning News*, September 21 and 25, 1997): "When board President Kathleen Leos announced Dr. Hughey's name, members of the mostly black audience seemed confused. 'What's the race? If he's not African-American, we're definitely opposed,' shouted Thomas Muhammad, a black activist." "Some say the current battle between blacks and Hispanics is, at least in part, a fight over who will control jobs and contracts in a school district with more than 17,000 employees and a $967 million annual budget. 'It's about power and it's about jobs,' said Jesse Diaz, a vice president of a league of United Latin American Citizens chapter."

23. These observations are based on ten years of interaction with thousands of teachers and administrators across hundreds of schools in a great many school districts where we have presented or implemented the Reading One-to-One tutoring program. See Farkas, *Human Capital or Cultural Capital?;* George Farkas, "Ten Propositions about Schooling, the Inheritance of Poverty, and Interventions to Reduce This Inheritance," *Research in Social Problems and Public Policy,* vol. 6 (1997), pp. 125–69; Farkas, "Reading One-to-One"; and Farkas and others, "Can All Children Learn to Read at Grade Level by the End of Third Grade?," in D. Vannoy and P. Dubeck, eds., *Challenges for Work and Family in the Twenty-First Century* (New York: Aldine de Gruyter, 1998).

24. See Adams, *Beginning to Read;* and Honig, *Teaching Our Children to Read.*

25. Catherine Snow and others, eds., *Preventing Reading Difficulties in Young Children* (Washington: National Academy Press, 1998).

26. See the literature cited in Adams, *Beginning to Read*; Sonya Simons, Vera Woloshyn, and Michael Pressley, eds., "Special Issue: The Scientific Evaluation of the Whole-Language Approach to Literacy Development," *Educational Psychologist,* vol. 29, no. 4 (Fall 1994); Honig, *Teaching Our Children to Read*; and Foorman and others, "The Case for Early Reading Intervention."

27. For further explanation, see "Focus: Reading Recovery, Preventing Reading Failure," *Effective School Practices,* special issue, vol. 15, no. 3 (Summer 1996).

28. These gross characterizations are violated in particular cases. Nevertheless, they represent real tendencies in the alignment of forces in the reading wars.

29. Further examination of the perennial appeal to educators of such constructivist ideologies of instruction would be useful. Examples include the cross-national adoption of whole language (for example, it dominates reading instruction in Mexico despite the strong phonetic basis of Spanish) and the popularity of constructivist mathematics instruction, which, despite its damaging neglect of drill to achieve automaticity in addition and multiplication, is strongly advocated by many mathematics instructional specialists in education schools and school districts.

30. Bonnie Grossen, Gail Coulter, and Barbara Ruggles, "Reading Recovery: An Evaluation of Benefits and Costs," in "Focus: Reading Recovery, Preventing Reading Failure," *Effective School Practices,* special issue, vol. 15, no. 3 (Summer 1996), pp. 6–24.

31. When we have discussed Reading Recovery practices with school district people over the past ten years, many have volunteered, "They're like religion." In particular, Reading Recovery practices include the following: instructional techniques are passed on by a shared experiential training, with the belief that only this training makes a true practitioner; beliefs are based on faith instead of scientific research—these include the belief that intervention can be restricted to first grade and that, once "discontinued," the student will not require further remedial assistance; an unwillingness to release data for secondary analysis by others; and the use of nonscientific techniques in much of their research, including selecting "those who can profit" for tutoring, and dropping from the study sample those who did not succeed in the program.

32. "Focus: Reading Recovery, Preventing Reading Failure"; and Honig, *Teaching Our Children to Read.*

33. With the exception of those trained by Reading Recovery, many district curriculum directors have little formal training, or even experience, in the curriculum field. In the districts we have visited, it is common for the curriculum director to have been promoted from many years as a principal or other district administrator, based largely on personal ties to the superintendent. In many Texas school districts, an experienced Reading Recovery teacher typically earns in excess of $40,000 per year. With fringes this totals $50,000 or more. If he or she can tutor eight children one-to-one per year, the cost is $6,000 per child. At these prices only a small percentage of at-risk students can be served, but this fact is typically ignored by administrators, even when they are offered much lower cost alternatives (Farkas, *Human Capital or Cultural Capital?*, chapter 12). For studies questioning Reading Recovery's research practices, claims to effectiveness, and unit costs, see Yola Center, K. Wheldall, and L. Freeman, "Evaluating the Effectiveness of Reading Recovery: A Critique," *Educational Psychology,* vol. 12 (1992), pp. 263–73; Yola Center, K. Wheldhall, and L. Freeman, "An Experimental Evaluation of Reading Recovery," *Reading Research Quarterly,* vol. 30 (1995), pp. 240–63; Foorman and others, "The Case for Early Reading Intervention"; Patrick Groff, "Questions and Conclusions from a Discussion of Reading Recovery," in "Focus: Reading Recovery, Preventing Reading Failure," *Effective School Practices,* special issue, vol. 15, no. 3 (1996), pp. 25–29; Grossen, Coulter, and Ruggles, "Reading Recovery"; T. Rasinski, "On the Effects of Reading Recovery," *Reading Research Quarterly,* vol. 30 (1995), pp. 264–70; and T. Shanahan and R. Barr, "Reading Recovery: An Independent Evaluation of the Effects of an Early Instructional Program for At-Risk Learners," *Reading Research Quarterly*, vol. 30 (1995), pp. 958–96.

34. Kathleen Kennedy Manzo, "District Misuse of California Reading Funds Alleged," *Education Week*, May 7, 1997. We have observed similar activities on a widespread scale in Texas.

35. For further discussion see Farkas, *Human Capital or Cultural Capital?*, chapter 12.

36. Statement of Dr. G. Reid Lyon at *Overview of Reading and Literacy Initiatives*, hearings before the Senate Committee on Labor and Human Resources, April 28, 1998.

37. However, the most recent reauthorization in 1994 was more prescriptive of program operations than had previously been the case. James Berke and Michael Kirst, *Federal Aid to Education: Who Benefits? Who Governs?* (Lexington, Mass.: Lexington Press, 1972).

38. The sources of the numbers for the earlier 1990s are Martin Orland and Stephanie Stullich, "Financing Title I: Meeting the Twin Goals of Effective Resource Targeting and Beneficial Program Interventions," in Margaret Wong and Kenneth Wong, eds., *Implementing School Reform: Practice and Policy Imperative* (Philadelphia: Temple University Center for Research in Human Development and Education, 1997), chapter 1; and J. Moskowitz, S. Stullich, and B. Deng, *Targeting, Formula, and Resource Allocation Issues: Focusing Federal Funds Where the Needs Are Greatest* (Department of Education, 1993). However, Title I allocations have been in flux during the later 1990s, with an expansion to higher grades. See *Promising Results, Continuing Challenges* (Department of Education, Planning and Evaluation Service, Office of the Undersecretary, 1999).

39. Orland and Stullich, "Financing Title I"; and *Promising Results, Continuing Challenges.*

40. Orland and Stullich, "Financing Title I"; and *Promising Results, Continuing Challenges.*

41. Orland and Stullich, "Financing Title I"; and *Promising Results, Continuing Challenges.*

42. Orland and Stullich, "Financing Title I"; and *Promising Results, Continuing Challenges.*

43. Puma and others, *Prospects.*

44. This is from Mary Ann Millsap and others, *The Chapter 1 Implementation Study*, interim report, prepared by Abt Associates Inc. (Department of Education, 1992), which seems to be the most recent available data. These are the numbers cited in Department of Education, Office of the Undersecretary, *Use of Federal Education Funds for Administrative Costs* (Washington, 1998.)

45. Orland and Stullich, "Financing Title I"; *Promising Results, Continuing Challenges*; and Ralph Frammolino, "Title I's $118 Billion Fails to Close Gap," *Los Angeles Times*, January 17, 1999.

46. Puma and others, *Prospects*, p. 40.

47. Puma and others, *Prospects*, p. 55.

48. See George Johnson and James Tomola, "The Fiscal Substitution Effect of Alternative Approaches to Public Service Employment Policy," *Journal of Human Resources*, vol. 12 (Winter 1977), pp. 3–26; George Johnson, "The Labor Market Displacement Effect in the Analysis of Net Impact of Manpower Training Programs," in Farrell Bloch, ed., *Evaluating Manpower Training Programs* (JAI Press, 1979); George Farkas, D. Alton Smith, and Ernst W. Stromsdorfer, "The Youth Entitlement Demonstration: Subsidized Employment with a Schooling Requirement," *Journal of Human Resources*, vol. 18, no. 4 (Fall 1983), pp. 557–73; and Edward M. Gramlich and Harvey Galper, "State and Local Fiscal Behavior and Federal Grant Policy," *Brookings Papers on Economic Activity*, no. 1 (1973), pp. 15–58.

49. Puma and others, *Prospects*, p. 53.

50. The services provided to each student average fewer than thirty minutes per day.

51. Orland and Stullich, "Financing Title I"; and *Promising Results, Continuing Challenges*.

52. Anyone doubting that one of the major activities of district administrators is getting, spending, and shifting funds only needs to spend time with them, as we have done. For a description of how Dallas administrators used the 1994 reauthorization to pull large amounts of Title I moneys out of principals' budgets, see chapter 12 of Farkas, *Human Capital or Cultural Capital?* Concerning the general attitude of administrators to the use of funds, consider the case of the previous Dallas schools superintendent. Upon coming into office she announced she was bringing the FBI into the district to weed out what she had discovered to be long-standing corruption. The investigators convicted her of using district funds to purchase furniture for her home, and she was sent to prison. As for administrators' attitude toward accountability, the Austin assistant superintendent has just been indicted for altering student identification numbers so that these students' scores on the state accountability examination Texas Assessment of Academic Skills would be void, and some schools would receive higher rankings from the state.

53. Republicans used to be relatively vocal on this subject. It was one of their principal concerns during the many debates over the Comprehensive Employment and Training Act (CETA) and other job training programs during the 1970s and 1980s. Apparently their interest in decentralizing Title I and converting it into block grants has reduced their concern for this issue. For estimates of the magnitudes of displacement under these programs, see Farkas, Smith, and Stromsdorfer, "The Youth Entitlement Demonstration"; and Johnson and Tomola, "The Fiscal Substitution Effect of Alternative Approaches to Public Service Employment Policy."

54. Pogrow, "Title I."

55. Barbara Wasik and Robert Slavin, "Preventing Early Reading Failure with One-to-One Tutoring: A Review of Five Programs," *Reading Research Quarterly,* vol. 28 (1993), pp. 179–200; Marcia Invernizzi and others, "At-Risk Readers and Community Volunteers: A Three-Year Perspective," *Scientific Studies of Reading*, vol. 1, no. 3 (1997), pp. 277–300; and Farkas, "Reading One-to-One."

56. Farkas, *Human Capital or Cultural Capital?;* Farkas, "Reading One-to-One"; D. Morris and others, "Helping Low Readers in Grades 2 and 3: An After-School Volunteer Tutoring Program," *Elementary School Journal,* vol. 91 (1990), pp. 133–50; D. Morris, "First Steps: An Early Reading Intervention Program," ERIC Document Reproduction Service No. ED 388 956 (1995); Connie Juel, "Beginning Reading," in R. Barr and others, eds., *Handbook of Reading Research*, vol. 2 (New York: Longman, 1991), pp. 759–88; Connie Juel, "What Makes Literacy Tutoring Effective?," *Reading Research Quarterly,* vol. 31 (1996), pp. 268–89; Marcia Invernizzi and others, "A Community Volunteer Tutorial That Works," *Reading Teacher*, vol. 50 (1996); and Invernizzi and others, "At-Risk Readers and Community Volunteers."

57. During the eight years in which Reading One-to-One has tutored more than ten thousand students in more than one hundred schools across more than twenty districts, teachers have never had a problem with pullout once they saw the program in operation. See Farkas, *Human Capital or Cultural Capital?;* and Farkas, "Reading One-to-One."

58. Puma and others, *Prospects*, p. 66.

59. For one example, see Program Z discussed in chapter 12 of Farkas, *Human Capital or Cultural Capital?*

60. Orland and Stullich, "Financing Title I"; and *Promising Results, Continuing Challenges,* executive summary, p. 3.

61. Wasik and Slavin, "Preventing Early Reading Failure with One-to-One Tutoring"; and Farkas, "Reading One-to-One."

62. Chester Finn, Marci Kanstroom, and Michael J. Petrilli, "Overview: Thirty-Four Years of Dashed Hopes," in M. Kanstoroom and C. Finn., eds., *New Directions: Federal Education Policy in the Twenty-First Century* (Washington: Thomas B. Fordham Foundation, March 1999).

63. Diane Ravitch, "Clinton's School Plan Is a Good Start: Let's Go Further," *Wall Street Journal,* January 20, 1999.

64. Personal communication to George Farkas from Chester E. Finn Jr., April 1999.

65. However, the ability of these bureaucrats to influence principals out in the schools, whose career advancement they control, should never be underestimated. See chapter 12 of Farkas, *Human Capital or Cultural Capital?*

66. Rebecca Herman, *An Educators' Guide to Schoolwide Reform* (American Institutes for Research), at www.aasa.org/Reform.

67. Paul T. Hill, "Getting It Right the Eighth Time: Reinventing the Federal Role," in M. Kanstoroom and C. Finn, eds., *New Directions: Federal Education Policy in the Twenty-First Century* (Washington: Thomas B. Fordham Foundation, March 1999), p. 147.

68. "Title I Revision: IRA's Position," *Reading Today* (February/March 1999), p. 8 (emphasis in original).

69. Farkas "Reading One-to-One"; Invernizzi and others, "A Community Volunteer Tutorial That Works"; Invernizzi and others, "At-Risk Readers and Community Volunteers"; Juel, "Beginning Reading"; Juel, "What Makes Literacy Tutoring Effective?"; Morris and others, "Helping Low Readers in Grades 2 and 3"; and Morris, "First Steps."

70. Debra Viadero, "A Direct Challenge," *Education Week* (March 17, 1999), pp. 41–43.

71. Chester E. Finn Jr., "The Federal Role in Education Reform: First, Do No Harm," testimony prepared for delivery to the Senate Committee on the Budget, February 11, 1998.

The Safe and Drug-Free Schools Program

LAWRENCE W. SHERMAN

What is the best relationship between knowledge and democracy? The Calvinists who founded America thought democratic processes should set goals, while knowledge specialists should decide how to accomplish those goals. But in an increasingly antinomian (literally "against law") age, many Americans view knowledge itself as a democratic commodity, in which citizens are entitled not only to their own opinions, but also to their own facts. That is, every citizen is entitled to decide what knowledge means and what kind of evidence constitutes knowledge of cause-and-effect relationships. This view is manifest in the widespread resentment of elite knowledge as a basis for policymaking and the reverence for intuitive inspiration of the people "in the trenches" who must face problems on a daily basis. In the terms of Digby Baltzell, it is a matter of Puritanism versus Quakerism, of objective erudition versus the unschooled subjective inspiration of the "inner light."[1]

This conflict lies at the core of the new federalism. Who knows best how to fix the nation's problems: the knowledge elites of the federal government in Washington or the grass-roots leaders of local government? Since the administration of Lyndon B. Johnson in the 1960s, elected offi-

The comments of William Galston, Ramon Cortines, David Kirp, Diane Ravitch, and Michelle Cahill helped shape this paper's final form. The development of the paper was supported by my colleagues in the Crime Prevention Effectiveness Program at the University of Maryland, Department of Criminology and Criminal Justice, including Michael Buckley, Denise Gottfredson, Doris MacKenzie, John Eck, Shawn Bushway, Peter Reuter, and Mary West, as well as by the program's patrons, Jerry Lee, Robert Byers, George Pine, and a private foundation.

cials of both parties have increasingly chosen the latter. As public confidence in Washington has plummeted, more power to spend federal funds has been passed down to state and local leaders. Substantial evidence exists that Americans have more confidence in their local governments than in Washington to fix public problems.[2] But scant evidence is available that local officials can achieve more success than federal officials. In coming years, the evidence on the question of achievement will begin to accumulate on a wide range of programs, from welfare reform to medicaid.

One early result is found in the Safe and Drug-Free Schools program. As a crucial test of grass-roots control, the news is bad. Since 1986, this program has given more than $6 billion to some fifteen thousand local school districts and fifty state governors to spend largely at their own discretion. No evidence shows that this half-billion-dollar-per-year program has made schools any safer or more drug-free. However, much of the money has been wasted on performing magicians, fishing trips, and school concerts—and on methods (such as counseling) that research shows to be ineffective. Both the Office of Management and Budget and the Congressional Budget Office have tried to kill this program. Yet both Republican and Democratic presidents have joined with opposition parties in Congress to keep the program alive.

This paper explores the causes of, and alternatives to, the democratized waste of the Safe and Drug-Free Schools funding. The causes are linked to the politics of "symbolic pork," or the spending of money on problems without needing to show any outcome from previous spending. This paper documents that claim with respect to the Safe and Drug-Free Schools program and then considers alternative ways to restructure the program to increase its effectiveness. One alternative is a Food and Drug Administration (FDA)-style, Washington-driven program based on the best knowledge available nationwide. Another is a local accounting model, in which every community develops performance and results measures for every expenditure. A third alternative, which I define as "evidence-based government," combines the best national knowledge with the best local outcome measures in a participatory process of accountability for risk-adjusted, value-added results.[3]

Whether a Washington-led program of research-based best practices for school safety could make schools any safer is hard to say. The idea of a federally approved menu of practices of proven effectiveness is similar to a Food and Drug Administration, testing all policies for their safety and effectiveness. Yet applying such a menu on a national scale presumes both the resources to support sufficient research and the generalizability of research results from the test communities to all or many other communities. Congress has never appropriated funds for the former, and many Americans refuse to believe the latter. Local leaders clearly prefer knowledge based on "our town" rather than on someone else's town, on the premise that every community is unique.

That premise suggests the local accounting model, in which each community invests in measurement of the impact of its federal expenditures. This approach is best exemplified by the "reinventing government" philosophy of the Government Performance and Results Act (GPRA) of 1994, which calls on all government agencies at the federal level to name their criteria for success and then report on how well they meet those criteria.[4] Under this model, school safety, or even achievement test scores, could be compared across different policies to find the most effective way to accomplish each goal. Trends in outcomes before and after the introduction of new policies may provide some clue as to their success. But this approach yields very weak evidence on cause and effect. Moreover, it disregards the huge differences in the level of risk of crime—and of academic failure—that are found from one school to the next, or one school district to another.

This paper proposes a model of evidence-based government that draws on both national and local evidence to compare schools with their expected performance outcomes, given the social context in which their students live. This is arguably the only fair way to compare outcomes across units of government and to show the "value-added" difference that each unit can make with its raw material. By comparing the difference schools make with their students, and not just the qualities students bring to school, federal programs can help reward the best practices that each school can undertake in its own context.

The Safe and Drug-Free Schools and Communities Act is part of a larger group of programs that arguably constitute symbolic pork. These programs differ from traditional pork barrel funds, which bring jobs or tangible benefits such as construction projects to one congressional district at a time. Symbolic pork puts money into every congressional district to symbolize federal concern about a problem, regardless of what effect the money has—or how small the amounts of money may be. Each member of Congress gets to say that he or she has voted for this program whenever constituents complain about crime or drugs in schools. By this logic, no member of Congress could ever vote against such funding, because that vote could imply indifference to problems of school safety and drug abuse. Nor can members easily vote to limit grass-roots control of the money, after a decade of predictable funding.

Such spending can even be "symbolic" rather than tangible in terms of the choice of problems it addresses. By choosing problems based on subjective concerns of the voters, instead of on the basis of objective knowledge, Congress may spend money on nonexistent or minor problems—government by anecdote as opposed to government by analysis. If voters were aroused by several blizzards, for example, despite evidence of declining snowfall nationwide, the passage of a national blizzard prevention program would constitute symbolic pork.

This analysis uses the metaphor of the Food and Drug Administration to argue for national evidence-based government. If there were an FDA for schools, what would it say about school violence and drugs? Guided solely by the best evidence available, what would one conclude about the severity and shape of the problems? Given the shape of the problems and the available policy evaluations, what would be the best policy? If an effective program were designed to be run from Washington based on the best national knowledge available, what would it look like? On what principles would the resources be allocated, how would what works be determined, and how would specific prevention methods be selected?

Problems and Solutions: Evidence-Based Analysis

Most schools are safe, although few are drug-free. The causes of violence and drug abuse are largely external to the schools themselves, although school management can make a moderate contribution to preventing those problems. Substantial research evidence suggests that putting the right kinds of programs into the small number of high-risk schools could succeed in making schools somewhat safer and more drug-free. While far more research is still needed, some old-favorite methods are known to be ineffective.

The rare problem of school violence is heavily concentrated in a small number of schools in urban poverty areas. Fixing the problem in urban schools would largely solve the nation's school violence problem. Mass murders have increased slightly in recent years—including the rare occurrences in nonurban schools—but overall rates of violent injury of high school students have remained virtually unchanged since 1985.

Drug abuse is more widespread than violence, but only moderately linked to schools. Most students who use drugs do so off school property. Schools are more commonly used for exchange of drugs than their consumption. Marijuana use by high school seniors has fallen and risen since 1985, cocaine use has fallen, and hallucinogen use has risen.

The causes of these problems are mostly beyond school walls, and schools at best can have moderate effects on them. But good evidence exists about how those effects can be achieved.

The Problems

While the problems of violence and drug abuse are different in their geography, neither of them has changed much in the past decade.

VIOLENCE IN SCHOOLS. On average, American schools are among the safest places on Earth. While the number of mass murder incidents nationwide rose from two in 1992–93 to six in 1997–98, the overall murder rate has always been far lower in schools than in environments outside schools. In 1992–94, the murder rate for children in schools was less than 0.45 per 100,000 person-years.[5] The overall U.S. homicide rate in those years was about 9 per 100,000, or twenty times higher than the rate in schools.[6] For children outside of school, the murder rate was more than 20 per 100,000.[7] Thus American children are, on average, forty-four times more likely to be murdered out of school than they are in school. Moreover, they are far safer sitting in American schools than they are living in low-homicide countries such as Australia, England, and New Zealand.[8]

Yet not all children are created equal in their risk of being murdered, either in school or out. School violence, like serious violence in general, is heavily concentrated in highly segregated neighborhoods where most adults are out of the labor force.[9] Homicide rates in some urban neighborhoods reach 180 per 100,000, or twenty times the national homicide rate and almost four hundred times the national risk of murder in school.[10] Fully 90 percent of all 109,000 schools nationwide report not one serious violent incident in a year. But 17 percent of schools in cities report

Table 1. High School Seniors Injured with Weapon at School
Percent

Year	*All students*	*All males*	*All blacks*
1985	5.9	8.8	8.9
1986	5.4	8.6	6.9
1987	4.9	7.7	5.6
1988	4.7	7.8	9.0
1989	5.6	8.0	11.3
1990	5.8	8.9	10.0
1991	6.5	8.7	9.6
1992	5.1	8.1	5.2
1993	4.7	7.0	6.4
1994	4.7	7.8	8.1
1995	4.9	7.5	8.7
1996	4.9	6.7	9.8
1997	5.2	7.9	7.1

Source: Lloyd D. Johnston and others, "Monitoring the Future," in Kathleen Maguire and Ann Pastore, eds., *Sourcebook of Criminal Justice Statistics, 1997* (Department of Justice, 1998), pp. 205–09.

at least one incident, compared with 11 percent on the urban fringe, 8 percent of rural schools, and 5 percent of schools in small towns.[11]

High schools and middle schools carry most of the risk of violence. In 1996–97, 21 percent of high schools and 19 percent of middle schools reported at least one serious violent event; only 4 percent of elementary schools did. This difference also tracks the age structure of serious violence outside of school.

Schools are more dangerous for teachers than for students. While students are victimized by serious violent acts at the rate of about 10 per 1,000 per year, teachers face more than twice that rate. Teachers in urban schools are victimized at the rate of 39 incidents per 1,000, about double the rates of 20 per 1,000 for teachers in suburban schools and 22 per 1,000 in rural schools.[12]

The rate of violence against students in schools has remained remarkably constant over the past fifteen years, despite the national doubling in the overall juvenile homicide rate during that time.[13] That conclusion is evident in the prevalence of high school seniors who reported to the annual University of Michigan survey that in the past twelve months, while they were "at school (inside or outside or on a schoolbus)," they had been injured with a weapon "like a knife, gun or club." While table 1 shows the disproportionate concentration of injuries among black seniors (which would be even greater absent the higher dropout rate among inner-city students), it also shows virtually no substantial change in rates of violence since the program started in 1987.

These rates of injury may seem high to most adults. But they are comparable to national rates. In 1995 the national rate of victimization by all violent crime was 5 incidents per 100 people. For crimes of violence with injury, the national rate for all ages was 1 incident per 100, but for persons aged sixteen to nineteen it was 3.3 per 100.[14] The shape of the violence problem in general is that it is heavily concentrated among young men and has been for centuries—both in and out of school.[15]

Public perceptions of the school violence problem may be driven less by these rates than by anecdotal evidence. The national concern over mass murders in schools clearly increases the perception of all schools as dangerous, at-risk environments. But from a policy perspective, the shape of the mass murder problem is a needle in a haystack. Predicting where such incidents will occur is virtually impossible, despite the tendency to have 20/20 hindsight about the predictability of each event after it has happened.[16] From a political perspective, extreme cases reaffirm the need for a program to fix the problem of unsafe schools, regardless of how safe they are in any objective sense.

DRUG USE IN SCHOOLS. Drug use in schools appears to be more prevalent and more widespread than violent crime but is still limited to a small fraction of all students. More than 91 percent of all high school students, and some two-thirds of current users of marijuana, say they do not use marijuana on school property. More common is acquiring drugs on school property. For 1995, the Centers for Disease Control Youth Risk Behavior Surveillance System (YRBSS) reports that 32 percent of all high school students have been offered, given, or sold an illegal drug on school property. This figure varies little by race: 31.7 percent for whites, 28.5 percent for blacks, and 40.7 percent for Hispanics.[17]

These data do not provide separate estimates for inner-city schools, so the shape of the drug problem cannot be directly compared with the shape of violence. However, the analysis of *where* children are at risk for these problems, and whether schools are above or below the average risk for any location in their communities, can be replicated. While some 42 percent of students claimed to have used marijuana at least once in their lifetime, and 25 percent report current use, only 8.8 percent report current marijuana use (any time in the last thirty days) on school property.

Table 2. High School Seniors Using Drugs in the Past Twelve Months
Percent

Year	*Marijuana*	*Cocaine*	*Hallucinogens*
1985	40.6	13.1	6.3
1986	38.8	12.7	6.0
1987	36.3	10.3	6.4
1988	33.1	7.9	5.5
1989	29.6	6.5	5.6
1990	27.0	5.3	5.9
1991	23.9	3.5	5.8
1992	21.9	3.1	5.9
1993	26.0	3.3	7.4
1994	30.7	3.6	7.6
1995	34.7	4.0	9.3
1996	35.8	4.9	10.1
1997	38.5	5.5	9.8

Source: Kathleen Maguire and Ann Pastore, eds., *Sourcebook of Criminal Justice Statistics, 1997* (Department of Justice, 1998), p. 237.

This latter figure also varies little by race, at 7 percent for whites and around 12 percent for blacks and Hispanics.

Overall the data suggest that schools may be largely drug-free even when their students are not. The data on drug transfers suggest that schools may be more a marketplace for drugs than a place for their consumption. That might still be a damning indictment if students could get drugs only at school. The widespread availability of drug markets outside school suggests that drug-free schools might never create drug-free students. Even so, availability of drugs at school does make some difference. Controlling for individual propensity to use drugs, individual decisions to use drugs increase when more students in a school say that drugs are easy to buy there.[18]

Surveys of high school seniors conducted each year since 1985 show how few changes have occurred in their drug use over the most recent twelve months since the advent of the program in 1987 (see table 2).

The Causes

The causes of youth violence and drug abuse in schools have only a modest connection to how schools are run. The fact that most youth violence occurs outside schools suggests that schools do a good job of protecting students against violence for seven hours a day. The best predictor of the safety of a school is the safety of its neighborhood.[19] Once the effect of neighborhood violence rates is controlled, little (although some) variability remains in the safety of each school. Only some of that variability can be explained by how the schools are run. Smaller schools are safer than larger schools. Schools with a sense of community and strong administrative leadership are safer than schools that lack these characteristics. It may be easier to create a sense of community in smaller schools, but size is only one factor in school climate.

The pessimistic view of the high correlation between community problems and school problems is compositional: The composition, or kinds of students each school has, determines its level of violence and drug abuse. Much like the conclusions of research on family factors in determining educational achievement, this view says that family and background factors of students shape the school safety climate and overwhelm good educators.[20] This argument concludes that it is futile to modify schools if the community is the prime source of school problems; modifying communities and their families would work far better and would naturally improve the schools.

Good evidence against that view comes from Gary and Denise Gottfredson's 1985 analysis of 1976 crime data from more than six hundred secondary schools.[21] This study measured characteristics of communities, students, and schools. Schools were measured by interviews with students, teachers, and principals. Their analysis shows that community structural characteristics (such as rates of unemployment and single-parent households) and student compositional characteristics (such as the number of parents in each student's home) were so highly correlated that they could not be separately estimated. Even after controlling for these characteristics, however, school climate still varied—and had a clear effect on rates of victimization in schools. For junior high schools, community factors explained 54 percent of the variance in victimization of teachers, but school factors explained an additional 12 percent. Community factors explained only 5 percent of the variance in junior high school victimization of students, while school effects explained 19 percent. Thus depending on the measure, school effects can be even greater than compositional or community effects on junior high crime rates.

School effects are somewhat weaker for senior highs, but still important. Community factors explain 43 percent of the variance in teacher victimization rates, while school factors explain an additional 18 percent of the variance. For student victimization rates, community factors explain

21 percent of the variance, while school effects explain another 6 percent of the variance.

If school characteristics matter, which ones affect rates of crime the most? The Gottfredsons found that three general factors may cause less crime: size and resources, governance, and student socialization. Specifically, schools have less teacher victimization, independent of community context, when they have

—More teaching resources,

—Smaller total enrollment (junior highs) or smaller student-teacher ratios (senior highs),

—More consistent and fair discipline,

—Less democratic teacher attitudes toward parent and student control (junior highs only),

—Less punitive teacher attitudes,

—More teacher-principal cooperation (senior highs only), and

—Higher student expectations that rules will be enforced (junior highs), and commitment to conventional rules (senior highs).

The Gottfredsons found similar factors also affect rates of student victimization, especially perceptions of the fairness and consistency of school discipline.[22]

Despite the independent effect of school factors on crime, school management is highly correlated with community characteristics. The most disorganized schools are found in the most disorganized communities. Does this mean that schools cannot be improved to reduce crime? No. But it does reflect the size of the challenge facing any policy trying to produce that result. That challenge can be met more effectively on the basis of experimental and quasi-experimental research that has compared a wide range of different strategies for enhancing school capacity to prevent crime and drug abuse.

The Solutions

How should the United States spend $500 million per year to foster safe and drug-free schools? Note that the question is not how much, if any, money to spend on this objective. Evidence-based government could help rank the relative importance of different issues, and even help allocate resources among them. Yet those decisions are increasingly the result of poll-driven politics, which is just another technology in the long history of democracy.[23] Criminologists might argue for redirecting the money to a general reconstruction of community, family, housing, and labor markets in small areas of the fifty-four cities producing more than half of all homicides in America.[24] But that option, for now, is off the table. If the money is inevitably to be spent on schools, the best evidence can still be used to design the best program. Doing that requires matching resources to risks, learning what works, and crafting policy from evidence.

MATCHING RESOURCES TO RISKS. The evidence shows highly uneven risks of violence, with most school violence found in a small percentage of schools. The evidence is less clear about the concentration of drug abuse. Thus it may make sense to split the efforts for controlling drugs and violence. This requires some criterion for weighing the relative importance of the two problems. One criterion is cost to the taxpayers. An estimated $20,000 in medical costs results from each nonfatal gun injury, most of which is borne by taxpayers. The number of drug-related auto accidents or violent crimes is much harder to estimate. But a 50-50 split between the two problems is probably as good an estimate as any.

Where should this country spend $250 million annually to foster safer schools? The evidence suggests the money should be put where the crime is, concentrating most of the funds in the schools with most of the violence, generally located in urban poverty areas. This strategy is made easier by the relative lack of resources in many of the most dangerous schools. The evidence on how to allocate the funds would have to be gathered carefully, to ensure that schools do not increase crime reporting just to get more money. Police records on neighborhood crime rates might be a better source of data.

Where should this country spend $250 million annually to foster drug-free schools? The evidence suggests that this objective requires far broader distribution of funds than for violence prevention. Nonetheless, an ample literature exists on the inequitable support for education across school districts. If federal funds are to make the most difference, a question still arises of whether all school districts should be funded equally per student, or on some measure of risk given each school's constraints. The "old" federalism would require extensive paperwork to demonstrate each school's need and a comprehensive proposal for federal officials to review. But that is what grass-roots solutions reject. Using measures of drug use, either the National Institute of Drug Abuse (NIDA) or the President's Office for Narcotics and Drug Control Policy (drug czar) could assign a risk level to every one of the fifteen thousand school districts in the nation and create three levels of risk: high, medium, and low. Then, for example, 60 percent of the funds should be assigned to the high-risk districts, 30 percent to the medium-risk districts, and 10 percent to the low-risk districts.

In a political process, resources can rarely be matched to risks, especially when the need is greatest among those with the least political power. But whatever principle is used to allocate resources across schools, the next question is how to spend the money in each school. Grass-roots political theory says each school or district should make that decision, without Washington telling it what to do. Evidence-based government says whoever makes the decision should do it based on good evidence. But doing that requires a clear definition of terms for learning what works: what constitutes good evidence.

LEARNING WHAT WORKS. Three schools of thought about evaluation research have emerged in recent years: the mainstream evaluation community, program advocates who reject the legitimacy of external evaluation, and antinomian critics of the scientific method. Each group has its own view about how to learn about what works. Yet all three agree that once what works has been determined, more of it should be done.

Mainstream evaluators continue to believe that good science and reliable measurement can reveal more about cause and effect than the opinions of people delivering the programs. This group, which includes myself, continues to press for randomized field trials, multisite replication, testing and refinement of microprocesses, and theory-based programs. Many of this group would prefer a combination of qualitative process evaluations and controlled impact analysis, although they are often accused of caring only for the latter. Their view of how to scale up from pilot to national program is cautious, with a preference for an incremental process of testing at each level of larger scale.

Program advocates learn what works from personal experience. They make things happen with remarkable success, overcoming obstacles that might restrain the growth of their programs. Evaluation is one such obstacle. They would not work so hard for their programs if they had any doubt as to the program's benefits. That viewpoint inevitably makes evaluation at best a distraction, and at worst a threat. Advocates often ask elected officials to observe their programs firsthand, talk to staff and clients, hear the testimonials, and feel the enthusiasm. That method of evaluation, to them, is a far more reliable indicator of success than whatever statistics might show, because statistics can show anything. Both this viewpoint and the evaluators' have been around for decades, and both are predictable.[25]

The newest school of thought may be called the antinomian critics of the scientific method. Lisbeth B. Schorr is an articulate exponent of this viewpoint, which stresses the difficulty of placing comprehensive, flexible programs into a controlled test.[26] The basic argument is that variability is essential to program success, but inimical to controlled testing. Therefore, controlled tests should be abandoned in favor of less rigorous research designs. Low internal validity designs are the only research possible for the kind of multitreatment, comprehensive, one-size-does-not-fit-all interventions that are needed. Tom Loveless has applied this perspective to education policy research, arguing against anyone trying to define "best practices" based on research results. He also stresses the responsiveness of each teacher to each student, arguing against research-based policy, which by definition constrains that virtue.[27]

From the perspective of mainstream evaluation, the antinomian view confuses the limitations of inadequate research funding with inadequate methods of science. The primary reason that variability within treatment group is problematic for evaluation is limited research funding. With larger sample sizes, more resources for consultation with practitioners, and other resources, the scientific method can use controlled tests of many variations and combinations of strategies. What evaluators call "Solomon" designs, with ten or twenty different treatment groups in a randomized comparison, can be taken out of the laboratory and put into field tests, given enough money and time to enlist the partnership and commitment of teachers. With 14,000 police agencies, 15,000 school districts, 109,000 schools, and more than 1,000,000 classrooms, more than enough cases are available for analysis. Even in big cities, where the numbers of governments get smaller, the number of contact points remains enormous.

Evidence-based government takes its inspiration (and its name) from evidence-based medicine.[28] That nascent field faces similar debates between evaluators, doctors, and antinomian critics of randomized trials. Yet medicine persists in seeking elegant simplicity for clarification of evidence, with a five-point scale of the strength of each study supporting each choice of medical treatment.[29] Similarly, the University of Maryland's Department of Criminology and Criminal Justice recently employed a five-point scale to rank the strength of evidence from each evaluation of crime prevention practices.[30] This scale was employed in a congressionally mandated review of the effectiveness of the $4 billion in state and local crime prevention assistance administered by the U.S. Department of Justice. The law required that the review "employ rigorous and scientifically recognized standards and methodologies."[31]

Following that mandate, the Maryland report defined its scientific methods scale as follows:

Level 1: Correlation between a crime prevention program and a measure of crime or crime risk factors at a particular time.

Level 2: Temporal sequence between the program and the crime or risk outcome clearly observed, or a "comparison" group present without demonstrated comparability to the treatment group.

Level 3: Before-after comparison between two or more units of analysis, one with and one without the program.

Level 4: Before-after comparison between multiple units with and without the program, controlling for other factors, or a with a nonequivalent comparison group that has only minor differences evident.

Level 5: Random assignment and analysis of comparable units to program and comparison groups.

Using this scale, the report then classified all crime prevention programs (defined as local methods, not federal funding "streams") for which sufficient evidence was available. The categories were what works, what doesn't work, and what's promising. Any program that did not meet the following standards was left in the residual category of what's unknown.

What works. These programs are reasonably certain to prevent crime or reduce risk factors for crime in the kinds of social contexts in which they have been evaluated, and for which the findings should be generalizable to similar settings in other places and times. Programs coded as "working" by this definition must have at least two level 3 evaluations with statistical significance tests and the preponderance of all available evidence showing effectiveness.

What doesn't work. These programs are reasonably certain to fail to prevent crime or reduce risk factors for crime, using the identical scientific criteria used for deciding what works.

What's promising. These are programs for which the level of certainty from available evidence is too low to support generalizable conclusions, but for which some empirical basis exists for predicting that further research could support such conclusions. Programs are coded as "promising" if they were found effective in at least one level 3 evaluation and the preponderance of the evidence.

What's unknown. Any program not classified in one of the three above categories is defined as having unknown effects.

The weakest aspect of this classification system is that no standard means is available for determining which variations in program content and setting might affect generalizability. In the current state of science, that can be accomplished only by the accumulation of many tests in many settings with all major variations on the program theme. None of the programs reviewed for the Maryland report had accumulated such a body of knowledge. The conclusions about what works and what doesn't work should therefore be read as more certain to the extent that the conditions of the field tests can be replicated in other settings. The greater the differences between evaluated programs and other programs using the same name, the less certain or generalizable the conclusions of any report must be.

In her chapter of the Maryland report, Denise C. Gottfredson reviewed available evidence on the programs designed to reduce violence and drug use in schools. Her work was not an evaluation of the Safe and Drug-Free Schools program, but its results can be summarized as a basis for an evidence-based program to accomplish those goals.

WHAT WORKS IN PREVENTION. Given the research on the causes of the problems of violence and drugs at school, most effective programs not surprisingly treat the whole school and do not just supplement the curriculum. Building on social organization theory, these programs have taken the holistic approach that all aspects of school life can affect violence and substance abuse. Whether school starts on time, for example, can affect student perceptions that discipline is fair and consistent, which in turn can affect the level of crime and drug abuse. The specific conclusions Gottfredson reached follow.

What works. Building school capacity to initiate and sustain innovation through the use of school "teams" or other organizational development strategies works to reduce delinquency and is promising for reducing substance abuse.[32]

—Clarifying and communicating norms about behavior through rules, reinforcement of positive behavior, and schoolwide initiatives (such as antibullying campaigns) reduce crime and delinquency and substance abuse.[33]

—Social competency skills curricula, such as Life Skills Training (LST), which teach over a long period of time such skills as stress management, problem solving, self-control, and emotional intelligence, reduce delinquency and substance abuse.[34]

—Training or coaching in "thinking" skills for high-risk youth using behavior modification techniques or rewards and punishments reduces substance abuse.[35]

What doesn't work. This list includes some of the most popular attempts at prevention that have been developed and promoted by strong advocates. These are in widespread use in schools, both with and without federal funding. They are based on what appear to their advocates to be reasonable theories and produce strong anecdotal evidence. But they all fail to show prevention effects in at least two studies at the Maryland scale level 3 or higher:

—Counseling and peer counseling of students fail to reduce substance abuse or delinquency, and can even increase delinquency.[36]

—Drug Abuse Resistance Education (D.A.R.E.), a curriculum taught by uniformed police officers primarily to fifth and sixth graders in more than seventeen lessons, has virtually no effect on prevention of drug abuse.[37] Available evaluations are limited to the original D.A.R.E. curriculum, which was modified slightly in 1993 and again in 1998, now extending from K-12 in Los Angeles.

—Instructional programs focusing on information dissemination, fear arousal, moral appeal, self-esteem, and affective education generally fail to reduce substance abuse.[38]

—Alternative activities and school-based leisure time enrichment programs, including supervised homework, self-esteem exercises, community service, and field trips, fail to reduce delinquency risk factors or drug abuse.[39]

What's promising. The following programs have only one level 3 or higher study showing that they work, but no studies of that strength showing that they do not work:

—"Schools within schools" programs (such as Student Training through Urban Strategies or STATUS) that group students into smaller units for more supportive interaction or flexibility in instruction have reduced drug abuse and delinquency.[40]

—Training or coaching in "thinking" skills for high-risk youth using behavior modification techniques or rewards and punishments may reduce delinquency and are known to work to reduce substance abuse.[41]

CRAFTING POLICY FROM EVIDENCE. Three decades ago under the old federalism, a highly trained civil servant in Washington might have taken this list and offered funding to schools that could propose plausible plans for replicating one or more of the programs that work. Each proposal would have been carefully reviewed, and perhaps regional federal officials might even have visited each site. If the program was not implemented as planned, some attempt might have been made to cut off the funds, but an appeal to a member of Congress might have stopped that quickly.

Under the new federalism, the law essentially limits civil servants in Washington to writing a check and enclosing with it a manual of recommended programs. The premise is that no one in Washington is close enough to local conditions to decide what kinds of programs are most appropriate for any given locale. While that may be true, proximity alone may not lead to the right answer. Local officials may have more information, but they may also be more susceptible to the enthusiasm of advocates selling what has proven to be snake oil.

Antinomian critics of the list of what works and what doesn't work will cite the uncertainty about generalizability of the results. So do the evaluators. Gilbert Botvin, the inventor of Life Skills Training—the most effective (but by no means the most widely used) drug prevention curriculum—examined the variability in the quality of implementation after teacher training. He found that the percentage of curricular materials covered in the classroom varied widely from school to school, from 27 percent to 97 percent, with an average of 68 percent. Only 75 percent of the students were taught at least 60 percent of the required content. Most important, the level of implementation directly affected results. When less than 60 percent of the program elements are taught, the program fails to prevent drug abuse.[42]

This "flexibility" of committed teachers is what the antinomians wish to preserve. Lisbeth Schorr, for example, objects to a McDonald's restaurant kind of formula for ensuring consistency across programs—largely on the empirically testable grounds that it cannot be delivered, but also on the grounds that theory-based flexibility will work better. Botvin's evidence partly falsifies the latter claim but may support the former claim. It is not clear that the means are yet available to ensure proper implementation of the programs that work, even if funding could be limited to such proven programs.

Lacking the means to ensure fidelity does not mean that they cannot be provided. Just as research can show what works and what doesn't work to prevent crime, it can also learn what works in program implementation. Here again, the limits of the scientific method could be confused with the current limits in funding. With adequate investment in the research and development (R&D) effort to learn how to implement effective programs, evidence-based teaching and evidence-based school leadership could be fostered in ways that reduce violence and drug abuse.

Had $6 billion been spent on such an R&D effort over the past twelve years, an effective means of encouraging grass-roots adoption of effective practices may have been developed by now. Instead, the $6 billion was given to local officials to spend any way they wanted. The results are not encouraging.

Symbolic Pork: The Return on Investment

The Safe and Drug-Free Schools program is based on two key principles. One is that everyone should get an equal share of money per student, regardless of need. The other is that interference from Washington should be minimal. Ironically, federal officials are the first to be blamed for any local program failures. A *Los Angeles Times* exposé in 1998 documented such failures extensively. Yet in his 1999 State of the Union address, President Bill Clinton received bipartisan applause when he called for continuing the program.

The Shape of the Legislation

The Safe and Drug-Free Schools and Communities Act, first enacted in 1986, was most recently reauthorized in 1994 under Title IV of the Elementary and Secondary Education Act.[43] The law divides the available funds on the basis of the number of students in each state. It gives 20 percent of each state's funds to governors to award as grants. The 80 percent balance of the money is allocated to each school district on the basis of enrollment.

The result of this formula is to spread the money thinly across the 14,881 school districts in the country, most of which participate in the program. Six out of every ten school districts receive $10,000 or less each year. Small districts may receive only $200 or $300, which does not even cover paperwork processing time. The Greenpoint Elementary School District in Humboldt County, California, received $53 in 1997 for its twenty students.[44]

Large school districts, in contrast, can spend the money on substantial administrative costs. The Los Angeles Unified School District received $8 million from the program in 1997 for its 660,000 students. It spent $2.2 million—28 percent—of the funds on the program's administration, including a $1,000 bonus to teachers who serve as program coordinators at each school.

School districts are also authorized to spend up to 20 percent of their funds for security measures, such as metal detectors or security guards. Schools in communities as safe as State College, Pennsylvania, have followed this suggestion in recent years, assigning police or guards to patrol the schools. So did Columbine High School in Littleton, Colorado, although to no effect in preventing a mass murder.

Administrative Rulemaking

In response to the March 1997 University of Maryland report on preventing crime, the U.S. Department of Education in July 1997 proposed revised guidelines to make the program more evidence-based. The proposed rules tried to limit the funding to activities for which some research showed effectiveness. These guidelines originally proposed that each state or school district "design and implement its programs for youth based on research or evaluation that provides evidence that the programs used prevent or reduce drug use, violence, or disruptive behavior among youth."[45] Yet, in the politics of the new federalism, even this proved too tough a standard to impose.

In June 1998, the department summarized the comments received on the proposed principles and published its final "nonregulatory guidance for implementing SDFSCA [Safe and Drug-Free Schools and Communities Act] principles of effectiveness." The comments indicate a strong grass-roots reaction against an attempt to invoke evidence-based government. The final rules show the compromises the Department of Education made to preserve the symbolism of evidence-based government without much reality:[46]

> Comments: Several commentators noted the lack of research-based programs in drug and violence prevention that meet local needs. One of those commentators stated that the high standard imposed by the SDFS [Safe and Drug-Free Schools] Principles of Effectiveness would create a "cartel" or monopoly since very few programs can meet the standard established.
>
> Discussion: While a significant body of research about effective programs that prevent youth drug use and violence exists, even more needs to be done to identify a broader group of programs and practices that respond to varied needs.
>
> Changes: Based on these concerns, the Secretary has modified the language accompanying this principle. These modifications broaden the scope of the term "research-based" approach to include programs that show promise of being effective in preventing or reducing drug use or violence.
>
> Comment: One commentator expressed concern that implementation of the SDFS Principles of Effectiveness may force rural LEAs [local educational agencies] to replace "old favorite" programs that they feel have been working for them with prevention programs that have been proven to work in other socio-economic areas—such as high-population LEAs—but may not be appropriate to their needs.
>
> Discussion: The Department plans to provide technical assistance to help LEAs obtain information about effective, research-based programs appropriate for an LEA's demographics. The purpose of the SDFS Principles of Effectiveness is to ensure that funds available to grantees under the SDFSCA are used in the most effective way. This allows LEAs to continue "old favorite" programs if they are effective or show promise of effectiveness.

The language of "promise" in the revised guidance raises the basic question of how "research-based programs" are defined. "Promise" is not defined the same way as in the Maryland report, with at least one level 3 impact evaluation showing a positive result. No definition of "research-based programs" is found anywhere in either the Principles of Effectiveness (which have the force of administrative rules) or the accompanying "Nonregulatory Guidance." In the final published version supplementing the *Federal Register* announcement, one section discussed (but did not define) the meaning of programs that show promise of being effective:

> Recipients that choose this approach should carefully examine the program they plan to implement to determine if it holds promise of success. Does

it share common components or elements with programs that have been demonstrated to be successful? Is the program clearly based on accepted research? Is there preliminary data or other information that suggest that the program shows promise of effectiveness?

If recipients decide to implement a promising program, at the end of no more than two years of implementation they must be prepared to demonstrate to the entity providing their grant that the program has been effective in preventing or reducing drug use, violence, or disruptive behavior, or in modifying behaviors or attitudes demonstrated to be precursors of drug use or violence.

This section is followed by a questions-and-answers section on how to evaluate programs, which provides this further detail:

Q53. What does "evaluate" mean?

A53. Evaluation is the systematic collection and analysis of data needed to make decisions. Periodically, recipients will need to examine the programs being implemented to determine if they are meeting established measurable goals and objectives. The nature and extent of such evaluation activities will vary, and should be selected after considering the methods that are appropriate and feasible to measure success of a particular intervention. . . .

Q55. Must evaluation efforts include a control group?

A55. No, recipients are not required to establish a control group.

Thus a close reading of these rules suggests that research-based or promising programs can mean anything that recipients say they mean. Expressed in terms of the Maryland scale, evaluations need not be any higher than level 1 or 2. Because no clear requirement exists for an outcome measure, some recipients might even interpret this language to allow goals to be defined in terms of inputs alone—so many students attending D.A.R.E. classes, for example. By failing to define the meaning of "research-based," the department continued the basic policy of letting recipients spend the money without regard to results. But it is not clear that Congress or the White House would have allowed the department to push much further if the grass-roots protests had become loud.

In the final language of the explanatory comments accompanying the principle of research-based programs, the department tried to please both the antinomians and the mainstream evaluators simultaneously by urging each school district to conduct its own extensive review of the scientific literature:

While the Secretary recognizes the importance of flexibility in addressing State and local needs, the Secretary believes that the implementation of research-based programs will significantly enhance the effectiveness of programs supported with SDFSCA funds. In selecting effective programs most responsive to their needs, grantees are encouraged to review the breadth of available research and evaluation literature, and to replicate these programs in a manner consistent with their original design.

How the Money Has Been Spent

Given the legislation and rules, the resulting expenditures were predictable. *Los Angeles Times* reporter Ralph Frammolino spent months learning what the Department of Education has no system for knowing: how the local education authority recipients spent the money. While neither a systematic audit nor a social scientist's coding of different categories of spending, Frammolino's research provides a level of detail that supports his basic conclusion: "Left to thrash about for any strategy that works, local officials scatter federal money in all directions and on unrelated expenses."[47]

Frammolino found many examples of schools spending money on entertainment that was, in theory, supposed to inspire students to stay drug-free. The theoretical basis of that claim is not clear in his examples:

—Several months before the March 1998 murders in Jonesboro, Arkansas, the school used program funds to hire a magician.

—One Washington-based magician makes two hundred performances annually with a drug awareness theme, of which some 25 percent are paid for with program funds. The $500 show lasts forty-five minutes, during which "we might cut a girl in half and talk about drugs damaging a body."

—The 1997 Miss Louisiana gives antidrug talks paid for by program funds, in which she sings the theme song from "Titanic" and Elvis Presley's "If I Can Dream."

—A school district outside Sacramento paid $400 for a speaker who described the life of Dylan Thomas and his death from alcohol.

Other program funds are spent on the "alternative activities" that Denise Gottfredson's review found ineffective. In Los Angeles, more than $15,000 was spent on tickets to Dodgers games and $850 was spent for Disneyland passes. In Eureka, Utah, officials spent $1,000 on fishing equipment for field trips in which students go fishing with a health teacher. The teacher said he thought students might learn to prefer fishing to drinking and trying drugs. In Virginia Beach, program funds paid for lifeguards and dunking booths for drug-free graduation activities.

Many dollars are spent in aid of classroom instruction, although the connection to violence and drug prevention is unclear. Hammond, Louisiana, police spent $6,500 in program funds to buy a remote-controlled, three-foot replica police car toy. In Michigan, a state audit found $1.5 million spent on full models of the human torso, $81,000 for large sets of plastic teeth and toothbrushes, and $18,500 for recordings of the "Hokey Pokey." These aids were used to teach sex education, toothbrushing, and self-esteem, respectively.

Enormous sums are spent on publications. More than half of the $8 million in Los Angeles went to buy books, including $3.3 million in character education books published by a small firm specializing in books reimbursed by the program. The books provide second to fifth graders with "lessons in character." These books are part of a program that is supposed to be taught for a minimum of twenty-four forty-minute sessions spread across the school year, teaching "pillars of character: respect, responsibility, fairness, and trustworthiness." Another $900,000 was paid for substitutes to replace 2,354 teachers who spent a day attending seminars on how to inculcate character in elementary schools, or to lead discussion groups with older "at-risk" students.

Frammolino reports that "student assistance groups" take about half the national budget for the program. In Los Angeles, 141 schools run 2,450 groups of high-risk students led by teachers given five days of training and a script. The students are pulled out of one class period per month to discuss their personal problems. They are not exposed to Life Skills Training, the research-based curriculum that San Diego school officials obtained $1 million in federal funds to implement—one of the few large districts known to have done so.[48]

Estimating Return on Investment

For the program funds spent on counseling, the return on investment for that money is reliably estimated to be zero. Mark Lipsey's 1992 meta-analysis of juvenile delinquency interventions found counseling near the bottom in effectiveness, with an average effect size of –.01. Gary Gottfredson's 1987 level 3 evaluation of peer counseling groups similar to the Student Assistance Program groups in Los Angeles found that they increased delinquency slightly, instead of reducing it.[49]

Whatever portion of program funds is spent on alternative leisure activities is also producing zero return for prevention. The evidence shows either no effects from such programs or increases in delinquency from mixing high-risk and low-risk youth in the absence of strong pro-social norms. These "old favorites" may appear effective to the teachers who lead them, but they can hardly tell what effect the programs have on delinquency when the teachers are not around. One program of such activities led by a street gang social worker kept offending rates high until the program's funding ran out. When the activities ended, the gang's cohesion declined, and so did its members' offending rates.[50]

The return from hiring magicians, singers, speakers, and other inspirational performers is unknown. It seems reasonable to dismiss these programs as a waste of money, if only because no plausible theory or indirect evidence suggests that these activities might prevent violence or drug abuse.

Estimating the return on investment in character education is a harder task. James Q. Wilson wrote after the Littleton murders that American schools were designed primarily for character education, a mission they have lost in recent years. He suggested that, if schools got serious about this task, they might be able to foster a climate less conducive to violence. However, whether mere books and lectures are enough to make character education the central mission of a school is not clear. The research on whole school organizational strategies may indicate the extent of the changes required. Nonetheless, both the character curricula and Wilson's larger hypothesis remain unevaluated. Both could be fruitful topics for increased research on school-based prevention.

The most profitable investment in the program's portfolio may be the Life Skills Training curriculum. To the extent that the curriculum is fully taught, it could be achieving up to 66 percent reductions in substance abuse.[51] Yet it is unknown how much program funding is allocated to LST. Far more money appears to be spent on the police-taught D.A.R.E. program, which has shown meaningful prevention effects in none of its evaluations to date. (The reason Botvin's LST program is much less widely used than D.A.R.E. is that he lacks an advocacy organization comparable to D.A.R.E.'s national corporation; Botvin's program is also taught by teachers, who have much less visual and telegenic appeal than uniformed police officers in classrooms.)

It is difficult to demonstrate much if any clear prevention benefit from the half-billion dollars or more per year in federal funding for the program. Even in the face of congressional concern, the program remains alive because of its political benefit. As Representative George Miller (D-Calif.) told Frammolino, "Every elected official wants these programs in their district. Once you succumb to that pressure, you're just dealing with a political program. You're not dealing with drug prevention or violence prevention." Or as Representative Peter Hoekstra (R-Mich.) observed, "Most of the numbers on Safe and Drug-Free Schools will tell you that the federal program has failed miserably."

Marrying Grass Roots with Evidence

Can this program be saved? Can it do something useful, rather than squandering tax dollars indefinitely? Answering that question requires a more general perspective on the new federalism and evidence-based accountability. It also requires acknowledging the limitations of divided government, with different parties in control of the executive and legislative branches. As long as government is divided, Congress has no incentive to grant strong powers to the executive branch to improve results. Success by the administration may be good for the country, but bad for party politics. This was true when the program started in 1986 with a Democratic Congress and a Republican president and remains true in 1999 with a Republican Congress and a Democratic president.

Many have argued that the program should simply be eliminated. That response is not useful, given the strong political forces keeping the program alive. In the wake of the 1999 school murders, the program is less likely than ever to be eliminated, no matter how much evidence may support that conclusion. The only useful question is how the program might be modified, within the political constraints that Congress and the president perceive, to make schools even safer and more drug-free than they already are.

There are at least four possible approaches to modifying the program within its political constraints. One is the FDA model of federally approved programs. A second is the agricultural extension agent model for applying national knowledge. A third is the Government Performance and Results Act model for local accounting indicators. But only the fourth alternative, evidence-based government, seems likely to combine knowledge and democracy for good results.

The FDA Model

One alternative is more detailed legislation on programs eligible for federal funds. Congress may not want the administration deciding what programs are eligible, which could work to the administration's political advantage. But Congress could conduct its own review of the literature or delegate that task to the National Research Council of the National Academy of Sciences. That review could develop detailed blueprints for a selection of prevention methods that research has found to be effective. Congress could use its report to enact a legislated list of eligible prevention methods, just as the Food and Drug Administration certifies drugs found to be safe and effective for public distribution. Congress could also develop a list of methods found to be ineffective, which could be barred from federal funding. Room for innovations could be created by reserving 20 percent of funding for previously untested programs, along with requirements that the funded innovations be rigorously evaluated (level 3 or higher) by an independent research organization or university.

The major problem with this approach is that the available research lacks legitimacy across a wide spectrum of grass-roots leadership. The most commonly heard example of this problem is the statement that "D.A.R.E. may not work in the places it was studied, but we know it is working in our local schools." Even if one accepts all the available research that supports lists of effective and ineffective programs, those lists are very short. Much of what the program spends money on has never been evaluated, at least not in the precise form that each locality employs. The lack of knowledge about locally popular programs further reduces the legitimacy of the FDA approach at the grass-roots level.

The Agricultural Extension Agent Model

A more democratic approach would simply put the available knowledge into the hands of grass-roots leaders, using the agricultural extension agent model. Since 1919, the U.S. Department of Agriculture has shared with the states the cost of hiring university employees to provide evidence-based farming advice directly to farmers. Congress does not have to review any literature to do this. It merely pays for an ongoing flow of data between universities and farms and back again. This partnership has helped make America the breadbasket of the world. The subject matter of farming may not be as contentious as that of running schools, but controversy may not be the key variable. In agriculture and education alike, the key to success may be a close personal relationship between a university extension agent and a local decisionmaker.

If school districts could rely on educational extension agents to provide them with free technical assistance on how to spend their program funds, that might move the schools voluntarily toward adopting the same list of proven programs that an FDA model might develop. The problem with Washington bureaucrats, or even researchers in other cities, is that they are faceless and impersonal. The virtue of extension agents giving advice is that they become well-known personalities, long-term colleagues in the same community. Even medical doctors ignore research evidence when it comes to them in the form of publications and resent its bureaucratic imposition in the form of managed care reimbursement rules. As a RAND study discovered, doctors usually change their practices only when another doctor they know and respect persuades them to—not when they read a new study in the *New England Journal of Medicine*.[52]

Commentaries on the extension agent model have suggested that the agents would not necessarily stick to the evidence. Some commentators indict schools of education as often indifferent to research evidence and prone to pushing the latest fads. Social integration of extension agents with the grass-roots leadership could put pressure on the agents to find research that "justifies" the decisions local leaders make, rather than objectively informing those decisions. And without a basis for increasing the availability of strong evaluation research, these agents of applied research would have too little research to apply.

The GPRA Model

A third alternative is to require that each school receiving federal funds account for the results of those funds using the federal Government Performance and Results Act standards. This model assumes that localities cannot do their own controlled field tests of prevention programs, but they can at least document trends over time in crime and drug abuse associated with those programs. Given the secret nature of much crime and delinquency, this would require schools to administer annual student surveys of self-reported victimization, offending, and drug abuse. Such instruments are readily available and would only require local competence in the administration and interpretation of such tests. Properly employed, these surveys could identify schools that showed greater or lesser success over time in preventing these problems, just as a certified public accountant statement shows how profit levels change over time in publicly held corporations.

The main limitation of this model is resources. As a recent RAND study suggests, local school leaders are unable to add such evaluations to their job descriptions. They already have far too many duties to start performing survey research. Their interpretation of the Safe and Drug-Free Schools and Communities program is that it asks them to provide evaluations without paying for the work.[53] This problem is summarized elsewhere as "There's no such thing as free evidence."[54] Even more important, however, is the scientific limitation of the GPRA local accounting model. Without explicit field tests employing control groups, the causal link between programs and trends in "outcomes" will remain tenuous. And even with a local evaluation staff assigned to such accounting tasks on a full-time basis, the common failure to adjust for student background characteristics can make trend analysis a poor indicator of how successful schools are with the cards they are dealt.

The importance of controlling for student background characteristics cannot be overestimated. It is shocking that the national standards reform movement has failed to identify this issue, thus allowing schools serving wealthy communities to look more successful than schools serving poorer communities. A strong link exists between the social capital of the community and the overall success of the school. To account for the value that schools add to their students beyond what students acquire at home, all performance measures should control for the expected rates of student failure or success. This is as true of drug abuse as it is of Scholastic Assessment Test (SAT) scores. Parental educational levels, parental employment rates and income, prevalence of two-parent homes, and other factors can be measured in student surveys. But proper statistical controls for these background factors require competent data analysts in each state and large school district, people whose full-time job is the collection and interpretation of valid local accounting data. Merely requiring schools to produce GPRA-style trend data comes nowhere near meeting these needs.

Evidence-Based Democracy

The fourth, and arguably best, approach to reforming the Safe and Drug-Free Schools and Communities program is to combine national knowledge, risk-adjusted local GPRA accounting, and grass-roots democracy. This approach starts with a participatory planning process of using data to hold programs accountable, one that includes representatives of schoolteachers, administrators, parents, school board members, students, and local taxpayers. Such a group can be called a planning committee, an oversight group, or a results task force. It could be operated at the margins of a school system, or it could be integrated into the ongoing supervision of the schools. It could meet in private, or it could hold annual public sessions in which each school principal is asked to account for the data assembled by the school district's own performance data analyst. Such high-visibility sessions could be as successful as the New York City Police "compstat" process or hospital "grand rounds" in focusing the organization on its outcomes, whether the outcomes measure crime and drug abuse or standardized achievement test scores.[55]

No matter how each local education authority chooses to use the data, the key element of this approach is to put the right kind of data in its hands. These data should include both the latest, most complete results of national research, as well as highly refined local trend data. Such data should look not only at measures of crime and drug abuse, but also at measures of program implementation and fidelity. School climate measures from annual surveys of students and teachers would be a critical component of the local accounting data, given the strong relationship in the literature between school organizational climate and all school-specific results. The measurement of educational practices allows local conclusions to be drawn about cause and effect of different programs and practices. The measurement of school-specific—and possibly even teacher-specific or class-specific—results net of the student background characteristics helps identify true success or failure. And this process has proven successful at the hospital level in diagnosing high failure rates and improving results.[56]

The use of these data would therefore constitute an iterative process of the kind proposed by W. Edwards Deming. Figure 1 shows how the process would draw on both national and local evidence on the relationship between practices and outcomes. The model is as applicable to drug

Figure 1. Continuous Program Accountability

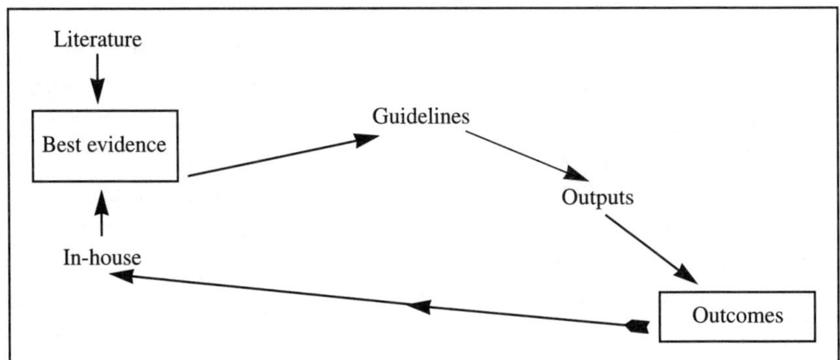

abuse rates as it is to SAT scores. Its success depends largely on the quality of the data, and the quality of the leadership using the data to improve performance.

The major limitation of this approach is cost. The approach may not be feasible in the majority of school districts that are too small to support a performance data analyst, although state agencies could provide local schools with a time-shared performance analysis service. Even in the larger districts, the approach requires new data collection and new knowledge rarely found in-house. It is striking that the U.S. Department of Education would put into print the suggestion that "grantees are encouraged to review the breadth of available research and evaluation literature, and to replicate these programs in a manner consistent with their original design." It is unclear how many local education authorities have staff with the time and the training needed to do all that properly. However, Ph.D.-level "performance accountants" could devote their entire careers to reviewing and explaining the results of ongoing school-based prevention and performance program evaluations. School-based prevention research is a highly specialized field that few university professors are equipped to discuss. Only this kind of infrastructure can provide the requisite level of expertise in comprehending, communicating, and applying the research.

If Congress wants to see local prevention programs based on sound knowledge, perhaps the best way to achieve that goal is to pay for it. Changing the program to earmark an additional 10 percent of funds for performance data accounting would put some $50 million into this function nationwide. But without such an appropriation, this approach is not likely to be implemented.

Implications for Reinventing Government and GPRA

As long as the Education Department is prohibited by law from "exercising any direction, supervision, or control over the curriculum or program of instruction of any school or school system," it makes little sense to hold the department accountable for results.[57] That is one example of the major flaw in GPRA in particular and in federal accountability in general in an era of grass-roots control. But the department could be empowered to measure results across local education authorities and use those measures for further pressure to adopt evidence-based government. That measurement could also be part of an amended Safe and Drug-Free Schools program. A university extension service associated with each school district could be charged with collecting standardized data from local police or other sources, all of which would be sent to Washington for analysis.

The method of outcome assessment is an important issue for making GPRA work. Perhaps the best way to ensure that performance measures are adjusted for student background characteristics is to require each state to produce a ranking of schools or school systems on standardized, background-controlled results. This ranking could allow schools in high-poverty areas to show more value-added results than schools in wealthy suburban areas. Aggregating such measures by state and nation could even allow the federal Safe and Drug-Free Schools and Community program to produce its own meaningful GPRA indicators for the nation's 14,881 school districts. The annual standing of each district (probably within category of urban, suburban, and rural schools) could become a point of pride in fostering an evidence-based culture of results guiding democracy at the grass roots.

Such rankings could also become a source of cheating. The more important evidence becomes, the more likely it is to be subverted. Thus, not surprisingly, a Texas school official was recently indicted for falsifying school test scores. That is one more reason to have a performance analyst symbolically clothed in the mantle of accounting, rather than science. Studies as such can always be discounted as irrelevant, but profit-and-loss statements carry overtones of serious business.

Conclusion

Other ways may exist to make the Safe and Drug-Free Schools program less wasteful and more useful. No matter how it is done, the fundamental challenge remains the same: marrying grass-roots federalism to a culture of evidence-based government. This marriage may be one of the few ways to overcome symbolic pork. It provides no solution to the mismatching of resources and risk. But it does begin to do what President Clinton proposed for federal education funding in his 1999 State of the Union address—to "change the way we invest that money, to support what works and to stop supporting what doesn't."[58]

Comment by Christina Hoff Sommers

Lawrence W. Sherman's "evidence-based" approach to school drug and safety problems is admirable and reasonable, but the difficulties of implementing his proposals should not be minimized. Many in the education establishment react with hostility and indignation to the very idea of an evidence-based policy, with the implied accountability that it entails. My more serious reservations pertain to his general approach of solving problems that vex U.S. schools by calling for yet more studies, more experts, more funding. Are more studies needed about how to improve the moral climate of schools? Schools would be much improved simply by applying what is already well known.

Sherman is on target when he shows how and why the current Safe and Drug-Free Schools program is failing. He notes that since 1986 the program has received more than $6 billion, yet "there is no evidence that this half-billion-dollar-per-year program has made schools safer or more drug-free." He cites several painful examples of how program monies have been spent wastefully. Some schools used funds for excursions to Disneyland, others for fishing trips and baseball games. Tens of thousands of dollars were spent on visiting magicians and other "edutainers." Drug Abuse Resistance Education (D.A.R.E.) is immensely popular with schools and parents. Uniformed policemen visit schools and warn students about the hazards of drugs. The trouble is it does not work. Neither does the ever-popular peer counseling; this program may actually encourage drug usage by bringing high-risk and low-risk teenagers together.

One questionable expenditure not mentioned by Sherman is a 1998 K-12 anti-harassment and anti-violence curriculum entitled *Quit It!* (It was developed jointly by the Wellesley Center for Research on Women and Educational Equity Concepts and distributed by the National Education Association (NEA).) Among its many unusual classroom exercises, *Quit It!* instructs teachers on how to introduce a new version of the game tag:

> Before going outside to play, talk about how students feel when playing a game of tag. Do they like to be chased? Do they like to do the chasing? How does it feel to be tagged out? Get their ideas about other ways the game might be played.

After students share their fears and apprehensions about tag, the teacher is advised to announce a new, nonthreatening version of the game called Circle of Friends—"Where nobody is ever 'out.' "

Somehow, the authors of *Quit It!* were able to convince officials in the Department of Education that this was a good use of federal funds targeted for reducing school violence. No one seems to have asked anyone to show that *Quit It!* is an effective program. No talk was heard of control groups or randomized field testing. It was funded, rushed into print, and distributed by the NEA to teachers—bearing the imprimatur of the Department of Education and the Safe and Drug-Free Schools and Communities Act. Somewhere today children are playing Circle of Friends.

Quit It! is just one of many examples of empirically baseless and socially useless government subsidized programs promoted by well-intended but misguided educators and government officials. Unfortunately, its approach is not atypical, and it shows how badly Sherman's reforms are needed. But it also reveals the irrational forces that any Sherman-inspired reformer will be up against.

Sherman's proposals depend critically on the availability of good data and solid research for grass-roots education groups to use when deciding on which programs to fund. He wants education experts to determine the "best practices" in pedagogy and programs, just as medical doctors routinely do, and to make this knowledge available to local schools. But Sherman may be overly optimistic about the prospects for getting responsible information from professional educators about best practices. Doctors are accustomed to changing their practices when negative evidence indicates the need for new practices. Educators are less sensitive and more resistant to empirical checks on their ideas, policies, and practices. Sherman is facing an uphill struggle.

Sherman says that his idea of having an evidence-based approach is inspired by the medical model for adopting new cures or disease-preventing measures. The Life Skills Training program, which Sherman cites as the best program for reducing drug abuse in the schools, was not developed by educators but by Gilbert Botvin at the Cornell Medical School. Sherman notes that Botvin's program, though relatively effective, is not much used when compared with other programs that have advocacy organizations behind them. In the world of contemporary education, having logic, reason, and evidence on your side is no guarantee of success.

Despite the difficulties in implementing it, Sherman's evidence-based approach is clearly the right way to go. He is well aware of popular antagonisms to intrusive central controls. So he resists all suggestions of sending out knowledge elites from Washington telling local communities how to run their schools. He proposes instead to bring good science to local citizens groups, or as he puts it, "marrying grass roots with evidence." In this respect, Sherman's approach is especially attractive.

At the same time, Sherman's persistent emphasis on data and new research appears excessive. In the area of teen drug abuse, a relatively new phenomenon, the argument is plausible that more research on how to control it is needed. The case is different for the more general problem of student behavior and school safety. Schools are much less safe than they were earlier in the twentieth century. Schools were doing something right that they are no longer doing. Sherman pays little attention to the body of historical experience on how to civilize children.

He casually dismisses the observation sociologist James Q. Wilson made in the wake of the Littleton, Colorado, school murders. Wilson points out that schools have abandoned their traditional mission of character education, suggesting that this is in part responsible for an amoral climate that made the violence possible. If schools took ethics education more seriously, Wilson believes, they could diminish violence. Sherman reacts to Wilson's suggestion with skepticism. He wants evidence. He says that Wilson's hypotheses remain "unevaluated."

I believe that Sherman's dismissal of Wilson's point is unwarranted. Prestigious educators in the 1970s deliberately turned their backs on the schools' traditional mission of moral education. Some, such as Harvard University's former dean of education, Theodore Sizer, talked dismissively of the "old morality." In a 1990 ethics anthology, he and his coauthor point to a consensus among leading thinkers on moral education: "The old morality can and should be scrapped."[59] At the same time, influential Harvard University moral psychologists derided the "the old bags of virtue" that schools had traditionally promoted. For the last three decades, educators have been participating in a moral deregulation that has radically changed society, by allowing the children in their care to "find their own values."

Setting children ethically adrift in this way was irresponsible and socially harmful. Children need clear, unequivocal rules. They need structure. They thrive on firm tutelage from the adults in their lives. Aristotle laid down what children need some twenty-five hundred years ago: clear guidance on how to be moral human beings. The kind of direct moral education that Aristotle recommended has had a long and successful history in Western culture. Sherman wrongly suggests that this is something whose usefulness still needs to be evaluated.

To be sure, the usefulness of direct moral education can be confirmed anew. Some of the old approaches are now being rediscovered by objective researchers. Sherman admires the careful and rigorous work of criminologists Gary and Denise Gottfredson. But much of what they recommend is common sense dressed up in sociological jargon. Here is one of the ways they say schools can reduce crime and delinquency: "Clarifying and communicating norms about behavior through rules, reinforcement of positive behavior, and school wide initiatives (such as antibullying programs)." Translated into everyday prose, this comes down to saying that schools should be focusing on moral norms and insisting on good behavior. It calls on the schools to once again take up their responsibilities to foster moral development, discipline, and accountability. At the risk of sounding like one of those antinomians that Sherman criticizes, are new studies and research needed to confirm that schools should be "communicating norms about behavior through rules"?

I agree with Sherman that far too much "symbolic pork" exists in current programs aimed at enhancing the safety of children in schools. Efforts should be made to find ways to marry the grass roots with evidence of what works. But much about what works is already known, particularly that schoolchildren are much safer when their teachers feel strongly responsible for their moral development. Much or most of the money annually given for programs to make schools safer should be used to promote the revival of the schools' mission of moral education. That kind of constructive diversion of funds, now largely wasted in fatuous ways, would also have a great deal of popular and political support. Sherman warns "There's no such thing as free evidence." But there is. It is the distilled product of centuries of experience and it is called common sense.

Comment by Bruno V. Manno

"Our goal in this crusade is nothing less than a drug-free generation." Thus spoke President Ronald Reagan on October 27, 1986, during a ceremony at which he signed a $1.7 billion law that contained $200 million for school-based drug prevention programs. And thus began the federal government's odyssey into a world that today has lost its focus, expanding from support for school-based drug prevention to programs as diverse as violence prevention, health education, after-school instruction in the arts, and the purchase of curricula that "promote the awareness of sensitivity to alternatives to violence through courses of study that include related issues of intolerance and hatred in history."[60]

Lawrence W. Sherman argues that twelve years after the inception of what is now called the Safe and Drug-Free Schools program, with expenditures totaling more than $6 billion and going "to some fifteen thousand local school districts and fifty state governors to spend largely at their own discretion. No evidence shows that this half-billion-dollar-per-year program has made schools any safer or more drug-free." To the contrary, "much of the money has been wasted on performing magicians, fishing trips, and school concerts—and on methods (such as counseling) that research shows to be ineffective."

His conclusion is buttressed by other investigations of this program. A recent analysis by Matthew Rees said, "Twelve years after its inception, the federal government has yet to comprehensively evaluate it. In other words, after spending a total of $6 billion on the Safe and Drug-Free Schools program, there's no way of knowing whether it's working or not."[61]

A 1996–97 General Accounting Office report on the program's accountability and oversight provisions pinpointed the problems associated with ascertaining whether it works or how to improve it. The study found that the program has innumerable loopholes in its requirements, placing an almost exclusive focus on local control and leaving the federal government with minuscule influence over how program funds are spent. No method was in place to collect comparable data that allows the U.S. Department of Education to reach valid conclusions about the program's overall effectiveness.[62] In short, the program is neither a typical categorical program with specific instructions on how to use federal money nor a block grant that permits local flexibility in implementation coupled with accountability for results.

Sherman argues that the program constitutes "symbolic pork"; that is, it sends taxpayers' dollars back into every congressional district to symbolize federal concern about a problem but does not require any evidence-based demonstration of positive results. Sherman points out the results of what I call a "spreading peanut butter" approach to distributing federal money: Fiscal disbursements reach 97 percent of the nation's school districts, with six out of ten school districts receiving $10,000 or less each year and small districts receiving only $200 or $300.

Are Schools Unsafe and Drug-Plagued Places?

Sherman presents a welcome corrective to the view that schools are dangerous settings for young people. His data show that, for most students, violence is a seldom-encountered experience concentrated in a few schools located in poor, segregated neighborhoods with many unemployed adults. Violent incidents occur mainly in middle and high schools, with the most likely victims being young men, particularly black seniors. Finally, violence is more likely to occur to teachers instead of students.

These facts may not change public perceptions about school safety and violence that stem from a few highly visible, dramatic, and tragic incidents such as the killings at Columbine High School in Littleton, Colorado. But they are strong enough to have prompted U.S. Secretary of Education Richard W. Riley to caution the public about these incorrect perceptions in an August 1999 "back to school" op-ed in the *Washington Post.* He said, "Tragically, there are many homicides that occur among our youth, but less than one percent of all homicides among school-age children (ages 5 to 19) occur in or around schools. New data indicate that violence among young people is on a downward trend and that the number of students being expelled from school for carrying a firearm decreased by one-third from the 1996–97 to 1997–98 school year."[63]

Sherman also shows that drug use is limited to a tiny percentage of students, though its reported use is more "prevalent and . . . widespread" among students than violent crimes. Drug use is only moderately associated with schools; schools are more likely to be a place where drugs are exchanged than consumed. And, not surprisingly, more consumption of drugs occurs in schools where drugs are easier to get.[64]

Sherman goes on to present convincing evidence that the causes of both violence and drug use are predominantly outside the school. But schools can contribute to modifying the effects of outside influences and overcome family background factors and community liabilities. How schools are run contributes to making schools safe and drug-free.[65]

What can schools do to decrease incidents of violence and drug use?

Sherman points to research that suggests effective prevention programs are schoolwide programs. They affect the climate and ethos of the school. Some of the key elements that foster a positive school climate that nurtures safe and drug-free schools include:

—School size. Small schools are safer than large schools, and programs that organize students in large schools into smaller educational groups ("schools-within-schools") are a promising approach to reducing school violence and drug use.

—Resources. Assets should be focused on enhancing teaching and curricula.

—Governance and management. Strong administrative leadership and teamwork are needed in schools.

—Socialization. Norms for behavior should be well known, and enforcement should be fair and consistent.

The line of inquiry that tries to understand what school practices reduce drug use and violence bears remarkable similarity to "effective schools" research. Effective schools have a clear, focused mission; a core curriculum with high expectations for all students (and teachers); an organizational climate that supports the school's mission and expectations; and strong leadership that provides the school with a measure of autonomy within which it shapes its own destiny.[66]

Recent analysis of the effective schools research goes beyond this list of attributes to explain how these characteristics are nurtured and sustained. These schools place a premium on a coherent vision and shared values about teaching and learning. They have "integrative capital."[67] In short, good schools are focused and coherent communities of learning where adults collaborate—especially educators and families—and share a set of ideas about what constitutes good teaching and how to exercise responsibility for nurturing learning and virtuous behavior in young people.

What Should Be Done to Fix the Progam?

Sherman's analysis and the additional information that I have cited lead me to conclude that:

—There is no evidence that the program is working.

—The program has weak-to-nonexistent accountability provisions and a diluted focus.

—Schools today are mostly safe and drug-free, with most violence and drug use concentrated in middle and high schools in urban areas.

—Schools are safer and more drug-free than their communities.

—Effective prevention programs are schoolwide, based on a unifying vision of the school and replete with a moral code that holds high expectations for learning and virtuous behavior.

Sherman suggests four paths to changing the program, given that political constraints will not allow its elimination.

1. Food and Drug Administration (FDA) model. The federal government would oversee a program that aims to reach scientific agreement on research-proven programs that would qualify for federal funds. Conversely, ineffective methods would be barred from federal funding.

2. Agricultural extension agent model. A (mostly) university-based research infrastructure would provide grass-roots leaders with knowledge of effective programs. School districts would receive technical assistance from educational extension agents on how to use their program funds to implement proven or promising programs.

3. Governance Performance and Results Act (GPRA) model. School districts would annually administer survey instruments to students and others in the district to document trends in crime and drug use. This would provide a modicum of evidence about program results.

4. Evidenced-based democracy model. Sherman's recommended approach is a hybrid of the other models that combines "national knowledge, risk-adjusted local GPRA accounting, and grass-roots democracy." It

would replace ineffective programs and methods with those that are proven to work or show promise of working. It combines knowledge of effective or promising programs with local documentation of trends in school crime and drug abuse and a participatory planning process.

Sherman's favored approach brings to mind two tried and mostly ineffective approaches to creating national knowledge and fostering grassroots democracy in education. First, his FDA and agricultural extension models are similar to the present U.S. Department of Education's Research and Development (R&D) Centers, Regional Educational Laboratories (the Labs), and Educational Resources Information Clearinghouses (ERIC). Second, the participatory planning process that is part of Sherman's evidenced-based model recalls the planning and oversight groups—the "stakeholder" committees—that are the bane of federal education programs such as Title I and Goals 2000.

NATIONAL KNOWLEDGE IN EDUCATION. The R&D Centers, the Labs, and ERIC have a long, complicated, and checkered history, beginning in the mid-1960s and then undergoing significant structural changes in 1972 with the establishment of the National Institute of Education (NIE) and in the early 1990s with the reauthorization of the Office of Educational Research and Improvement (the earlier reconstituted NIE). The theory underlying this approach was that the (mostly) university-based R&D Centers would produce research-based knowledge; the federal regional labs would work with states (and districts) in field testing and disseminating new knowledge; and ERIC would be a collection of clearinghouses that would store knowledge and information on best practice for use by education stakeholders and community members bent on improving education.

Maris A. Vinovskis has conducted several studies of the work of these federally supported programs. He aptly summarized these federal investment as "generally disappointing and limited."[68] In another report he said, "The evaluation of the quality of the research and development work produced by the centers and the labs ... paint[s] a mixed, but, overall, a rather disappointing picture of the conceptual and technical soundess of much of their work."[69]

Why such a gloomy picture?

Vinovskis hits the nail on the head: "Much of the research and development produced by educational scholars is ... methodically and conceptually second-rate."[70] Another article on the status of education research calls that research a "black hole, . . . weak and inconclusive . . . [and] especially lacking in rigor." The result is that "education reform is often shaped by political whim and pedagogic fashion."[71]

This aversion of educators to creating a sound research base for "what works" and then using it in teaching and learning manifests itself in the implementation of the drug-free program. Analysts at the Research Triangle Institute funded by the U.S. Department of Education to investigate some elements of the program concluded: "Drug prevention approaches that have been shown to be effective are not widely used, while approaches that have not shown evidence of effectiveness or have not been evaluated properly are the most common approaches currently in use."[72]

GRASS-ROOTS DEMOCRACY IN EDUCATION. One of the primary reasons that ineffective programs have made their way into schools is that stakeholder groups and influential constituencies have come to regard federal funds as pork barrel entitlements for their favorite programs whether or not these programs are effective. Symbolic pork invariably becomes traditional pork. In other words, federal money always becomes a jobs program for some group of beneficiaries, making it nearly impossible to eliminate these programs and the power centers they create.

In education, most operational power rests with the producers of education, not with consumers, taxpayers, or citizens. Most decisions are made by an education establishment that includes the two big teacher unions; groups representing principals, superintendents, and the other school employees; state departments of education; textbook publishers and software vendors; colleges of education; the custodians, bus drivers, and cafeteria workers; and so forth. They are frequently joined by (slightly sheepish) business groups and by a docile Parent-Teacher Association (PTA). These expert professionals and their legion of supporters place the schools largely beyond the self-correcting reach of community politics. They mask a system of bureaucratic and interest groups politics that derives its sustenance from the pork barrel funds they receive.

HOW SHOULD THE PROGRAM BE STRUCTURED? Most schools are safe and drug-free, and the money spent on this program is mostly wasted. Furthermore, education R&D, its dissemination apparatus, and the producers of education are not likely to vanish before the present reauthorization of the Safe and Drug-Free Schools program. This seems to argue strongly for getting rid of the program. But if that action is not politically feasible, then the program should be made into a genuine categorical program or block grant program. Either approach should include statutory language with stringent accountability provisions, reflecting Sherman's GPRA model. For example, there should be a statutory requirement that states annually collect effectiveness data demonstrating program results.

In the categorical approach to the program, at least the following additional elements should be federal requirements:

—Focus the program more clearly on supporting activities and services that foster safe and drug-free schools.

—Direct most of the money to the source of the problems—middle and high schools in poor urban neighborhoods.

—Target federal funds to treat the whole school and reflect those proven core attributes that foster coherent, small, and purposive schools.

—Allow some small percentage of money for communitywide safe and drug-free prevention efforts, because this is the source of many problems that occur in the schools. (An example of the kind of program is the effort to create "violence-free zones" undertaken in Washington, D.C., by the National Center for Neighborhood Enterprise and the Alliance of Concerned Men in what was formerly known as the "most murderous" section of the city. Since January 1997, youth homicides have been eliminated where twelve had occurred within the prior three years.)[73]

Two options exist for a block grant approach to restructuring the program. One approach would keep a distinct program but narrow the scope (for example, exclude areas such as health education from funding) and require the use of proven or promising programs. States and communities would be free to spend the money as they want, as long as they annually report on and demonstrate positive program results. States would determine what actions to take if a school district's program is not effective.

Another block grant approach could link the program with the "super ed-flex" idea being advanced in Congress under a legislative proposal called the Academic Achievement for All Act (also known as "Straight A's"). Under this approach, up to fourteen K-12 federal categorical education programs would be combined into a block grant with teeth. In essence, the federal government would enter into a contract with interested states to swap rules and regulations for results, defined primarily as evidence that students are progressing to or achieving high levels of student learning.

This approach differs from the traditional approach to creating a federal block grant in education. First, this block grant would be voluntary. States would not be required to participate. States or school districts that did not wish to consolidate their funding in this way could continue to receive categorical funding under the new reauthorization of the Safe and Drug-Free School program. But those who do participate could consolidate their federal dollars and spend that money as they want. Second, this block grant would require that states commit themselves to results—students learning more, with evidence to show it. For example, student academic results could be measured using the National Assessment of Educational Progress (NAEP).

The three options I propose accept Sherman's GPRA model in that they require evidence of program effects. But they would minimize the drawbacks of Sherman's evidence-based model: national knowledge and grass-roots democracy in education—that is, what I call second-rate knowledge and producer control under the guise of stakeholder participation.

Notes

1. Digby Baltzell, *Puritan Boston and Quaker Philadelphia* (New York: Free Press, 1979).

2. Gary Orren, "Fall from Grace: The Public's Loss of Faith in Government," in Joseph F. Nye, Philip D. Zelikow, and David C. King, eds., *Why People Don't Trust Government* (Harvard University Press, 1997), pp. 81, 83.

3. Lawrence W. Sherman, *Evidence-Based Policing*, Second Ideas in American Policing Lecture (Washington: Police Foundation, 1998).

4. David Osborne and Ted Gaebler, *Reinventing Government: How the Entrepreneurial Spirit Is Transforming the Public Sector* (Penguin, 1993).

5. During those two years, sixty-three students aged five though nineteen were murdered. The denominator for these murders was about 50 million students in school for about 6 hours per day (after adjusting for absenteeism) for about 200 days per year × 2 years = 2,400 hours per student. Because one full person-year = 365 days × 24 hours = 8,760 hours, each student represented an estimated 0.274 person-years (2,400/8,760 = 0.274) × 50 million = 13,698,630 person-years. The rate of murder was therefore 0.45 per 100,000 person-years. This overstates the rate by about 50 percent, because almost all murders are committed against people who are awake at the time, and the person-year calculation assumes that people never go to sleep. If people sleep about one-third of each day, the corrected rate of homicide is only 0.30 per 100,000. These calculations were

derived from raw data in *Annual Report on School Safety, 1998* (Department of Justice and Department of Education, 1999), p. 9.

6. Federal Bureau of Investigation, *Crime in the United States: The Uniform Crime Report,* 1992, 1993, 1994 (Department of Justice).

7. The obverse of the calculation of the school-hours denominator is that the 50 million students spent 0.726 of their time (1 – 0.274 = 0.726) = 36,300,000 person-years out of school. During those years, (7,357 – 63 =) 7,294 children aged five to nineteen were murdered out of school, for a rate of 20.09 per 100,000. *Annual Report on School Safety*, p. 9.

8. Heather Strang, *Homicide in Australia, 1990–91* (Canberra, Australia: Australian Institute of Criminology, 1993).

9. See William J. Wilson, *When Work Disappears* (Alfred A. Knopf, 1996); and Douglas S. Massey and Nancy A. Denton, *American Apartheid: Segregation and the Making of the Underclass* (Harvard University Press, 1993).

10. Lawrence W. Sherman and Dennis P. Rogan, "Effects of Gun Seizures on Gun Violence: Hot Spots Patrol in Kansas City," *Justice Quarterly,* vol. 12 (1995), pp. 673–93, especially p. 679.

11. *Annual Report on School Safety,* p. 11.

12. *Annual Report on School Safety,* p. 10.

13. Federal Bureau of Investigation, *Crime in the United States: The Uniform Crime Reports* (Department of Justice, annual).

14. Kathleen Maguire and Ann Pastore, eds., *Sourcebook of Criminal Justice Statistics, 1997* (Department of Justice, 1998), pp. 178–81.

15. James Q. Wilson and Richard Herrnstein, *Crime and Human Nature* (Simon and Schuster, 1985).

16. Sheryl Gay Stolberg, "By the Numbers: Science Looks at Littleton, and Shrugs," *New York Times,* May 9, 1999, section 4, p. 1.

17. Maguire and Pastore, *Sourcebook of Criminal Justice Statistics,* p. 234.

18. Gary D. Gottfredson, *Exploration of Adolescent Drug Involvement: Report to the National Institute of Juvenile Justice and Delinquency, U.S. Department of Justice*, grant 87–JN–CX–0015 (Johns Hopkins University, Center for the Social Organization of Schools, 1988).

19. Denise Gottfredson, *Schools and Delinquency* (Cambridge University Press, forthcoming), chapter 3.

20. Denise C. Gottfredson, testimony before the Senate Committee on Health, Education, Labor, and Pensions, May 6, 1999.

21. Gary D. Gottfredson and Denise C. Gottfredson, *Victimization in Schools* (New York: Plenum, 1985).

22. Gottfredson, *Schools and Delinquency*, chapter 3.

23. Robert Dahl, *On Democracy* (Yale University Press, 1998).

24. Lawrence W. Sherman and others, *Preventing Crime: What Works, What Doesn't, What's Promising* (Department of Justice, 1997), at www.preventingcrime.org.

25. Carol H. Weiss, *Evaluation Research: Methods of Assessing Program Effectiveness* (Englewood Cliffs, N.J.: Prentice-Hall, 1972).

26. Lisbeth B. Schorr, *Common Purpose: Strengthening Families and Neighborhoods to Rebuild America* (New York: Anchor Books, 1997).

27. Tom Loveless, "The Use and Misuse of Research in Educational Reform," in Diane Ravitch, ed., *Brookings Papers on Education Policy, 1998* (Brookings, 1998), pp. 279–317.

28. Sherman, *Evidence-Based Policing.*

29. Michael Millenson, *Demanding Medical Excellence* (University of Chicago Press, 1997).

30. Sherman and others, *Preventing Crime*.

31. H. Rept. 104–378, 104th Cong., 1 sess., Section 116.

32. Denise C. Gottsfredson, "An Empirical Test of School-Based Environmental and Individual Interventions to Reduce the Risk of Delinquent Behavior," *Criminology*, vol. 24 (1986), pp. 705–31; Denise C. Gottfredson, "An Evaluation of an Organization Development Approach to Reducing School Disaster," *Evaluation Review*, vol. 11 (1987), pp. 739–63; and D. J. Kenney and T. S. Wilson, "Reducing Fear in the Schools: Managing Conflicts through Student Problem Solving," *Education and Urban Society*, vol. 28 (1996), pp. 436–55.

33. G. R. Mayer and others, "Preventing School Vandalism and Improving Discipline: A Three-Year Study," *Journal of Applied Behavior Analysis,* vol. 16 (1983), pp. 355–69; D. Olweus, "Bully/Victim Problems among Schoolchildren: Basic Facts and Effects of a School Based Intervention Program," in D. J. Pepler and K. H. Rubin, eds., *The Development and Treatment of Childhood Aggression* (Hillsdale, N.J.: Lawrence Erlbaum Publishers, 1991); and D. T. Olweus, "Bullying among Schoolchildren: Intervention and Prevention," in R. D. Peters, R. J. McMahon, and V. L. Quinsey, eds., *Aggression and Violence throughout the Life Span* (Newbury Park, Calif.: Sage, 1992).

34. G. J. Botvin and others, "A Cognitive Behavioral Approach to Substance Abuse Prevention," *Addictive Behaviors*, vol. 9 (1984), pp. 137–47; R. Weissberg and M. Z. Caplan, "Promoting Social Competence and Preventing Anti-Social Behavior in Young Adolescents," University of Illinois, Department of Psychology, 1994; Institute of Medicine, *Reducing Risks for Mental Disorders: Frontiers for Preventive Intervention Research* (Washington: National Academy Press, 1994); and W. B. Hansen and J. W. Graham, "Preventing Alcohol, Marijuana, and Cigarette Use among Adolescents: Peer Pressure Resistance Training versus Establishing Conservative Norms," *Preventive Medicine*, vol. 20 (1991), pp. 414–30.

35. J. E. Lochman and others, "Treatment and Generalization Effects of Cognitive-Behavioral and Goal-Setting Interventions with Aggressive Boys," *Journal of Consulting and Clinical Psychology*, vol. 52 (1984), pp. 915–16; B. H. Bry, "Reducing the Incidence of Adolescent Problems through Preventive Intervention: One- and Five-Year Follow-Up," *American Journal of Community Psychology*, vol. 10 (1982), pp. 265–76; and Mark Lipset, "Juvenile Delinquency Treatment: A Meta-Analytic Inquiry into the Variability of Effects," in T. Cook and others, eds., *Meta-Analysis for Explanation: A Casebook* (New York: Russell Sage Foundation, 1992).

36. Gottfredson, "An Empirical Test of School-Based Environmental and Individual Interventions to Reduce the Risk of Delinquent Behavior"; and Gary Gottfredson, "Peer Group Interventions to Reduce the Risk of Delinquent Behavior: A Selective Review and a New Evaluation," *Criminology*, vol. 25 (1987), pp. 671–714.

37. C. Ringwalt and others, *Past and Future Decisions of the D.A.R.E. Program: An Evaluation Review, Draft Final Report*, award 91–DD–CX–K053 (Washington: National Institute of Justice, 1994); D. P. Rosenbaum and others, "Cops in the Classroom: A Longitudinal Evaluation of Drug Abuse Resistance Education (DARE)," *Journal of Research in Crime and Delinquency*, vol. 31 (1994), pp. 3–31; and R. R. Clayton, A. M. Cattarello, and B. M. Johnstone, "The Effectiveness of Drug Abuse Resistance Education (Project DARE): Five-Year Follow-Up Results," *Preventive Medicine*, vol. 25 (1996), pp. 307–18.

38. G. Botvin, "Substance Abuse Prevention: Theory, Practice, and Effectiveness," in M. Tonry and J. Q. Wilson, eds., *Crime and Justice*, vol. 13: *Drugs and Crime* (University of Chicago Press, 1990).

39. Botvin and others, "A Cognitive Behavioral Approach to Substance Abuse Prevention"; W. B. Hansen, "School-Based Substance Abuse Prevention: A Review of the State of the Art Curriculum 1980–1990," *Health Education Research,* vol. 7 (1992), pp. 403–30; J. G. Ross and others, "The Effectiveness of an After-School Program for Primary Grade Latchkey Students on Precursors of Substance Abuse," *Journal of Community Psychology,* OSAP special issue (1992), pp. 22–38; M. Stoil, G. Hill, and P. J. Brounstein, "The Seven Core Strategies for ATOD Prevention: Findings of the National Structure Evaluation of What Is Working Well Where," paper presented at the Twelfth Annual Meeting of the American Public Health Association, Washington, D.C., 1994; and *An Evaluation of a School-Based Community Service Program: The Effects of Magic Me*, technical report, available from Gottfredson Associates Inc., Ellicott City, Md.

40. Denise C. Gottfredson, "Changing School Structures to Benefit High-Risk Youth," in P. E. Leone, ed., *Understanding Troubled and Troubling Youth* (Newbury Park, Calif.: Sage Publications, 1990).

41. B. H. Bry, "Reducing the Incidence of Adolescent Problems through Preventive Intervention."

42. Botvin, "Substance Abuse Prevention"; and Gottfredson, testimony before Senate Committee on Health, Education, Labor, and Pensions.

43. Sections 4111–4116, 20 U.S.C. 7111–7116.

44. Ralph Frammolino, "Failing Grade for Safe Schools Plan," *Los Angeles Times*, September 6, 1998, p. 1.

45. *Federal Register*, July 16, 1997 (62 FR 38072).

46. *Federal Register*, vol. 63, no. 104, June 1, 1998, p. 29902.

47. Frammolino, "Failing Grade for Safe Schools Plan."

48. Botuin, "Substance Abuse Prevention."

49. Denise C. Gottfredson, "School-Based Crime Prevention," in Lawrence W. Sherman and others, *Preventing Crime: What Works, What Doesn't, What's Promising* (Department of Justice, 1997), pp. 5–46, 47, at www.preventingcrime.org.

50. Malcolm Klein, *Street Gangs and Street Gang Workers* (Englewood Cliffs, N.J.: Prentice-Hall, 1971).

51. Frammolino, "Failing Grade for Safe Schools Plan."

52. As cited in Millenson, *Demanding Medical Excellence*.

53. Melissa A. Bradley, Michael Timpane, and Peter Reuter, "Focus Groups: Safe and Drug-Free Schools Program Conference Draft," RAND Corporation Aspen Institute Wye River Conference on Prevention of Drug Abuse and Violence among School Children, July 21–23, 1999.

54. Lawrence W. Sherman, "Ten Principles of Evidence-Based Government," University of Pennsylvania, Fels Center of Government, 1999.

55. Sherman, *Evidence-Based Policing.*

56. Millenson, *Demanding Medical Excellence*.

57. Department of Education, Safe and Drug-Free Schools and Communities Act, State Grants for Drug and Violence Prevention Program, Nonregulatory Guidance for Implementing SDFSCA Principles of Effectiveness, May 1998.

58. *New York Times*, January 20, 1999, p. A22, Washington edition.

59. Nance F. Sizer and Theodore Sizer, eds., *Moral Education: Five Lectures* (Harvard University Press, 1970), p. 5.

60. Matthew Rees, "Title IV: Neither Safe Nor Drug-Free," in Marci Kanstoroom and Chester E. Finn Jr., eds., *New Directions: Federal Education Policy in the Twenty-First Century* (Washington: Thomas B. Fordham Foundation, 1999), p. 83.

61. Rees, "Title IV," p. 79.

62. Carlotta C. Joyner, *Safe and Drug Free Schools: Balancing Accountability with State and Local Flexibility* (General Accounting Office, 1997).

63. Richard W. Riley, "Safe in Our Schools," *Washington Post*, August 15, 1999, p. B7. See also Phillip Kaufman and others, "Indicators of School Crime and Safety, 1998," *Education Statistics Quarterly*, vol. 1, no. 1 (Spring 1999), pp. 42–45; and Edward Walsh, "Fewer Students Were Expelled for Firearms, U.S. Reports," *Washington Post*, August 11, 1999, p. A3.

64. Similar conclusions are presented in Paul E. Baron and Richard J. Coley, *Order in the Classroom: Violence, Discipline, and Student Achievement* (Princeton, N.J.: Educational Testing Service, 1998). They used data from the Department of Education and the Department of Justice.

65. Barton and Coley, in *Order in the Classroom*, said, "The strongest predictor of school crime was the nature of the surrounding community." Quoted matter on p. 8; see also pp. 11–19.

66. For an excellent summary of this line of inquiry, see Marshall S. Smith and Stewart C. Purkey, "Effective Schools: A Review," *Elementary School Journal*, vol. 83 (March 1983), pp. 427–52.

67. Paul Hill and Mary Beth Celio, *Fixing Urban Schools* (Brookings, 1998), pp. 31–38.

68. Maris A. Vinovskis, "Improving Federal Educational Research, Development, and Evaluation," testimony presented at a Joint Hearing before the House Committee on Education and the Workforce and the Senate Committee on Health, Education, Labor, and Pensions, June 17, 1999, p. 5.

69. Maris A. Vinovskis, *Changing Federal Strategies for Supporting Educational Research, Development, and Statistics* (Department of Education, 1998), p. 70.

70. Vinovskis, *Changing Federal Strategies for Supporting Educational Research, Development, and Statistics*, p. 69. See also Vinovskis, "Improving Federal Educational Research, Development, and Evaluation," p. 6; and Maris A. Vinovskis, "Missing in Practice?: Systematic Development and Rigorous Program Valuation at the U.S. Department of Education," paper prepared for the Conference on Evaluation of Educational Policies, American Academy of Arts and Sciences, May 13–14, 1999.

71. D. W. Miller, "The Black Hole of Education Research," *Chronicle of Higher Education*, August 6, 1999, p. 1.

72. E. Suyapa Silvia and Judy Thorne, *School-Based Drug Prevention Programs: A Longitudinal Study in Selected District* (North Carolina: Research Triangle Institute, 1997), p. E23.

73. National Center for Neighborhood Enterprise, *Violence-Free Zone Initiative* (Washington, 1999).

Goals 2000 and the Standards Movement

ROBERT B. SCHWARTZ *and*
MARIAN A. ROBINSON

AMERICA FINALLY HAS a national education strategy. That strategy is called standards-based reform. Virtually every state in the union has developed, or is in the process of developing, new academic standards that specify what students are expected to know and be able to do in the core academic subjects at key grade levels; assessments that measure progress against those standards; and accountability systems that, at a minimum, provide annual public reports on school and district performance. Although enormous variation is evident in the quality of state standards and assessments and in the sophistication of state thinking about implementation, we believe that a broad enough consensus exists across the states on the core elements of this strategy to warrant our characterization of standards-based reform as America's de facto national education policy. Even within the states that have experimented most boldly with choice, charters, and vouchers, these initiatives are playing out in the context of a broader standards-based strategy. The injection of competition and market pressures may make state standards and accountability even more necessary to track the use of public funds in different settings.

We want to thank the following people for sharing with us their knowledge, experience, and files about Goals 2000: Tom Fagan, former director of the Goals 2000 Office; Jack Jennings, Center for Education Policy; Jack McDonald, Council of Chief State School Officers; and George Erhart, General Accounting Office. The views presented in this paper are those of the authors alone and do not necessarily reflect the views of these individuals or of Achieve Inc.

To what degree, if any, is the emerging national education strategy a product of federal policy? In virtually every other developed nation, this question would be incomprehensible. Most everywhere else, national governments, even in federalist systems, are clearly responsible for setting national policy; that is what education ministries do. In the United States, where education is among the unenumerated responsibilities left to the states under the Constitution and where more than 90 percent of education funding derives from state and local tax revenues, the federal government's role has historically been carefully circumscribed. Education has only fitfully been seen as an issue worthy of serious national attention. The current reform period, generally acknowledged to have begun with the release of *A Nation at Risk* in 1983, is striking for several reasons, not least for its staying power. Education reform has not only remained on the national radar screen for most of this period, but it also has now moved to the very top of the domestic political agenda.

The Goals 2000: Educate America Act, the centerpiece of the Clinton administration's education reform program, provides a fascinating case study of the challenges facing an activist administration in trying to craft federal legislation that can provide national direction and leadership in a highly decentralized education system. Goals 2000 represented a very different federal strategy than ever seen before. Despite the relative modesty of its funding, especially when judged against large categorical programs such as Title I, it was audacious not only in proposing to use federal funds to leverage whole system reforms at the state level, but also in creating new national structures to guide the states toward a national strategy. Although the nationalizing elements of Goals 2000, especially the role originally envisioned for the National Education Standards and Improvement Council (NESIC), never came into being, the funds provided for state and local systemic improvement under Title III of the act have played a significant role in many jurisdictions in helping education leaders move forward with the standards agenda. In the main body of this paper we will review the available data about how Goals 2000 funds have been used by states and localities as well as the evidence about impact. Our principal interest, however, is in examining the lessons to be learned from the demise of the nationalizing aspects embodied in Title II of the act, for that story might help bring an understanding of under what conditions, if any, federal policy can bring about a more coherent national strategy for improving the performance of America's schools and students.

The Evolution of Goals 2000

Goals 2000 had an unusual political and legislative history. It began not in Washington, D.C., but in Charlottesville, Virginia, at the 1989 National Education Summit, with the creation of the first-ever national education goals. While President George Bush convened the Charlottesville summit, the impetus for the creation of national goals came from the National Governors' Association (NGA). Even before the release of *A Nation at Risk*, education-minded governors, especially in the South, realized that without a comprehensive strategy to improve the knowledge and skills of their young people, their states' long-term economic prospects would be bleak. In releasing *A Nation at Risk*, President Ronald Reagan asserted that the poor performance of the education system imperiled the nation's economic security, but that this was the states' problem to fix. The states accepted the challenge, and over the next six years an unprecedented flood of education initiatives emanated from virtually every statehouse in the nation.

Fourteen months after the release of *A Nation at Risk*, the Education Commission of the States issued a report on new state legislation and policy aimed at education renewal. *Action in the States* identified forty-four states that had raised graduation requirements; thirty states that had developed new regulations governing learning outcomes, curriculum content, and frameworks; forty-five states that had strengthened teacher certification and evaluation requirements; and twenty-seven states that had implemented initiatives to provide more instructional time. More than 250 task forces were helping forty-six states develop comprehensive state action plans to improve educational outcomes of students.[1]

By August 1986, when the governors gathered in Hilton Head, South Carolina, for their annual meeting, virtually every governor, regardless of his or her initial interest in education as an arena for policy action, had been compelled to place education reform at or near the top of the state's political agenda. That summer's NGA meeting, hosted by Governor Richard W. Riley of South Carolina and chaired by Governor Lamar Alexander of Tennessee, focused entirely on education. Organized principally around the release of a report that was the product of seven gubernatorial task forces on such topics as school readiness, leadership, teaching, technology, and parental involvement and choice, the meeting provided an occasion for the governors not only to talk with one another and with such national leaders as Albert Shanker of the American Federation of Teachers and Secretary of Education William Bennett about their efforts to stimulate reform in their own states, but also to propose collectively to their education communities a new public bargain. *Time for Results*, the report released at Hilton Head, was important for its message to the education community—"We will let up on regulating inputs and give you more flexibility and control over resources, in return for your commitment to be held more accountable for results"—as well as for its public message that the nation's governors had now come center stage on education.[2] The number of state leaders from both parties who could speak knowledgeably and passionately about education issues and who had initiated significant enough reform programs by 1986 to lay claim to the title of "education governor" was substantial, and that list was to grow even longer by the end of the decade.

Hilton Head was in a sense a trial run for Charlottesville three years later. *Time for Results* demonstrated the ability of the governors to work together across party lines on education issues and to speak with a unified public voice. As activist governors worked on reform initiatives in their own states (and discovered, incidentally, that being an "education governor" was good politics as well as good policy), the idea of creating some kind of national framework within which states could focus their efforts began to take shape.

Bush's invitation to the NGA to join him in an education summit in late 1989 provided the occasion for the governors to advance the idea of national education goals. Governor Terry Branstad of Iowa, who was chair of the NGA at that time, had earlier asked Governors Bill Clinton of Arkansas and Carroll Campbell of South Carolina, who had succeeded Richard Riley, to cochair a task force on national goals, and their work drove the agenda of the summit.

The idea of national goals for education emerged first from a bipartisan group of governors, not from Washington, and the proponents of national goals saw them principally as useful guideposts for state action, not as a stimulus for new federal initiatives. Eight years of Reaganism had so diminished state expectations about the federal role in education that the principal anxiety expressed by governors of both parties at Charlottesville was that Bush's "read my lips, no new taxes" pledge during the 1988 campaign would make it politically difficult for them to ask their own electorates to continue to finance ambitious state reforms. There was virtually no expectation at Charlottesville of significant federal help; the policy statement issued by the governors and president spoke only about the need for more regulatory flexibility in existing federal programs.

A year after the summit, Bush brought new leadership into the Education Department, which lost little time in bringing forth a bold new proposal to provide national leadership for the implementation of national goals. America 2000, announced in April 1991 and carefully labeled a national strategy instead of a federal program, had four principal features: (1) a grass-roots organizing component, designed to promote the development of community-level support for achieving the national goals; (2) "break-the-mold" New American Schools, whose design and development would be supported by a new privately funded corporation, but whose implementation in each congressional district would be federally funded; (3) demonstration grants to support school choice through tuition vouchers; and (4) voluntary American Achievement Tests at grades four, eight, and twelve. The voluntary national tests were to be based on world-class standards, the model for such standards presumably being the widely acclaimed standards published two years earlier by the National Council of Teachers of Mathematics.[3]

In retrospect, three things are striking about the America 2000 package. First is the care taken to protect the administration from attacks from the right, with the inclusion of vouchers, strong private sector participation, and the disclaimer about the federal role (a strategy, not a program). Second is the focus on communities as the locus of activity instead of states, and the concomitant reluctance to acknowledge or connect with the systemic reform efforts already under way in the states. Third is the courage displayed in advancing the idea of national achievement tests. As John F. Jennings noted in his detailed account of the legislative history of the standards movement, this feature of America 2000 was the domestic equivalent of President Richard Nixon's trip to China. It legitimized the idea of national standards and tests as a public policy issue, and it enabled grateful Democratic advocates of national standards such as Albert Shanker and Claiborne Pell, senator from Rhode Island, to endorse the bill.[4]

The legislation submitted by the Bush administration did not seek legal authority from Congress to create new standards and tests, instead taking a backdoor route of merely notifying Congress that discretionary funds would be used for this purpose. While this tactic proved effective in helping the administration jump-start the work of professional associations in developing national standards, it increased friction within Congress as it considered the America 2000 legislation. The final bill so watered-down the administration's original legislation that even the bill's authors were less than enthusiastic. Democrats remained skeptical about the standards and testing strategy; Republicans worried about an expanded federal role; and administration officials were unhappy about the lack of support for the New American Schools. In the last days of the congressional session, a filibuster in the Senate, led by the most conservative Republican senators, killed the America 2000 legislation.

The congressional response to America 2000 was a reminder of just how difficult it is to craft a federal leadership role in education that can generate broad bipartisan support, especially when the focus shifts from programs targeted to specific groups of students in need of federal protection to a strategy aimed at raising the achievement of all children. The very components of America 2000 designed to insulate the administration from criticism from conservative Republicans (for example, choice and break-the-mold schools) raised alarms among the liberal Democrats on the House Education and Labor Committee, and both groups looked with some suspicion on the proposal for national tests. (As the Fordham Foundation president Chester E. Finn Jr. noted wryly when the Clinton administration's national test proposal ran aground, "Republicans don't like 'national,' Democrats don't like 'test.' ") Perhaps it was never in the cards for a Democratic Congress to enact a Republican president's education agenda, especially heading into an election year, but some of the political dynamics that stalled America 2000 were still in play two years later when President Bill Clinton introduced his own program to help the country move forward to meet the ambitious goals set in Charlottesville.

Clinton's proposals were significantly influenced by the 1992 report of the National Council on Education Standards and Testing (NCEST), a blue-ribbon group initiated by Secretary Alexander, authorized by Congress, and cochaired by Governors Roy Romer of Colorado and Campbell of South Carolina. Its charge was to advise the federal government on the desirability and feasibility of establishing national standards and tests. It recommended moving forward with national standards and a national system of assessments (not a single national test). These recommendations, however, were arrived at after very tough and contentious debates, revolving around two key issues. The first was the question of whether there should be standards for schools and school systems as well as for students, and, if so, where they should be set. The council finally resolved that both school delivery standards and system performance standards were needed. Unlike student content and performance standards, however, these should not be set nationally; instead, they should be "developed by the states collectively from which each state could select the criteria that it finds useful for the purpose of assessing a school's capacity and performance."[5] This Rube Goldberg–like solution foreshadowed the difficulties Congress was later to have in addressing this issue (now re-renamed opportunity-to-learn [OTL] standards) in Goals 2000.

The second contentious issue stemmed from the council's attempt to reconcile its recommendation to create voluntary national standards with its recommendation for a voluntary system of assessments that would respect the ability of individual states (or groups of states) to design or select their own tests, all of which would somehow be linked to national standards.

To make such a mixed system of centralized standards and decentralized assessments work, some kind of central coordinating structure was necessary. NCEST recommended that the National Education Goals Panel, established by Bush and the governors in 1990 to monitor progress toward the goals, be reconfigured to assure bipartisan balance and that a new council be created under the panel's jurisdiction that would certify both standards and criteria for assessments. This new entity, the National Education Standards and Assessment Council (NESAC), would be appointed by the goals panel to give it some political insulation, while still making it accountable publicly. NESAC's membership would be one-third public officials, one-third educators, and one-third other citizens.

As the recommendations of NCEST moved to the White House and then to Congress, and ultimately got fought out in the course of enacting Goals 2000, the political challenge of fashioning a federally created council to provide national coordination and quality control on standards and assessment proved virtually insurmountable, and this crucial feature of the NCEST report never came into being.

Despite the surface similarities between America 2000 and Goals 2000—similarities the Clinton administration played up in seeking Republican support—Goals 2000 represented a fundamentally different vision of educational reform and of the federal role in stimulating and leading that reform. What were the primary influences shaping that vision? First, and probably most important, virtually all the key administration players brought a strong orientation toward the leadership role of states and a shared belief that, without coherent state policy grounded in high expectations for all students, the nation would be unlikely to make much progress in improving student performance. Second, a clear conception of what coherent state policy might look like had begun to emerge, drawn both from a series of influential articles by Marshall S. Smith and Jennifer O'Day of Stanford University and from the reform strategy unfolding in California under the leadership of State Superintendent of Public Instruction Bill Honig. The Smith and O'Day articles on systemic reform argued for a much stronger alignment between goals for student learning and curriculum, instructional materials, assessments, and teacher preparation and professional development programs. They called for clear, high academic goals and stronger instructional guidance from the top of the system, coupled with substantial decentralization to schools and communities to determine the best means of accomplishing those goals.[6] California's ambitious curriculum frameworks, its use of statewide adoption policies to push the textbook publishers to produce aligned texts, its creation of a statewide network of content-based professional development centers to help teachers implement the frameworks, and its development of challenging new assessments to measure student learning against the frameworks—these elements constituted an unfolding existence-proof that American states might be able to create the kind of coherent, aligned educational policies associated with more centralized European and Asian systems.

In the Goals 2000 legislation put forth by the Clinton administration, the states were the locus of standards and assessment, with national standards serving only as exemplars to guide the development of state standards and benchmarks against which to judge them.[7] In contrast to America 2000, national standards were to have no independent weight at the community level, for no national tests would be derived from them.

In this spirit, the heart of Goals 2000 was its state grants program, designed to provide support both for such state-level activities as standards and assessments development and for district-level planning and implementation of standards-based reform. The legislation acknowledged that many states were already well launched on systemic reform and encouraged the states to use the new federal funds to help implement reform plans and programs already under way. The legislation required no regulations and granted the secretary broad waiver authority, again to signal the administration's conception of Goals 2000 as a vehicle to facilitate the implementation of a state-defined reform strategy, not as a new freestanding federal program with its own rules and regulations. As long as states bought into the underlying principles of standards-based, systemic reform and committed to a broad-based planning process, virtually no strings were attached to the use of Goals 2000 funds.

The flexibility deliberately built into the design of the state grants section (Title III) of Goals 2000 made it extremely hard to attribute results to the expenditure of federal dollars. Unlike the typical federal education program, Goals 2000 addressed neither an identifiable target population (for example, children whose first language is not English) nor an identifiable problem (for example, safe, drug-free schools). Its purpose was to help states raise academic expectations and improve academic achievement for all students. In this sense, it was path-breaking legislation, for it asserted a national interest in improving the performance of the whole enterprise. Given how circumscribed the federal role in education has been historically, and the modesty of the federal share of education funding, any attempt to take a much more prescriptive posture than that adopted in Goals 2000 about how federal funds should be used in support of state-based reforms would probably have been doomed to failure.

That Goals 2000 was finally enacted in 1994 is largely a consequence of the broad support it enjoyed from virtually every major education and business organization, the bipartisan congressional interest in creating a role for itself in the national education reform movement sparked by the Charlottesville summit, and the fact that Democrats controlled both houses of Congress. Congress addressed the anxiety about a broadened federal role by including language explicitly prohibiting federal mandates and control and reaffirming the responsibility of the states and communities for setting educational policy.

The legislation aimed to define the elusive federal-state partnership first envisioned by the governors during the 1989 National Education Summit. In exchange for flexibility and minimal regulation, the states would be held accountable for improvements in student performance. Within a standards-based reform context then, Goals 2000 attempted to channel federal resources in support of state-driven systemic education reform.

Supporting State and Local Education Systemic Improvement

The core of Goals 2000 is Title III, through which states received funds to realign their systems, as they saw fit, to achieve the national goals. The funds would help states and local communities through a transition phase as they improved their basic services and engaged in restructuring and realigning their systems around emerging standards. Compared with long-standing federal formula-grant programs, Title III employed a number of innovative approaches to refashion federal support for state reform initiatives. First, multilevel planning grants were made to both states and their local districts, and they were designed to encourage a combination of top-down and bottom-up planning. In the first grant year, states could use up to 40 percent of the funds to support state-level system building activities, with 90 percent of funds in subsequent years designed to support competitive grants to local districts and schools to implement state standards.[8] Second, the federal funds were designed to be "responsible block grants," a term coined by Secretary Riley. While the law designated a broad use of funds for coordinated improvement activities, it allowed states to develop their own criteria, ones that presumably reflected state priorities, for awarding subgrants. Third, Goals 2000 also included an experimental program, the Education Flexibility Partnership, that extended to six states (expanded to twelve states under the 1996 amendments) the secretary's authority to temporarily waive regulations in nine federal programs.

State-Level Grants

Since 1994, states have received more than $2 billion in formula-based Goals 2000 grants for education reform activities. For the most part, congressional appropriations for Goals 2000 steadily increased from the initial $92 million in 1994 to more than $490 million by 1999. Allocation levels dropped slightly under the intense scrutiny of the 104th Congress, from $358 million to $336 million, as conservative Republicans incorporated the Goals 2000 program into their broader strategy to reduce deficit spending and eliminate avenues for federal intrusion in school-level decisionmaking. By 1997, however, in the wake of the public backlash against the federal government shutdowns, Goals 2000 allocations sharply rebounded to $471 million. After some initial resistance from a handful of states, virtually all are now participating in Goals 2000, with annual federal grants ranging in size from $370,000 to Wyoming in 1994 to $54.7 million to California in 1997.[9]

The most systematic, though largely descriptive, review of how states used their Goals 2000 funds comes from a 1998 study by the General Accounting Office (GAO), *Goals 2000: Flexible Funding Supports State and Local Education Reform.* The GAO reported that, between 1994 and 1997, collectively states used about $109 million for state-level reform activities to help plan and build the key components of a new standards-based system. Specifically, about 44 percent of these state-level funds supported personnel to manage the states' subgrant programs as well as other state-sponsored education reform activities. States also used about 28 percent of these funds to contract with state and national experts to help develop new standards and assessments, to devise new curricula aligned with new standards, and to conduct necessary research and development activities. About 9 percent of funds supported training and conference costs associated with state education improvement panel activities and the training of teachers and administrators.[10]

These broad categories of state activity mask the multiplicity of ways that states were able to weave Goals 2000 funds seamlessly into their respective reform strategies. Each state's story is different, but Texas provides an illustrative example of how a large state employed Goals 2000 funds to advance its own standards-based reform agenda. Between 1994 and 1997, Texas received about $102 million in Goals 2000 funds with more than $6 million supporting state-level reform activity. Texas explicitly connected its support of Goals 2000 with the statutory assurances that barred any federal intervention in state affairs. Upon joining, the state refashioned Goals 2000 as Academics 2000, an administrative two-step to avert a conservative backlash for accepting federal dollars.

The seeds of current reform efforts date back before Goals 2000 to 1983, when the Texas state legislature first directed the state Board of Education to develop essential elements of instruction by course and grade level for each content area in the state's required curriculum. Academics 2000 supported the development of Texas Essential Knowledge and Skills (TEKS), which the state board adopted in 1997 to replace the essential elements for English language arts and reading, mathematics, science, and social studies, among other subject areas. Texas employed an exhaustive and iterative public outreach effort to develop TEKS, with fifteen subject-area teams, two public comment periods, state board of education review committees as well as Internet, newsletter, and regional education service centers for dissemination during the process. The state began implementing the new essential knowledge and skills in 1998–99 through textbook adoption policies, state assessments, and professional development activities.

In 1996 Goals 2000 funds helped establish two statewide educator development centers for training and professional development in English language arts and social studies. These centers help districts and schools implement TEKS and disseminate models for exemplary instructional strategies and effective staff development. An important part of the Texas accountability system, though not supported by Goals 2000 funds, is the Texas Assessment of Academic Skills (TAAS), first administered in 1993. The TAAS forms the basis of the state's Academic Excellence Indicator System, which tracks school performance and reports data by student race and poverty. Under the new Professional Development Appraisal System established in 1998, teacher evaluations are linked with schoolwide student performance, and schools and districts are rated and accredited based on performance indicators. Clearly, Goals 2000 cannot be credited with having built Texas's systemic reform strategy, but its funds supported the development of essential building blocks, without which the state's progress would likely have been much slower.[11] Because Texas had a clear education reform plan, it was able to use its Goals 2000 funds strategically. Texas presents just one example of the many approaches states employed in building their standards-based systems.

District-Level Grants

Most Goals 2000 funds supported reform efforts at the district and school level. States distributed these funds through competitive processes based on their own criteria, focused on three broad categories of activity established by the law: local school improvement, preservice teacher education reform, and professional development. From 1994 to 1997, more than one-third of the 14,367 school districts nationwide received a Goals 2000 subgrant. Because states had discretion in determining the size of district grants, the average size of awards varied, ranging from $10,000 to more than $200,000.

Goals 2000 subgrants paid for a variety of education improvement activities, which the GAO found to be aligned with the state education reform strategy as intended. Two-thirds of subgrants supported local education reform activities, such as developing improvement plans, updating curriculum frameworks, involving parents and communities in reform efforts, and professional development. About 10 percent supported technology acquisition. The remaining funds, less than one quarter, supported preservice training for college students who plan on becoming teachers, efforts to align local curriculum with standards and select appropriate assessment systems, and a mixture of activities that cut across these categories.[12]

Texas also serves as an example of how states were aligning the local subgrants with their own improvement priorities. Through its Academics 2000 program, Texas awarded a total of $96 million in competitive grants to 833 districts between 1994 and 1997.[13] To meet its goal that all elementary students exhibit grade-level performance by the end of fourth grade, Texas strategically dedicated its subgrant program to improving early childhood and elementary student achievement. The first two years of subgrant awards addressed proficiency in reading, English language arts, mathematics, social studies, and science, with the last three cycles of awards targeting elementary reading improvement to complement the Texas Reading Initiative. In addition, Texas was one of the first Education Flexibility Partnership states, with one of most active waiver programs in the country. According to a 1998 GAO report on the Ed-Flex program, between 1995 and 1997 the Texas education agency issued eight statewide waivers from federal record-keeping and administrative requirements, and another forty district waivers, some of which allowed for more targeted use of teacher training funds. Texas expects all districts receiving waivers for Title I monies to show annual gains in test scores so that in five years 90 percent of all students will pass the state's assessments in reading and mathematics.[14]

What Is Known

While a broad sense exists of how states and districts used their Goals 2000 monies to further their systemic reform plans, little evidence is available by way of student performance to indicate whether such activity improved student learning. Given Title III's flexibility and its goal of seamless integration with state improvement activities, it may be impossible to link Goals 2000 dollars to any concrete state outcomes. Nonetheless, a review is instructive of what systematic information is known on the general and, where possible, specific effects of the federal program on state and local reform efforts.

The 1998 GAO study of Goals 2000 commended the Title III state and local grants program, reporting to lawmakers "that in its present form, Goals 2000 accomplished what Congress intended." Because most states had begun their state education reform strategy before 1994, Goals 2000 funds provided an "additional flexible resource for promoting coordinated improvements in state and local education systems." According to GAO, some states reported that federal funds accelerated the pace of reform. For example, an official in Nevada characterized Goals 2000 funding as a "catalyst" that sparked the development of content and performance standards in each grade, stating that his state did not even have the terminology for standards-based reform before Goals 2000. Missouri officials claimed Goals 2000 was the "vehicle that got schools and universities talking for the first time." In other states, officials thought Goals 2000 monies helped to improve the quality of key standards components under development. An Oregon official reported that Goals 2000 funding made the difference between "doing it and doing it right," explaining that the state might have settled for standards only half as good without the additional funds to bring in experts and to partner with colleges to create institutes for helping teachers use the content standards. Other states found Goals 2000 funding valuable because it enabled their state to respond quickly to evolving problems and opportunities. One New York official explained that "it allows you to change the tire while the car is moving."[15]

Beyond the GAO's broad review of state activity, however, a dearth of research exists around how Goals 2000's flexibility and multilevel grant process have contributed to widespread use of standards as the new systemic building blocks that support improved teaching and learning. Available research comes from Education Department–supported contracts with research and policy analysis firms—surveys of state and district officials and annual analyses of state progress reports submitted to the Goals 2000 program office—designed to gather baseline information on state and district reform activities.

In 1997 Policy Studies Associates (PSA) conducted a survey of state officials and federal program directors to collect information on the early implementation of Goals 2000 and eight other programs reauthorized under the Improving America's Schools Act (IASA). Survey results, reported in *Living in Interesting Times: Early State Implementation of New Federal Education Laws*, suggest that the policy framework and emphasis on flexibility for results proffered by Goals 2000 has helped reduce policy fragmentation and increase coordination across federal and state programs. Cross-program communication and consolidated planning were widely present at the state level and growing in acceptance at the district level. State officials reported that the new consolidated plan option "had sparked new ideas" about how formerly disparate programs might work in tandem, including the integration of so-called monitoring activities.[16] Most Goals 2000 coordinators reported that states were also actively reviewing their own laws and regulations to identify those that might impede reform or serve as barriers to local flexibility.

A more cautious finding from the PSA survey reveals that program administrators were slow to embrace the student performance orientation promoted by the Goals 2000 policy framework. While states reported that they were actively dismantling their old monitoring systems, few state administrators were sending a strong message to their districts that accountability for student performance would replace the compliance monitoring of the past. With the exception of Title I directors, less than 20 percent of survey respondents used student performance data in ways that helped to focus attention on student performance to improve program quality. This contrasted sharply with the 91 percent of directors who reported that such student data were in hand. In terms of technical assistance, rather than actively assessing local capacity to respond to new legislation, many administrators were relying on districts to know when they needed help. Many waited to be "invited" in, with only 13 percent of program managers reporting visits triggered by information about student performance. According to PSA, "technical assistance remained largely responsive to program-specific issues, rather than a cross-cutting agenda of standards, assessment, whole-school improvement, and data-driven decision-making."[17] These findings were confirmed in a separate report to the department summarizing state Goals 2000 progress reports, 1995–97, by Policy Studies Associates. Forty percent of the state progress reports did not include information on student performance at the state or local level. Of those that did, about one-third reported aggregate data from all districts receiving Goals 2000 funding or reported grant purposes, such as number of teachers trained and partnerships facilitated.[18]

The 1997 Urban Institute study *Reports on Reform from the Field: District and State Survey Results* represents the first systematic feedback from the field on the state of reform, broadly construed, since the passage of Goals 2000. For the purposes of the discussion here, it provides a snapshot of how states and districts are struggling with both planning and initiating standards-based reform. Through surveys of fifty state officials and twenty-seven hundred district administrators, the Urban Institute collected information about state and district views on reform, their progress, and their technical assistance needs.[19] Survey findings indicated that state and district improvement efforts appeared to be working in concert, as intended under standards-based reform, with both state and district officials reporting a clear and strong influence of state-level policies on district-level progress. Districts that were located in states that either were early leaders in standards-based reform—Kentucky, Maryland, and Oregon—or had received a Goals 2000 subgrant reported a "high understanding of the elements of standards-based reform" and that "reform would require greater change on their part." Compared with districts in other states or those that had not received a Goals 2000 grant, these districts have a "clear understanding of what reform entails." Early reform districts and Goals 2000 districts were also more likely to report greater progress than other districts. Districts in early reform states appeared to have a closer and more helpful relationship with their states. Districts not in early reform states or receiving Goals 2000 subgrants appeared slightly behind in planning for and implementing standards in schools and classrooms.

The study revealed additional challenges. Both district- and state-level administrators reported issues associated with assessments and accountability as those that would require the greatest change on their part, in which they are making the least progress, and where they needed the most help. They also reported a need for information about how to provide effective technical assistance to districts and schools that are not making adequate progress in student performance.

The Urban Institute survey found that size and poverty level were important factors in determining the level of district understanding of, and engagement in, standards-based reform. Districts with the greatest poverty reported substantial difficulty in establishing standards and aligning curricula. While high-poverty districts appeared well connected to helpful sources of assistance regarding federal programs, they did not seem to have the connections needed to help with standards-based reform. High-poverty districts also reported needing a great deal more assistance in a number of areas, but particularly in providing technical assistance to schools not making adequate progress. In addition, the study found that smaller districts appeared disadvantaged as well, reporting significantly lower levels of understanding of the various elements of reform and less progress. They also did not appear well connected to helpful sources of information and assistance, which may stem from having smaller, less specialized staff that can attend to reform.

Districts reported that state agencies, professional associations, and education publications were the most helpful sources of technical assistance for standards-based reform, with the federal government being the least helpful. However, state officials found federal sources of information and assistance very helpful in their reform efforts, thus affirming the underlying design of Goals 2000, which channels federal resources through states, not districts. The study characterized the department's technical assistance efforts as "transparent" and recommended its continued support of education reform partnerships and consortia as mechanisms for disseminating information and providing technical assistance.[20]

The GAO report on Goals 2000 also included site visits to ten states. State officials applauded the design of Goals 2000 with its emphasis on broad functions rather than specific programs. One state official reported that such flexibility allowed districts and schools to work together on designing comprehensive, coherent implementation strategies, ones free of the "stovepipe" mentality of previous disparate programs. While it is no surprise that state officials endorsed the flexibility of the grant, they did resist the idea of block grants, welcoming instead some degree of broad guidelines. Their resistance stemmed from concerns that any attempt to combine Goals 2000 funds with other federal funding into a more general block grant would increase the risk that resources would not support education reform. They did not want unencumbered funds, preferring instead the clear but broad parameters used in Goals 2000.[21]

While the several Goals 2000 reports discussed in this paper provide a sense of the sheer number of educators, policymakers, and parents who have become mobilized around developing standards-based systems and improving teaching and learning, they reveal little about whether the federal funds have contributed to the creation of state and local systemic reform policies and programs that are likely over time to lead to substantial improvements in student performance. For states such as Texas that made strategic use of Goals 2000 funds to advance a coherent reform agenda and are now seeing significant student learning gains, it is relatively easy to declare the program a success. But in the vast majority of states, where as yet little evidence is seen of substantial progress in student performance and there is a less coherent reform strategy, anecdotal reports from satisfied state and local officials constitute an unacceptably weak indicator of program effectiveness. Absent some federal mechanism for exercising quality control over the systemic reform work of states, "responsible block grants" look little different from revenue sharing. Goals 2000 as enacted contained an important provision that was designed to provide some measure of quality control over the setting of state standards, the foundation piece of any systemic reform strategy, but that provision never became operational.

National Education Reform Leadership, Standards, and Asssessments

The most problematic and controversial component of the Goals 2000 was the national leadership provision outlined in Title II of the act. This title authorized two federally funded entities to provide leadership and technical assistance to states engaging in voluntary systemic reform. The law codified the existing National Education Goals Panel and created a new National Education Standards and Improvement Council. With the establishment of these two relatively modest, broadly based, quasi-governmental organizations, lawmakers hoped to promote "coherent, nationwide, systemic education reform."[22] That only one of these entities exists today, the National Education Goals Panel, illustrates the governmental tensions and political pitfalls in formalizing federal leadership functions around strategic planning for national education reform.

Because the goals panel had already been in existence since 1990 and had a carefully circumscribed mission—to report on state and national progress toward meeting the national education goals—the decision to incorporate it along with the goals in the new legislation was relatively straightforward. Its membership was expanded to ensure a bipartisan balance among its governors, congressional representatives, and state legislators, and its mission was made proactive; it was to work "to establish a system of high academic standards and assessments" and to help build "a national, bipartisan consensus to achieve the Goals," as well as to report annual progress. One could argue that its reporting function could have gotten it in trouble, especially with low-performing states, but the annual data on state performance against the goals were sufficiently weak and inconclusive in the early years to obviate this danger. Consequently, the panel's work suffered more from public inattention than from controversy—hardly a fatal disability in the eyes of Congress.

Unlike the existing goals panel, the proposed National Education Standards and Improvement Council was designed to break new ground. Its purpose was to promote the development and use of high-quality national and state standards and assessments, support research and development work where appropriate, and provide, at the request of states, a review and certification of state standards and assessments. The law also provided for NESIC to develop national opportunity-to-learn standards and to certify such standards from states, if voluntarily submitted. Although independent, all NESIC decisions could be overridden by a two-thirds vote of the goals panel. Together these two entities would provide the necessary technical and political leadership for state and local reform efforts.

Dramatic shifts in party power at the federal level between 1993 and 1996 complicated the creation of the NESIC as policymakers and interest groups gained new opportunities to pursue alternative agendas and redefine problems related to education. The 1996 amendments to Goals 2000 withdrew authorization for NESIC, even before its members had been appointed, thus removing any levers for quality control available to the Department of Education or to Congress. Without an entity such as NESIC, the sole national leadership functions were left to the goals panel and to the department's capacity to leverage programmatic funds and to use its education bully pulpit.

The Rise and Fall of NESIC

NESAC, the national council first proposed in the 1992 NCEST report, was to be nonfederal, nonduplicative of existing entities, bipartisan, representative of government at all levels, and accountable to the public. The council would coordinate a national system of standards and assessments, issue guidelines, ensure technical merit, and certify state and national products with a "Good Housekeeping seal of approval."[23] Its powers, particularly around the controversial concept of opportunity to learn, were strategically limited, however. While NESAC could develop "national school delivery standards," it could not certify them, thereby defusing the potential litigation that concerned conservative congressional leaders. The provision also eased liberal Democrats' concerns that any system that included testing would address students' opportunities to learn the standards. As conceptualized and designed, the proposed NESAC appeared a viable bipartisan structure that would help guide the emerging national interest in standards-based systemic reform.

The NCEST report's recommendations quickly infiltrated the ongoing congressional and public debate over Bush's America 2000 proposal. Shortly following the report's release, a group of four dozen prominent educators, scholars, and civil rights leaders issued a joint statement aimed at "hitting the brakes" on the drive to create a single national test—a stand that reinforced the NCEST recommendation of a national system of assessments while condemning the president's plan. The signers were prestigious education leaders and experts, including Gregory R. Anrig, president of the Educational Testing Service, James Comer of Yale University, Marion Wright Edelman of the Children's Defense Fund, and Marshall Smith of Stanford University, who also served on NCEST, among others.[24]

Lawmakers in the Democratically controlled Congress expressed reservation at NCEST's endorsement of a national system of testing and a coordinating body that would facilitate its development. Their misgivings stemmed from concurrent debates over the reauthorization of federal education research programs and a widely circulated report from the Office of Technology Assessment that called for more research on high-stakes testing. The report reinforced liberal Democrats' concerns about the negative consequences of testing for disadvantaged populations and under-resourced schools. Consequently, as a condition for receiving federal funding under America 2000, liberal lawmakers wanted to elevate service delivery standards to the same level of importance as content standards. Encouraged by an election-year push, they added an amendment to Bush's education bill that required any assessment of student learning to also include assessments of school resources. The Bush administration vowed to veto the bill, calling it a "federal recipe book" that would dictate to local school boards "day-to-day decisions about curriculum, discipline, teacher training, and textbooks."[25] The growing conflict over the role of national assessments and system delivery standards led to a legislative stalemate, and Bush's education bill was allowed to die quietly in the Senate.

A political window opened for the national goals effort when the 1992 presidential election swept Arkansas governor Bill Clinton into the White House, for the premise was that a Democratically controlled Congress would be eager to move from confrontation to cooperation with the White House on education legislation. As a key participant in the Charlottesville summit, Clinton was strongly committed to the governors' 1989 collective pledge to achieve the national goals. Drawing directly from the NCEST recommendations and his vision of a new federal-state partnership, Clinton incorporated NESAC into his Goals 2000 legislative proposal, with council members to be appointed by the goals panel.

The president and his education secretary, Richard W. Riley, quickly learned just how brief their honeymoon would be. Democratic lawmakers, frustrated by twelve years of jousting with a Republican White House, were not about to roll over and enact an education bill that many perceived as a warmed-over version of America 2000.[26] The House Education and Labor Committee chair immediately declared Clinton's proposal a "non-starter" and sent it back to the White House for revisions. Administration officials dutifully redrafted the legislation, renaming a somewhat repositioned version of NESAC, now called the National Education Standards and Improvement Council (NESIC), to minimize conflict around any mention of testing. The composition of NESIC changed as well: Appointment authority shifted to the president, with the goals panel reduced to offering nominations alongside the Speaker of the House and Senate majority leader. These changes would provide the Democratically controlled Congress and, to a lesser extent, the White House more control over NESIC. Clinton's initial proposal called for the council to be comprised of "eminent Americans." The revised proposal allocated the twenty seats on the council principally to representatives of interest groups: five professional educators, five representatives of business, labor, and postsecondary institutions; five public members such as participants in advocacy groups, civil rights, and disability groups, or state and local policymakers; and five education experts. The Senate version of NESIC was similar but composed of nineteen members.[27]

The contentious debate in the previous Congress over opportunity-to-learn standards was re-ignited in the early deliberations of Goals 2000. Representative Jack Reed (D-R.I.) attached a controversial amendment to the Goals 2000 bill that required states, as a condition of receiving federal funds, to take corrective action if opportunity-to-learn standards were not implemented in local school districts. Representative William D. Ford (D-Mich.), chair of the House Education and Labor Committee, followed with a demand that such standards be "equal to or slightly ahead of any testing or standards." Furthermore, the House bill authorized a national commission to develop national opportunity-to-learn standards that NESIC would then certify. These actions sparked conservative anger; if NESIC could certify OTL standards, it would pave the way for federal control in schools and fuel lawsuits from civil rights groups. This would mark the first step on a "slippery slope toward federal control of education and serve as the basis for new unfunded mandates directed at states."[28]

At this stage of the national debate, the governors were well invested in education reform and were particularly watchful of congressional actions. They were skeptical of the numerous "voluntary" provisions emerging in the bills. They believed that such mechanisms for content standard certification could, by a turn of the wrist in Congress, quickly become mandatory. In a letter to Secretary Riley, Governor Campbell blamed Congress for destroying the new vision of a federal-state partnership that would support flexibility for results. He wrote that "throughout the [legislative] process, the pressure has always been to prescribe more and more federal requirements, and to switch performance based accountability to accountability based on inputs." From his perspective, the House bill came "dangerously close to derailing our hard-won emphasis on student achievement." Furthermore, by giving the power to NESIC it "leads us inevitably toward a federalization of what has been, until now, a pact that recognized and respected the preeminent role of states in education reform."[29]

The governors' displeasure increased as Congress authorized the national goals. Two additional goals regarding parent involvement and teacher professional education were included, extending the original national goals from six to eight. Although neither was controversial, their addition illustrates how control of the goal-setting process, as well as its implementation strategy, had shifted from the governors to the federal government, specifically the interest groups that surrounded the legislative process. As the Goals 2000 bill went to conference, Governor Campbell called upon the president to pull the federal government "out of the goals/standards movement because the federal government cannot seem to contribute without wanting to control." He reasoned that "governors and parents should not have to fight for their rights in a very complicated subject area every time Congress passes an education bill." These protests proved moderately effective. In the final version of Goals 2000, NESIC was authorized to develop voluntary national OTL standards but given no authority to certify those standards, and the state requirement to develop OTL standards was dropped. Multiple sections of the law assured the voluntary nature of NESIC's review authority.

With the passage of Goals 2000, Congress and the executive branch, not the governors, would control the standard-setting process. After repeated attempts by both President Bush and the governors to exclude congressional participation, Congress was hesitant to lose NESIC. Access to any goals-related entity presented a long-sought opportunity to institutionalize its role and interests. As a result, lawmakers kept the panel and designed it to secure channels of influence and future policy choices. Now the dominant group in Washington, the Democratic 103rd Congress structured NESIC to maximize input from current Democratic leadership. Congressional leaders altered the composition of the panel so that majority leaders of both the House and Senate could make nominations. And they shifted final appointment authority from the goals panel to the Democratic president, reducing the goals panel's role to simple veto power over NESIC's decisions. A generous sprinkling of the term "voluntary" throughout the legislation seemed to placate conservative fears about NESIC's authority, particularly in reference to NESIC's certification powers over standards and assessments.

But the new nomination process for its nineteen members required a complex formula: seven from the secretary, and twelve from the Speaker of the House, majority leader of the Senate, and the goals panel. These elected policymakers would have to make nominations based on a set of appointment categories that clearly represented organized interests: professional educators; education experts; representative of business, labor, and postsecondary institutions; and the public and advocacy groups. Additional constraints further complicated the process: At least one member must represent business, but the other eighteen could all be educators; "to the extent feasible," NESIC should "reflect the diversity of the United

States" and "be equally divided between two major political parties"; and one-third must have "experience or background in the educational needs of children who are from low-income families, from minority backgrounds, have limited-English proficiency, or have disabilities."[31] The president had much latitude in determining whether the panel would be dominated by interest groups. Because NESIC was designed as a congressionally authorized federal agency, in future years lawmakers could continue to redefine and expand its functions and powers, as happened a few months later in the reauthorization of the Elementary and Secondary Education Act (ESEA). Under the new law, states could not receive federal funds for K-12 education until either the secretary of education or NESIC approved their state reform plans.

Following its authorization, the nomination process for NESIC proved slow and cumbersome. Less than two months following the enactment of Goals 2000, the department received more than three hundred nominations, with names flowing in daily. This growing list was supplemented by an internal solicitation of nominations from senior department officials who oversaw civil rights enforcement, bilingual education, adult and vocational education, and special education—all long-standing programs with special interests. The goals panel also culled through nearly two hundred names provided by panel members and interest groups, all requiring background checks. The process seemed to encourage interest group lobbying with its appointment categories and diversity considerations. For example, the National Alliance of Business openly expressed the hope that four or five business representatives would serve on NESIC. Concerned with maintaining the legitimacy of the standards review council, the governors wanted to see the "best and brightest" selected, particularly nationally recognized names, but also people still in the classroom and in schools. The nomination process backlogged. With a pending election in November, the president and Secretary Riley decided "to wait and see" and consequently found themselves facing a radically altered political landscape as they contemplated completing the appointment process. In late December 1994 as a last-ditch attempt to preserve their influence before the Republican Congress took charge, congressional leaders sent the president their nominations, with the secretary's following soon thereafter. But President Clinton was well aware that if he appointed NESIC in light of the forthcoming turnover in Congress, the council would have no legitimacy and would encounter numerous challenges to its establishment and efforts.[32]

As Congress debated Goals 2000, the media prophesied "standards in collision" and speculated that NESIC's first job would be to "introduce some order into the standards-setting process."[33] National standards development projects in arts, civics, geography, science, U.S. history, and social studies, which the Bush administration funded, released their documents late in 1994. In a parallel effort, states themselves were engaged in a bevy of standards-setting activities, as were several of the nation's largest school districts. Apprehension about the large number of organizations developing standards turned to concerns about the quality of work being produced and who could safeguard it. If in place, NESIC would review and certify the standards. But NESIC was still only an idea—stalled by its cumbersome nomination process. As the field awaited NESIC's appointment, other national groups volunteered to fill the void. These groups sought private funds to find "areas of commonality among various standards" and to rework them "into more manageable documents for teachers."[34]

While federal involvement might improve the situation, signs were that it might also aggravate it. Critics connected the poor quality of some of the national standards projects with their federal funding source. Federal financial and political support proved unreliable, as evidenced by the department's refusal to continue funding the national English language arts project, citing lack of progress. The release of the national history standards in November 1994 created a political furor, culminating in a 99-1 sense of the Senate resolution denouncing their political correctness and opposing their certification.[35] Although the history standards were subsequently revised to incorporate most of the concerns raised by critics, the controversy underscored the political difficulty of making standards "national." It also raised questions about the federal government's ability to address quality, especially in standards that were developed with federal assistance. (The history standards were revised based on the recommendations of a foundation-funded panel of experts, convened by the Council of Basic Education, a respected nonpartisan, not-for-profit, private organization.)

With the election of 1994, for the first time in forty years the GOP captured control of both houses of Congress. Republicans also gained control of nineteen state legislatures and a majority of governorships, reflecting a nationwide endorsement of their political platform.[36] In terms of education policy, it marked the Republicans' first time in power since the advent of all major federal K-12 education programs. They were determined to roll back the federal role in education, and Goals 2000 was their target: a "symbol in the larger ideological clash over state and federal rights." They believed that it would lead to a national curriculum set in Washington and that NESIC would set school-level policies, bringing the federal government right into their children's classrooms.[37]

As new Republican lawmakers descended upon Washington in January 1995, they exhibited remarkable cohesion. At the request of the new Speaker of the House, Newt Gingrich (R-Ga.), the conservative Heritage Foundation developed a briefing book for new lawmakers that called for the evaluation of every federal education program, the elimination of the federal education department over five years, and the "scrapping" of NESIC and the goals panel. Conservatives viewed the standards panels as "politically controlled" and feared that NESIC would essentially operate as a nineteen-member national school board.[38] The Christian Coalition charged that Goals 2000 would bring the federal government deeply into public schools, burden them with new regulations, and "bully them about how to teach everything from sex education to 'politically correct' history."[39]

Some conservative critics charged that the national standards movement had been "hijacked" by the education establishment of teachers, administrators, and other "politically correct" education experts. For these critics, the debate about education reform was too removed from parents and citizens. The nomination process for NESIC did not guarantee the participation of lay persons, reinforcing conservative claims that, as currently constructed, NESIC would facilitate the continued domination of education reform by education experts. Moreover, because the consensus-building process at the 1989 National Education Summit around goals occurred behind closed doors and the 1992 presidential campaign prompted little debate about education, as all three candidates endorsed national standards and examinations, public debate about national goals had been severely limited. Bipartisan support of education reform may have helped precipitate the conservative backlash.

Unlike the 103rd Congress, which simply wanted input into the design of the national goals and their related structures, conservative lawmakers entering the 104th Congress wanted it all eliminated. Within its first month in power the GOP-controlled Congress held hearings on the controversial history standards to air its dismay at the use of federal monies to create a national, as well as an unpatriotic, curriculum. The controversy over the history standards fueled conservative efforts not only to reevaluate NESIC, but also to eliminate it and any possibility that a federal entity outside the control of Congress could influence school curricula. The new chair of the House Education and Labor Committee, Representative William Goodling of Pennsylvania (a former principal and school superintendent), pledged to "rethink the whole thing—whether the federal role has already grown too large, whether we'll need NESIC."[40]

With NESIC under attack, only a few voices were raised in its defense. Speaking on behalf of the business community, the National Alliance of Business stressed the importance of bipartisan leadership in the standards-setting process and that such leadership should not be sacrificed to "any incidental political debate on structures or other issues." Gordon Ambach, executive director of the Council of Chief State School Officers, told Congress it would be a "terrible mistake" to eliminate NESIC, citing the need for an "objective and prestigious" national council to add legitimacy to the standards documents being developed by the states. But these voices were few. As Christopher Cross, president of the Council for Basic Education, observed, NESIC had "no real constituency" that considered its services vital. Existing educational organizations were already beginning to fill the void and provided feedback to states on their standards. Chester Finn observed that the "marketplace should make these judgments" with states and communities buying or rejecting standards as they see fit.[41]

In early 1995 Representative Goodling introduced legislation to eliminate NESIC as a way to "put a stop to an unwarranted federal intrusion into education while preserving education standards developed by State and local school districts." In presenting his proposal on the House floor, Goodling stated that NESIC "has generated great controversy about continued local control of education." He continued:

> The distance between standards and curriculum is not great. Currently there is a prohibition on the federal government dictating curriculum to States and school districts and there is good reason to be wary of Federal involvement in certifying education standards. The seriously flawed and justifiably controversial history standards illustrate how the standards-

setting process can go awry and point out the dangers of having a Presidentially appointed unaccountable body certifying education standards.

In spite of this controversy, Goodling pledged his support of standards-based reform as "the most promising strategy for improving education for all children in our Nation."[42] Understanding that the choice was now between saving NESIC and risking all of Goals 2000, Clinton and Riley signaled their acceptance of Goodling's bill, and NESIC was effectively dead.

The demise of NESIC did not end the discussion among the states about the need for some kind of credible external review body to which they could turn. Governor Romer of Colorado liked to wave his state's draft standards in the air at Washington meetings and say, "I may not need anyone to certify these standards, but I still need someone who can tell me how they stack up against those of other states and nations with whom we compete." This being America, three different private organizations jumped into the standards review business, and by the end of his term in office Governor Romer's new question was, how was he to make sense of the disparate grades Colorado standards received from the American Federation of Teachers, the Council for Basic Education, and the Thomas B. Fordham Foundation?[43]

The Balance Sheet

Has Goals 2000 been successful? The legislation begins by specifying the following purposes: "to improve learning and teaching by providing a national framework for education; to promote the research, consensus building, and systemic changes necessary to ensure equitable educational opportunities and high levels of educational achievement for all students; to provide a framework for reauthorization of all federal education programs."

If the principal measure of success is the degree to which a law fulfills its stated purpose, Goals 2000 deserves high marks. To begin with the easiest purpose to assess, Goals 2000 has provided a framework to guide the reauthorization of the Elementary and Secondary Education Act (retitled Improving America's Schools Act) and the Individuals with Disabilities Education Act (IDEA). In both cases the legislation has used the lever of common high academic standards with aligned assessments to challenge "the conspiracy of low expectations" that have led to watered-down academic programs for too many disadvantaged or disabled students. Both laws now push states and districts to include virtually all children within a single, coherent overall reform strategy and encourage schools to adopt schoolwide improvement strategies aimed at helping all students meet the same high standards of performance. Even the Higher Education Act reauthorization shows the influence of Goals 2000, in that teacher education programs will now be expected to prepare their students to teach in a standards-based environment.

The second purpose, promoting systemic changes aimed at both equalizing educational opportunities and improving achievement, is more difficult to measure. The evidence from the several reports cited earlier suggests that states and districts have used Goals 2000 funds to support the broad purposes of systemic reform, but the more important question is whether the kinds of reforms most states are putting in place, and the initiatives to which Goals 2000 funds are being directed, will improve equity and achievement.

The decentralized U.S. system perhaps inevitably results in at least fifty different answers to that question, depending not only on how far along the systemic reform path a state was in 1995 and how strategic it has been in the use of its Goals 2000 funds, but also on such fundamental issues as the quality of its standards and tests, the strength of its teacher preparation programs and professional development strategies, and the capacity of its state education department to mobilize useful technical assistance to low-performing districts and schools.

This leads to the larger question, which is how, if at all, judgments about the effectiveness of Goals 2000 can be disentangled from the assessment of the status and success of standards-based reform. In political terms the standards-based strategy has to be judged successful; it has become America's de facto national education strategy. Forty-five states as of 1999 have academic standards in place in the four core academic subjects, with four more states well along in the development process. Virtually all states are moving to align their assessments to their standards, with a majority of states reporting such assessments already in place. Seventeen states have professional development policies aligned to standards under development or in place. Thirty-six states issue report cards on district and school performance, and nineteen states have policies or programs in place to address the problem of persistently low-performing schools.[44] If "providing a national framework for educational reform" (the act's first stated purpose) is taken to mean providing a common vision of systemic reform for the states with higher academic standards for all, aligned assessments, and clearer accountability for results at the center of that vision, then the number of states that have adopted policies to move them in this direction in the last five years has to be taken as an extraordinary indicator of success.

But presumably the framers of the law had something more in mind by "providing a national framework" than offering up the national goals and an operational definition of systemic reform, for they sought to create a national reform leadership function through Title II. Part of that leadership function is provided by the National Education Goals Panel, which through its annual reports aims to keep public attention focused on national and state progress toward meeting the goals. But the more important part was to be able to provide guidance and feedback to the states on the quality of their reform and improvement strategies, beginning with their standards, and over time to help shape a more national consensus on how best to "ensure equality of educational opportunities and high levels of educational achievement for all students." The loss of NESIC crippled the government's ability to impose some measure of quality control on what has become essentially a block grant program for state and local systemic reform. Without some mechanism for establishing and implementing performance standards for states, some way to help them know whether their standards, tests, and implementation strategies are "good enough," the national leadership function envisioned in the act cannot be fulfilled.

The loss of NESIC may have signaled the political difficulty of creating a federal mechanism for providing quality control for what is essentially a state-based movement, but NESIC's demise is hardly the end of the story. In 1996 the nation's governors, led by two Charlottesville veterans (Tommy Thompson of Wisconsin and Bob Miller of Nevada) came together with fifty corporate chief executives at a second National Education Summit, this time in Palisades, New York, to renew their commitment to raise standards and improve academic performance in their states. At this summit there was no longer any talk of national standards—even President Clinton, the invited luncheon speaker, asserted his conviction that standard setting must be left to the states—but there was significant discussion about the continuing need of states to have some way to benchmark their standards and tests against the best national and international work. Out of this summit came a decision to create a new organization, Achieve, to respond to this need.

Other organizations were already attempting to fill one piece of the NESIC vacuum, the rating of state standards, and a consortium of state-based organizations led by the Council of Chief State School Officers came together to provide advice and assistance to states on standards issues. Achieve focused its initial efforts on the development of a rigorous benchmarking process to provide states an in-depth analysis of the quality and rigor of their standards and the alignment between their standards and tests. By the end of 1999, six states will have been through Achieve's benchmarking process, with several more states in the pipeline.

Achieve came into being at least in part as a private sector alternative to NESIC, designed to help states move toward a common standard for assessing the quality of their reform strategies. Given the tensions that developed between the governors and both Congress and the administration during the Goals 2000 legislative process, it is conceivable that even if NESIC had survived the governors would have sought to develop a standards review vehicle more responsive to state needs and interests. Resistance runs deep to the federal government's assuming any role that touches on the academic core of what is taught and learned, as was evident again in 1997 when the administration's voluntary national testing proposal ran aground in Congress. As with the review of standards, the states seem to prefer a bottom-up strategy for getting comparative data about student performance, as witness the ten-state consortium that has recently formed under Achieve's sponsorship to develop a joint middle grades mathematics improvement project, with a common syllabus, professional development strategy, and assessment.

Achieve's early experience in promoting rigorous external reviews of state standards and cross-state collaboration on curriculum and assessment issues is only the latest example of a private nongovernmental agency exercising national education leadership in ways that are difficult for the federal government, at least in the current political climate. By and large, the strongest "nationalizing" forces fueling the movement for higher standards have been such nongovernmental entities as the National Board for Professional Teaching Standards, the National Center on Education and the Economy, the American Federation of Teachers, The

Business Roundtable, and the major disciplinary organizations such as the National Council of Teachers of Mathematics. Some of these organizations receive federal funds; others, such as Achieve, are privately funded. The common denominator is that they can assert a national interest in education without having to defend themselves against the charge of wanting to become a national school board. As long as the federal education agenda is limited to the protection of particular groups of underserved students or clearly identifiable and circumscribed national problems, the federal government can assert the national interest without raising red flags. When the agenda shifts to programs aimed at raising academic achievement for all students, the underlying ambivalence about the federal role comes to the fore, and the distinction between federal and national takes on greater significance. The governors and their allies in the states have the political legitimacy to call for a national education strategy, as they have done since the mid-1980s, without triggering anxieties about the erosion of state and local control, for it goes without saying that they will protect state sovereignty. The federal government almost by definition does not enjoy that trust and legitimacy in advocating for a national education strategy, and it is difficult to imagine circumstances in which the federal government will be allowed to assume a more activist leadership role in what continues to be a state-based systemic reform movement.

What Next?

On balance, Goals 2000 has succeeded in accomplishing much of its core mission. It was designed to catch the wave of a predominantly state-based movement and to provide flexible funds to help states do better and faster what most were already committed to do anyhow. Despite the political controversy that swirled around it in its first years, Goals 2000 has proven to be an immensely popular program in the states, precisely because it is so flexible and has so few constraints on the expenditure of its funds. It has had, as its architects hoped, a significant impact on the redesign of Title I and the other large-dollar federal programs. For all of these reasons, it would be eminently defensible for the Clinton administration to declare victory and withdraw. Virtually all the states are now well launched on the reform path Goals 2000 was created to support, and those that are still back at the starting line are unlikely to be much influenced by additional rounds of modest federal funding.

If one asks more difficult questions, however, and reminds oneself that the fundamental purpose of systemic reform, and of Goals 2000, is "to ensure equitable educational opportunities and high levels of educational achievement for all students," then it ought to be obvious that this movement is still in its infancy and that by and large most states and districts have barely begun to put in place the kinds of changes in curriculum, instruction, teacher preparation, professional development, and school organization that will be necessary if higher standards are going to lead to better performance. Preliminary indications are that standards-based reforms, if implemented thoughtfully and sustained over several years, can produce significant gains in student performance. The recent goals panel-sponsored RAND report on the factors underlying the rapid achievement gains in North Carolina and Texas has captured significant attention among state policymakers, as has Richard Elmore and Deanna Burney's analysis of the instructional improvement strategies that have led to such impressive results over the last several years in New York City's Community District 2.[45]

With a relative handful of exceptions, however, most states and school districts have barely begun to address the formidable implementation challenges presented by the adoption of new standards, and in too many jurisdictions the standards themselves are so problematic that they are not worth aligning with.

The range of issues that will be front and center in the next phase of standards-based reform—how to build capacity for continuous organizational learning, how to address the most fundamental opportunity-to-learn issues for the kids who are furthest behind, how to substantially strengthen the knowledge and skills of the education work force—are probably best addressed in federal policies not through an extension of the relatively open-ended, "responsible block grant" provisions of Title III of Goals 2000, but through the more focused, targeted large-dollar programs in ESEA. If a continuing role exists for Goals 2000—and we confess to ambivalence on this score—it is in keeping before the country the unifying vision represented by the goals themselves and in asserting the need for continuing national leadership and direction for the systemic reform movement. Instead of proposing the creation of new federal mechanisms to provide such leadership, perhaps any new legislation should identify the kinds of issues on which states and districts are most in need of credible advice and assistance, put resources to seek such help in the hands of states, and allow the market to do its work. In such a strategy, special incentives should be offered to encourage collaboration and peer learning across states, and perhaps even across national boundaries. Education has clearly become a major national issue, but in the U.S. system, for better or worse, it remains a state and local responsibility. The lessons of the past decade, in particular the path from Charlottesville through Goals 2000 to the present, are that a national education strategy has to be driven by the states, working in conjunction with a wide variety of nongovernmental national organizations. It may be awkward, inefficient, messy, and, from an international perspective, irrational, but it seems to be the way Americans do education.

Comment by Michael W. Kirst

Robert B. Schwartz and Marian A. Robinson offer a significant contribution to the historical understanding of the federal role in establishing and moving toward national goals. The Goals 2000 legislative debate was the most high-profile initiative of the early Clinton administration but has faded from the limelight as the administration and the Republican Congress have pursued other issues. I agree with the authors that it would be best for the administration to declare victory (whether justified or not) and move on to new grant approaches. Goals 2000 has been lost as a Clinton priority and overtaken by more general aid strategies such as class-size reduction and school construction. The year 2000 is almost here, so another target date is needed to meet the goals if this focus is to continue.

As the paper reveals, it is impossible to isolate the distinctive contribution of Goals 2000 legislation to the rapid spread of standards-based state and local policy. Goals 2000 has helped, but how much is uncertain. The state-level funding was only 10 percent of the total, but it added flexible state money for test and standards development as well as systemic initiatives that state categoricals rarely permit. But 90 percent of the money was allocated to local school districts and its effectiveness was problematic. The General Accounting Office did not provide the authors with the grant applications, and the summary statistics do not reveal much. The California local grants were often add-on projects that did not focus on broad Goals 2000 activities or systemic reform. Small amounts of Goals 2000 money could easily get lost in a blizzard of state initiatives in California and other states. As education has become the nation's top issue, states have passed many bills to fix education, in addition to Goals 2000.

Goals 2000 was headed in the same direction as the recent intensive state reform activity on standards. Goals 2000 reinforced three key reforms that have had mixed results:

1. Challenging academic standards for what all students should know and be able to do. Forty-six states by 1999 had done this in most academic subjects—a remarkable change in the historic state role.
2. Aligning policies—such as testing, teacher certification, and professional development—and accountability programs to state standards. All states but Iowa and Nebraska had statewide student achievement tests in 1999, and most were addressing the other systemic components.
3. Restructuring the governance system to delegate overtly to schools and districts the responsibility for developing specific instructional approaches that meet the broadly worded academic standards for which the state holds them accountable. Only a handful of states have done this.

Known as standards-based systemic reform, the overarching objectives of this policy approach are to foster student mastery of more rigorous, challenging academic content and to increase the emphasis on its application. More data are available on what states did to galvanize standards-based reform than local districts, but local districts got 90 percent of the Goals 2000 money.

Goals 2000 was one aspect of a multipronged federal strategy to stimulate systemic standards-based reform. The National Education Goals Panel (NEGP) began in 1991 to monitor progress on meeting the education goals that came out of the 1989 Charlottesville, Virginia, education summit between President George Bush and the governors. But the NEGP role is not clearly linked in the paper to the Goals 2000 legislative evolution. Is there a rationale for continuing NEGP as a separate federal organizational unit, or should it fade away like Goals 2000? It is not clear why the U.S. Education Department—specifically, its National Center for Education Statistics—could not update progress toward the goals after 2000, which is the main task of NEGP.

Goals 2000 legislation was eclipsed in 1995 by Clinton support for a voluntary national test (VNT). This proposed fourth-grade reading and eighth-grade math test, however, has never been authorized, because of bipartisan opposition. Clinton tried to use the VNT as another installment in the attempt to enhance the federal role in standard setting. A logical successor to Goals 2000, it ended up stymied by a rare congressional coalition of conservative Republicans, blacks, and Hispanics. The Republicans were wary of excessive federal control from the VNT, and the minority Democrats were concerned about lack of opportunity to learn the content of the federal test in low-income schools.

This inability to build a federal policy upon and around Goals 2000 has left a murky view of the proper federal role. Goals 2000 envisioned the federal role as featuring systemic reform. Consequently, recent reconsideration of the systemic concept has added to the political problems associated with aligning national tests with national standards. The current federal role is a mélange of categorical widgets that have accumulated over the past thirty-five years. In 1970 the federal role seemed to focus upon special-needs students (Title I, handicapped, bilingual) rather than general unrestricted aid to schools. But recent Clinton initiatives are general-aid oriented, such as class-size reduction and construction. Even more narrow categories are increasing such as after-school and computer grants. Goals 2000 clearly has not been an overall framework for a new and improved federal role. Standards-based reform began at the state level in the 1980s, briefly was a federal issue through Goals 2000 and the VNT, and now appears to have returned to the states for the foreseeable future. The federal role remains confused and opportunistic, but Goals 2000 does not seem to be the answer to the problems.

Comment by David L. Kirp

For more than thirty years, the idea of a national education strategy has been bruited by academics and public officials. Yet, while Washington has reshaped specific policy domains—the education of the handicapped is one example, racial discrimination another—no overall strategy has been adopted. Goals 2000, the major education initiative of the first Clinton administration, was meant to change that.

Robert B. Schwartz and Marian A. Robinson conclude that this effort has been a real, albeit mixed, success. My reading of the evidence, including the material the paper presents, is more pessimistic. Strategy, even something akin to systemic reform, may exist in certain instances, and standards are a critical component of that strategy. But it is at the state, not the federal, level that the push for standards, as part of a larger vision of change, was initiated in the 1980s; and it is at the state, not the federal, level that the movement has blossomed.

The current federal undertaking has spawned too many diverse programs with too little coherence to be characterized as a strategy. Far from embodying the New Deal or the Great Society redux, Goals 2000 is simply another example of the varieties of state initiative-taking—what Louis Brandeis called the laboratories of democracy in action. The kindest reading of the Goals 2000 story is that Washington has been a cheerleader, occasionally a booster, in this effort. A less charitable view would treat the doings inside the Beltway as essentially irrelevant.

The idea of systemic reform, first put in place by Bill Honig in California and later fleshed out in a series of influential articles by Marshall S. Smith and Jennifer O'Day, represented a radical departure from the conventional education policy wisdom. The received view, developed by Charles E. Lindblom and Herbert Simon, among others, holds that change is almost invariably incremental in character: Policymakers do not optimize, they satisfy.[46] By contrast, systemic reform is far more ambitious in its intention to align the various elements of education policy, including standards, curriculum, textbooks, assessment, and training. Implicit in this approach is the belief that to do good incrementally, as through the proliferation of categorical programs, might be the enemy of the (systemic) best. As well, the strategy for effecting systemic change has been drawn from the "reinventing government" school of thought.[47] Good management practice, carried out by smart entrepreneurial professionals, is supposed to carry the day. Politics is conspicuously absent from this analysis.

In the design of real policies, however, politics is present in all its messiness—hence the jibe about the similarities between politics and sausage making. Although a goals and standards agenda was advanced during the Bush administration, it was never taken up in Congress. A window of opportunity opened briefly with the 1992 election of Bill Clinton.[48] By the time that window had shut, Congress had authorized funds for Goals 2000, $2 billion to date, to encourage state and district innovation. But the idea of a national policy was a nonstarter, as were national standards; even a voluntary national test conjured visions of Washington as schoolmaster.

What happened in the states and school districts following passage of the Goals 2000 legislation is far less readily summarized—inevitably so, given the design of the legislation. At the state level, where 25 percent of the money was allocated, federal aid sometimes contributed to reforms that were already being implemented. In those instances, Washington could claim credit (a favorite activity of politicians), but the federal aid amounted to no more than piling on.[49] Elsewhere, Goals 2000 changed the rhetoric but not the behavior of state agencies. Only in a handful of states, those on the cusp of change, has the Goals 2000 money made a difference, and even those effects are hard to specify. The General Accounting Office report on the program does not make a convincing case.

At the district level, where the bulk of the money has been spent, the impact of the legislation is even harder to estimate. More than sixteen thousand school districts have received slices of the Goals 2000 pie, some getting as little as $25, and they have used it for an endless array of programs, from installation of new technology to restructuring. The proliferation of activities subsidized by Goals 2000 funds means that the program is really an umbrella under which seemingly any money-spending scheme can be situated. The response of the school districts has not been a random phenomenon. Districts' willingness to change policy direction is a key factor, as is their capacity to change. Hard-pressed urban school districts are, because of their disorganization, least able to take advantage of this potential opportunity to reinvent themselves, while smaller and more stable districts can extract the most from these marginal dollars. This is a familiar phenomenon in the implementation of any policy innovation—Chicago's school reforms, for instance, or Arizona's charter schools—that depends on a bottom-up strategy of change.[50] Almost invariably, the best do better while the gap widens between best and worst. To them who have, more shall be given, as the Book of Matthew says; the more, the more, in contemporary argot.

Another important if familiar lesson from the Goals 2000 experience is that states and school districts are much better at redesigning organizations, or at least organizational charts, than they are at setting standards. And they are much, much better at setting standards than at holding anyone—students, teachers, administrators—accountable for failing to meet those standards. Stories of reconstituted schools or school districts placed in state receivership make headlines because they are rarities. Changing practice in the high-visibility, high-stakes world of education is a lot harder than rearranging the proverbial deck chairs.

The ultimate goal of Goals 2000 is to boost academic performance. All the other changes, from better texts to reinvigorated teacher training, represent means to that end. But how could anyone even begin to measure the impact of such an amorphous program on student achievement? Why would anyone contemplate that Goals 2000 might be one of those unusual instances when the null hypothesis was shown to be wrong, when there was a discernible and sustained impact of government policy on student performance? In this context, the strategy of Goals 2000, described by New York senator Daniel Patrick Moynihan years ago and in a not dissimilar context as "feeding the sparrows by feeding the horses," is hardly promising. Goals 2000 has had no apparent impact on achievement, except perhaps in those states and school districts where the standardized tests drive everything in the academic life of the school.

Predicting the future is hazardous business. The best-case scenario looks like this: Prodded by parental and political pressure, states do a better job of setting meaningful standards of achievement; those standards are vetted by a national agency; and accountability for failure, on the part of both students and professionals, becomes more widely accepted. For all the high hopes surrounding Goals 2000, the federal role will remain marginal. The emerging policy is federal, not national, in character, with fifty flowers blooming in the garden of education. The Clinton administration has already moved on. Its 1999 education initiatives, including reducing class size and building new schools, have nothing to do with Goals 2000, while for his part, Vice President Al Gore seems fixated on Internet access—closing the "digital divide."

In short, the idea of incremental change, which systemic reform was meant to bury, turns out to be alive and thriving. Such changes, rather than the brave new world of systemic reform, represent the most likely legacy of education's nearly two-decades-long run on the national policy stage.[51]

Notes

1. Education Commission of the States, *Action in the States* (Denver, Colo., 1984).

2. National Governors' Association, *Time for Results: The Governors' 1986 Report on Education* (Washington, 1986).

3. For a comprehensive description of the Bush-Alexander strategy, see *America 2000: An Education Strategy* (Department of Education, 1991).

4. John F. Jennings, *Why National Standards and Tests?* (Thousand Oaks, Calif.: Sage, 1998).

5. National Council on Education Standards and Testing, *Raising Standards for American Education: A Report to Congress, the Secretary of Education, the National Education Goals Panel, and the American People* (Government Printing Office, January 24, 1992).

6. See Marshall S. Smith and Jennifer O'Day, "Systemic School Reform," in S. Fuhrman and B. Malen, eds., *The Politics of Curriculum and Testing* (Bristol, Pa.: Falmer Press, 1991); and Jennifer O'Day and Marshall S. Smith, "Systemic Reform and Educational Opportunity," in S. Fuhrman, ed., *Designing Coherent Education Policy* (San Francisco, Calif.: Jossey-Bass, 1993).

7. In a speech delivered at a Brookings Education Policy Conference in 1994, Marshall S. Smith, then undersecretary of education, said: "*State* [italics in original] content and performance standards that establish challenging academic expectations for all students are the heart of the Administration's systemic reform strategy." See Marshall S. Smith, "Education Reform in America's Public Schools: The Clinton Agenda," in Diane Ravitch, ed., *Debating the Future of American Education: Do We Need National Standards and Assessments?* (Brookings, 1995).

8. P.L. 103–227, Title III.

9. As of October 25, 1995, Alabama, Montana, New Hampshire, Oklahoma, and Virginia chose not to participate in Goals 2000. The 1996 amendments to the law attracted the remaining states by (1) eliminating the requirement that states submit their reform plans to the secretary of education for approval; (2) permitting districts to apply directly to the secretary for funding, provided they have approval to participate from their state education agency; and (3) permitting the use of Goals 2000 funds for technology. Alabama, New Hampshire, and Virginia joined Goals 2000 at the state level. Montana and Oklahoma allowed their local educational agencies to apply directly to the Department of Education for their respective Goals 2000 allotment, with the department distributing funds on a competitive basis. Since 1996, all states, the District of Columbia, and U.S. territories, in some form, have been participating in Goals 2000. See the funding history of the Goals 2000 program in Department of Education, *Goals 2000: Reforming Education to Improve Student Achievement,* report to Congress (Department of Education, Office of Elementary and Secondary Education, April 30, 1998).

10. General Accounting Office, *Goals 2000: Flexible Funding Supports State and Local Education Reform,* HEHS–99–10 (Washington, November 1998).

11. From the Council of Chief State School Officers, *Goals 2000: Educate America Act State Profiles* (Washington: Council of Chief State School Officers, State Leadership Center, November 1995); Council of Chief State School Officers, *Status Report State Systemic Education Improvements*, under the State Education Improvement Partnership (Washington, September 1998); and Texas State Department of Education, *Texas America 2000* (http://www.tea.state.tx.us/A2000/, cited April 7, 1999).

12. General Accounting Office, Goals 2000, pp. 8–13; and Department of Education, *Goals 2000*, p. 10.

13. General Accounting Office, *Goals 2000*, p. 26.

14. From the General Accounting Office, *Ed-Flex States Vary in Implementation of Waiver Process,* HEHS–99–17 (Washington, November 1998); Texas State Department of Education, *Texas America 2000*; and General Accounting Office, *Goals 2000*, p. 26.

15. General Accounting Office, *Goals 2000*, p. 14.

16. Leslie M. Anderson and Brenda J. Turnbull, *Living in Interesting Times: Early State Implementation of New Federal Education Laws*, prepared by Policy Studies Associates for the Department of Education, Planning and Evaluation Service, under Contract EA94053001 (Government Printing Office, October 1998).

17. Anderson and Turnbull, *Living in Interesting Times,* p. viii.

18. Policy Studies Associates, *Synthesis of 1997 Goals 2000 State Annual Performance Reports* (Washington, March 1999).

19. Jane Hannaway and Kristi Kimball, *Reports on Reform from the Field: District and State Survey Results*, prepared by the Urban Institute for the Department of Education, Planning and Evaluation Service, under Contract EA94053001 (Government Printing Office, 1997).

20. Hannaway and Kimball, *Reports on Reform from the Field.*

21. General Accounting Office, *Goals 2000.*

22. P.L. 103–227, Section 2, Purpose.

23. National Council on Education Standards and Testing, *Raising Standards for American Education.*

24. Washington Roundup, "Group Urges 'Hitting the Brakes' on National Test," *Education Week* (January 29, 1992).

25. Julie A. Miller, "Legislation to Create National System of Standards, Assessments under Fire," *Education Week* (March 25, 1992); and Diane Ravitch, *National Standards in American Education: A Citizen's Guide* (Brookings, 1995), p. 146.

26. Congressional Quarterly, *Congressional Quarterly Annual Almanac* (Washington, 1993), p. 3.

27. Ravitch, *National Standards in American Education,* p. 154.

28. Jennings, *Why National Standards and Tests?,* pp. 56–58; Julie A. Miller, "Administration Readies Reform, Assessment Bill," *Education Week* (March 24, 1993); and Ravitch, *National Standards in American Education*, pp. 150–52.

29. Carroll A. Campbell Jr., governor of South Carolina, letter to Richard W. Riley, U.S. secretary of education, June 3, 1993, quoted in Ravitch, *National Standards in American Education*, p. 152.

30. Carroll A. Campbell Jr., governor of South Carolina, letter to Bill Clinton, president of the United States, March 1, 1994, quoted in Ravitch, *National Standards in American Education*, p. 153.

31. P.L. 103–227, Part B, Section 212, National Education Standards and Improvement Council.

32. Lynn Olson, "Board Seen Setting Tone for Standards Efforts," *Education Week* (May 18, 1994); and Lynn Olson, "Two Months and Counting: Naming of Standards Panel Behind Schedule," *Education Week* (November 2, 1994).

33. Debra Viadero, "Standards in Collision," *Education Week* (January 19, 1994).

34. Groups volunteering to fill the National Education Standards and Improvement Council (NESIC) void included the Council for Basic Education, the Council of Chief State School Officers, and the National Center for Improving Science Education. See Viadero, "Standards in Collision."

35. Karen Diegmueller, "Backlash Puts Standards Work in Harm's Way," *Education Week* (January 11, 1995); and S. Res. 66, *Congressional Record,* January 20, 1995, p. S1282.

36. Congressional Quarterly, *Congressional Quarterly Annual Almanac* (Washington, 1994); and Karen Diegmueller, "Standards: Running Out of Steam," *Education Week* (April 12, 1995).

37. For the historic significance of the 104th Congress, see Congressional Quarterly, *Congressional Quarterly Annual Almanac* (Washington, 1995), pp. 1–3. Rene Sanchez, "GOP's Power of the Purse Put to the Test: Education Goals Program Targeted for Early Demise," *Washington Post,* September 26, 1995, p. A1.

38. Lynn Olson, "G.O.P. Victories Energize Conservative Think Tanks," *Education Week* (December 7, 1994); and Lynn Olson, "Undo School Programs, Heritage Urges," *Education Week* (December 7, 1994).

39. Sanchez, "GOP's Power of the Purse Put to the Test," p. A1; and Linda Feldman, "Conservatives Question 'True Goal' of Goals 2000 Education Guidelines," *Christian Science Monitor,* June 8, 1995, p. 1.

40. Lynn Olson, "Bills to Scrap NESIC Likely to Hold Sway," *Education Week* (February 8, 1995); and Diegmueller, "Backlash Puts Standards Work in Harm's Way."

41. Jennings, *Why National Standards and Tests?,* p. 161; and Lynn Olson, "The Future Looks Cloudy for Standards-Certification Panel," *Education Week* (January 11, 1995).

42. *Congressional Record,* February 24, 1995, p. E432.

43. See American Federation of Teachers, *Making Standards Matter* (Washington, 1998); Scott Joftus and Ilene Berman, *Great Expectations?: Defining and Assessing Rigor in State Standards for Mathematics and English Language Arts* (Washington: Council for Basic Education, January 1998); and Chester E. Finn, Michael J. Petrille, and Gregg Vanourek, *The State of State Standards* (Washington: Thomas B. Fordham Foundation, July 1998).

44. "Quality Counts: Rewarding Results, Punishing Failure," special report, *Education Week* (January 11, 1999); and "The State of the States: A Progress Report," in *1999 National Education Summit: Briefing Book*, prepared for the 1999 National Education Summit, sponsored by Achieve Inc., held in Palisades, N.Y., September 30–October 1, 1999.

45. David Grissmer and Ann Flanagan, *Exploring Rapid Achievement Gains in North Carolina and Texas* (Washington: National Education Goals Panel, November 1998); and Richard Elmore and Deanna Burney, *Investing in Teacher Learning: Staff Development and Instructional Improvement in Community School District # 2, New York City* (New York: National Commission on Teaching and America's Future, August 1997).

46. See, for example, Charles E. Lindblom, *The Intelligence of Democracy: Decision-making through Mutual Adjustment* (New York: Free Press, 1965); and Herbert Simon, *Administrative Behavior* (New York: Free Press, 1976). See also Hugh Heclo, *A Government of Strangers* (Brookings, 1977); and Robert Behn, "Management by Groping Along," *Journal of Policy Analysis and Management*, vol. 8, no. 3 (1988), pp. 643–63.

47. David Osborne and Ted Gaebler, *Reinventing Government* (New York: Perseus, 1992).

48. John Kingdon, *Agendas, Alternatives, and Public Policies* (New York: Addison Wesley, 1995).

49. Eugene Bardach, *The Skill Factor in Politics* (Berkeley and Los Angeles: University of California Press, 1972).

50. Richard Elmore, "Backward Mapping: Implementation Research and Policy Decisions," *Political Science Quarterly*, vol. 94, no. 4 (1979–80), pp. 69–83.

51. The other major legacy is the movement to greater choice in education, whether through intra- and inter-district public school options, the explosion of charter schools, or the revival of vouchers.

The Federal Bilingual Education Program

CHRISTINE H. ROSSELL

Since the 1960s, the U.S. Department of Education has enthusiastically embraced bilingual education. At the time this love affair began, no research evidence supported bilingual education as the best means for limited-English proficient (LEP) children to learn English and other subjects that a child will be tested on in English. Nor did any agreement exist on the definition of the target population or even on what bilingual education is. Some thirty years later, there still is no consistent evidence available to support bilingual education as the best means for LEP children to learn English and other subjects that they will be tested on in English, nor any agreement on the definition of the target population or bilingual education. Yet, the federal government's enthusiasm for bilingual education seems undiminished.

What is bilingual education? There are currently three different basic instructional programs for LEP students: (1) native tongue instruction, characterized by learning to read and write in the native tongue and learning subject matter in the native tongue and eventually transitioning to English, (2) structured immersion—all-English instruction in a self-contained classroom containing English language learners, and (3) regular classroom instruction with English as a Second Language (ESL) instruction in a pullout setting—all being implemented in school districts around the country and all called "bilingual education" by federal, state, and local administrators, legislators, reporters, and educators.[1] Only the Spanish speakers, however, are receiving bilingual education through native tongue instruction, according to the theory (the program described above), and not even all of them are. Thus, there is no single treatment called "bilingual education" that is implemented in the same way and understood to be the same thing by everyone.

The Origin of Title VII

Bilingual education began as a part of the civil rights movement of the 1960s. Senator Ralph W. Yarborough (D-Texas) catalyzed Hispanic support for federal intervention on behalf of linguistic minority students by painting a picture of Hispanics as disadvantaged minorities who had been the victims of discrimination. In the 1960s, an almost 40 percentage point gap in high school completion rates existed between whites and Hispanics, favoring whites, and an almost 10 percentage point gap existed between blacks and Hispanics, favoring blacks. Given that Hispanic immigrant children were all being taught in English, the problem seemed obvious to their advocates. Instruction in English was the cause of their low achievement, and the loss of their native tongue was a civil rights violation that could be remedied by bilingual education.

Congress embraced this logic by passing three statutes that addressed the educational and civil rights of linguistic minority students: (1) the Bilingual Education Act of 1968, also known as Title VII of the Elementary and Secondary Education Act (ESEA), (2) Title VI of the Civil Rights Act of 1964, and (3) the Equal Educational Opportunities Act (EEOA) of 1970. Administrative agencies, such as the Office for Civil Rights (OCR) and the Office of Bilingual Education and Minority Language Affairs (OBEMLA), were created as a result of this legislation and directed to implement these provisions.[2] The federal courts also reviewed several lawsuits brought by language minorities claiming that school districts had violated these federal laws by ignoring the language barrier.[3]

The 1968 Bilingual Education Act was the first and most important piece of federal legislation devoted exclusively to the needs of language minority students. Although the 1964 Civil Rights Act and the 1965 Elementary and Secondary Education Act dealt with the problems of children disadvantaged by segregation and poverty, Hispanics and their advocates felt they were uniquely disadvantaged by language and culture and that this was not addressed in programs for poor children and children of color.

Hispanic advocates had high hopes for the 1968 Bilingual Education Act, but in the end, it was nothing more than a modest grant-in-aid program designed to promote research and experimentation in bilingual education. The policy declared:

> In recognition of the special educational needs of the large numbers of children of limited English-speaking ability in the United States, Congress hereby declares it to be the policy of the United States to provide *financial* [emphasis added] assistance to local educational agencies to develop and carry out new and imaginative elementary and secondary school programs designed to meet these special educational needs. (Section 702)

School districts that did not want federal funds did not have to implement bilingual education or any other program for limited-English proficient children. Nor were the federal funds at that time sufficient to be much of a carrot, because the amount of money authorized for the fiscal year ending June 30, 1968, was a mere $15 million, increasing to $30 million in fiscal 1969 and $40 million in fiscal 1970.

Defining the Eligible Population

The original bill filed by Senator Yarborough identified the eligible population as Spanish speakers. This met with considerable opposition, and so the final bill encompassed all language groups:[4]

> For the purposes of this title, "children of limited English-speaking ability" means children who come from environments where the dominant language is other than English. (Section 702)

Because some children who come from non-English-speaking families are fluent in English and high in achievement, this definition broadened the target group considerably.

Title VII was reauthorized in 1974, 1978, 1984, 1988, and 1994 and will be reauthorized again in 1999. The 1974 amendments (section 703) narrowed the definition of the eligible population to those who were of "limited-English-speaking ability," not just from a non-English-speaking family. The 1978 amendments changed the term to "limited English proficiency" (section 7003) and added American Indians and Alaskan Natives to the eligible population of students. The 1978 amendments also added reading and writing to the difficulties children might have in English that would deny them the opportunity to learn successfully in classrooms where the language of instruction is English.

The 1984, 1988, and 1994 reauthorizations did not change this definition in any important way, and the amount of funds to be allocated has continued to depend on the number of LEP students claimed by a school district. The general presumption of Title VII has been that determining who is LEP is a rational process. The 1994 reauthorization requires no specific identification or assessment procedures, and the Clinton administration's 1999 proposal to reauthorize the Elementary and Secondary Education Act is similarly silent.[5] In their grant applications, school districts simply have to present data on the number of children and youth of limited-English proficiency in the school or school district to be served and their characteristics, such as language spoken, dropout rates, proficiency in English and the native language, academic standing in relation to the English-proficient peers of such children and youth, and, where applicable, the recency of immigration.

The only problem identified in the legislation is the consistency of national estimates, and this only surfaced in the last reauthorization. The 1994 act specified in section 7132 (b) (3) that the secretary of education may establish (through the National Center for Education Statistics in consultation with experts in bilingual education, second language acquisition, and English as a Second Language) a common definition of limited-English proficient students for purposes of national data collection.

Neither the 1994 legislation nor the Clinton administration's 1999 proposal recognized that, because school districts receive more money for students if they are identified as LEP, a fiscal incentive exists to overidentify. The Clinton proposal dutifully recites a Council of Chief State School Officers' report that, between 1990 and 1997, the number of LEP students increased by 57 percent to roughly 3.4 million and the LEP population more than doubled in eighteen states.[6] These statistics are cited as unimpeachable proof of the need for federal aid to school districts with LEP students.

The fiscal incentive to overidentify comes not only from federal funds, which are about 7 percent of funding for public schools, but also from state funds tied to the number of LEP students.[7] State funds are almost half of school district revenues. Because a below-average student brings in more state and federal revenues if he or she is identified as LEP, a rational actor will want to identify such a student as LEP.[8]

But the problem of identifying LEP students is bigger than simply a fiscal incentive to overidentify. The procedures used by school districts to identify students as limited-English proficient are inherently illogical. And they cannot be made logical.

The selection procedures used by school districts are reducible to two steps: (1) a home language survey is administered to all students to identify the pool of potential LEP students; and (2) the students identified in the home language survey are tested on several measures of academic performance and are classified accordingly.

The decision to exit a student from bilingual education or special language assistance involves procedures similar to those used to determine eligibility. Students are reclassified as fluent-English proficient (FEP) if they score at or above a certain percentile on an English language test that has been normed on an English-speaking population. The decision to reclassify is tempered by staff judgment, either the child's classroom teacher or a team of professionals employed by the school district.

The Home Language Identification Survey

The home language survey is the first step in the process of identification of LEP students. The Boston home language survey is typical of those used by school districts around the country. It asks parents to fill in basic demographic data such as their country of birth and highest grade completed and to indicate the language they understand best. Parents are asked to respond to the following questions about the home environment:

1. What language(s) are spoken and/or understood by people living in your home?
2. What was the first language your child spoke?
3. What language does your child use when speaking with you?
4. What language does your child use when speaking with brothers and sisters?
5. What language does your child use when speaking with other family members?
6. What language does your child use when speaking with friends in the neighborhood?

If a parent's answer is a language other than English for any one of these questions, the child is considered potentially LEP and referred for testing. In other words, if a parent answers English and Cantonese to question 1, but English only to all other questions, the child is referred for testing even though he or she speaks only English.

The New York City home language survey is similar but has two additional questions about the language the child reads and the language the child writes in. The questions about language use are a little more discriminating in that they are modified by the clause "most of the time." The scoring process is a little more complicated as well. But the outcome is the same. A child who reads and writes only in English can be classified as potentially LEP simply because English and Cantonese are spoken in the child's home most of the time. In short, the home language survey does not try to determine if the child in question is fluent in English. The wording of the questions are intentionally broad because their goal is to identify children who come from language minority backgrounds, not children who are limited in English.

Norm-Referenced Tests

The overinclusiveness of the home language survey would not be a problem if the subsequent steps accurately identified who was not fluent in English. Unfortunately, they do not. However, were it not for the home language survey, many fluent-English-speaking children would be classified as LEP by the tests that are used.

Children identified by the home language survey must take a standardized test normed on an English-speaking population. The first norm-referenced test they take is an English proficiency test. If they pass the English proficiency test, they may take a standardized achievement test of reading, language, and math in English. If they are Spanish speakers, they may also take these tests in Spanish. These are the same tests LEP students will take later when being evaluated for reclassification as fluent-English speakers.

A point on this normal curve—typically between the 20th and the 50th percentile—is selected as the point at which a student is defined as limited-English proficient. Given that the tests are normed on an English-speaking population, it is not possible for all students to achieve the score that classifies them as fluent-English proficient even if they know no language other than English. If the classification criterion is the 36th percentile, at a minimum 36 percent of the children who take the norm-referenced test will always be classified as LEP even if they are fluent in English and they will never be reclassified no matter how good the program is. This is a mathematical principle.

An important question is why do so many school administrators establish criteria for limited-English proficient students that cannot be met even by all of the English-speaking norming population? One reason is ignorance. Educators seem to have been misled by the constant criticism they receive from intellectuals, policymakers, and reporters who castigate them for such sins as having "only half their students at grade level." In my discussions with school personnel, I have found them to be almost universally ignorant of the fact that nationally it is only possible to have half the student population at grade level.[9]

Another reason that people adopt a standard for LEP students that cannot be met by 36 percent of the students in their school district is confusion. Educators apparently believe that children who score below average—any score below the 50th percentile—are children who are in academic difficulty. Because the home language survey identifies those who are from a home where a language other than English is spoken, many educators believe that setting a standard such as the 36th or 40th or 50th percentile identifies children who are academically in trouble because they come from a home where a language other than English is spoken.

This, however, is wrong. The 40th percentile is that point at which 40 percent of the population scores—no more and no less. All of the students, including those scoring below the 40th percentile, could be extremely smart and highly knowledgeable (for example, by comparison with previous generations). Conversely, all the students, including those scoring above the 99th percentile, could be stupid and ignorant (for example, by comparison with previous generations). Percentiles, or any score computed to differentiate children, simple are not relevatory. They are rank orders, not absolute standards, a fact that is usually not known or, if known, forgotten.

Oral Proficiency Tests

In virtually every school district in the country, students identified by the home language survey as potentially LEP have to take an oral proficiency test and, if they are older (for example, assumed to be literate), a written English proficiency test. Typically a kindergarten and often a first-grade student will take only an oral proficiency test.

On the face of it, oral English proficiency tests would seem to be better than a written test at determining whether a child knows enough

English to function in a regular classroom because the child does not have to know how to read to take an oral proficiency test. Unfortunately, oral English proficiency tests are no better than written English proficiency and standardized achievement tests, and for many of the same reasons.

Oral proficiency tests are known to be unreliable (the same outcome is not reached in subsequent tests of the same child) and invalid (they do not accurately determine who is LEP).[10] Like standardized achievement tests administered to the English-speaking student body and written English proficiency tests administered only to the LEP students, oral proficiency tests cannot tell the difference between a student who does not know English and a student who does not know the answer. They are normed on an English-speaking group and the same arbitrary cutoff points are used.

Several experiments have been conducted in which oral proficiency tests have been administered to English monolingual students. Between 40 and 50 percent of these children who know no language other than English received a score that classified them as limited-English proficient.[11] Other studies have found that the tests classify students as limited in their native language, as well as in English.[12] In addition, the tests do not agree with each other. A student can be classified as limited-English proficient by one test, but not by another.[13]

An experiment in Chicago suggests that even above-average students are not immune from being classified as limited-English proficient by an oral proficiency test. The Chicago Board of Education administered the Language Assessment Scales (LAS) to students who spoke only English and were above the citywide Iowa Test of Basic Skills (ITBS) norms in reading. Almost half of these monolingual, above-average, English-speaking children were misclassified as non- or limited-English speaking. Moreover, there is a developmental trend. Seventy-eight percent of the English monolingual five-year-olds, but only 25 percent of the fourteen-year-olds, were classified as LEP.[14]

Teachers are better than tests in determining whether a child is proficient in English, but even they make mistakes and for the same reasons.[15] Like the tests, teachers can become confused as to whether a child does not understand English or does not know the answer, particularly if the teacher does not know the child very well.

Some school districts conduct dual language testing for Spanish speakers. In New York City, for example, as a result of the ruling in *Aspira of*

New York, Inc., et al. v. *Board of Education of the City of New York, et al.*, students were classified as LEP if they scored below the 20th percentile in English and also scored higher in Spanish than in English. Dual language testing reduces error, but it does not eliminate it because tests in two different languages are not equivalent. The 40th percentile on a Spanish proficiency test is not the same ability level as the 40th percentile on an English proficiency test. For one thing, the tests are normed on different populations—Spanish speakers in the case of a Spanish proficiency test and English speakers in the case of an English proficiency test—and for another it is not yet known how to make questions equally difficult in two languages.

Even if it were, few educators would be able to resist concluding that a language minority student who scores at the 10th percentile in Spanish and the 11th percentile in English is limited-English proficient. Educators are as confused as the general public as to what tests mean and most of them appear to believe that a low score has some absolute meaning.

Even if a language minority student is accurately identified as LEP upon entering the school system, a classification criterion of the 40th percentile guarantees that at a minimum 40 percent of the students will never get reclassified as FEP no matter how good the program is and no matter how proficient they are in English.

Moreover, the cutoff point can be manipulated to produce more or fewer LEP students. If a school district or state changes its criterion from the 20th to the 40th percentile, it can in one fell swoop double the number of limited-English proficient children.

The experience of New York City and New York state illustrate this. The city and state identification standards for LEP students, which were different for Hispanic and non-Hispanic students, changed three times from 1975 to 1999. The initial criterion for Hispanic students was determined in 1975 as a compromise between the defendant city school board that wanted fewer students identified as LEP and the Hispanic plaintiff group that wanted more students identified as LEP. The *Aspira* consent decree established the 20th percentile on the English Language Assessment Battery (LAB) to identify Spanish-speaking students as LEP, but only if the student scored higher in Spanish than in English.[16]

Three years later the city established the 20th percentile for non-Hispanic language minority students in an agreement with OCR. At the same time, the state of New York was recommending to school districts that they use the 23rd percentile to identify LEP students.

In 1989 the state changed the criterion to the 40th percentile on the recommendation of administrators in the state bilingual education department who believed that the 23rd percentile was too low. They argued that students from language minority families who scored between the 23rd and 40th percentile were having difficulty in English and should be helped. Because 17 percent of the English-speaking population scores between the 23rd and 40th percentile, they, too, would be having trouble in English.

Figure 1 shows that the number of LEP students in the New York City public schools increased by about thirty-five thousand from 1987–88 to 1990–91 as a result of the 1989 change in the LEP standard from the 20th to the 40th percentile. Then the opposite occurred in 1996—the LEP enrollment declined—when the city decided to start using the home language survey as a screening device for Hispanic LEP students. Although

Figure 1. Limited-English Proficient Enrollment Trends in the New York City Public Schools, 1987–88 to 1997–98

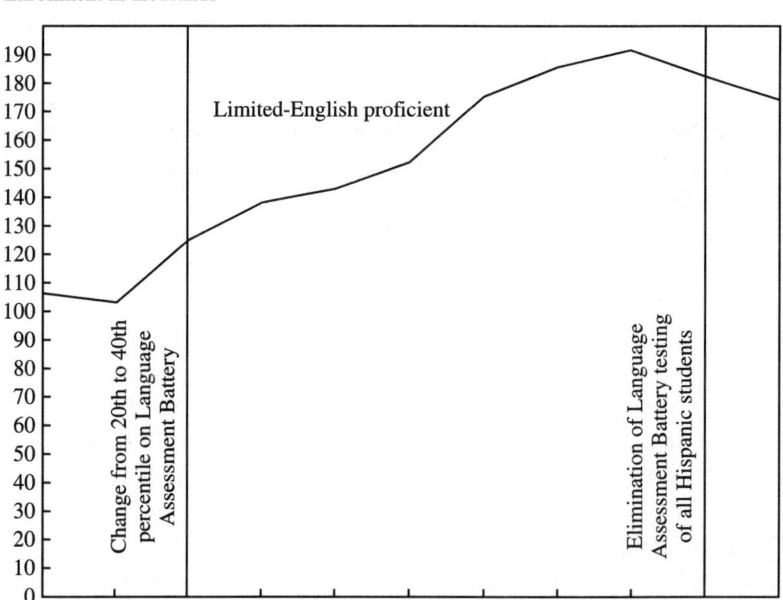

the original *Aspira* consent decree required dual language testing (but not a home language survey), sometime during the 1980s the city had stopped using the results of the Spanish proficiency test to classify LEP students. As a result, whether Spanish-speaking students who scored low on the LAB even spoke Spanish was not known. Because LEP enrollment declined by about seventeen thousand students when the home language survey was instituted as a screening device for Hispanic students, at a minimum, about seventeen thousand Hispanic students who had been classified as LEP because of low test scores presumably came from English-speaking families.

This example illustrates how school districts and states can increase or decrease the number of LEP students simply by changing the standard. Moreover, they do this on a regular basis without any rationale other than the desire to help students who are below average by classifying them as LEP. Almost no one seems to appreciate that being below average, and below grade level, is an affliction of half the student population in the United States and that this is not a reflection of the quality of education or the quality of the students.

In short, the procedures and criteria used by every school district in the United States identify more children as LEP than there are because they cannot tell the difference between a child who does not speak English and a child who has not learned the subject matter and thus does not know the answer. Second, the criterion used—for example, the 40th percentile normed on an English-speaking population—guarantees that at a minimum 40 percent of the students who are administered an English proficiency test will be classified as LEP no matter how fluent they are in English. Unfortunately, there seems to be little or no understanding of this.

The determination of LEP status is made at the local level, but the states and the federal government also make estimates of the number of LEP students. The state governments estimate the LEP population in their state from the numbers given them by their school districts, which are typically based on local standards, although many states recommend standards for school districts to use if they want to receive state funds.

The federal government and researchers also estimate the LEP population. They do this in two ways: first, by aggregating state statistics that typically are based on local statistics, and second, by using decennial census counts. The census counts are based on responses to two questions:

Figure 2. Limited-English Proficient Estimates of Population in the United States, Fiscal 1978–97

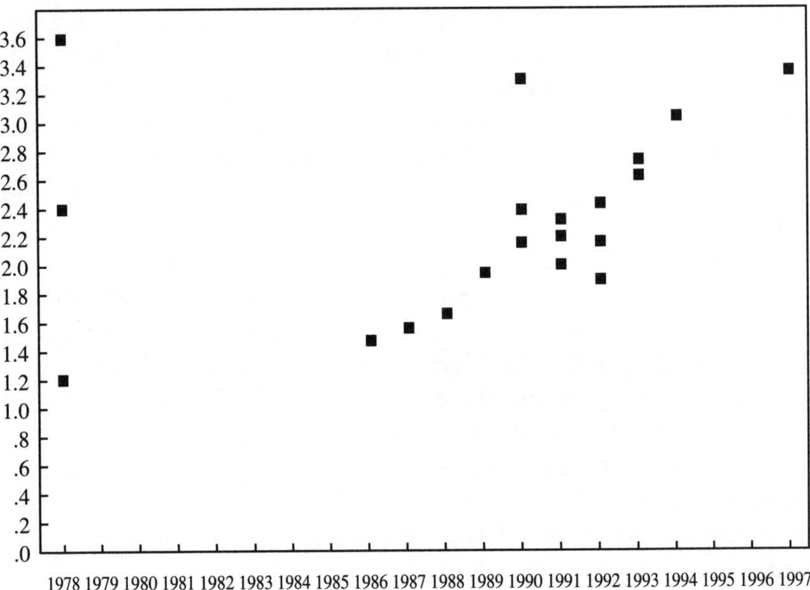

languages used in the home and reported ability to speak English. Respondents are asked to rate whether household members speak English "very well," "well," "not very well," and "not at all."

As shown in figure 2, the national estimates that have been generated over the last two decades vary wildly because the standard used varies.[17] If the highest estimate generated in 1978—3.6 million in the Children's English and Services Study—is compared with the lowest estimate in that year, there is a 2.4 million-student disagreement. In later years, there seems to be less disagreement, but this is misleading. All of the estimates are inaccurate because they are all based on the notion that a student from a language minority family who is below average is LEP. Thus, unquestionably, the true number of LEP students is much smaller than the national, state, and local school district estimates, and the only uncertainty is exactly how much smaller. Unfortunately, critics of the process do not understand this.

Kris Anstrom criticizes the census counts because they do not take into account reading and writing in English.[18] But taking into account reading and writing in English would decrease, not increase, the reliability of the designation because household members would have even greater problems estimating proficiency in reading and writing than in speaking. It is easier to determine how household members speak English than how they read or write it. Moreover, what does it mean to not read or write English very well? My fellow professors would probably designate half of their English monolingual college students as not reading or writing English very well. In short, this is an area where adding English proficiency skills would make the evaluation less, not more, reliable. But what is particularly troubling is the unquestioning belief, common in the social sciences, that greater specificity and higher standards make the determination more reliable. They do not.

Oona M. Cheung, Barbara S. Clements, and Y. Carol Miu recommend a national standard for limited-English proficiency that includes a family language other than English and whether the student is below that of an academically successful peer with an English language background.[19] This guarantees that at a minimum half of all language minority students will be classified as LEP because "academically successful" is typically defined as being at grade level, and only half of all students can be at grade level.

Cheung, Clements, and Miu further recommend a definition for fluent-English speaking students that is basically reading, listening, writing, and speaking at the age and "grade appropriate level." Once again, this guarantees that half of all language minority children will be classified as LEP and never reclassified given that only half of all children in the United States can be at a "grade appropriate level." Thus, Anstrom is wrong in her belief that a national standard would provide a more accurate estimation of the LEP population. The only thing a national standard might possibly do is provide a consistent inaccurate estimate for national programs.

The Recommended Program

From the beginning, Title VII has favored bilingual education. In the original 1968 Bilingual Education Act, bilingual education was one of several programs that a school district could adopt to help LEP students, although it was favored among second language programs. By 1974 bilingual education was not just a favored option, but also almost a requirement for receiving Title VII funds. The Reagan administration hardly made a dent in this. The 1984 reauthorization under the Reagan administration added only that in some school districts bilingual education might be impractical because of small numbers of LEP students of the same language or because of unqualified staff. The 1984 reauthorization also specifically declared it to be the policy of Congress "to encourage the establishment of special alternative instructional programs" defined as

> programs of instruction designed for children of limited English proficiency in elementary and secondary schools. Such programs are not transitional or developmental bilingual education programs, but have specially designed curricula and are appropriate for the particular linguistic and instructional needs of the children enrolled.[20]

The act allowed up to 4 percent of overall funds (or up to 10 percent if more than $140 million was appropriated in a single fiscal year) to go to these special alternative instructional programs that did not use the native tongue. However, 75 percent of funds for instructional programs (Part A) were still allocated to transitional bilingual education programs and 21 percent to maintenance bilingual education under the Reagan administration.

The 1988 reauthorization under the Reagan administration continued to favor bilingual education but included further provisions to allow school districts to use different approaches to the education of LEP children. Part A authorized 75 percent of total grant funds to school districts for transitional bilingual education but increased to 25 percent the amount of grant funds that could go to special alternative instructional programs that did not use the native tongue. In addition, a three-year limit was placed on a student's participation in a transitional bilingual education program or in alternative instructional programs, although under special circumstances, a student could continue in a program for up to two additional years. Thus, the Reagan administration only slowed the bilingual education juggernaut.

The 1994 reauthorization under the Clinton administration earmarked $215 million for fiscal year 1995, gave funding priority to programs that provide for the development of bilingual proficiency both in English and another language, but kept the 25 percent maximum allocation for programs that did not use the native tongue. What is different from the reauthorizations under the Reagan administration, however, is that the Democrats added the requirement that alternative educational programs must be justified either by small numbers of language minority students (although no minimum is mentioned) or a lack of teachers with native language skills (after demonstrating an effort to obtain such).

The 1999 Clinton administration proposal continues to favor bilingual education and even cites the 1998 National Research Council review to support its position.[21] But it also opened a small crack in the bilingual education armor by its many references to the goal of learning English and achieving to high state standards and by its proposal to change the name of the National Clearinghouse for Bilingual Education to the National Clearinghouse on the Education of Children and Youth with Limited English Proficiency.

Although Title VII favors bilingual education, not an ounce of evidence in 1968, and no consistent evidence in the thirty years since, proves its superiority. Moreover, only Spanish speakers seem to receive it, although no recognition is made of this troubling fact in either the educational literature, the legislation, or the regulations.

The theory underlying bilingual education is the facilitation theory, developed by Jim Cummins, which argues that children will be more cognitively developed if they learn to read and write in their native tongue before they learn English. This theory was created a decade after bilingual education was implemented in the 1960s. It is a limited theory, however, because it ignores the issue of the great variation in written language. In particular, it is silent on how to teach Asian children to read and write in their native tongue and why doing so is desirable. The majority of Asian languages use an ideographic system of writing, instead of an alphabet, and have no similarity to English in appearance, thus reducing the number of skills that are transferable, such as sight recognition of words, sounding out of words, and so forth. These languages also take much longer to master than English. In other words, learning to read in the native language, if it is ideographic, may be harder than learning to read and write in the second language, if the latter is English or another phonetic, alphabetic language. As a result, I have not yet found any nonalphabetic bilingual education programs that teach initial literacy in the native language, although many are taught in self-contained classrooms, are called bilingual education, and receive bilingual education funding.

I also have not found any non-Roman alphabet bilingual education programs, even if the alphabet is phonetic (for example, Hebrew, Arabic, the Indian dialects, Russian, and Khmer), that teach initial literacy in the native language. Educators apparently believe that it is too difficult and confusing to teach initial literacy, particularly to young children, in a language with a completely different alphabet from English. For one thing, the transferability of the skill of sight recognition of words is diminished. For another, some of these dialects have more than one alphabet and the rules regarding the combination of consonants and implied or missing vowels are different from English and other Roman alphabet languages so that teaching such languages in an already full day is too formidable a task.

None of the federal and state laws nor bilingual education theory recognizes this. Title VII notes the impracticality of bilingual education for some language groups, but only "due to the presence of small numbers of students of a particular native language or because personnel who are qualified to provide bilingual instructional services are unavailable."[22] To my knowledge, I am the only academic to question the applicability of the facilitation theory to the non-Roman alphabet languages. I suspect this is because to acknowledge that the most academically successful of the language minority children—the Asian students—are instructed almost completely in English would raise too many questions regarding the efficacy of native tongue instruction.

What little research evidence there is indicates that bilingual education, defined as native tongue instruction and native tongue literacy transitioning to English, is, on average, the least effective approach to educating limited English children if one's goal is English language achievement and subject matter knowledge that a student will be tested on in English. Table 1 shows outcomes reported in seventy-two studies that met the standards for a scientific study; that is, they had a treatment and control group and, if there was no random assignment, controlled for pretreatment differences.[23] The effect of transitional bilingual education is compared with "submersion" or doing nothing, English as a Second Language, structured immersion, and maintenance bilingual education—on second language (usually English) reading, language, and mathematics.[24]

Table 1 also shows the effect of structured immersion compared with ESL pullout. Studies are repeated in more than one category of outcome if they had different outcomes at different grade levels or for different

Table 1. Methodologically Acceptable Studies Demonstrating Program Superiority, Equality, or Inferiority by Achievement Test
Percent unless otherwise indicated

Outcome	*Reading*[a]	*Language*	*Math*
TBE versus submersion (do nothing)			
TBE better	22	7	9
No difference	45	29	56
TBE worse	33	64	35
Total number of studies	60	14	34
TBE versus ESL			
TBE better	0	0	25
No difference	71	67	50
TBE worse	29	33	25
Total number of studies	7	3	4
TBE versus submersion/ESL			
TBE better	19	6	11
No difference	48	35	55
TBE worse	33	59	34
Total number of studies	67	17	38
TBE versus structured immersion			
TBE better	0	0	0
No difference	17	100	63
TBE worse	83	0	38
Total number of studies	12	1	8
Structured immersion versus ESL			
Immersion better	100	0	0
No difference	0	0	0
Total number of studies	3	0	0
TBE versus maintenance bilingual education			
TBE better	100	0	0
Total number of studies	1	0	0

Source: Christine H. Rossell and Keith Baker, "The Educational Effectiveness of Bilingual Education," *Research in the Teaching of English*, vol. 30, no. 1 (February 1996), pp. 1–74.

Note: Studies are listed in more than one category if there were different effects for different grades or cohorts. There were 72 methodologically acceptable studies. TBE = transitional bilingual education; ESL = English as a Second Language.

a. Oral English achievement for preschool programs.

cohorts.[25] Those not in the table are excluded because they did not assess alternative second language learning programs or they did not meet the methodological criteria.[26]

Table 1 indicates the percentage of studies showing a program to be better than the alternative it is compared with, the percentage showing no difference, and the percentage showing the program to be worse than the alternative it is compared with. This is repeated for each achievement test—

reading, language, and math. The total number of studies assessing the particular achievement test for each category of comparisons is shown below the percentages.[27]

TBE VERSUS SUBMERSION. Table 1 indicates that for second language reading, 22 percent of the studies show transitional bilingual education (TBE) to be superior, 33 percent show it to be inferior, and 45 percent show it to be no different from submersion (doing nothing).[28] Altogether, 78 percent of the studies show TBE to be no different from or worse than the supposedly discredited submersion technique.

In a standardized achievement test of language, a test of a student's understanding of grammatical rules, transitional bilingual education does even worse than it does in reading. Seven percent of the studies show transitional bilingual education to be superior, 64 percent show it to be inferior, and 29 percent show it to be no different from submersion. Altogether, 93 percent of the studies show TBE to be no different from or worse than doing nothing at all.

These more negative findings for language than for reading suggest that a child is less dependent on school for many of the skills learned in reading—decoding, vocabulary, and understanding concepts—than for grammar. The fine rules of grammar apparently are learned mostly in school and, because they are more complex, are more influenced by school time on task.

In math, 9 percent of the studies show TBE to be superior, 35 percent show it to be inferior, and 56 percent show it to be no different from TBE. Altogether, 91 percent of the studies show it to be no different from or worse than the supposedly discredited submersion technique in developing math proficiency.

TBE VERSUS ESL. Although many so-called submersion situations probably have an ESL program in which students are pulled out of the regular classroom and taught English in small groups for a period a day or a few times a week, it is generally not specified in the evaluations. Nevertheless, many of the studies classified above as submersion could include an ESL pullout component. In seven studies, transitional bilingual education is specifically compared with reading achievement in the regular classroom with ESL pullout. None of these studies shows TBE to be better than ESL pullout in reading. Five studies (71 percent) show no difference between transitional bilingual education and ESL in reading, and two studies (29 percent) show TBE to be worse than the regular classroom with ESL pullout. Of the three studies that examined language achievement, none showed TBE to be superior, two showed no difference between TBE and ESL, and one showed TBE to be worse. Of the four studies that examined math, one showed TBE to be superior, two showed no difference, and one showed TBE to be worse.

TBE VERSUS SUBMERSION/ESL. Because the suspicion is that many, if not most, of the so-called submersion alternatives had an ESL component, also shown in table 1 are the outcomes for a category that combines submersion and ESL studies. Because of the small number of studies that specifically examine ESL pullout, virtually no difference turned up in the findings—81 percent of the studies show TBE to be no different from or worse than submersion or ESL in reading, 94 percent show TBE to be no different from or worse than submersion or ESL in language, and 89 percent show TBE to be no different from or worse than submersion or ESL in math.

TBE VERSUS STRUCTURED IMMERSION. Table 1 also compares TBE with structured immersion. Most of these studies are of the Canadian immersion programs that come in several carefully documented types—early immersion (late bilingual), delayed immersion (early bilingual), dual immersion, and so forth. In many cases, the programs had to be translated using U.S. terminology. Twelve studies had reading outcomes, one study had language outcomes, and eight studies had math outcomes. No studies showed TBE to be superior to structured immersion in reading, language, or math. In reading, 83 percent of the studies showed TBE to be worse than structured immersion and 17 percent showed no difference. In language, the one study showed no difference. In math, five studies showed no difference and three studies showed TBE to be worse than immersion.

STRUCTURED IMMERSION VERSUS ESL. Three studies compared structured immersion with ESL specifically. These studies all showed structured immersion to be superior to ESL in reading.

TBE VERSUS MAINTENANCE BILINGUAL EDUCATION. The final category in table 1 compares transitional bilingual education with maintenance bilingual education. This study by Marcella Medina and Kathy Escamilla showed that transitional bilingual education produced significantly higher English reading achievement than maintenance bilingual education, although the authors did not acknowledge it.[29]

Confronted with the kind of evidence presented in table 1, the advocates of bilingual education have sometimes contended that the issue is learning in a language, not learning a language. These data, however, do not show TBE to be superior in either learning a language or learning in a language—in this case, math. Moreover, no research evidence exists on the effects of TBE on learning other subjects such as geography, social studies, and history because standardized achievement tests are not given in these content areas. Thus, any assertion regarding the superiority of TBE in these areas is anecdotal. Moreover, the math findings for TBE suggest an important problem: Subject matter is taught in the native tongue, but the student is tested on his or her understanding of that subject in English. For many students the difficulty of having to translate what was learned in another language could be great enough that the subject matter lost in the translation may equal or surpass what is lost in submersion before the second language is mastered enough to understand subject content. However, the solution is not to test LEP children in their native tongue because the primary goal of Title VII is for students to reach the highest level in a subject in English that they are capable of.

An important limitation of these studies is that they are short term—even the longest one is only five years and the average is one to two years. If the superiority of bilingual education is evident only after six or seven years, these studies are not a good test of the efficacy of bilingual education. However, because the two scientific longitudinal studies—the J. David Ramirez and others study and the El Paso Independent School District studies—did not find bilingual education to be superior and the latter found it to be inferior, it is safe to say there is not yet any evidence that bilingual education is superior even after many years.[30]

But it is important to point out that some scientific studies find bilingual education to be superior. These superior bilingual education programs seem to have two things in common—the native tongue instruction does not reduce the time on task in English (either because the school day or year is expanded or because nonacademic subjects are eliminated to accommodate the native tongue instruction) and the students make a quick transition to English reading and writing. Because learning to read in one's native tongue is easier than in a foreign language, programs that include native tongue reading instruction can apparently be very good programs so long as there is no reduction or only a brief reduction in English language instruction. Moreover, the positive effect of native tongue reading instruction is most likely if there is no time-consuming native tongue writing instruction. Unfortunately, bilingual education programs typically reduce English language instruction to include copious amounts of time on native tongue literacy. Students can get stuck trying to master native tongue literacy and spend their entire elementary career in a bilingual education program.

What Is the Goal?

When confronted with the evidence that bilingual education is on average less effective in teaching English and subject matter that one will be tested on in English, supporters of bilingual education have sometimes countered that the goal of bilingual education is bilingualism, not English language development. However, the theory supporting bilingual education does not have bilingualism as a goal. The argument is that learning to read and write in one's native tongue produces the greatest cognitive development and that will be evidenced in the second language (that is, English). Bilingualism may be a by-product of that process or even a means of achieving that goal, but it is not the goal.

The federal legislation has been somewhat conflicted on this issue. Knowing more than one language has been a goal of Title VII, although not the primary goal, from the beginning. The 1994 reauthorization states that one of the purposes of Title VII is "developing bilingual skills and multicultural understanding," and the 1999 Clinton administration proposal continues this goal.[31] To achieve this, Title VII includes a program called Foreign Language Assistance, which funds programs of foreign language study for all elementary and secondary school students. The problem is that this program dilutes Title VII's limited resources and changes its purpose from a compensatory education program for children who do not speak English to an enrichment program that might benefit affluent, upper-middle-class children who want to learn another language. This seems to be an unfortunate waste of scarce resources.

Conclusions

I have four general conclusions about the major problems with Title VII and four recommendations for changing the statute.

The Target Group

Accurately identifying who is LEP is not possible.

As the research and statistics on the wildly fluctuating LEP population in the United States suggest, the category is unreliable and the percentages are a function of the criterion used. Different school districts use different criteria, and no logic exists to any of them, which is probably why there is no agreement. The same school districts change the criteria over time and thus are able to increase or decrease at will the number of LEP children they have. Nor is it possible to establish a criterion that would prevent this.

Because the underlying intent of Title VII is to help children who enter school from a home where there is less English than in other homes because the family speaks a language other than English, why not make this the criterion for eligibility? Determining language minority status is easier than ascertaining whether a child is limited-English proficient, because the former can be revealed by a home language survey. The home language survey could be administered in two stages:

1. Administer a short home language survey in English to all entrants into the school system to find children who come from a family that speaks a language other than English (families who cannot respond to the survey in English are automatically classified as language minority).

2. Administer a longer home language survey to language minority families to determine how limited the parents feel their child is in English and how proficient they think their child is in the non-English language (families who cannot respond to the survey in English are automatically classified as language minority).

Children are identified as language minority background from the parents' inability to respond to the survey in English or from the parents' responses to the survey. The primary source of identification would be the first-stage survey, whereas the second-stage survey would be used for clarification. Children would never be reclassified because their identification would not be as limited-English proficient, but as language minority, a classification that is not dependent on misleading test scores. They would have this identification all their school career, thus avoiding the impossible task of deciding when a child is, or is not, LEP.

Some error will occur in determining who is language minority, but far less than in determining who is LEP, because the former would not depend on tests. Moreover, if children are assigned to short-term structured immersion classes or regular classrooms with extra help as is happening in California with Proposition 227, the negative effect of misclassification would be minimal.

For those who think that to stop collecting LEP statistics and reclassification rates is extremely dangerous, I can only emphasize how dangerously misleading these statistics are. The number of LEP students is a function of the criterion used, which differs from school district to school district. In every school district in the country, the criteria include in the LEP category large numbers of fluent-English speakers and exclude smart children who need extra help with their English. Furthermore, the reclassification rates that school districts and programs are held accountable for are not achievable by all students no matter how good the program is. Moreover, because they are annual rates, they are only a snapshot in time, which makes them even more meaningless. What is the point of collecting and making policy decisions on statistics that are meaningless? Using these statistics is dangerous because it lulls school districts, states, and the federal government into thinking they are making rational decisions based on sound data when they are not. Because the enterprise cannot be rationalized, it should be abandoned, and a simpler, more reasonable one adopted.

Title VII funds would go to school districts based on the number of language minority children they have as determined by the home language survey. School districts would be eligible for additional funds under Title I if these children were also poor and low achieving.

Recommendation 1. The phrase "limited-English proficient" or "limited-English speaking," and any other phrase referring to the ability of a child in English, should be stricken from Title VII and the rest of the Elementary and Secondary Education Act, and the term "language minority" should be substituted.

The Program

No consistent research evidence supports bilingual education as a superior alternative for educating supposedly LEP children. Moreover, it is an especially risky program given how difficult accurately classifying a child as LEP is. A child who does not speak Spanish could be placed in a Spanish bilingual program and taught in a language he or she does not understand or speak, supposedly to improve his or her English. More commonly, a fluent-English speaking child could remain in a Spanish bilingual program his or her entire elementary career because he or she cannot score above the exit criterion. Even if the facilitation theory is correct, being taught in Spanish cannot help a child's English language achievement if Spanish is not his or her native tongue. Nor is being taught in Spanish helping the English language achievement of a Spanish-speaking child who already knows English.

A prudent approach to the conflicting research and controversy would be to eliminate program recommendations from Title VII. A particular program need not be specified to help language minority children, and it would be prudent to refrain from doing so, given how little research backs up any particular one, how controversial the research and its conclusions are, and how quickly the sands of social science research can shift. Authorizing money for children who might need extra help is one thing; that is based on common sense and the heart. However, specifying exactly what kind of extra help this should be is foolhardy when social science research findings change and school districts can modify any program any way into whatever makes sense for them.[32] Moreover, Title VII seems to be the only part of the Elementary and Secondary Education Act that calls for a specific, and controversial, educational program that is opposed by most Americans, most language minority parents, and most Hispanics.[33]

Recommendation 2. Eliminate all references to bilingual education programs and to developing bilingual skills. Title VII should refer only to programs that provide high-quality instruction to language minority children to meet the performance standards expected of all children.

The Legislation

Title VII is badly written. It is far too long and full of redundant and fragmented programs and agencies as well as self-evident, repetitive statements and assertions such as

> the assistance provided under the application will contribute toward building the capacity of the applicant to provide a program on a regular basis, similar to that proposed for assistance, which will be of sufficient size, scope, and quality to promise significant improvement in the education of students of limited-English-proficiency, and that the application will have

> the resources and commitment to continue the program when assistance under this subpart is reduced or no longer available. (Section 7116 (h) (5))

This could be reduced to one sentence: The local educational agencies (LEAs) will be expected to continue systemwide enhancements funded under Title VII. Everything else in that paragraph has already been stated a number of times before and after that in the text of the legislation.

Title VII is also full of false statements about the superiority of bilingual education. In many cases, assertions are made for which absolutely no supporting research exists. Many statements are puzzling and why they are in the legislation is a mystery, unless the goal of each administration is simply to add text.

The Clinton administration's 1999 proposal continues this tradition. As occurs often in journalism and in educational policy, the opinions of intellectuals and academics are confused with research findings. Not only are many of the same spurious claims made, but new ones have been added. The Clinton administration included the statement that educational technology has the "potential" to improve the education of language minority and limited-English proficient students and therefore the federal government should foster development of that technology. But many things have the potential to help many students. What is the point of including this statement in Title VII?

Foreign language training is another one of these issues that does not belong in Title VII. The original goal of Title VII was to help immigrant children gain proficiency in English. Foreign language training may not even belong in ESEA, which, after all, is a compensatory education bill. The Emergency Immigrant Aid Act program is also redundant if the definition of the target population is changed to language minority. Title VII needs to be simplified, not further complicated. Unfortunately, the Clinton administration has not made any progress in this; it has made matters worse.

Recommendation 3. Reduce Title VII to a few pages stating that:

—Money is to be allocated to school districts based on the number of children from language minority families, and this money should be spent on educational programs, additional staff, and in-service teacher training that have a high likelihood of improving their education.

—A certain percentage of this money can be spent on schoolwide programs and districtwide programs.

—State and local funds are not to be reduced if a Title VII award is made.

—The school districts should be required to show the number of language minority children that they have and that they spent the money on extra staff, in-service training, and programs that have a likelihood of improving the education of language minority children.

—Title VII will fund research and evaluation conducted under the auspices of the federal government, but school districts are not required to do it themselves, although they must collect and provide the data to be used in the evaluations.

—Title VII will fund the National Clearinghouse on Bilingual Education (or the proposed National Clearinghouse on the Education of Children and Youth with Limited English Proficiency).

The Research

The quality of research in this field is terrible. Not all of this is the fault of the school districts that receive funding, however. Doing good research is extremely difficult and expensive, and few people are trained in it. Title VII, for example, includes a research and evaluation component—a minimum of 5 percent of the funds are reserved for program evaluation by school districts. Unfortunately, the 1994 reauthorization appears to advocate an invalid research design when it suggests that school districts compare the academic achievement of LEP students with that of non-LEP students. This is the wrong design and the wrong comparison because LEP children are defined by their low achievement. If they are high achieving, they are not classified as LEP, even if they come from a language minority family. Simple examinations of the two would compare low-achieving children to high-achieving children and be meaningless.

Other misleading statements are in Title VII. Section 7115 states that the secretary shall terminate grants to eligible entities under this section if the secretary determines that "the program evaluation required by section 7123 indicates that students in the program are not being taught to and are not making adequate progress toward achieving challenging State content standards and challenging State student performance standards; or in the case of a program to promote dual language facility, such program is not promoting such facility." The problem is that only an expensive and sophisticated evaluation would be able to do this, and few individuals have those skills. The statement also implies that this is a simple process of looking at progress over time. It is not.

Because few people in federal, state, or local government understand research design, federal program legislation should not include statements about the characteristics of program evaluations because they are almost always wrong.

But school districts should not be required to evaluate their own programs because they do not know how to do it. Millions of dollars are wasted every year on local evaluations that are not scientific and cannot determine program effectiveness. The federal government should require only that school districts that accept Title VII funds keep and be willing to turn over anonymous student-level data upon request for program evaluation by trained and experienced researchers. The legislation should not specify more than that because it is too often wrong or misleading.

Title VII could offer extra funds to school districts willing to conduct experiments that would enable researchers to understand the effects of different programs. Such an experiment would begin with random assignment of Hispanic language minority children to different instructional environments such as a mainstream classroom with ESL pullout, a transitional bilingual education program, and a structured immersion program. Random assignment would eliminate the need for a pretest (a measure of academic achievement or intelligence before enrollment in the program). A pretest is extremely difficult to obtain because most children are tested in the spring, after they have spent a year or more in a program or school. With random assignment, a pretest need not control for the ability differences of students that might cause them to be chosen for various programs because they are not selected for their characteristics. With random assignment, any differences in outcomes will be the result of the program instead of the characteristics of the children that caused them to be assigned to the program.

For those who worry about the issue of parental consent for random assignment, the California experience with Proposition 227 indicates that most parents look to the schools for guidance and will do what they say. If the school administration tells them their child should be in a traditional bilingual education program, most Hispanic parents will agree. If, a day later, the school administration finds that it does not have enough students assigned to the traditional bilingual education to have a whole class, the same Hispanic parents will agree to have their child taught in all-English classes. Thus, random assignment is likely to be accepted by Hispanic parents so long as it has the support of the school administration.

But random assignment is not a solution to determining program effectiveness if the children in the programs are tested at different rates. If there are differential testing rates, the program with the lower testing rate will always, all other things being equal, have an unfair advantage over the program with the higher testing rates because the students who would score the lowest are deemed "not ready" to take the test and are excluded from testing.

A bias currently exists in the program evaluations because the students in all-English programs are tested at higher rates than the children in bilingual education programs. Even if there is random assignment to the two programs, evaluations comparing all-English programs with bilingual education programs will be biased against the all-English programs. Therefore, a valid research design must include not only random assignment to the two programs, but also universal testing. To know the true effects of programs, all children must be tested with standardized achievement tests even if they do not know any English.

The Clinton administration's proposal for testing in English after three years of education in the United States is an improvement over the 1994 reauthorization, which had no timetable for testing in English. It is still, however, naïve in failing to understand that, if no testing is done at the beginning of a program, the ability of a statistical evaluation to determine the effect of a program will be severely limited. This is particularly true because of much lower testing rates for students in bilingual education than in all-English programs in their first three years.

Although the Clinton administration's 1999 proposal is also an improvement over the 1994 reauthorization by explicitly stating that the goal of Title VII is to learn English and to achieve to challenging state content and performance standards and by requiring annual testing, it reduces the positive effect of this by encouraging native tongue testing if that would "more accurately reveal" what a child knows. The Clinton proposal specifically singles out Spanish-speaking LEP students when it specifics there should be "tests written in Spanish for Spanish-speaking students with limited English proficiency, if those tests are more likely than tests written in English to yield accurate and reliable information on what those students know, and can do, in subjects other than English."[34] The problem again is that the LEP students in bilingual education programs will be taking tests in Spanish, if that is their native tongue, and the LEP students in all-English programs will be taking them in English, thus biasing any program evaluation in favor of bilingual education. Given that no one believes that achievement in Spanish is the ultimate goal, valid program evaluations must be of English language achievement with equal percentages of students in each program taking tests in English.

Recommendation 4. School districts should be required to collect basic statistics for individual language minority students and to provide it on demand to federal researchers, but they should not do the program evaluations themselves. The federal government should provide a fiscal incentive to school districts to do random assignment to programs and universal testing. The school districts would be required to provide achievement and other data on individual students to the federal government so that experienced researchers could do statistical analysis to determine program effects.

Given the inconsistency in the research and the lack of strong effects in any direction, assigning students randomly to alternative treatments would not be unethical. Random assignment and universal testing would go a long way toward producing a research study that could do this, and the federal government could make a huge contribution by including funding for it in Title VII.[35]

Title VII can be improved by changing the target group from limited-English proficient students to language minority students; eliminating the support for a specific, and controversial, program—bilingual education—that is only implemented for Spanish speakers; reducing the redundancy and turgid prose of the legislation itself; encouraging school districts to do random assignment and universal testing by awarding additional funds for these experiments; and funding national research studies. In general, Title VII should be simplified—it has grown from six pages to thirty-five pages in thirty years and has become only more fragmented and irrational. Unfortunately, the Clinton administration's proposal worsens this problem by adding verbiage. The bill as it stands now could be cut to less than ten pages and lose nothing of substance.

Comment by Catherine E. Snow

In these comments on Christine H. Rossell's paper about the federal bilingual education program, I will respond specifically to her principal conclusions and her four recommendations. I acknowledge the line of reasoning that underlies those recommendations, and in some cases I agree with both the reasoning and the conclusions. Who could disagree, after all, that the language of federal legislation is often characterized by poor writing, redundancy, and irrelevancies? However, Rossell and I differ in basic orientation to the issues and in the knowledge bases we bring to this topic. Furthermore, Rossell makes some basic misstatements in her paper, misstatements that are in some cases so egregious that it would be remiss of any discussant to let them pass unchallenged.

Political Science versus Developmental Psychology

Rossell is a political scientist whose major focus in her discussions of bilingual education seems to be to identify obstacles to the rational implementation of policies and unpredictabilities in the process by which policies have been decided upon. I am a developmental psychologist, interested in the conditions under which children develop to their full capacities, and in particular the conditions under which the largest possible percentage of children will successfully learn to read. Teaching children to read is, in my view, the most important task schools face, because failure in reading will doom children in most other school-related domains. Furthermore, learning to read is the first serious task children face in school, and success or failure in this task has a long-term impact on children's views of themselves as students and learners.

Thus, my primary interest is how to ensure success in reading—or, to put the issue in the public health perspective adopted by the Committee on the Prevention of Reading Difficulties in Young Children, which I chaired, how to minimize risk of reading failure. Learning to read is, in a sense, a natural act for a normally developing child in a literate culture with good schooling. Factors that enhance the risk that children will not follow this normal developmental pathway, as reviewed in the committee's report, include living in poverty, arriving at school not speaking English, attending schools with generally poor performance, and having poorer than average language and preliteracy skills on school entry.[36] The superordinate prevention strategies identified by the committee were: (1) ensuring that all children have access to excellent, language- and literacy-rich, preschool environments, and (2) ensuring that all children have access to excellent reading instruction.

What constitutes excellent reading instruction? The answer the committee gave to that question derives from its definition of reading: Reading is the act of constructing meaning from print. In other words, good readers of English use the alphabetic principle—that letters map in regular ways onto sounds—fluently and automatically to access word meaning and construct textual meaning. Excellent reading instruction must give children opportunities to grasp the alphabetic principle, in the context of a continual focus on reading for meaning, and must ensure that children have enough practice in reading to become automatic at the identification of words and to become skilled users of strategies for comprehension.

So what is the relevance of this view of reading to policies for bilingual education? The committee report concluded that the relevance was great—that this view of reading dictated that instruction that involves teaching children to read in a language they do not understand cannot constitute good instruction. Getting to the meaning is the whole point of reading, and children (particularly children from homes with low levels of parental education and little literacy exposure) can be expected to become confused and discouraged if expected to learn to read meaningless words. Furthermore, recognizing the words one starts out reading is an enormous support to the acquisition of the details of the alphabetic principle for most children. Children who cannot use meaning to support their reading during the initial stages of mastering the alphabetic principle are, inevitably, facing a much harder task than children being taught to read meaningful words.

At slightly more advanced stages, as well, knowing the language in which one is reading is crucial to developing sophisticated comprehension strategies and to spending enough time on task to develop fluency and automaticity with word recognition and the implementation of comprehension strategies. Enthusiasm for the practice of reading is a major input to developing fluency and success. Young children are unlikely to be enthusiastic or to engage in the practice they need if they are reading mostly incomprehensible texts.

Thus, the report on preventing reading difficulties made the following recommendation concerning reading instruction for children who arrive at school not knowing English and not knowing how to read: that such children be taught to read in their native language if that is feasible (that is, if instructional materials and qualified teachers are available, and if such children are sufficient in number to justify native language reading instruction), while also receiving instruction focused on building oral proficiency in English, and that transition to English reading instruction take place only after a reasonable level of oral proficiency in English had been achieved. For children for whom these conditions do not hold, the committee recommended that formal reading instruction be postponed until some reasonable level of proficiency in English has been achieved and that the schools design programs to provide rich English language and preliteracy environments for such children, to ensure the most rapid possible acquisition. Furthermore, research should be undertaken to address the question of what constitutes "sufficient oral proficiency in English" to serve as a safe basis for reading instruction.

Two important points must be made about these recommendations. First, they are designed to reduce risk of reading failure. The committee recognized that children can learn to read in a language in which they have very low oral proficiency. Many millions of children have demonstrated that this is possible, not just in U.S. schools but also in colonial school systems across the world. However, such an approach is inherently more risky—more children will fail under this approach than if taught to read under conditions where meaning can be used as a support. The level of school failure that is normal in third-world countries with universal second language reading instruction simply cannot be tolerated in the United States.

Second, this recommendation applies only to children who cannot read on arrival at school. The committee did not make any recommendation concerning the value of bilingual education for older arrivals who can already read in their native language, nor for precocious readers who enter first grade reading fluently in their native language. However, much research suggests that such children can learn to read in the second language relatively quickly and then use second language literacy as a resource for second language oral acquisition.

Specific Claims That Deserve Response

In responding to quotations from Rossell's paper, I recognize that some are less than central to the arguments she is making but nonetheless feel it is imperative to note when they are misleading or unfounded. In each case, her statement is provided in italics.

The U.S. Department of Education has enthusiastically embraced bilingual education. This claim is based on the distribution of funds available through the Bilingual Education Act and its successors. The largest part of these funds has typically been reserved for bilingual programs. But the total funding available has never been sufficient to serve most of the children who would have qualified for and benefited from bilingual programs. Thus, one could with as much justification argue that the Department of Education has failed to support bilingual education enthusiastically.

There is no treatment called "bilingual education" that is implemented in the same way and understood to be the same thing by everyone. This claim is true. The three program types noted in Rossell's paper fail to reflect the full range of program types or of variation within types. A major problem with the evaluations of bilingual programs, which as she notes are often exemplars of the worst in educational research, is that the variation within program type, which is often as great as that between program types, has not typically been taken into account. Many of the studies Rossell cites in her research synthesis would be rejected as fatally flawed by others who demand at least some information about classroom practices before evaluating a program's outcomes.

A major issue in thinking about these program labels is to realize that program labels do not distinguish educational experiences of children efficiently. The program labels mostly refer to classroom configurations—what mix of languages do the children in the classroom speak as native languages, and what language capacities are expected of the teacher? Thus, a transitional bilingual program is defined by the presence of children dominant in one language and a teacher with at least some competence in that language (and, one hopes, in English as well). Details of pedagogy, of distribution of instructional activities over the two languages, and of curriculum are all left undefined by the program category.

"Structured immersion" is described by Rossell as "all-English" instruction in a self-contained classroom containing (exclusively) English language learners. Here, again, classroom configuration rather than explicit models for what to teach and how to teach it defines the program type. No one knows what should be going on in a structured immersion classroom, only that it should be going on primarily in English. Structured immersion is the program type that has been mandated in California by Proposition 227 and that is being proposed for Massachusetts and other states under Proposition 227-like legislation. No one has been trained in how to teach children in structured immersion settings. All that is prescribed is to restrict the use of the children's native language to a minimum. In many parts of the country, places where all the English language learners come from the same language background, structured immersion may not differ much in practice from programs labeled as transitional bilingual in which, as observational research shows, the children's native language may also be used rather little.

What does this mean? At a minimum, it implies that evaluations that compare programs called structured immersion with programs called transitional bilingual, but that provide no data on pedagogical activities and language use in the classroom, are worthless. More depressingly, all the complaints about the level of academic and English language accomplishments of children in transitional bilingual programs almost certainly will be replicated for structured immersion programs.

Only the Spanish speakers . . . are receiving bilingual education through native tongue instruction, according to the theory. This claim reflects Rossell's beliefs that children who arrive at school speaking languages other than Spanish do not receive reading instruction in their native languages and that native language reading instruction is the key defining element of bilingual education. Both these claims could be challenged—on factual and theoretical grounds, respectively.

The majority of children receiving "bilingual education according to the theory" in the United States are Spanish speaking. Also, the majority of language minority children eligible for bilingual education but not receiving it "according to the theory" are Spanish speaking. Because 85 percent of non-English-speaking children in the United States speak Spanish, bilingual education not surprisingly has been developed largely with their needs in mind. Furthermore, the proximity of Spanish-speaking countries and the availability of Spanish language materials facilitate the introduction of initial Spanish reading instruction, which is undeniably more widespread than initial instruction in other languages. The force of this observation in Rossell's argument is not, however, entirely clear. Even if only Spanish speakers were benefiting from native language reading instruction within bilingual programs, this does not constitute any indictment of the policy from an educational perspective.

In fact, though, sizable numbers of children who speak languages other than Spanish are receiving traditional bilingual education in which literacy is first introduced in the native language. Rossell and I spoke in the fall of 1998 at a meeting at Simmons College where we heard half a dozen bilingual teachers stand up and say that they were teaching children initial reading in languages ranging from Haitian Creole to Chinese.

The second aspect of this claim is that teaching reading in the native language is the key defining element of bilingual education. While not contesting the importance of native language literacy instruction to effective bilingual programs, I would disagree that this has been the primary justification within the intellectual history of the bilingual education movement. Rossell identifies a single theory as justifying bilingual education—Jim Cummins's theory of facilitation, or a common underlying proficiency. This theory has been widely cited in documents explaining the value of bilingual education, in particular in California where it has been combined with another theory, S. Krashen's notion of "comprehensible input" in informing educational practice.[37]

But facilitation is only one take on the value of bilingual education and, as Rossell's exposition reveals, the theory postdates the movement. The major intellectual input to bilingual education was practical wisdom—observations within the Coral Way program that bilingual education was possible—combined with a certain level of desperation concerning the academic accomplishments of non-English-speaking children. Justifications for bilingual practice have ranged widely, for example:[38]

—Basic humanity. It is neither kind nor nurturant to little children to put them in strange situations where they cannot communicate.

—Cultural continuity. Building on the skills and capacities children bring from home presupposes creating greater connections between home and school in language and in other ways.

—Achievement motivation. Children who are academically successful and well adjusted during their first year of formal schooling continue to show better school outcomes.

—Bilingualism. The children's home language skills constitute resources that should be exploited.

—Sociolinguistic realities. In many immigrant communities, both the ancestral language and English are used widely, and thus if schools are part of those communities, both languages will be used in school, though perhaps for different purposes.

I would argue, perhaps agreeing with Rossell, that the most urgent justification for bilingual programs is the value of native language literacy as an academic protective factor, but it is a misrepresentation to think that this is the only rationale for bilingual programs that has ever been proposed.

The procedures used by school districts to identify students as limited-English proficient are inherently illogical. Rossell has identified a number of cases in which school districts have shifted their judgment of who was limited-English proficient (LEP) and some practices of identification and of decisionmaking that are less than exemplary. The "technology" of language proficiency assessment is relatively new, and her worst cases (from twenty years ago) reflect that. It is wrong, though, to suggest that all of the variation in identification rates she notes reflect incoherent identification procedures. The rise in the LEP population between 1987 and 1995 noted in her figure 1 is what would be predicted from immigration rates during those years.

Rossell is right that determinations must be made of whom bilingual programs are meant to serve and how best to identify those children. She proposes, in effect, a secondary prevention strategy—cast a wide net that requires little in the way of individual testing or screening, and provide prevention services to all within those risk groups, because enhanced education cannot hurt those who do not need it. Much can be said for this model as a mechanism for distributing money. Less can be said for it if it becomes a mechanism for ignoring the specific educational needs of language minority children. Furthermore, within the language minority population, different children may need access to different prevention strategies. If teaching children to read occurs optimally in a language they speak well, then before assigning language minority children to English-medium classrooms where formal reading instruction will be offered, whether they speak English well enough must be ascertained. How can this be done? By judicious use of some of the tests that Rossell discusses. She complains about those tests on various grounds. However, that some native English speakers perform poorly on the same tests does not indict their usefulness as predictors of reading outcomes. Those low-scoring native English speakers no doubt would also profit from special educational treatments—but different ones than the non-native speaker needs.

The basic logic here is simple if one avoids being misled by Rossell's confused psychometric presentation. A six-year-old child who knows only three hundred words in English is going to have trouble in an English-medium first grade where the teacher is focusing on teaching reading. The child with a three-hundred-word vocabulary in English does not have a stable set of phonological distinctions, knows too few words to develop the phonological analysis skills basic to learning letter-sound correspondences, and will encounter many words critical to understanding first-grade texts that he or she does not know the meaning of. If such a child is a native English speaker, I would recommend English language enrichment combined with emergent literacy activities to promote prereading skills. If this child also knows six thousand words in Spanish, then the child should be given formal reading instruction in Spanish so that he or she can master the alphabetic principle and automaticity in letter and syllable recognition and develop the habit of reading, while acquiring more oral skills in English. If this child has become an on-grade-level reader in Spanish by the end of first grade, introducing English reading material at that point is likely to promote oral English development as well.

Nationally it is only possible to have half the student population at grade level. This claim, which Rossell not only makes but also excoriates others for failing to understand, is patently wrong. Rossell fails to display an understanding of the not-very-subtle distinction between norm-referenced and criterion-referenced measures. On norm-referenced measures, some test takers will always score below average. On criterion-referenced tests, however, everyone in a class, a school, or a nation can "pass." Grade level for reading is a criterion—established as a function of curricula and consensual standards. Rossell likely would counter that the curricula and the consensus standards shift to reflect average performance. Standards do shift—in the current period of educational reform, standards are being shifted upward, with the result that more than half the children in the nation are failing to meet many of them. If grade-level standards were averages, as Rossell seems to think they are, such an outcome would also be impossible.

Educators apparently believe that children who score below average . . . are children who are in academic difficulty. Rossell accuses educators of being as confused as the general public as to what tests mean and of appearing to believe that a low score has some absolute meaning. She is right that low scores on norm-referenced tests have no absolute meaning. But they do have power nonetheless, as predictors of academic outcomes and of literacy achievement. One could construct a language test on which first-grade children with excellent language and literacy skills score as low as the 10th percentile (the Scholastic Assessment Test [SAT] for college-bound high school students, for example). But if language minority or English-speaking students are scoring at the 10th percentile on valued age appropriate tests of vocabulary, knowledge of grammar, and oral comprehension in English, they are going to have trouble learning to read and will need adapted programs. All of Rossell's smoke and mirrors about the relativity of norm-referenced tests do not change those basic facts. The shift she notes in New York state's criterion for classification as LEP from the 23rd to 40th percentile may have reflected the reaction of wise practitioners to this finding. Whether the 40th percentile on the Language Assessment Battery (LAB) represents a level of English that is high or low depends on the norming sample. A cutoff at the 60th percentile would be justifiable, if children scoring at the 59th percentile were "having difficulty in English." No absolute meaning is attributable to either high or low scores, but that does not imply that test scores are meaningless. Rossell's university no doubt imposes as an entrance requirement for non-native English speakers a score on the Test of English as a Foreign Language (TOEFL) that is well above the 70th percentile for that test—and then occasionally still admits students whose English proves not to be adequate for the academic demands of a U.S. university.

School districts and states can increase or decrease the number of LEP students simply by changing the standard. Moreover, they do this on a regular basis without any rationale other than the desire to help students. School districts can change incidence of students classified as LEP or any other category by changing cutoff points. Rossell acknowledges that they do this through a desire to help students. While being below average on a universally administered test is the fate of half its takers, scoring below average on a test normed on non-native English speakers is not a likely fate for native speakers of English. Being below grade level could, in principle, afflict all or none of any given population. Again, Rossell confuses norms with criteria, and norms for the language minority population with norms for the entire population.

[Facilitation theory] ignores the issue of the great variation in written language. In particular, it is silent on how to teach Asian children to read and write in their native tongue and why doing so is desirable. Essentially, Rossell is claiming that learning to read Asian languages could hardly develop skills that transfer to English. Rossell is general in her reference to Asian languages, which fall into a number of different language groups and use a variety of orthographies. Vietnamese and Korean, for example, use alphabetic writing systems—in the first case the Roman alphabet; Khmer's writing system is described as "alpha syllabic"; Japanese uses a syllabic system that displays many of the principles of alphabet writing but at a slightly less abstract level; the languages of the Indian subcontinent mostly use consonant-centered alphabetic systems.[39] Thus, Rossell seems to have generalized Chinese morpho-syllabic orthography (which is borrowed for use in sophisticated Japanese and Korean writing, but not for initial literacy instruction) to the entire continent. Nor do the data suggest that it is harder to learn to read in syllabic or morpho-syllabic orthographies. Initial reading in such systems is much easier, though acquiring full literacy (two thousand to twenty thousand Kanji) in morpho-syllabic systems does take some years.

The key issue here, though, is whether transfer of literacy skills from a first to a second language occurs only when the two languages share a writing system. From my own infinitely greater difficulty trying to learn to read Arabic and Hebrew as compared with Spanish and Dutch, I can sympathize with Rossell's intuition-based claim, that transfer to new alphabetic systems is less extensive than transfer within alphabetic systems. Unfortunately a systematic research base does not exist from which to argue either side of this case. However, there clearly are things one learns from knowing how to read in Chinese that could be useful in learning to read English—the analyzability of print, the need to access a phonological representation of words being read, something about the difference between spoken and written language, the value of literacy skills, and so on. And knowing any alphabetic system prepares one for the phonological analysis of words that constitutes the basis for any other alphabetic system—and often is a great barrier to young readers of English because English has a deeper orthography than most alphabetic languages. I must agree with Rossell that it may not be worth the time and effort to teach children to read first in a language in which they will not have ongoing opportunities to read. Transfer of skills from first to second language literacy may require more than initial literacy accomplishments in the first language. In this case, given the absence of realistic opportunities to become an advanced or fluent reader in some languages because of absence of reading materials or ongoing support and instruction, some children perhaps should postpone formal literacy instruction until after the development of sufficient English proficiency.

Although Title VII favors bilingual education, not an ounce of evidence in 1968, and no consistent evidence in the thirty years since then, proves its superiority. The claim that research fails to confirm the value of bilingual education, central to Rossell's paper and to her work in this area, is demonstrably false. She and I agree that much of the research on this topic is execrable. She has included many of those studies in the overview presented in table 1. A. C. Willig and J. P. Greene reviewed far fewer studies in their meta-analyses because they identified crucial design flaws in many of the seventy-two studies Rossell allows to "vote" in her method.[40] Such flaws ranged from including graduates of transitional bilingual programs in the putative control group to failing to distinguish between Canadian (elite, elective) and U.S. immersion programs. The flaws in Rossell's approach to synthesizing research on bilingual education have been repeatedly discussed in numerous venues. Despite her willingness to stretch her methods so as to disfavor bilingual education as a model, her results do not demonstrate that bilingual programs are bad for children. The scores come out about even for the various programs across the various assessments offered. A fairer presentation of data and a stricter selection limited to well-designed studies make clear that bilingual education is much better for children entering school without literacy skills in English.

Four Recommendations

First, eliminate reference to limited proficiency in English and substitute "language minority" as the criterion for distributing Title VII funding. This proposal would increase the population base for distributing Title VII funding and would streamline the process of estimating the numbers of children eligible. Though it would not solve all problems of identification, it would simplify identification and could reduce error. If elimination of consideration of children's language skills did not extend to the decisions made about their educational program, but was limited to determining a basis for distribution of funding, it might be sensible and deserves a trial.

Second, eliminate reference to specific educational programs in Title VII. This recommendation is based on a claim with which I categorically disagree, that research cannot be used to justify bilingual approaches to educating language minority children with limited skills in English. Thus, while I endorse the underlying notion that states and districts should be required to use solid research evidence in justifying their decisions about education, I cannot endorse this recommendation. Bilingual programs offer the best education to many children. Their quality needs to be improved, as Rossell points out. But the United States is not responding to the evidence that math and science programs are often ineffective by eliminating them. Instead, efforts are made to improve them. The same approach should be adopted for bilingual education.

Third, rewrite Title VII to eliminate redundancies and irrelevancies. Rossell and I agree entirely that Title VII is badly written. The impact of this on schools and children is not, however, so negative that major efforts to call in the language police need to be launched.

Fourth, Title VII legislation should require school districts to collect and make available outcome data, not to carry out evaluation studies. Like Rossell, I am appalled at the money and time wasted in carrying out evaluations of educational programs, generally with inadequate designs and insufficient resources to do a good job. However, requiring school districts to provide outcome data to outside evaluators will hardly solve the problem of generating good evaluations. A major issue in evaluating educational programs (those for language minority children and all others) is knowing what is going on inside the classroom. Program labels are not enough. Thus, I agree that evaluation efforts need to be rethought but do not agree that the solution offered by Rossell is adequate.

Comment by Charles Glenn

Christine H. Rossell has amply demonstrated what bilingual education guru Jim Cummins once called an "entry and exit fallacy in bilingual education." That is, the methods used to identify which children are to be placed in separate bilingual education programs do not identify reliably those whose educational needs derive primarily from the dominance of a language other than English. Instead, they identify children whose proficiency in oral and written English is below national norms, whatever the reason. The same arbitrary criterion makes it difficult to return children, once designated as limited-English proficient, to the educational mainstream.

The key to a more sensible policy was suggested by Catherine E. Snow, who pointed out that a continuum exists of need and of language development that includes, at some point, every student in school. Because this is self-evidently true, it would make sense to abandon the labeling and educational segregation of some language minority students on the basis of an arbitrary cutoff point. My study of a dozen nations with large numbers of immigrant children found that only in some American states and in some highly controversial programs in Sweden is it considered appropriate to educate these children separately from the majority after an initial transition period of (in most cases) a year of intensive instruction in the language of the host society.[41]

Educational segregation is more harmful to language minority students than to any of the groups for which serious efforts have been made to integrate—female students, black students, special needs students. A case can be made, I believe, for single-sex schools, for schools with a special focus on the needs of African American youth, for schools concentrating on a particular disability. No convincing case can be made, I submit, for herding together language minority children whose most urgent educational task is to become effectively integrated into U.S. society. Language minority students have a compelling need to be with peers for whom English is the first language if they are to learn the language well.

They also have a compelling need to be held to the same educational standards as other students. Too often they are subjected to what I call "Jim Crow educational standards," which almost guarantee that they will not be able to participate in secondary and higher education on equal terms. Blame for these separate but unequal expectations must be shared by educational progressives and conservatives alike. The progressives have recoiled from holding language minority children to expectations that seem culturally insensitive and threatening to their self-esteem, which has led to bilingual education becoming a sort of comforting cultural bubble-bath for too many students who deserve to be challenged instead. Conservatives, meanwhile, have sometimes focused so single-mindedly on the acquisition of English that other academic objectives are neglected. Even as a technique for teaching English, this is unwise. Proficiency in a language, beyond an elemental level, is developed by using it for real tasks that matter, such as mastering academic materials, not for artificial exercises.

The fundamental mistake made by both sides in the debate over educating language minority children is to focus on language instead of education as the central issue. As both Rossell and Snow seem to agree, effective education can be provided either through use of the home language or through structured immersion. Either can be done well or badly. A couple of years ago, I served as a reviewer for the National Research Council's (NRC) study of thirty-five years of evidence on the teaching of language minority children.[42] The NRC report concludes that, despite countless research studies and evaluations (costing hundreds of millions of dollars), one approach is not superior to the other. "It is clear," the authors note,

> that many children first learn to read in a second language without serious negative consequences. These include children in early-immersion, two-way, and English as a second language (ESL)-based programs in North America, as well as those in formerly colonial countries that have maintained the official language [of the colonizer] as the medium of instruction, immigrant children in Israel, children whose parents opt for elite international schools, and many others.... The high literacy achievement of Spanish-speaking children in English-medium Success for All schools ... that feature carefully-designed direct literacy instruction suggests that even children from low-literacy homes can learn to read in a second language if the risk associated with poor instruction is eliminated.[43]

Later in the report, the authors candidly conclude, "We do not yet know whether there will be long-term advantages or disadvantages to initial literacy instruction in the primary language versus English, given a very high-quality program of known effectiveness in both cases.[44]

The emphasis should now shift to ensuring that whichever method is chosen in particular circumstances be implemented by competent teachers following a demanding curriculum and with accountability for clear and measurable results. What will that take? Some concrete measures should be reflected in federal and state educational policy for language minority students.

First, the principal and teachers in each school should be responsible for planning and implementing the education of all the students in that school and should have broad discretion about the instructional methods that they use. Development of both oral and written language is a continuous process alongside the other tasks of schooling, and only those directly involved with students should be diagnosing what each needs at a particular time and prescribing the challenges and the support that will best meet those needs. Only those working in the school can develop an effective combination of integration for common tasks and separation for special help.

To make this possible, state and federal programs supporting the education of language minority students should not prescribe teaching methods or the language used but should hold schools accountable for the measurable, steady progress of these students in all required academic subjects.

Second, teachers and school administrators should receive specific training in strategies for language development, including how to diagnose and prescribe for the needs of language minority students. States should make this an important requirement of teacher and administrator certification, and coherent pre-service and in-service training in these skills should be a priority for federal funding. Additional research is not needed to determine what the necessary skills are. Much is already known about good practices in promoting language development; what is not known about, and perhaps will never be known about in view of the complexity and variation of all the factors involved, is what a complete model of good schooling for language minority children would be. Those practices should be taught to every teacher and administrator, not just to those who are preparing to work in separate bilingual programs.

The fine print of the National Research Council report concedes that "we need to move away from thinking about programs in such broad terms and instead see them as containing multiple components—features that are available to meet the differing needs of particular students."[45]

Perhaps some day a general model will emerge for the education of language minority children, though I am skeptical about that. Those who work in pedagogy as an academic discipline have long sought to make the field an exact science comparable to the natural or, more modestly, to the social sciences, with strong and reliable predictive power. If such a general theory of learning "linguistic, social, and cognitive skills" (as the NRC study wistfully puts it) is ever developed, it should take language minority children into account. May it happen, and soon.

But until that glad day comes, the interests of language minority children will be better served by principled and theory-based experimentation on effective schooling of poor children of whatever ethnic background, taking language into account in how they are assessed and taught, than by putting faith in research on second-language acquisition. A fair amount is already known about how to develop bilingualism among middle-class children, especially if their parents are bilingual, but very little is known about how to overcome the academic underachievement of Latino youth or why they are outperformed by youth from other immigrant groups. Do they have more in common with underachieving African American students?

I would put my money on schools that are effective by other measures to be effective also for language minority students, but only if they are set free to tackle problems for every student without programmatic preconditions.[46]

Third, such a strategy of school-level freedom and accountability requires that language minority students be included in all assessments of academic progress. In some limited instances this will appropriately be done through assessment in their home language, but the great difficulty of making assessments in different languages comparable, and the implicit message that students are not expected to demonstrate proficiency in English, creates a danger of returning to Jim Crow standards. In general, it is preferable to assess language minority students in English, while making allowances in reporting and using the results for the challenges they face.

Because schools will choose different strategies for language minority students, parents should be allowed to choose among schools. For some, the maintenance and development of the home language in school will be much more important than it will be for others. Surveys have found, again and again, that Latino parents tend to want the school to help maintain their children's Spanish (though not at the expense of time devoted to English), while Asian and other language minority parents prefer to do that at home or through after-school community groups. Parents should be able to opt for a school that supports their own educational goals.

Finally, schools would be enriched if they provided elective and supplemental—not transitional—language support in a variety of world languages to students whose parents speak those languages as well as to students whose parents do not. In place of the touchy-feely multicultural activities in so many schools, it would be much healthier for students of different ethnic backgrounds to tackle together the difficulties and the rewards of a language, and thus to learn from one another.

Notes

1. There are variations on these models, and they form a continuum.

2. The Office of Bilingual Education and Minority Language Affairs (OBEMLA) has undergone several name changes since it was first established as the Office of Bilingual Education in 1974. Rachel F. Moran, "Of Democracy, Devaluation, and Bilingual Education," *Creighton Law Review*, vol. 26 (1993), pp. 255–319.

3. See Christine H. Rossell and J. Michael Ross, "The Social Science Evidence on Bilingual Education," *Journal of Law and Education*, vol. 15 (Fall 1986), pp. 385–419.

4. See Arnold H. Leibowitz, *The Bilingual Education Act: A Legislative Analysis* (Rosslyn, Va.: National Clearinghouse for Bilingual Education, 1980).

5. The complete text of the Clinton administration's proposal to reauthorize the Elementary and Secondary Education Act, called the Educational Excellence for All Children Act of 1999, can be found at http://www.ed.gov/offices/OESE/ESEA/legislation and a summary at http://www.ed.gov/offices/OESE/ESEA/prospectus/overview.html.

6. Council of Chief State School Officers (CCSSO), *State Education Indicators with a Focus on Title I* (Washington, 1998). These statistics are presented state by state for 1989–90 and 1996–97 and must be added to get the total for the nation. The growth rate shown in the CCSSO report after adding up each state is higher than that cited in the Clinton proposal. It is 72 percent.

7. Department of Education, National Center for Education Statistics, *Digest of Education Statistics,* NCES 93–292 (Washington, 1993); and Department of Education, National Center for Education Statistics, *The Condition of Education,* NCES 93–290 (Washington, 1993).

8. Contrary to popular belief, however, typically little fiscal incentive exists to enroll a limited-English proficient (LEP) child in bilingual education. The LEP identification is the source of extra state revenues, not the program that the child is placed in. With regard to federal funds, although three quarters of the federal Title VII funds are earmarked for bilingual education programs, the money received is only a small portion of the cost of these programs. Thus, it is hard to imagine that a rational actor would implement a bilingual education program solely for the money.

9. The concept of grade level and reading below grade level is almost universally misunderstood, not only by laymen, but also by educators. Grade level is simply the average achievement for a particular grade; it has no absolute meaning. It is not possible, for example, for all students in the norming population to be at grade level because it is not possible for all students to be at or above average, only half can be.

10. J. David Ramirez, Sandra D. Yuen, and Dena Ramey, *Second Year Report: Study of Immersion Programs for Language Minority Children* (Alexandria, Va.: Sra Technologies, 1986). See also Keith Baker and Christine Rossell, "An Implementation Problem: Specifying the Target Group for Bilingual Education," *Educational Policy,* vol. 1, no. 2

(1987), pp. 249–70; and Christine Rossell and Keith Baker, "Selecting and Exiting Students in Bilingual Education Programs," *Journal of Law and Education*, vol. 17, no. 4 (1988), pp. 589–623.

11. Robert Berdan, Alvin So, and Angel Sanchez, *Language among the Cherokee: Patterns of Language Use in Northeastern Oklahoma*, part 1: *The Preliminary Report* (Los Alamitos, Calif.: National Center for Bilingual Research, 1982); Bureau of the Census, *1984 Analysis Data for the Office of Planning, Budget, and Evaluation: Decision Resources* (Department of Education, 1984); and C. Perlman and W. Rice Jr., "A Normative Study of a Test of English Language Proficiency," paper presented at the annual meeting of the American Educational Research Association, San Francisco, Calif., 1979.

12. Sharon E. Duncan and Edward A. De Avila, "Relative Language Proficiency and Field Dependence/Independence," paper presented at the annual meeting of Teachers of English for Speakers of Other Languages (TESOL), Boston, 1979.

13. D. Ulibarri, M. Spencer, and G. Rivas, *Comparability of Three Oral Language Proficiency Instruments and Their Relationship to Achievement Variables* (California State Department of Education, 1980); G. Gillmore and A. Dickerson, *The Relationship between Instruments Used for Identifying Children of Limited English Speaking Ability in Texas* (Houston, Texas: Education Service Center, Region IV, 1979); Robert A. Cervantes, *Entry into and Exit from Bilingual Education Programs* (Washington: E. H. White Inc., 1982); and Sol Pelavin and Keith Baker, "Improved Methods of Identifying Who Needs Bilingual Education," paper presented at the annual meeting of the American Research Association, Washington, D.C., 1987.

14. Perlman and Rice, "A Normative Study of a Test of English Language Proficiency."

15. Nancy L. Russell and Alba A. Ortiz, "Assessment of Pragmatic Skills of Kindergarten Limited English Proficient Children in a Dialogue Model of Communication," paper presented at the annual meeting of the American Educational Research Association, San Francisco, Calif., 1989; and Southwest Regional Laboratories for Educational Research and Development (SWRL), *Development of Entry/Exit Criteria and Associated Assessment Procedures for Bilingual Education Projects* (Los Alamitos, Calif., 1981).

16. *Aspira of New York, Inc., et al.* v. *Board of Education of the City of New York, et al.*, F. Supp. 1161 (1975).

17. The sources are as follows: Fiscal 1978 (2.4 million): Michael J. O'Malley, *Children's English and Services Study: Language Minority Children with Limited English Proficiency in the United States* (Rosslyn, Va.: InterAmerica Associates, 1981), cited in Robert E. Barnes and Anne M. Milne, "The Size of the Eligible Language-Minority Population," in Keith A. Baker and Adrianna A. de Kanter, eds., *Bilingual Education* (Lexington, Mass.: D.C. Heath and Company, 1983), p. 13; (3.6 million): O'Malley cited in Barnes and Milne, "The Size of the Eligible Language-Minority Population," p. 11; and (1.2 million): Barnes and Milne, "The Size of the Eligible Language-Minority Population," p. 14, table 1-2. Fiscal 1986 (1,472,042), fiscal 1987 (1,553,918), fiscal 1988 (1,656,180), fiscal 1989 (1,946,107), fiscal 1990 (2,154,781), fiscal 1991 (2,232,500), fiscal 1992 (2,430,712), and fiscal 1993 (2,735,952): Allison Henderson, Brenda Donly, and William Strang, *Summary of the Bilingual Education State Education Agency Program Survey of the States' Limited English Proficient Persons and Available Educational Services 1992–1993* (Westat Inc. and Development Associates, September 1994), p. 9, figure 2-1. Fiscal 1990 (3,307,500): D. August and K. Hakuta, *Federal Education Programs for Limited English Proficient Students: A Blueprint for the Second Generation* (Stanford Working Group, 1993), cited in Kris Anstrom, "Defining the Limited-English Proficient Student Population," *Directions in Language and Education, National Clearinghouse of Bilingual Education*, vol. 1, no. 9

(Summer 1996), http://www.ncbe.gwu.edu/ncbepubs/directions/09.htm; and (2,388,243): figure from Department of Commerce, *1990 Census of Population and Housing Summary Tape File 3C* (Bureau of the Census, Data User Services Division, 1990) cited in Paul J. Hopstock and Bonnie J. Bucaro, *A Review and Analysis of Estimates of the LEP Student Population*, submitted by Special Issues Analysis Center (Arlington, Va.: Development Associates Inc., 1993). Fiscal 1991 (2,314,079): Howard Fleischman and Paul Hopstock, *Descriptive Study of Services to Limited English Proficient Students*, vol. 1: *Summary of Findings and Conclusions* (Arlington, Va.: Development Associates Inc., 1993), p. 3; (1,997,742): Paul Hopstock and others, *Descriptive Study of Services to Limited English Proficient Students*, vol. 2: *Summary of Findings and Conclusions* (Arlington, Va.: Development Associates Inc., 1993) cited in Anstrom, "Defining the Limited-English Proficient Student Population." Fiscal 1991 (2,198,778), fiscal 1992 (2,429,815), fiscal 1993 (2,620,747), and fiscal 1994 (3,037,922): Brenda Donly, Allison Henderson, and William Strang, *Summary of the Bilingual Education State Education Agency Program Survey of the States' Limited English Proficient Persons and Available Educational Services 1993–1994* (Westat Inc. and Development Associates, September 1995), p. 11, table 2-1. Fiscal 1992 (2,160,000): H. Puma and C. Jones, *Prospects: The Congressionally Mandated Study of Educational Growth and Opportunity: Interim Report* (Abt Associates Inc., 1993), cited in Anstrom, "Defining the Limited-English Proficient Student Population"; and (1,892,845): ALEC Foundation and U.S. English, *Bilingual Education in the United States, 1991–92* (Washington, 1994), p. 7. Fiscal 1997 (3,358,163): Council of Chief State School Officers, *State Education Indicators with a Focus on Title I.*

18. Anstrom, "Defining the Limited-English Proficient Student Population."

19. Oona M. Cheung, Barbara S. Clements, and Y. Carol Miu, *The Feasibility of Collecting Comparable National Statistics about Students with Limited English Proficiency* (Washington: Council of Chief State School Officers, September 1994).

20. 1984 Elementary and Secondary Education Act (ESEA), Section 703 (6).

21. Catherine E. Snow, M. Susan Burns, and Peg Griffin, eds., *Preventing Reading Difficulties in Young Children* (Washington: National Academy Press, 1998).

22. 1984 ESEA, Title VII, Section 702 (7).

23. Citation information on the studies in table 1 can be found in Christine H. Rossell and Keith Baker, "The Educational Effectiveness of Bilingual Education," *Research in the Teaching of English*, vol. 30, no. 1 (February 1996), pp. 7–74, especially appendix A and appendix C. For a summary of these results and other issues, see Christine H. Rossell and Keith Baker, *Bilingual Education in Massachusetts: The Emperor Has No Clothes* (Boston, Mass.: Pioneer Institute, 1996).

24. A more detailed discussion of these results can be found in Rossell and Baker, "The Educational Effectiveness of Bilingual Education."

25. A cohort is a group of students who are followed across grades in their progression through school. Thus, a group of students who started kindergarten in 1960 and graduated from high school in 1974 would be one cohort. A second cohort might be a group of students who started kindergarten in 1961 and graduated from high school in 1975.

26. These studies are listed in alphabetical order in complete citation format in Rossell and Baker, "The Educational Effectiveness of Bilingual Education," appendix B and references.

27. The "voting method" is used to evaluate the literature's findings. In the voting method, the percentage of studies showing each program's outcome is calculated. A theoretically preferred method is meta-analysis—a statistical analysis of the effects of bilingual education across all studies. But because of the lack of information in these studies by

which to estimate a common outcome measure, the two meta-analyses that have been conducted have had only a small number of studies. Ann C. Willig's 1985 meta-analysis included only thirteen of the thirty-nine acceptable studies of transitional bilingual education from Keith Baker and Adrian de Kanter's 1981 study. Jay P. Greene's 1997 meta-analysis of Rossell and Baker's 1995 study analyzed only eleven of the seventy-two studies. Both Willig and Greene concluded that bilingual education was superior. See Ann C. Willig, "A Meta-Analysis of Selected Studies on the Effectiveness of Bilingual Education," *Review of Educational Research*, vol. 55, no. 3 (1985), pp. 269–317; Keith Baker and Adrian de Kanter, *The Effectiveness of Bilingual Education Programs: A Review of the Literature, Final Draft Report* (Department of Education, 1981); and Jay P. Greene, "A Meta-Analysis of the Rossell and Baker Review of Bilingual Education Research," *Bilingual Research Journal*, vol. 21, nos. 3 and 4 (1997), pp. 103–21.

28. Oral progress in preschool or kindergarten is included in this category because a reading test for these grades is inappropriate.

29. Marcello Medina and Kathy Escamilla, "Evaluation of Transitional and Maintenance Bilingual Programs," *Urban Education*, vol. 27, no. 3 (1992), pp. 263–90. J. David Ramirez and others also examined maintenance bilingual education (late-exit bilingual education) but unfortunately did not directly compare it with transitional bilingual education (contrary to media reports and their own conclusions). Although their graphs appeared to show that the students in late-exit bilingual education were way behind the students in transitional bilingual education although beginning to catch up, no statistical analysis was performed to determine if they would ever catch up. See J. David Ramirez and others, *Final Report: Longitudinal Study of Structured Immersion Strategy, Early-Exit and Late-Exit Transitional Bilingual Education Programs for Language-Minority Children*, report to the Department of Education (San Mateo, Calif.: Aguirre International, 1991).

30. Ramirez and others, *Final Report*; El Paso Independent School District, *Interim Report of the Five-Year Bilingual Education Pilot 1986–87 School Year* (El Paso, Texas: Office for Research and Evaluation, 1987); El Paso Independent School District, *Bilingual Education Evaluation: The Sixth Year in a Longitudinal Study* (El Paso, Texas: Office for Research and Evaluation, September 1990); and El Paso Independent School District, *Bilingual Education Evaluation* (El Paso, Texas: Office for Research and Evaluation, November 1992).

31. ESEA, Title VII, Section 7102 (b) (2).

32. Descriptions of these varied interpretations can be found in Rossell and Baker, *Bilingual Education in Massachusetts,* chapter 4; and Christine Rossell, "Teaching Language Minorities: Theory and Reality," in Diane Ravitch and Joseph Viterriti, eds., *City Schools: Lessons from New York* (Johns Hopkins University Press, forthcoming 1999).

33. See Rossell and Baker, *Bilingual Education in Massachusetts,* chapter 7.

34. Clinton administration proposal, p. VII-7.

35. See also Rossell and Baker, *Bilingual Education in Massachusetts*, for a detailed description of how a research study should be conducted and what variables it should include.

36. C. E. Snow, M. S. Burns, and P. Griffin, eds., *Preventing Reading Difficulties in Young Children* (Washington: National Academy Press, 1998).

37. J. Cummins, "The Role of Primary Language Development in Promoting Educational Success for Language Minority Students," in *Schooling and Language Minority Students: A Theoretical Framework* (California State University at Los Angeles, National Evaluation, Dissemination and Assessment Center, 1981), pp. 3–49; and S. Krashen, *Language Acquisition and Language Education* (Prentice-Hall International, 1989).

38. C. E. Snow, "Rationales for Native Language Instruction in the Education of Language Minority Children: Evidence from Research," in A. Padilla, H. Fairchild, and C. Valadez, eds., *Bilingual Education: Issues and Strategies* (Newbury Park, Calif.: Sage, 1990).

39. E. Schiller, "Khmer Writing," in P. T. Daniels and W. Bright, eds., *The World's Writing Systems* (New York: Oxford University Press, 1996), pp. 467–73; and W. Bright, "The Devanagan Script," in P. T. Daniels and W. Bright, eds., *The World's Writing Systems* (New York: Oxford University Press, 1996), pp. 384–90.

40. A. C. Willig, "A Meta-Analysis of Selected Studies on the Effectiveness of Bilingual Education," *Review of Educational Research*, vol. 55, no. 3 (1985), pp. 269–317; and J. P. Greene, "A Meta-Analysis of the Effectiveness of Bilingual Education," University of Texas at Austin and Thomas Rivera Policy Institute, 1998.

41. Charles L. Glenn with Ester J. de Jong, *Educating Immigrant Children: Schools and Language Minorities in Twelve Nations* (New York: Garland, 1986).

42. Diane August and Kenji Hakuta, eds., *Improving Schooling for Language-Minority Children: A Research Agenda* (Washington: National Research Council, 1997).

43. August and Hakuta, *Improving Schooling for Language-Minority Children*, p. 60.

44. August and Hakuta, *Improving Schooling for Language-Minority Children*, p. 179.

45. August and Hakuta, *Improving Schooling for Language-Minority Children*, p. 158.

46. Thomas P. Carter and Michael L. Chatfield, "Effective Schools for Language Minority Students," *American Journal of Education*, vol. 97 (1986), pp. 200–33.

The Federal Role in Teacher Professional Development

JULIA E. KOPPICH

THE REAUTHORIZATION OF the Elementary and Secondary Education Act (ESEA) provides an opportune occasion to take a fresh look at the federal role in teacher professional development. Funds designed to improve teachers' professional prowess currently are tucked into a number of federally funded programs—programs, for example, for students living in poverty, for children with little or no English language proficiency, and for schools engaged in so-called whole school reform.

The largest federal professional development appropriation, and the only federal effort devoted entirely to this purpose, is the Eisenhower program. Initiated a decade and a half ago, Eisenhower has undergone substantial changes over the years in terms of level of funding, purpose, and mission.

Lessons learned from Eisenhower, considered alongside contemporary research on the type of teacher support likely to have the greatest impact on improving practice to raise student achievement, can inform a new federal role in teacher professional development. In brief, this new role would:

—Concentrate federal professional development dollars specifically and exclusively to support teachers' subject matter knowledge and mastery of subject-based pedagogy; and,

—Require that accountability for such dollars be based on an assessment of teachers' contributions to improving student learning.

This paper is not an evaluation of federally funded professional development, a comprehensive appraisal of the Eisenhower program, or a thorough review of relevant research. The purpose here is to put forth a set of ideas designed to spark discussion about ways in which a segment of federal dollars might more effectively be used to improve student achievement.

The First Eisenhower: 1984–94

The Eisenhower program was born in August 1984 as Title II of the Education for Economic Security Act (EESA). *A Nation at Risk*, the report of the National Commission on Excellence in Education, had been released the previous year warning that "a rising tide of mediocrity" threatened to engulf the nation's schools.[1]

Nearly three decades earlier, in 1957, Russia's successful launch of *Sputnik*, the first man-made satellite to orbit the earth, had been the impetus for the National Defense Education Act (NDEA). Then, policymakers feared that inadequate science and mathematics programs in the nation's public schools had allowed the Soviets to gain the technological upper hand. The threat was perceived to be a military one. If Russia could launch a satellite, Americans worried, surely it had, or soon would have, the technological capability to initiate a successful nuclear strike against the United States.

In the 1980s, the fear was economic, not military. Japan, a country once known for the shoddy quality of its goods, when "Made in Japan" meant "made to fall apart," began to surge ahead of the United States in the competition to claim dominance in the global marketplace. The cold war had ended. The trade wars had begun.

In times of national crisis, America often turns to its schools for salvation. Title II of EESA was part of this response. If schools did a better job preparing students in mathematics and science, policymakers reasoned, the logical spillover would be that Americans could begin to gain a leg up on the global competition in a world increasingly dependent on advanced technology.

Title II federal funds were allocated specifically to advance professional development for mathematics and science teachers in elementary and secondary schools. Funding was justified on the basis of the presumption that increasing teachers' knowledge and skills in these areas would have a beneficial effect on improving students' math and science achievement levels.

The original intent of Title II was purposely both broad and specific. While funds were targeted to improve mathematics and science education, the program allowed school districts maximum flexibility within the bounds of math and science to design staff development programs to meet teachers' needs.[2] The program was funded at $100 million in 1985, but Congress cut the Title II budget in 1986 to $46 million.

Two years later, in 1988, the program was reauthorized as part of the Hawkins-Stafford Elementary and Secondary School Improvement Amendments to ESEA. Officially named the Dwight D. Eisenhower Mathematics and Science Education Act at that time, funding was increased to $110 million.

In both the 1984 and 1988 authorizations, the lion's share of Eisenhower dollars was distributed to states.[3] Money was allocated by means of a funding formula that took into account two factors: (1) a state's overall student population, and (2) the number of students eligible to receive ESEA Title I funding. Eisenhower, then, was established as a state entitlement.

Seventy-five percent of each state's Eisenhower allocation was designated as a "pass through" from the state's education agency (for example, state department of education) to local school districts. The remaining 25 percent was directed to a state-selected "state agency for higher education" that administered competitive grant programs among those of the state's colleges and universities interested in conducting Eisenhower-related activities for elementary and secondary school teachers. This setup—a proportional funding split between K-12 and higher education and a specific focus on improving mathematics and science education—would last until 1994 when Eisenhower was again reauthorized.

In the Midst of Reform

The first decade of the Eisenhower program, from 1984 to 1994, fell squarely in the midst of two cycles, or "waves," of the education reform movement that had been launched in 1983 with the release of *A Nation at Risk*. From the mid-to-late 1980s, the first wave of reform, national and state-level education policy discussions and actions centered primarily on four aspects of education improvement: (1) developing and implementing higher and more rigorous academic standards for students, (2) designing new curricula around these standards, (3) ensuring that all students take larger numbers of academic courses—more math, more English, more science, more history, and (4) creating new kinds of assessments aligned with new standards and curricula.

These reform activities, despite their fervor and energy, produced decidedly mixed results. On the one hand, the intense focus on standards, curriculum, and assessments began to shift policymakers' and educators' attention away from educational inputs and toward measurable student outcomes. On the other hand, early reform efforts were based on the notion that if educators continued to do what they had always done—but did it harder, faster, and generally under stricter state scrutiny—improved student achievement would result. When this did not prove to be the case, reformers rededicated themselves to change and refocused their efforts on improving the conditions of teaching.

The late 1980s to about the mid-1990s marked the second reform cycle. *A Nation at Risk*, in criticizing teachers' limited professional decisionmaking authority and the relatively low level of teachers' salaries, had declared, "The professional working life of teachers is on the whole unacceptable."[4] But little policy attention had been paid during the first cycle of reform to the work conditions that shaped the teaching career. By the end of the 1980s, policymakers and reformers began to zero in on the conditions of teaching. Many states raised teachers' salaries; teachers were provided with modestly expanded decisionmaking authority; and some limited opportunities were created for teachers to take on new professional roles without leaving the classroom.

The notion here was that if teaching began more closely to resemble a profession, with better compensation and a taste of the kind of discretion professionals in other fields enjoy, more competent people would be attracted to teaching and good teachers, who often left after just a few years in the classroom, would remain. Improving student achievement was the desired result. But despite much hard work and many good intentions, after a decade of these efforts, student achievement in the United States was not showing much improvement.

Results of the Third International Mathematics and Science Study (TIMSS) revealed the United States to be the only country that scored above the international average at fourth grade and below at eighth grade. Eighth graders ranked nineteenth out of twenty-five countries; at the twelfth grade, U.S. students ranked near the bottom in math, above only students from Cyprus and South Africa. In science, eighth graders ranked twelfth out of twenty-five countries; at twelfth grade, they ranked sixteenth out of twenty-one countries. National Assessment of Educational Progress (NAEP) results were discouraging as well. They showed 40 percent of fourth-grade students scoring below the basic level in reading, nearly the same percentage of eighth graders scoring below the basic level in math. Likewise, more than 40 percent of twelfth graders scored below the basic level in science.

These first two cycles of education reform, then, framed the policy context for the first two Eisenhower authorizations. Policymakers and reformers concentrated on building policy structures to support education improvement—higher standards, new curricula, better tests—and altering some of the conditions of classroom teaching.

An Appraisal of the First Eisenhower Decade

A 1991 national evaluation of the Eisenhower program conducted by SRI International, as well as other evaluative work of the early Eisenhower years, offered a mixed picture of program results. On the credit side, Eisenhower cut a wide swath through the population of targeted K-12 teachers. Nearly one-third of all elementary and secondary teachers with responsibility for math and science instruction participated in some Eisenhower-funded activity during the 1988–89 school year.[5]

On the other side of the ledger, however, state departments of education and local school districts clearly had made the choice, in the way they expended Eisenhower funds, to trade quality for quantity. As the SRI team reported, state- and district-level Eisenhower funds generally were paying for low-intensity in-service training, averaging just six hours or less per participant.[6] Most of this staff development was both generic and benign, focused on building awareness among teachers about emerging math and science standards, for example, or enabling elementary and secondary teachers to attend math- or science-related conferences. SRI found little evidence that these activities were having much impact on improving teaching or, by extrapolation, on increasing student achievement.

The picture for higher education Eisenhower professional development was somewhat brighter. College- and university-based Eisenhower projects, reported SRI, typically were more intensive than were their state or local school district counterparts. Each participant in an Eisenhower higher education program received approximately sixty hours of professional development, a tenfold increase over state department of education and local school district programs.

Moreover, college and university Eisenhower projects tended to be less generic, paid significantly more attention to the content of mathematics and science instruction, and were better designed than were district or state activities to have an impact on classroom practice. This latter finding may have, at least in part, resulted from the fact that more than half the Eisenhower college and university project directors made their academic homes not in schools of education, but in departments of mathematics, science, or related fields.

SRI's evaluation, while critical of many of the district and state uses of Eisenhower dollars, nonetheless attributed a number of advantages to the program:

1. Eisenhower had a wide reach. All states, nearly all school districts, and a substantial fraction of colleges and universities received funds.

2. The money was easy to obtain and flexible to use. With the exception of the higher education portion, which was allocated on a competitive basis, Eisenhower dollars were an entitlement to states and districts and allowed a wide range of professional development activities to be subsumed under the Eisenhower umbrella.

3. Eisenhower dollars substantially increased the array of math and science professional development opportunities available to teachers. The funds, for example, were a key resource in promoting teacher participation at state and local math and science professional meetings. For many teachers, especially at the elementary level, Eisenhower-funded meeting attendance was the first, and perhaps the only, opportunity to participate in sessions focused on mathematics and science education.

4. The program simultaneously targeted elementary and secondary education as well as higher education, thus encouraging collaboration among various sectors in the improvement of mathematics and science instruction.

Federal professional development dollars, then, in the form of the Eisenhower program, showed some modest benefits. However, measurably contributing to improving student achievement did not seem to be among them.

Eisenhower's next reauthorization, in 1994, came in the midst of once again shifting education policy priorities. These priorities, as reflected in the new Eisenhower, profoundly influenced the shape of the program.

A New Reform Wave

By the mid-1990s, even though the American economy had made a near-complete recovery, American education had not. The focus on standards, curriculum, assessments, and the conditions of teaching clearly had wrought some educational benefits. Policy talk and action centered on implementing academic standards and new forms of student assessments. To some extent, more, and more capable, people were being attracted into teaching. In some states and districts, improved teaching conditions were beginning to staunch the flow of good teachers from the profession. Yet improved student achievement—the pot of gold at the end of the education reform rainbow—still lagged badly.

The policy tide began to shift again. Improving the quality of teaching catapulted to the top of federal and state education policy agendas. The rationale for this new attention to teaching quality was echoed in the common-sense mantra of the National Commission on Teaching and America's Future: "What teachers know and can do makes the crucial difference in what students learn."[7]

Improved teaching quality, as played out in policy, came to encompass three fundamental elements:

1. Better teacher preparation through more rigorous licensing requirements and teacher competency tests;

2. Standards for both beginning and accomplished teaching, enunciating what beginning teachers should know and be able to do through the Interstate New Teacher Assessment and Support Consortium (INTASC) standards and, likewise, what accomplished experienced teachers know and can do as demonstrated through certification by the National Board for Professional Teaching Standards; and,

3. Higher quality professional development, using research about effective teacher learning to shape programs designed to increase teachers' expertise in ways that lead to improved student performance.

The emphasis on higher quality teaching derived in large measure from a recognition on the part of policymakers and educators that when expectations changed for students, in terms of meeting tougher standards, they changed for teachers as well. If teachers were to be responsible for helping all students reach high standards, they would need to know more about the subjects they teach and about how to communicate that subject matter effectively to students.

This, then, was the education reform milieu that surrounded the next Eisenhower reauthorization.

The Second Eisenhower: 1994 to the Present

The Eisenhower professional development program was reauthorized in 1994, this time as part of the Improving America's Schools Act (IASA). Expanded in scope and purpose, the program was renamed the Eisenhower Professional Development Program. Mathematics and science were removed from the name.

In reauthorizing Eisenhower, Congress declared:

> The federal government has a vital role in helping states and local agencies to make sustained and intensive high-quality professional development in the core academic subjects . . . an integral part of the elementary and secondary education system.

Thus, the new Eisenhower was to include professional development for teachers in all core academic subjects, those being defined by the federal government as arts, civics and government, economics, English, foreign languages, geography, history, mathematics, and science. Moreover, not only was Eisenhower funding to encompass the sweep of core subjects, but, responding to the SRI critique about generic activities of brief duration, program dollars were now also to buy "sustained and intensive" support for teachers.

In the 1994 reauthorization, the government enunciated a new set of principles that would undergird Eisenhower programs and funding:

1. All students can meet high academic standards.

2. Students in poverty should be taught to the same high standards as other students.

3. Schools must be held accountable for students' progress in meeting the standards.

These principles derived from two federal—as well as state—policy thrusts that complemented, or were complemented by, the focus on improving the quality of teaching. Namely, no students should be allowed to fall through the academic cracks, and districts and schools must shoulder greater responsibility for improving student achievement.

The Hope for a Coordinated Strategy

The White House viewed a reauthorized Eisenhower as part of its continuing effort to assist the nation in meeting the education goals first announced in 1989 as a result of President George Bush's education summit for governors held in Charlottesville, Virginia.

In particular, the Clinton administration saw expanded Eisenhower efforts as critical to achieving Goal 4:

> By the year 2000, the nation's teaching force will have access to programs for the continued improvement of their professional skills and the opportunity to acquire the knowledge and skills needed to instruct and prepare American students for the next century.

and to assisting students to meet Goal 3:

> By the year 2000, American students will leave grades four, eight, and twelve having demonstrated competency in challenging subject matter including English, mathematics, science, history, and geography.

and Goal 5:

> By the year 2000, U.S. students will be first in the world in science and mathematics achievement.

The federal government's intent was that Eisenhower-funded teacher professional development would become part of states' systemic education reform efforts, focused around standards, curriculum, and assessments. The new federal legislation encouraged districts to coordinate Eisenhower activities with other ongoing education reform efforts and admonished them to construct professional development programs so as to maximize their impact on teachers' classroom performance.

Federally promulgated examples of activities authorized under the 1994 Eisenhower included providing seed money for agencies and organizations to expand their capacity to offer professional development; encouraging the creation of professional networks; supporting teachers with professional development time and money; supporting partnerships among schools, consortia, school districts, and colleges and universities; and developing and identifying model professional development programs. In addition, Eisenhower funds could be used to align states' teacher licensing requirements with new standards; recruit underrepresented groups, such as minorities and women, into mathematics and science teaching; and train teachers in the effective use of educational technology.[8] Finally, the legislation also authorized the secretary of education to waive many of Eisenhower's statutory and regulatory requirements to increase state and local decisionmaking authority.

As part of the reauthorization, the administration originally requested from Congress a 1995 funding level of $800 million, on the assumption that Eisenhower could move beyond math and science if the program had a significantly increased annual appropriation. Congress approved a substantially lower amount, just under $252 million, and added the proviso that, in any given year, the first $250 million of Eisenhower funding must be dedicated to mathematics and science professional development.

By 1998, Eisenhower funding had reached $335 million. More than three quarters of those funds (78 percent, or $261 million) were sequestered for math and science purposes. Of the remaining nearly $74 million, the federal government required that 7 percent, or approximately $5 million, be used to improve reading instruction. States and districts were free to determine how to deploy their share of the final 15 percent, or $69 million.

Distributing the Dollars

In addition to expanding the scope and purpose of the program, the 1994 Eisenhower reauthorization also altered, to some extent, the way in which state and local funds are distributed. Despite the SRI finding that college and university Eisenhower offerings tended to have greater impact on improving teaching, the new regulations increased the states' Eisenhower allocation from 75 percent to 84 percent of the dollars and reduced the college and university share from 25 percent to 16 percent.

Money continues to be allotted on a formula grant basis, calculated by using a state's previous year's Title I funding and the total number of students—both public and private—in the state.[9] States use the same allocation formula to distribute money to school districts as the federal government uses to distribute money to states; that is, a combination of total pupil population and the number of Title I–eligible students. Any district whose share of Eisenhower funds is less than $10,000 must be part of a consortium of similarly funded districts.

Current regulations also require that states "pass through" no less than 90 percent of Eisenhower funds to local school districts. Of the remaining 10 percent, 5 percent may be preserved by the state for administrative costs incurred as a result of overseeing the program. Only 5 percent may be used for state-level activities, which the federal government suggests include revising teacher licensing requirements, providing teachers with financial incentives to seek advanced certification through the National Board for Professional Teaching Standards, and developing and supporting regional and statewide teacher networks.

Districts are required to use at least 80 percent of their share of funds for school-based professional development. The remaining 20 percent may be used for districtwide activities. Local activities, like those at the state level, must be tied to state academic standards and designed to improve teachers' classroom practice.

The 1994 reauthorization also includes a cost-sharing provision. At least one-third of the cost of district-provided Eisenhower professional development must come from sources other than Eisenhower funds. Finally, though Eisenhower money is an entitlement, each school district must—at least every three years—submit to the state education department an application detailing how the district intends to use its funds.

College and university Eisenhower dollars continue to be disbursed on a competitive basis by a designated state higher education agency. In addition to institutions of higher education, nonprofit organizations, such as museums, may compete for these funds.

The Accountability Provision

For the first time in Eisenhower's history, the 1994 reauthorization includes a form of accountability for the dollars. Each school district must develop specific measurable performance indicators designed to assess the degree to which Eisenhower-funded professional development is meeting its avowed purposes.

Sample indicators suggested in the regulations include the following:

—Teachers show evidence that participation in Eisenhower professional development activities improved their knowledge and skills.

—District-level Eisenhower professional development is aligned with content and student performance standards.

—Significant proportions of teachers from historically underrepresented groups and teachers of high-poverty children are involved in Eisenhower-funded activities.

Every three years, states and districts must prepare a report for the federal government documenting progress on the performance indicators.

A Preliminary View of the Effects of the 1994 Reauthorization

Information about how the Eisenhower program has operated, and what its effects have been since the 1994 reauthorization, is just beginning to trickle in.[10] A new three-year national evaluation, commissioned by the U.S. Department of Education from the American Institutes of Research (AIR), is under way and is slated to be completed by April 2000.

Despite the relative paucity of data, some information is known. Using data gleaned from the first of AIR's evaluation reports, consisting of case studies in six districts, and reports the states submitted to the federal government describing their uses of Eisenhower funds, a preliminary picture of the current Eisenhower program can be constructed. Three features seem evident:

1. Eisenhower in most states still focuses largely, although not exclusively, on mathematics and science.

States report that 76 percent of their Eisenhower dollars are dedicated to math and science professional development, as is 60 percent of college and university Eisenhower funds.

While the intent of the 1994 Eisenhower changes was to integrate that program with other education reforms, according to the AIR study, Eisenhower's relationship to other state and district education reforms is essentially to support the math and science components of these efforts. AIR posits that much of the continuing math and science focus results from the fact that many state and district Eisenhower coordinators are math and science specialists. Moreover, while professional development dollars are available in a number of the core academic areas, Eisenhower remains one of the few reliable sources of professional development for mathematics and science education.

2. Eisenhower funds support a wide, and perhaps expanding, array of professional development opportunities for teachers. However, the extent to which Eisenhower programs are designed to have an impact on teachers' classroom practice remains an open question.

More than 96 percent of the nation's school districts receive Eisenhower funds. Some Eisenhower-funded activities—workshops, institutes, conferences, university courses—are traditional. Others, such as coaching, mentoring, and teacher study groups, are less so.

While AIR reports that Eisenhower activities are more sustained and intense than was previously the case, states' reports suggest otherwise. According to the states, more than half the professional development funded through Eisenhower (56 percent) lasts one day or less.

In addition, AIR notes that Eisenhower-funded activities generally are aligned with state and district standards, as was intended by the 1994 reauthorization. However, while professional development in the core subject areas is the federally intended thrust of Eisenhower, only a small portion of the program's funded activities emphasizes subject matter per se. Many Eisenhower programs, apparently, are still of the SRI-criticized generic variety.

3. Federal efforts to hold states and districts accountable for the results of Eisenhower-funded professional development have met with less than successful results.

In planning Eisenhower activities, states report that districts often take into account student test scores as a way of pinpointing teacher needs. However, little district- or state-wide planning and evaluation are based on locally developed performance indicators, as the Eisenhower program now requires. States report confusion about how to develop indicators and how to design a measurement system for program-specific professional development. The bottom line, according to AIR's preliminary findings, is that little accountability exists for the results of Eisenhower-funded professional development.

One could conclude, after reviewing these findings, however preliminary, that the Eisenhower program should simply be allowed to sunset and that the prospect of federally funded professional development having a beneficial effect on teachers' classroom practice is dim. That conclusion, however, would be premature. A look at the way in which one state—California—deployed its Eisenhower dollars before and after the 1994 reauthorization provides some valuable lessons.

The Eisenhower Program in California

California is a state that often exemplifies Mr. Toad's wild ride. Seemingly in perpetual motion, the state's citizens both grimace and gloat when non-Californians are heard to remark, "Everything that happens anywhere in the country begins in California."

A Little State Context

The state's numbers are impressive, and daunting. The world's seventh largest economy, California is home to one of every eight American schoolchildren. Nearly 6 million kindergarten through twelfth-grade students are enrolled in the state's public schools, and that number is expected to increase by another 15 percent over the next decade.

Twenty-five percent of California's schoolchildren live below the federal poverty line. Eight of every twenty qualify for free and reduced-price lunches.

By the turn of the century, Hispanic students (who now compose 40 percent of the school population) will be the majority. Many of these children come to school with limited or no English language skills. Currently, one quarter of all California children enter school not speaking English. In the 650,000-student Los Angeles Unified School District alone, nearly half the children (46 percent) districtwide, and 60 percent at the elementary level, have limited proficiency, or none at all, in English.

Like many states, California is experiencing a teacher shortage. The problem is an immediate, not a prospective, one. Increasing enrollment, coupled with policies such as class-size reduction, has created a situation in which thirty-one thousand teachers—10 percent of the state's teaching force—are teaching on emergency permits.

Despite its $30 billion annual price tag for public education, California's per pupil expenditures are below the national average. While California in the 1960s ranked among the top ten states in annual per pupil spending, the state spends less of its personal income on schools now than it did a generation ago. Compounding the school funding dilemma, local citizens have virtually no ability to raise money for their schools. As a result of a combination of court decisions and voter initiatives, local revenue raising is limited to special use taxes (called parcel taxes), which require a two-thirds affirmative vote to be enacted.

California's reputation as a trend setter is well earned and remains intact. For years, government by initiative has been one of the state's favorite pastimes. Californians have enacted amendments to the state's constitution to reduce property taxes (the now-famous Proposition 13), cap state and local spending, require a minimum percentage of state revenues to be dedicated to public schools, abolish affirmative action in public education and employment, deny educational services to the children of illegal immigrants (the courts, so far, have prohibited implementation of this), restrict bilingual education, and most recently, ban the slaughter of horses for human consumption. As former *Sacramento Bee* editorial page editor Peter Schrag notes, "California does very little of consequence without excess."[11]

A Reform Roller Coaster

California was once ahead of the education reform curve. By 1983, when higher academic standards were just a twinkle in the policy eye of most states, California had already begun the hard work of creating standards, developing curriculum frameworks, and rethinking student assessment.

But California's road to education change has been anything but smooth. For good or ill, the vagaries of politics often have held sway over reform. The state has been blessed, or cursed, with vocal, and sometimes colorful, high-level policy actors who have latched on to the education cause in a variety of ways: governors who have taken a particular interest in—some would say launched a vendetta against—public schools; an activist legislature prone to specify instructional pedagogy in policy; a governor-appointed state board of education, which in recent years has flexed its policy muscles and fanned the flames of the much-publicized "curriculum wars," most recently fought over mathematics; and constitutionally elected state superintendents of public instruction with their own agendas rarely in accord with the governor, state board, or legislature.

When Gray Davis was elected governor in November 1998, the first Democrat in sixteen years, he vowed to make education his top priority. Immediately upon being sworn into office, the new governor called the legislature into a special session devoted to education. Four statutes emerged: establishment of statewide reading institutes; peer review as a means to reshape teacher evaluation; a high school exit examination for all students; and a new statewide, school-by-school accountability system.

Davis had run on a platform of improving California's sadly sagging public school system. The shift in the 1980s to more rigorous academic courses in the core areas (spurred, at least in part, by the state university system's tougher admission requirements) had resulted in larger percentages of students enrolling in more academic courses, more students taking Advanced Placement classes and passing the tests, and slight increases in Scholastic Assessment Test (SAT) scores. Nonetheless, putting a positive spin on student achievement results stretched the bounds of credulity to the breaking point.

National Assessment of Educational Progress results placed California second to last, tied with Mississippi and only slightly ahead of Louisiana in reading. Fourth and eighth graders placed well below the national average in both science and mathematics. Results of the new statewide exam, given for the first time in 1998, were not much more encouraging. Students scored below the national average in reading, math, and science, and they lagged well behind in spelling.[12]

Eisenhower in California: 1984–94

Teacher professional development in California, as elsewhere, tends to be low-impact and generic. A 1987 study of teacher professional development statewide had concluded that most of what passed for staff development in California was unlikely to influence positively teacher practice. Most professional development programs offered in districts and by the state were organized in ways that reinforced existing patterns of teaching and conventional structures of schools, did little to expand teachers' horizons in terms of rethinking their instructional strategies, and tended to be offered as single sequence, one-shot activities with little follow-up and coaching and insufficient lasting effect.[13]

The Eisenhower program, however, in the decade from 1984 to 1994, had a different flavor. California used federal dollars to support state and local efforts to improve mathematics and science education by focusing on the content of mathematics and science instruction.

Whereas the SRI nationwide assessment of Eisenhower had shown that many states and districts were using these federal dollars for professional development nominally centered on generic math and science, a 1993 evaluation of California Eisenhower by Policy Analysis for California Education (PACE), a joint University of California at Berkeley–Stanford University education think tank, revealed a different pattern. Eisenhower money in California was being used specifically to leverage the state's mathematics and science frameworks.[14]

California had adopted frameworks in the mid-1980s with much fanfare and little or no teacher professional development. Teachers were simply instructed to "Go forth and teach" what amounted to an entirely new curriculum in most of the core subject areas. Eisenhower dollars were used to partially fill the professional development gap in math and science.

Districts reported that the state's mathematics and science curriculum frameworks were the most significant factor affecting school districts' planning for and use of Eisenhower money. Eisenhower-funded professional development, in other words, was shaped by state policy regarding what California expected students to know and be able to do in the areas of science and mathematics and, by extension, what the state expected teachers to know and be able to teach in these areas. Cited by three quarters of the state's nearly one thousand school districts as the primary source of funding for math and science improvement activities, Eisenhower-funded professional development contributed to steady, albeit slow, changes in mathematics and science teaching.

The power of Eisenhower in California is again illustrated by the ways in which the state made use of dollars that remained in Sacramento with the Department of Education and those that were part of the higher education allotment.

The competitive portion of California's Eisenhower program is administered by the California Postsecondary Education Commission (CPEC). Nonprofit organizations and all three of California's systems of higher education—community colleges, the state university system, and the University of California (UC)—vie for CPEC-held Eisenhower funds.

Before 1994, the California Department of Education and CPEC pooled their resources to administer joint state competitions and encourage cooperation among colleges, universities, nonprofit organizations, and local school districts. Math and science projects involving UC Berkeley's Lawrence Hall of Science and San Francisco's interactive science museum, the Exploratorium, for example, resulted from such collaborations. Professional mathematicians and scientists became involved in the public schools in programs designed to help teachers gain more math and science knowledge and use that knowledge in implementing the state standards and frameworks.

CPEC–Department of Education grant awards were substantial, generally in the range of $250,000 a year for each of three years. These amounts were, in the words of one California Department of Education official, "large enough to really get something started—to create communities of people who could continue into the future."

Four of these initiatives illustrate this point:

—Teaching Opportunities for Partners in Science (TOPS) was a joint project of Columbia Community College and the San Joaquin County Office of Education. The goal of the project was to improve the delivery of science education to students in twenty-four rural school districts in four California counties. TOPS placed twenty-six retired scientists in elementary schools to provide specific science content expertise and offer professional development to teachers based on science education activities developed by the teachers, scientists, and local community college faculty.

—The Los Angeles Mathematics Initiative was part of a cities and urban district initiative focused on metropolitan areas in which at least 70 percent of the students were members of racial and ethnic minority groups. The Los Angeles initiative funded teacher mathematics academies, each of which lasted a minimum of four days and focused on a particular curricular strand, such as fractions or problem solving, that was part of the state standards and frameworks. Academy instructors were experienced classroom teachers with math backgrounds who were available following the sessions to serve as ongoing resources to teachers as they implemented in their classrooms what they had learned in the academies. In addition, the Los Angeles initiative established a math resource center in each school, consisting of a library of math curriculum materials and a directory of experts and organizations willing to provide assistance to classroom teachers.

—The Informal Science Education Centers Initiative was a cooperative effort of a range of nonprofit organizations, including museums, aquariums, planetariums, and zoos. One of the projects resulting from this initiative was led by San Francisco's Exploratorium in consortium with San Francisco State University and San Francisco City College. The first awardee of grant money founded the Mission Science Workshop, a community-based interactive science center that provided monthly in-service programs for area teachers, a two-week summer science institute, and field trips for teachers to learn how to use neighborhood resources for teaching science. This effort was so successful that the National Science Foundation awarded a multimillion-dollar grant to establish ten similar community-based science centers around the state.

—The Teacher Achievement Award Program (TAAP) provided seed money to teachers and teams of teachers to develop and implement science curriculum based on the California science standards. Teachers were given resources and time to begin to put flesh on the bones of the science curriculum framework. Some projects not only were implemented in California classrooms, but they received national recognition as well. One TAAP grantee was awarded the Disney Science Teacher of the Year prize for developing a multimedia curriculum exploring nuclear fusion.

Summing Up the First Decade

The first decade of the Eisenhower program in California concentrated heavily on improving mathematics and science education by improving the subject matter knowledge and subject-based pedagogy of classroom teachers, particularly those at the elementary level. Eisenhower-funded professional development took the long view. Built into the program was the recognition that teaching improvement leading to student achievement gains required steady, sustained effort; that the communities of mathematics and science professionals had much to contribute to this work; and that professional development needed to be grounded in expectations about what teachers needed to do in the classroom to help students meet specific academic standards.

Following the 1994 reauthorization, Eisenhower in California began to show a different face.

A Shift in Focus: 1994 to the Present

No new evaluation of Eisenhower has been conducted in California since the PACE study of the early 1990s. But anecdotal evidence suggests that, since the 1994 federal reauthorization, the federal shift in Eisenhower has been reflected in the state.

While state officials report that most of California's $35 million in Eisenhower funding continues to be directed to math and science education, tracking Eisenhower footprints in school districts is difficult. With little federal direction, there is little state support for mathematics and virtually none for science education.

California's state-level Eisenhower program, which formerly was staffed by three to four math and science specialists, is now overseen by one staff person as part of his general responsibilities for the state's Coordinated Compliance Review for all state and federal funds. For inexplicable reasons, the program is crowded into the Department of Education's overtaxed Secondary Education Unit, even though a heavy emphasis of the program has been at the elementary level.

Many elementary schools in the state have now all but eliminated their science programs. They are likely to reappear once the state again tests students in science. But that will not be for another couple of years, and even then, fifth grade is the only elementary grade at which science will be tested.

In a way, the state behaves schizophrenically. While the Department of Education does not promote a math and science focus, neither does it encourage districts to spend Eisenhower money for subjects other than math and science professional development. But federal Title I regulations make the state's suggestions somewhat empty.

Schoolwide Title I schools—those in which half or more of the students are Title I–eligible—are allowed to waive all Eisenhower regulations. As a result, in some California Title I schools, 95 percent of Eisenhower funds are spent, for example, on reading improvement.

Reading is the singular professional development focus in the state. Programs to help teachers teach reading better tend to center on strategies for reading instruction, certainly a worthy endeavor in itself. But this is reading divorced from content. The state is likely to pay a price for all but abandoning improving teacher knowledge and skill in the other core academic areas.

The California Postsecondary Education Commission–administered programs have fared little better and, in some ways, represent a sadder story. Some of the competitive grant programs continue to survive on their own momentum, but without state support or funding.

California's higher education Eisenhower program has been transformed into the Eisenhower State Reading Grant Program, with most of the CPEC Eisenhower money devoted to this purpose. In an effort to be all professional development things to all people, remaining Eisenhower higher education dollars are funding the California Reading and Literature Program, Mathematics and Science Implementation Projects, and planning grants for arts, civics and government, economics, English, foreign languages, geography, and history. Individual grants are no longer awarded in the $250,000 range; the average is now $20,000, or up to $50,000 for statewide collaborative grants, hardly enough to make a difference or sustain a program.

In sum, Eisenhower in California has become more like, than unlike, the state's other professional development efforts. Programs once content-rich are now significantly more process focused. Professional development dollars that formerly were targeted to increasing teachers' subject matter knowledge and subject-based pedagogy in mathematics and science are now typically folded into funds expended on more generic professional development offerings.

California is concentrating on reading improvement. To be sure, there is nothing wrong with focusing dollars on improving reading instruction. This is a need and a priority. The danger is in assuming that teaching reading, to the exclusion of academic content, is sufficient.

As new state tests come on line, mathematics, science, and other academic subjects will once again be spotlighted. But structures that were in place, at least in math and science, to support increasing teacher knowledge and skill in these areas, once dismantled, will be difficult and time-consuming to reconstruct. The clear and consistent message Eisenhower formerly communicated—that improving mathematics and science education is an important goal—has been lost in the policy noise of the moment.

Lessons from Eisenhower

When the Eisenhower program was first initiated in 1984, it was meant to concentrate these federal professional development dollars on improving mathematics and science education. The problem was not that states and districts purposely frittered away the dollars, but that they did not then, and do not now, target Eisenhower dollars in ways that are likely to contribute to improving student achievement.

This situation does not result from inattention or malice, but more likely from two conditions: (1) lack of knowledge on the part of state and local policymakers about how to deploy professional development dollars most effectively and (2) little or no required accountability for the funds.

The 1994 Eisenhower reauthorization did not improve this situation. If anything, it probably made it worse. Expanding the focus to all core subjects has had little impact on the nature of professional development offerings. Too broad a focus is akin to no focus at all. Even in places such as California, where Eisenhower-funded professional development funds once were concentrated on increasing teachers' subject matter knowledge and skills in the designated academic content areas, expansion of the program served to dilute its focus and likely mitigate its impact.

Finally, federal accountability requirements, while well intended, are not serving their expected purpose. Indicators are vague and difficult for states to define. They are categorical in nature, centered only on the Eisenhower program even though federal regulations encourage coordination of Eisenhower with other education reform efforts. And Eisenhower accountability, as measured by progress on Eisenhower-specific indicators, are yet another add-on for states, a kind of paperwork requirement for federal funds that, in the real world of schools and districts, seems artificial and forced.

The Eisenhower program, in its current guise, is too broad, particularly given the level of funding. Moreover, the program ignores research on the critical link between teachers' subject matter knowledge and appropriately constructed professional development. Combining a sharper focus with research-based practice can chart a new, and predictably more effective, role for federally funded professional development.

Learning from Research

It seems axiomatic: Teachers cannot teach what they do not know. Studies reveal the importance of teacher preparation and expertise. Teacher qualifications—qualifications in these studies being defined as performance on basic skills tests and completion of teacher education coursework and clinical experiences—are said to account for 50 to 90 percent of the variation in student achievement.[15] Yet more important, beyond these general standards, studies confirm that teachers' subject matter knowledge counts.

Conventional wisdom long held that what teachers need to know and understand about a subject is, by and large, determined by the grade level they teach. Elementary teachers, according to this view, do not need to possess in-depth knowledge of mathematics or science or history because the level at which they teach these subjects is so basic. Even high school teachers, it was presumed, need not be experts, but only modestly conversant with the subjects they teach given that many courses are merely introductory or simply survey the broad landscape of a subject without digging too deeply into any aspect of it.

These assumptions derived from a time when teaching was thought to be a generic activity, a set of learned skills independent of subject matter. Given a standard kitbag of instructional techniques, the thinking went, anyone could teach anything to anybody. Research has shown these assumptions—both about the importance of subject matter competence and the art of teaching—to be mistaken.

A critical link exists between teachers' own knowledge of subject matter and the skills that enable them to translate subject content into effective classroom learning activities.[16] What teachers know and understand about content shapes their choices about instructional materials and strategies. What teachers know about content also significantly influences the level of skill they are able to bring to the tasks of diagnosing student needs, developing interventions when students falter academically, and assessing student progress.[17]

Teaching is now a harder, more intellectually demanding job in a system of standards-based education. The need to know, and know well, their subjects is an ever clearer imperative for elementary and secondary teachers. Yet many teachers in American classrooms today are not well-versed in any subject. Many others are teaching out-of-field.

Underpreparation and the Persistence of Out-of-Field Teaching

More than half the nation's teachers hold bachelor's degrees in the field of education. These individuals completed undergraduate majors that may have required them to know a little about a number of subjects, but not very much about any of them. This problem is particularly acute among elementary instructors. Two-thirds of teachers in grades kindergarten through five majored in education.[18] Among middle school teachers in grades six to eight, many of whom are teaching in subject-specific departments, nearly one-half hold degrees only in education.

Even when teachers hold degrees in a specific academic area, often that is not the subject they are assigned to teach. In any given year, out-of-field teaching is occurring in more than half the secondary schools in the United States. In each of the fields of English, mathematics, and history, every year well over 4 million secondary-level students (grades seven to twelve) are taught by teachers with neither a major nor a minor in the field they are teaching.[19] Mathematics and science, the fields for which the Eisenhower professional development program originally was designed, provide a vivid illustration of the problem:[20]

—One-third of all secondary mathematics teachers have neither a major nor a minor in math. Fully half the eighth graders in public schools are taught by teachers with neither a math major nor minor.

—Twenty percent of science teachers have no major or minor in any science field. Half of those teaching physical science (chemistry, physics, earth science, space science) lack a major or minor in any of these areas. A third of the teachers teaching life sciences (for example, biology) have neither a major nor minor in any of the life sciences.

The problem of teacher misassignment is additionally compounded by issues of poverty, race, and student achievement levels:

—In high-poverty schools, 43 percent of the math teachers have no major or minor in math, compared with 27 percent in low-poverty schools.

—In schools with high concentrations of poor students, nearly two-thirds of the physical science teachers (65 percent) have neither a major nor a minor in physical science, compared with about 50 percent in low-poverty schools.

—Students in schools with the highest minority enrollments have less than a 50 percent chance of being taught by a mathematics or science teacher with a license or degree in the field they teach.[21]

—More than a third of low-track math students are taught by teachers with no math major or minor, compared with 20 percent in the upper track.

Even teachers who are teaching in areas they have studied do not necessarily feel adequate to the task before them. A recent study found that just 36 percent of teachers overall (including those who are teaching subjects for which they are ostensibly prepared) report feeling very well equipped to implement state or district curriculum and performance standards.[22]

One can reasonably conclude, therefore, that teacher subject matter knowledge makes a difference; teaching to the more rigorous academic standards now in place in most states requires teachers to have deeper content knowledge; and many teachers lack adequate subject matter knowledge or are assigned to teach subjects other than the ones for which they are prepared. These findings point to a critical role for well-defined professional development programs.

Making Professional Development Matter

It was long believed that the support of practicing teachers was a matter of providing periodic, and generally brief, staff development experiences designed to acquaint teachers with new requirements or promising programs or help them solve particular problems of practice. This description still defines standard professional development fare for most teachers.

Data from the 1993–94 federal Schools and Staffing Survey, for example, reveal that more than 70 percent of teachers participated in staff development programs lasting less than a day, which introduced them to state standards or equipped them with information about particular strategies, such as cooperative learning.[23] Only about a third of teachers reported participating in long-term professional development or programs focused on the subjects they were teaching.[24] Most teachers, when they receive anything at all, are treated to professional development lite.

Something of a consensus, derived from research, has emerged about what constitutes effective professional development.[25] Programs that are likely to increase teacher knowledge and skill and contribute to improving student learning have a set of common qualities:

1. Curriculum-centered and standards-oriented. Professional development needs to be about something, and that something is not process. Effective staff development programs revolve around the subjects teachers teach, the curriculum for which they are responsible, and the standards they are to help students meet.

2. Provide opportunities for teachers to become deeply immersed in subject matter. Teaching is an intellectual pursuit, requiring engagement in content. Good professional development recognizes and honors this.

3. Continuous, sustained, and cumulative. One-shot workshops, one-day courses, and one-time lectures do little to improve teaching practice. To have effect, staff development programs need to be both long term and long range.

4. Directly linked to what teachers do in their schools and their classrooms. Effective professional development makes the connection between subject matter and pedagogy, between the content of instruction and instruction itself. And it is practical. It provides information and techniques teachers can readily apply in their classrooms.

There is also agreement that teachers need different kinds of support—and different kinds of professional development—at various stages of their careers. A novice just entering teaching needs the fundamentals, such as classroom management and lesson planning. A teacher with a bit of experience is prepared to delve more deeply into subject matter and different forms of pedagogy. A seasoned veteran can profit greatly from well-designed professional development but does not need—and is unlikely to accept—the same kinds of in-service training as the beginner.

Effective professional development, which engages teachers in serious content-based discussion of pedagogy and curriculum, has been shown to improve teacher practice in ways that contribute to improved student achievement. District 2 in New York City has marshaled professional development resources from the district's general fund budget, has focused them on improving teaching in designated content areas, and has begun to see results.[26]

David K. Cohen and Heather C. Hill, in an extensive research project, studied California elementary teachers and their efforts to implement the state's mathematics frameworks. Many of these teachers were underprepared to teach the required mathematics curriculum.

Teachers who participated in generic workshops, such as cooperative learning, or professional development that had a mathematics theme but dealt little with mathematical content or pedagogy—for example, Family Math, which helps teachers involve their students' parents in math learning, or EQUALS, which deals with gender, class, and racial inequalities in math classrooms—did not change their practice in ways that would impact student performance. However, when teachers were provided with ongoing professional development structured around specific mathematical concepts they would be required to teach, such as fractions, teacher practice improved and student achievement increased.[27] The content of professional development, concluded Cohen and Hill, makes a difference to teachers' practice, and that practice makes a difference to student achievement.[28]

A New Vision for Federally Funded Professional Development

Teacher professional development is an appropriate use of federal funds. While education is not a constitutionally mandated federal responsibility, the federal government does have an obligation, in preserving the social and economic health of the nation, to promote and support education improvement.

Federal support of professional development sends an important message: Continuous teacher learning is a key determinant of improving student achievement. That message is particularly important to states and districts in times of fiscal crunch when professional development too often is the first budget category to be eliminated.

This is not to imply that just any professional development will do. Federally dedicated resources need to be put toward purposes with some track record of proven effectiveness.

As the Cheshire Cat said to Alice, "If you don't know where you're going, any road will take you there." If the federal government cannot articulate a clear and consistent purpose for professional development dollars, then results of those expenditures are likely to reflect that fogginess of intent.

With the foregoing in mind, a two-pronged proposal is offered for federal professional development dollars:

1. Target federal professional dollars specifically and exclusively to support increasing teachers' subject matter knowledge and mastery of subject-based pedagogy.

2. Base accountability for federal professional development dollars on teachers' contributions to improving student learning in targeted subject areas.

Targeting the Dollars

A tempting case can be made that states should have complete latitude to determine how best to improve teacher practice in their own locales. To some extent, states know better than the federal government, districts know better than states, and schools know better than districts. Nonetheless, the temptation to allow complete professional development freedom should be avoided.

If there is one crying professional development need—one need that, if remedied, offers the most promising prospect of improving student performance—it is increasing teachers' knowledge of the subjects they teach and enhancing their repertoire of subject-based pedagogical skills. Without teachers who are well versed in their subjects and know how to teach those subjects to their students, nothing much else in the realm of reform matters. All of the governance changes, political exhortations, system tweakings, and process foci combined will not make as much difference in ratcheting up levels of student learning.

Should federal professional development dollars specify the subjects to which states, and districts, ought to pay attention? The answer is both yes and no.

To abandon totally the focus on improving mathematics and science education seems foolhardy. These subjects are unquestionably important, both in their own right and in the ways in which studying math and science equips students with important and transferable skills, such as developing an inquiry orientation to learning and understanding the sequential nature of problem solving.

However, states ought to have some freedom to choose. They ought to be able to decide how to spend subject-based professional development dollars to meet particular state needs or priorities.

Here, then, is a possible way to proceed:

Increase the federal professional development appropriation to at least $800 million. Require that the first $500 million focus on math and science. Math and science achievement are still far from where they ought to be. Moreover, federal funding remains one of the few sources of dollars for math and science teacher professional development.

Allocate at least an additional $300 million for academic areas other than math and science. Not all of this $300 million would need to come from a new federal appropriation. The federal government should review all of its current professional development funding, all of the dollars in various pots and programs, and give serious consideration to consolidating that funding into a single law, provision, or title.[29] In other words, decategorize professional development so that these education improvement dollars are not defined program by program.

Require states, in requesting federal professional development funds, to indicate the content area or areas, in addition to mathematics and science, on which they plan to focus. States might choose English, or history, or any of the other academic content areas. States must be clear about how they intend to concentrate their federal professional development dollars. And then they must know that they will be held responsible for results those dollars produce.

Tackling the Accountability Conundrum

The federal government should reasonably be expected to know what it is paying for. Determining how to assess the federal investment in professional development is the accountability conundrum.

Evaluating professional development is a tricky proposition. Too often appraisal revolves around whether participants enjoy the program, think it might be useful, and learn something new. Sometimes professional development is assessed on the basis of whether teachers acquire new knowledge and skills, and even whether classroom practice changes. But the real test for teacher professional development is, "Do students learn more?"[30]

An indicator system, such as that of the Eisenhower program, is not adequate. These indicators are both overly program-specific and viewed by states as just another federal paperwork requirement not linked to states' own education improvement work.

Ultimately, then, the measure of success of professional development is the extent to which it contributes to improved student performance. That link, between professional development and student learning, is not forged by a simple one-to-one correspondence. Most often student achievement is measured by scores on standardized tests. That is somewhat problematic in itself: Tests are not necessarily aligned with state standards and curriculum; they display only a sample of student performance; and performance itself often is affected by a host of context variables, such as sociodemographics, home support, and student attendance patterns, which are not readily amenable to education solutions alone.

Moreover, the research in this area—measuring the effects of teaching, and teacher learning, on student achievement—is in its infancy. Nonetheless, an accountability system must be created that has the reasonable prospect of linking federal professional development funds to improved student learning. Under this proposal, each state, to receive professional development funds, would designate how it plans to measure student achievement. States might choose to use NAEP results, or a state test aligned with that state's standards, or a state test that includes some NAEP questions. Or states might use a combination of indicators—test scores plus portfolios of student work, for example.[31]

Not all states will choose the same indicators, but all states will select some performance indicators. Measurements of progress or achievement ought to be those already in play, or soon to be in play, as part of the state's own learning improvement plan.

Student achievement needs to be at the heart of states' accountability systems, but accountability should not become another federally imposed state burden. Accountability needs to be genuine, but the process ought to be a seamless component of states' ongoing education improvement efforts and the results of those efforts.

Each state would regularly report student achievement in mathematics, science, and other state-designated subjects for which federal professional development funds are claimed. Should there be little or no demonstrable improvement in these areas, and should the state be able to offer no satisfactory explanation for this situation, then federal professional development funds would be at risk.

Federal professional development dollars would be converted to an "as long as" entitlement. As long as student achievement in designated subjects increases, the state would be entitled to receive funds. The success of professional development would be measured on the basis of student learning gains.

The suggested changes will not be easy to achieve. States and districts will need to pay considerable attention to developing appropriate indicators and to building state and local capacity to offer competent professional development. Right now, good professional development programs—whether offered by states, school districts, colleges and universities, or private providers—are few and far between. Increasing the capacity of states, districts, and teachers themselves to judge the quality of professional development offerings, to take advantage of those that enhance teachers' subject matter knowledge and subject-based pedagogy and reject those that do not, will be essential.

Finally, accountability needs to be a two-way street. In addition to data the states submit, the federal government could conduct a periodic nationwide review of the ways in which its professional development dollars are being deployed. The government might select a random sample of states and school districts or select some number of states and districts that seem to be showing the greatest gains in student achievement. The purpose would be to chronicle what teacher professional development looks like in these places and then feed back to states information about promising practices. In this way, the states would be the beneficiaries of an added return on their accountability investment. These findings might also have the ancillary effect of helping to shape federal research and development priorities.

An Opportune Time

This paper began with the assertion that now is an opportune time to rethink federal professional development programs and priorities. A more focused approach that concentrates on increasing teachers' subject matter knowledge and subject-based pedagogy, and holds recipients of these federal dollars accountable for improving student learning, seems both sensible and worthwhile.

If the United States is truly serious about improving student achievement, then it must be equally serious about the ways in which resources are dedicated to this purpose. The federal government has a golden opportunity to demonstrate its commitment to ensuring that all students are given a real chance to achieve at the high levels for which policymakers have been so aggressively advocating. Rethinking the way in which federal professional development dollars are apportioned is a good place to begin.

Comment by Thomas Toch

Julia E. Koppich has framed the teacher training issue correctly: Students cannot be expected to master today's higher standards without having teachers capable of teaching the higher standards. It is that simple.

Koppich also draws attention to the biggest flaw in the federal response to the standards movement—the superficiality of too many Eisenhower-funded programs. More than half of all Eisenhower-sponsored training lasts one day or less. Inevitably, training of such duration tends to have little lasting influence.

To counter such superficiality, a problem that is endemic in teacher professional development, I would argue for the sorts of intensive summer institutes that flourished under the National Defense Education Act of 1958, intensive programs that had a sanguine effect on the quality of math and science instruction in the late 1950s and early 1960s.

Furthermore, improving instruction in reading in the elementary grades should be a high priority of the Eisenhower program. I do not take issue with Koppich regarding the importance of subject matter content in staff development. But many elementary school teachers do not know how to teach reading well, even though learning how to read is the cornerstone of elementary education and thus the most important thing that goes on in elementary classrooms. Considerable energy must be put into that fundamental building block of K-12 education.

There is also a larger reality regarding the Eisenhower program. Vast amounts of professional development monies—monies not counted as such—are being frittered away through the single salary schedule. That salary system, pervasive in public education, awards salary increases strictly on the basis of years of experience and college credits beyond the initial degree required for certification. Some 100,000 masters degrees are issued in education each year, most of them to classroom teachers. If those teachers receive a modest $3,000 a year raise for earning their degrees, the cost to taxpayers is about $300 million—or almost as much as the annual congressional appropriation for the Eisenhower program.

The money is not well spent. Nearly half the courses that teachers take on their way to their masters degrees are about school administration, which has nothing to do with what is going on in their classrooms. So, by and large, that money is wasted as a professional development resource. To address this structural problem in public education, Congress could offer financial incentives to several states to uncouple the salary increases from college course credits and link them, instead, to intensive summer institutes.

Congress should also consider expanding the scope of the Eisenhower program to include other teacher-quality initiatives, such as, for example, signing bonuses to encourage teachers to work in hard-to-staff schools. Congress already has embraced the incentive notion by permitting states to spend up to 5 percent of their Eisenhower monies on financial incentives for teachers to obtain advance licensing through the National Board for Professional Teaching Standards.

Another model is the Yale-New Haven Teacher Institute, which has been around for two decades. It brings together New Haven public school teachers with senior Yale faculty in semester-long seminars. The topics of the seminars are proposed by the New Haven public school teachers. The collaborations culminate in curriculum units that are widely used in the New Haven public school system. Another significant payoff of the program is that it has reduced teacher attrition in New Haven. Teacher attrition rates and the consequences of professional development on those rates are an additional way to evaluate the effectiveness of professional development programs, including the Eisenhower program.

As Koppich points out, Congress has sought and largely failed to measure the payoff of the Eisenhower program. Drawing trustworthy cause-and-effect relationships between a teacher training initiative and a state standardized basic skills test scores is, to put it mildly, an inexact science. Many factors influence student achievement. Drawing a straight line from a particular training program to a test score is very difficult. Greater accountability in schools is a primary goal, but basic skills test scores should not be used in ways that are indefensible.

If Congress wants to know whether it is getting its money's worth in the Eisenhower program, it should fund studies that seek to isolate the influence of intensive professional development on student achievement. It should do the same sorts of studies on trends in teacher attrition and other indicators. In the absence of positive results from such studies, Koppich's notion of requiring states to demonstrate achievement gains as a condition for receiving future Eisenhower funding may be premature.

Pennsylvania uses another way of evaluating professional development. It measures the results of Eisenhower-funded programs not on the basis of student achievement, but by the extent to which the programs improve teachers' grasp of their subjects. It tests teachers before and after they enroll in Eisenhower programs, then bases a portion of future program funding on the results. That seems to be a defensible method of accountability.

Koppich's thoughtful discussion of the Eisenhower experience in California suggests that the movement to raise standards in the nation can be a catalyst to the improvement of teacher staff development. California districts, as Koppich points out, have spent many of their Eisenhower dollars ensuring that teachers have mastered the state's new, more rigorous math and science instructional frameworks. Rigorous state curriculum standards, it seems, give badly needed pedagogical direction to local schools.

Comment by Michael Podgursky

The federal government currently spends roughly $350 million on Title II Eisenhower programs, which provide subsidies for teacher professional development. Julia E. Koppich proposes to increase this spending to at least $800 million annually based upon her belief that a research-based consensus about "what works" has emerged. In these comments I make two points. First, little evidence exists that spending on professional development raises student test scores. Second, even if the research did show such a relationship, allowing school administrators to decide how to spend their budgets is probably better than using federal categorical programs to regulate spending.

Quality of the Research

Part of Koppich's case for expanded federal expenditures rests on an extraordinary claim: "Teacher qualifications . . . account for 50 to 90 percent of the variation in student achievement." Were this true, it would certainly make a prima facie case for larger expenditures on teacher training. Even if only a small fraction of professional development dollars were spent wisely, the returns in terms of student performance would be very large. However, I am aware of no reliable study of individual student achievement that supports such a claim. In general, the education production function studies conclude that teachers matter, but they do not explain half the variation in student test scores, and it is difficult to pin down what it is about teachers (at least what can be measured in surveys) that matters.[32]

The two studies cited by Koppich certainly do not support such a strong claim for teacher qualifications. Ronald Ferguson's widely cited study of Texas school districts did find that teacher scores on a test of verbal ability were associated with higher student test scores, after controlling for other district-level characteristics. The combined explanatory power of all the regressors in his models, including numerous controls for socioeconomic characteristics, approached 50 percent of interdistrict variation. However, even if he had found that teacher characteristics alone explained 50 percent of interdistrict variation, that says virtually nothing about explained variation in individual student test scores. The reason is that more than 90 percent of variation of student test scores occurs within school districts.[33] All of this intradistrict variation is averaged away in Ferguson's data. The second study cited, by Parmalee P. Hawk, Charles R. Coble, and Melvin Swanson, compares the general math and algebra scores of students taught by eighteen math-certified and eighteen non-math-certified (that is, out-of-field) teachers in several North Carolina schools. No regression results were reported in this study; the authors simply compared mean test scores between the two groups of students. However, if a simple analysis of variance decomposition is computed based on the statistics reported in the article, teacher math certification explained just 3.6 percent of the variation in student test scores in general mathematics, and less than 1 percent of the variation in student algebra scores.[34]

Koppich then argues that a body of research supports a consensus about what works in teacher professional development. However, the studies that Koppich cites do not provide strong evidence in support of the hypothesis that expenditures on professional development raise student test scores. She cites claims that a case study of New York City's Community District 2 shows that professional development "has been shown to improve teacher practice in ways that contribute to improved student achievement." This case study by Richard F. Elmore, relying on interviews and site visits, describes a variety of factors that Koppich believes have contributed to the test score gains. Yet a descriptive case study of a single school district, while suggestive, cannot be considered strong causal evidence. Many variables changed during the period under consideration, making it difficult to isolate the specific contribution of professional development per se. Moreover, some of the proposed explanations (for example, "oversight and principal site visits") have nothing to do with professional development as traditionally defined.

Koppich claims that a study by David K. Cohen and Heather C. Hill of California schools shows that ongoing professional development centered on concepts teachers are required to teach raises student test scores. This study does report evidence of a positive relationship between school-level mathematics test scores on the California Learning Assessment System (CLAS) and teacher opportunities to learn (OTL) about the assessment for a relatively small sample of California elementary schools.[35] However, even if the limitations of the authors' data are ignored and a causal interpretation is accepted, it is not clear how widely such results will generalize. CLAS was a new, and rather unusual, type of open-ended mathematics assessment. When teachers were given the opportunity to learn about it, their students did better. The question of whether professional development gains would have persisted over time as students and teachers became more familiar with the test is not answered. Moreover, the majority of teachers in the Cohen and Hill sample who were given an opportunity to learn about the test apparently did so in the type of short, one-shot workshops that Koppich criticizes, instead of the "continuous, sustained, and cumulative" programs she favors. Koppich cites a second study of CLAS test scores by David Wiley and Bokhee Yoon, which finds some associations between measures of teacher OTL and student performance. However, these were simple differences in means, without controls for the socioeconomic status of students. Wiley and Yoon therefore present their findings with a caveat that undermines Koppich's thesis: "When one compares OTL and student performance, one does not find a causal relationship because of several complicating factors. Many factors—including home environment and socioeconomic status—have equal or greater impact on student performance than the quality of schools (e.g., OTL)."[36]

Title II funding has also been provided to the National Board for Professional Teaching Standards to develop programs for identifying "accomplished teachers" on the basis of portfolios, self-prepared videotapes, and other open-ended assessments. The National Commission on Teaching and America's Future has proposed that 105,000 teachers be certified over the next several years. The Clinton administration endorses this goal as well. Yet no evidence is available to date that the students of teachers who pass National Board certification learn more than those who do not.

In short, I do not believe that there exists a strong body of research demonstrating that Title II–type professional development programs produce improvements in student performance.

Are Subsidies Justified?

Even if there were a large body of research showing that expenditures on teacher professional development raise student test scores, that does not in itself explain why a categorical federal program is needed to subsidize it. School administrators must make decisions as to how to allocate their spending to meet their educational performance objectives. To justify federal categorical aid, some compelling argument should be made that, left on their own, with the information at their disposal, schools underinvest in professional development as compared with other productive expenditures.

Consider an agricultural analogy. Many inputs will increase farm productivity: fertilizer, improved seed, mechanization, irrigation, better training for farm managers, and so forth. Suppose that a body of research demonstrates that a new type of fertilizer improves yield. Should the federal government subsidize the use of this farm fertilizer? Isn't it sufficient to simply publicize the findings and let farmers act accordingly? The case for a subsidy rests on identifying a "market failure," that is, some systematic reason that farmers are underinvesting in fertilizer as compared with other inputs.

I do not know the optimal level of expenditures on professional development. Clearly, proponents of Title II-type programs believe that schools are not spending enough on it. The National Commission on Teaching and America's Future proposes that 1 percent of state and local outlays should be spent on such programs (plus matching federal grants), for a total of $2.75 billion in 1996 dollars, but it offers no evidence that this expenditure is the best use of these funds.[37] However, as with the farm analogy, proponents of subsidies need to explain why the federal government is in a better position to know the optimal mix of spending than a local school administrator. As compared with federal or state regulators, local school administrators have much better information about the most pressing needs in their schools. If they are held accountable for performance in the school, why shouldn't they decide on the level and composition of spending on professional development?

A 'Market Test'

Many states are attempting to increase accountability of public schools through the development of academic standards and assessments, expanded school choice, charter schools, and performance contracting. These efforts focus regulatory oversight where it ought to be—on educational outcomes. By contrast, Koppich's proposals continue past practices of focusing on school inputs. Not only is the record of such policies a poor one, but if measures to enhance school accountability are to succeed, constraints that prevent local administrators from using resources as they judge best also must be removed.

For example, currently, the Title II categorical program in effect tells schools: "Here is $2,000, but you can spend it only on National Board certification for a teacher" ($2,000 is the current per teacher fee charged by the National Board). A better approach would be to make such programs pass a "market test." Hold schools accountable and let them spend their budgets as they see fit. If National Board certification is worth $2,000, then schools will buy it, just the way they buy textbooks, computer software, teaching modules, and other education inputs. If it is not, they will not. Why is a federal subsidy required? The same argument can be made for any other type of teacher professional development outlays.[38]

Federal programs that provide aid to schools in the form of narrow, categorical assistance distort market prices and restrict how local administrators can allocate their budgets. In so doing, they undermine state-level efforts designed to increase accountability and efficiency in public K-12 education spending.

Notes

1. National Commission on Excellence in Education, *A Nation at Risk: The Imperative for Educational Reform* (Government Printing Office, 1983).

2. Activities for foreign language and computer educators were also funded under Title II, but the majority of the dollars was spent for mathematics and science.

3. Title II Eisenhower consists of three component parts. Part A is composed of federal activities (currently the National Eisenhower Clearinghouse and support for the National Board for Professional Teaching Standard's continuing research and development). Part B is the state share. Part C is money for federal demonstration projects of promising practices. This paper focuses only on Part B.

4. National Commission on Excellence in Education, *A Nation at Risk*, p. 22.

5. James B. Stedman, *Eisenhower Professional Development Program: Moving beyond Math and Science* (Congressional Research Service, 1994).

6. Michael Knapp and others, *The Eisenhower Program and the Reform of Mathematics and Science Education: A Necessary But Not Sufficient Resource*, National Study of the EESA Title II Eisenhower Program, prepared under contract to the Department of Education (Menlo Park, Calif., and Washington: SRI International and Policy Studies Associates, 1991).

7. National Commission on Teaching and America's Future, *What Matters Most: Teaching for America's Future* (Columbia University, Teachers College, 1996).

8. Catalog of Federal Domestic Assistance, found at aspe.os.dhhs.gov/cfda/p.841.htm/ 2/24/99.

9. As a result of the 1997 U.S. Supreme Court decision in *Agostini* v. *Felton* (521 U.S. 203), federal dollars, under some circumstances, can support activities involving private school students and their teachers.

10. Information for this section is taken from two sources: Carin A. Celebuski and others, *Dwight D. Eisenhower Professional Development Program: Analysis of Data from the 1996–97 Annual Performance Reports*, draft version (Washington: Westat, 1999); and Beatrice F. Birman, Allison L. Reeve, and Cheryl Sattler, *The Eisenhower Professional Development Program: Emerging Themes from Six Districts*, prepared for the Department of Education (Washington: American Institutes of Research, 1998).

11. Peter Schrag, *Paradise Lost: California's Experience, America's Future* (University of California Press, 1998).

12. Between 1994 and 1998, California suspended its statewide student testing program. In 1998 the state began to offer a still-developing statewide test consisting of the Stanford 9 achievement exam with augmented questions keyed to California's standards.

13. Judith Warren Little and others, *Staff Development in California: Public and Personal Investments, Program Patterns, and Policy Choices* (San Francisco and Berkeley, Calif.: Far West Laboratory for Educational Research and Development and Policy Analysis for California Education, 1987).

14. Julia E. Koppich and others, *The Eisenhower Mathematics and Science Education Program* (Berkeley, Calif.: Policy Analysis for California Education, 1993).

15. See Ronald Ferguson, "Paying for Education: New Evidence on How and Why Money Matters," *Harvard Journal of Legislation*, vol. 28 (Summer 1991), pp. 465–98; and P. Hawk, C. R. Coble, and M. Swanson, "Certification: It Does Matter," *Journal of Teacher Education*, vol. 36 (1985), pp. 13–15.

16. For a more complete treatment of the relevant research, see Julia E. Koppich and Michael S. Knapp, *Federal Research Investment and the Improvement of Teaching, 1980–1997*, paper prepared for the Department of Education, Office of Educational Research and Improvement (Seattle, Wash.: Center for the Study of Teaching and Policy, 1998).

17. See, for example, Linda Darling-Hammond and Deborah Ball, *Teaching for High Standards: What Policy Makers Need to Know and Be Able to Do* (New York: National Commission on Teaching and America's Future, in cooperation with the Consortium for Policy Research in Education, 1997).

18. See Robin R. Henke and others, *America's Teachers: Profile of a Profession, 1993–94*, prepared by MPR Associates (Department of Education, Office of Educational Research and Improvement, 1997); and Laurie Lewis and others, *Teacher Quality: A Report on the Preparation and Qualifications of Public School Teachers* (Department of Education, Office of Educational Research and Improvement, 1999).

19. Richard Ingersoll, "The Problem of Underqualified Teachers in American Secondary Schools," *Educational Researcher*, vol. 28 (March 1999), pp. 26–37.

20. Unless otherwise specified, these data are taken from Ingersoll, "The Problems of Underqualified Teachers in American Secondary Schools."

21. Jeannie Oakes, *Multiplying Inequalities: The Effects of Race, Social Class, and Tracking on Opportunities to Learn Mathematics and Science* (Santa Monica, Calif.: RAND Corporation, 1990).

22. Lewis and others, *Teacher Quality*.

23. Henke and others, *America's Teachers*.

24. Lewis and others, *Teacher Quality*.

25. See, for example, Consortium for Policy Research in Education, *Policies and Programs for Professional Development of Teachers: A 50-State Profile* (Philadelphia, 1997).

26. Richard F. Elmore, *Investing in Teacher Learning: Staff Development and Instructional Improvement in Community School District #2, New York City* (New York: National Commission on Teaching and America's Future, in cooperation with the Consortium for Policy Research in Education, 1997).

27. See David K. Cohen and Heather C. Hill, *Instructional Policy and Classroom Performance: The Mathematics Reform in California* (Philadelphia: Consortium for Policy Research in Education, 1998).

28. In addition to Cohen and Hill, *Instructional Policy and Classroom Performance*, see Richard F. Elmore, *Investing in Teacher Learning: Staff Development and Instructional Improvement in Community School District #2* (New York: National Commission on Teaching and America's Future, 1998); and David Wiley and B. Yoon, "Teacher Reports of Opportunity to Learn: Analyses of the 1993 California Learning Assessment System," *Educational Evaluation and Policy Analysis*, vol. 17, no. 3 (1995), pp. 355–70.

29. There might be a few exceptions to the dollars in a single professional development law dedicated to subject matter and subject-based pedagogy. For example, professional development for special education teachers, particularly for teachers of severely handicapped children, may have a different, and legitimate, purpose.

30. For an explanation of the levels of evaluation of teacher professional development, see Thomas R. Guskey, "New Perspectives on Evaluating Professional Development," paper presented at the annual meeting of the American Educational Research Association, Montreal, Canada, April 1999.

31. Lining up student achievement tests with teacher professional development, and vice versa, may take some time. Thus, for a while—perhaps two years—states might be authorized to assess professional development on the basis of teacher learning. They might, for example, take a page from Pennsylvania's book and administer to teachers professional development pre- and post-tests designed to gauge acquired knowledge.

32. For example, see Dan D. Goldhaber and Dominic J. Brewer, "Why Don't Schools and Teachers Seem to Matter?: Assessing the Impact of Unobservables on Educational Productivity," *Journal of Human Resources,* vol. 32, no. 3 (Summer 1997), pp. 505–23. Using data from the NELS88, these authors regress tenth-grade math test scores on eighth-grade scores and an extensive set of controls for the socioeconomic characteristics of the student and his or her school. This yields an R^2 of 0.763. When they add a vector of twenty teacher characteristics and behaviors (for example, math major, certification in math, experience, uses National Council of Teachers of Mathematics methods) the R^2 rises only marginally to 0.768. In other words, after controlling for socioeconomic characteristics and a pretest, the independent contribution of teacher characteristics to explained variation is very small (0.5 percent). This does not mean that teacher characteristics do not matter;

some of the measured teacher characteristics were statistically significant. What it does show is that a substantial correlation exists between measured teacher characteristics and socioeconomic characteristics of students and schools. This is why it is not possible to uniquely partition explained variation into a part resulting from socioeconomic conditions and a part resulting from teachers or schools.

33. For example, a recent study by Steven C. Rivkin, Eric A. Hanushek, and John F. Kain, "Teachers, Schools, and Academic Achievement," Amherst College, 1998, finds that, in 1995, interschool variation in Texas explained just 5.5 and 3.3 percent of variation in Texas Assessment of Academic Skills (TAAS) grade school scores in mathematics and reading, respectively. Because school districts are simply aggregations of schools, these figures represent upper bounds on the share of total variation, which could be accounted for by interdistrict variation.

34. The National Commission on Teaching and America's Future has made similar assertions concerning the explanatory power of teacher credentials. National Commission on Teaching and America's Future, *Doing What Matters Most* (Columbia University, Teachers College, 1997). An extensive critique of these claims may be found in Dale Ballou and Michael Podgursky, "Reforming Teacher Preparation and Licensing: What Is the Evidence?," *Teachers College Record* (forthcoming 1999).

35. David K. Cohen and Heather C. Hill, in *Instructional Policy and Classroom Performance: The Mathematics Reform in California* (Philadelphia, Pa.: Consortium for Policy Research in Education, 1998), analyze fourth-grade mathematics test scores averaged at the school level for a sample of 162 public schools. It is a cross-section sample with one observation per school. The variables representing professional development and other conditions at the school were derived from a survey of teachers at the schools. However, only two to four teachers per school were surveyed in the estimation sample.

36. David Wiley and Bokhee Yoon, "Teacher Reports on Opportunity to Learn: Analyses of the 1993 California Learning Assessment System (CLAS)," *Education Evaluation and Policy Analysis*, vol. 17, no. 3 (Fall 1995), pp. 355–70.

37. National Commission on Teaching and America's Future, *Doing What Matters Most*, p. 121.

38. The recent teacher quality "manifesto" from the Fordham Foundation makes a good case for greater flexibility and less regulation of teacher labor markets. See Fordham Foundation, *The Teachers We Need and How to Get More of Them* (Washington, 1999). With respect to Title II spending, see John R. Phillips and Marci Kanstoroom, "Title II: Does Professional Development Work?," in Marci Kanstoroom and Chester E. Finn Jr., eds., *New Directions: Federal Education Policy in the Twenty-First Century* (Washington: Fordham Foundation, 1999).

Federal Support for Technology in K-12 Education

GARY CHAPMAN

THE FIRST IBM PERSONAL COMPUTER (PC) was released in August 1981; a year later, *Time* magazine named the personal computer its "Man of the Year." A year after that, in 1983, the U.S. government and its research partners implemented the technical decisions that created the Internet. The world has not been the same since.

By 1999, about 250 million people around the globe had personal computers, and about 100 million used the Internet. The computer industry sells tens of millions of PCs every year, and the number of Internet users has doubled every year since 1988. This rate of growth is expected to continue for some years to come, so early in the twenty-first century more than a billion people are expected to be on-line.

This is one of the most remarkable, rapid, and significant technological transitions in history. Not only has a new and uniquely capable technology been distributed around the world, but also work and the economy have been reorganized around this technology, at least in modern societies. This transition is a hinge in human history equivalent in significance to the Industrial Revolution. Computers and computer networks have forever altered the way humans work, communicate, play, entertain themselves, and educate their children.

Nevertheless, despite this immense transformation of modern, industrial societies, and the significance of computational technologies, no agreement exists on how to use this technology in education. Computers and the Internet have spread rapidly in K-12 schools in the United States, perhaps more rapidly in the past few years than in the rest of society. But still no widespread consensus has been reached on whether computers and the Internet will have a large, small, positive, negative, or inconsequential effect on learning in young people. One reason for this lack of consensus may be that, while the proper role of computers and networks in K-12 education is being determined, what learning means is being rethought. And both these trends are set into the context of near-universal public concern that K-12 schools are not performing as well as they should, which has made school reform a potent political issue throughout the United States. Information technologies have become a complex and controversial component of new ideas about school reform.

Furthermore, the Internet is an increasingly controversial aspect of modern life because of the way it can carry objectionable communication such as pornography, hateful and violent speech, information about making bombs and using drugs, dangerous and obscene appeals to young people from pedophiles, and numerous other threats. The Internet is largely unregulated, despite recent attempts to change this; it is global, which means that local means of control are weak or even useless; it can be anonymous and even deceptive; it is a source of hoaxes, fraud, and misinformation; and it can be a tool for illegal activities such as pirating music, software, or movies, or unauthorized entries into sensitive computer systems. All of these problems are vexing enough for adults, but they are particularly troublesome when millions of young people are introduced into cyberspace, a relatively new feature of on-line communication. The tools that teachers, administrators, and parents have for controlling students' use of the Internet are few and relatively unrefined, so far. This means that teachers and parents are faced with a new educational task, in addition to their traditional pedagogical roles: teaching kids about how to use this technology responsibly while exploring ways to use it to improve general learning. The combination of these two pedagogical tasks is a significant burden on the teaching profession as well as on parents.

The current debate about the role of computers and the Internet in K-12 education and in the lives of young people is occasionally acrimonious, but it is healthy. It can be viewed as part of a larger debate over the proper role of technological tools throughout society. The negative features of Internet communication, for example, are counterbalanced by its enhancement of democratic discourse and by its rich and deep resources of information. Computer-based work can be dull and demeaning, or it can be rewarding and creative. Computer-assisted instruction could produce a generation of technological drones or a renaissance of gifted, competent, and diversely talented lifelong learners. The information age could be one of hardening inequalities, a two-tiered society of the skilled and unskilled, or it could be an era of democratic equality and justice. Figuring out how to use new technologies, in proper balance with other normative goals, is a challenge for all institutions and individuals, including K-12 schools and teachers. For all these reasons, the current debate about computers and the Internet in schools is highly important.

The Current State of Information Technologies in the United States

U.S. schools have used personal computers and related technologies since the earliest days of the PC era, beginning about twenty years ago. The Apple II computer was a staple of many schools for a long time. Most schools have gone through successive generations of personal computers of various brands.

The Internet has catalyzed a new push for getting computers and network connections into K-12 schools. In the 1980s the Internet was used almost exclusively by scientists, academics, researchers, and a handful of people in private businesses. It was then a text-based system typically run on large computers using the Unix operating system, which was, and still is, a difficult operating system requiring a good deal of specialized skill. Internet servers were limited to authorized research centers, which restricted the number and kind of people who could get Internet accounts. The National Science Foundation, which took over management of the Internet from the Department of Defense in 1983, prohibited the use of the Internet for commercial purposes, which again limited its use and appeal.

All of this changed in the early 1990s. First came the appearance of the World Wide Web, which introduced both graphics and an easy-to-learn user interface to the Internet. The standards that made Web pages accessible via the Internet quickly transformed the entire system. The Web also introduced hypertext to the Internet, a technology that made the Internet a vast interlinked library of information.

In 1993 the National Science Foundation lifted its prohibition on commercial activity on the Internet, and this had an equally transformative effect on computer networking. Within a few years, the Internet became the most innovative and essential way of doing business in the "new economy." Now, millions of businesses are providing goods and services on the Internet, and "electronic commerce" is expected to explode in the next few years.

The result of these recent developments is that the Internet is now commonly viewed as the basic platform for nearly all future communications, including voice, data, video, music, radio, government services, and commercial enterprise. The United States is moving toward an Internet-based economy. More and more jobs require familiarity with computers; the U.S. Department of Labor estimates that, in the early twenty-first century, three quarters of all jobs in the U.S. economy will entail daily use of a computer.

Because all of this has emerged only within the past few years, the Internet is a new and largely unfamiliar technology to most Americans. About half of all U.S. homes have a personal computer, and about 30 percent of adult Americans, or about 60 million Americans, use the Internet. There are also about 10 million Americans under the age of eighteen in cyberspace. But because of the growth rate of new users, at any given time, only about half of all new users have been on-line more than a year. Consequently, about half of all Internet users are just developing their technical skills and adjusting to a new way of communicating.

"Surfing" the Web—learning how to "point and click" in a Web browser and how to navigate between Web pages—or learning how to send e-mail is not difficult. The ease of use that has become part of the Internet in the last five years is the major reason for its new popularity. But more advanced skills are difficult to acquire and consequently rarer. But these skills are in high demand. Leaders of technology companies are increasingly concerned that the U.S. educational system is not producing enough skilled workers to meet this demand and that the economy will suffer.

The United States will need ninety-five thousand new technology workers a year through 2005, but only 24,553 college graduates received degrees in computer science in 1994, and the trend lines point to a flat or even downward trajectory for that figure. Bachelor's degrees in computer science have fallen more than 40 percent since 1986. In more advanced degree programs, about half of all students in technology and engineering are from other countries.[1] Among mid- to large-sized firms, there was a shortage of about 190,000 information technology workers.[2] The number of Americans seeking technology-related degrees declined by 5 percent since 1990.[3] Many technology workers find their way to high-tech employment through degree programs other than computer science, but the computer science field is the traditional bellwether of skilled worker availability.

Because of this concern in industry, attention has focused on the exposure of young people to information technologies in K-12 education. Most industry leaders believe that early development of skills in computers, programming, and networking is essential to pursuing further education in college, in job training, or in other educational modes before getting a job in the high-tech industry. And most industry leaders—although not all of them—are convinced that fluency and competency with computers and the Internet will be essential skills in the new network-based economy. Industry leaders say that they need "problem solvers," a different kind of worker than in the past, and that skill with computers helps foster this quality in young people.

This message has been echoed by President Bill Clinton. He said in his 1996 State of the Union address, "Our . . . challenge is to provide Americans with the educational opportunities we'll all need for this new century. In our schools, every classroom in America must be connected to the information superhighway, with computers and good software, and well-trained teachers. We are working with the telecommunications industry, educators and parents to connect 20 percent of California's classrooms by this spring, and every classroom and every library in the entire United States by the year 2000."[4]

In 1997 the President's Committee of Advisors on Science and Technology (PCAST) also stressed the economic imperative of training young people in technical fields:

> In an era of increasing international economic competition, the quality of America's elementary and secondary schools could determine whether our children hold highly compensated, high-skill jobs that add significant value within the integrated global economy of the twenty-first century or compete with workers in developing countries for the provision of commodity products and low-value-added services at wage rates comparable to those received by third world laborers. . . .
>
> While a number of different approaches have been suggested for the improvement of K-12 education in the United States, one common element

> of many such plans has been the more extensive and more effective utilization of computer, networking and other technologies in support of a broad program of system and curricular reform. During a period in which technology has fundamentally transformed America's offices, factories, and retail establishments, however, its impact within our nation's classrooms has generally been quite modest.[5]

Much of the current attention paid to the use of computers and networks in K-12 schools has been motivated by concerns about the changing economy and the preparation of young people for new kinds of jobs. This trend tends to influence how computers and the Internet might be used in schools. Parents may press schools to use computers to prepare their children for jobs. Local industry leaders often demand training that supplies them with skilled workers. This has led to a debate about the proper balance between education and training, not only in K-12 schools but in universities and colleges as well.

Controversies about the use of computers by young people are at least in part related to diverse opinions about how to deal with inequality and whether the changes in society and the economy brought about by computers and the Internet are beneficial or not. A great many people are ambivalent about the information age, given the upheavals it entails. Many people believe that while information technologies have speeded up things, and perhaps made businesses more efficient, they have not contributed to a great improvement in the quality of life. For many people, the quality of life in the United States has declined in recent years, with more violence, rougher discourse, greater inequality, a dearth of public leadership, and little improvement in race relations. Some Americans believe that the computer and Internet bandwagon in K-12 schools is an expensive distraction from finding solutions to more basic problems confronting society.

Critics point out that numerous technological fads have been evident in schools throughout the twentieth century, most of them ineffective, and that the fundamentals of learning have not changed. Most of these critics are advocates of traditional models of well-rounded, liberal education instead of models driven largely by contemporary technologies. They also argue that the pace of change in the information age makes technical skills exceedingly ephemeral—what young people are taught about computers is likely to be obsolete within a few years, long before they enter the work force. That makes it all the more important, say critics, for young people to build sustainable skills of critical inquiry, curiosity about the world, historical knowledge, scientific literacy, judgment, and other skills that may not be aided by computers.

For all these reasons, educators and administrators face a daunting challenge: to find the proper balance between building job-related technological skills and fostering the "whole person" in K-12 education. This debate is not new, but it is under new intense pressure because of the strong push to get computers and the Internet into K-12 schools throughout the nation. The novelty of these technologies, especially the Internet, means that their potential impact on learning in young people is not yet known. The intensity of the current debate, and the stakes attached to its resolution, make most teachers and school administrators desperate for some guidance. This is the challenge for experts and policymakers.

Information Technologies in K-12 Schools

In contrast to the Internet, personal computers are a conventional and long-established technology in U.S. K-12 schools. Ninety-eight percent of U.S. schools own personal computers.[6] The number of computers in public schools has doubled in six years, to 7.4 million in 1998.[7] About 82 percent of K-12 schools have Internet access, up from 64 percent in 1997.[8] In March 1999 President Clinton announced that more than half (51 percent) of instructional rooms in K-12 public schools in the United States had access to the Internet, and the president repeated his pledge that all classrooms will be wired by the end of 2000.[9]

In 1997 the ratio of students to computers, on average nationwide, was 10 to 1, an all-time low, and was reported as 6 to 1 in a U.S. Department of Education report in February 1999 (from 1998 data).[10] The ratio decreases as the grade level increases, so high school students have greater access than elementary school students.

Spending on educational technology in K-12 schools was more than $5 billion in 1998, up from $2.1 billion in 1992.[11] This is, however, only a third to a fifth of the annual spending figure recommended by most experts, including PCAST.[12]

Many computers in schools are not Internet-capable, however. Even in 1999, about 8 percent of computers in schools were Apple IIs, which were nearly twenty years old.[13] Many old DOS-based machines also were in use as well as computers that cannot run the basic applications required for accessing the Internet. In 1997 the nationally averaged ratio of multimedia computers to students was 24 to 1, or nearly five times the recommended ratio of 5 to 1 advocated by the U.S. Department of Education. The lowest ratio was in Florida at 8.5 students per multimedia computer, and the highest average was in Louisiana, at 62.7.[14]

The biggest deficit in support for computer-assisted learning in U.S. schools is in teacher training. While many teachers are doing innovative and valuable things with computers in the classroom, the vast majority of K-12 teachers are inexperienced users. The PCAST panel on educational technology estimated that only about 15 percent of K-12 school budgets for technology is allocated to training, compared with the 30 percent the panel recommended.[15] In 1997 only 15 percent of teachers had received at least nine hours of training in computing technology.[16] Teachers typically do not have enough time either to take training in computer technology or to develop coursework integrated with the technology. Moreover, technology training for teachers is commonly limited to technical curricula designed to foster familiarity with hardware, software programs, or networks, a limited approach that many teachers find too narrow. Teachers often report being intimidated by the technology, or reluctant to use it, because some students are expert with computers and the Internet, and few teachers are comfortable revealing a lack of competence in the classroom. Keeping up with the technology is also a formidable challenge, given the pace of change in the industry and other demands on teachers' time.

Another problem for teachers is a relative dearth of high-quality educational software. The U.S. Department of Education estimated in 1996 that twenty thousand educational software packages were available for the K-12 market.[17] That number has certainly increased since 1996. But the academic software market is fragmented across many disciplines and grade levels, and software has to work on a wide diversity of machine capabilities. Software developers usually do not create programs for computers that are obsolete, but this category represents a large portion of the installed base of computers in U.S. public schools. Some states require educational software developers to do their own testing of efficacy, which is expensive and time-consuming, adding to the cost of development.[18] Also, educational software that is demonstrably effective requires high levels of funding for research and development, an investment that may be unrecoverable in a highly segmented market. Sophisticated programs may require training for teachers, too, a burden added to the training they may need for basic computer literacy. And all software programs require some level of technical support, an increasingly expensive requirement.

Another technology-related problem facing schools is one that is vexing all institutions in the United States, in the private, public, and nonprofit sectors: the shortage of well-trained technical support personnel. The shortage in software and networking specialists is the most acute. Software and networking specialists are the highest paid salary category of all engineering specialties; they earned an average of $64,000 in 1997. This group was also receiving annual pay increases of 6 percent, higher than any other engineering category.[19] Salaries for such personnel are even higher in technology-intensive areas such as the San Francisco Bay area, Boston, or Austin, Texas. The average pay for teachers from 1996 to 1997, in the country's largest one hundred cities, was $44,649.[20] That is 70 percent of the average for software and networking specialists. Public schools often find it difficult to pay these specialists the salaries they can get in the private sector.

The result is that schools and districts often wind up with fewer tech support personnel than they need, and this makes their technology unreliable and frustrating to many teachers and students. Some schools attempt to supplement their technical staff with student help, but this has liabilities. Schools may be reluctant to entrust expensive equipment to students, labor laws may be applicable, and insurance clauses may also be relevant. There is, unfortunately, no way to skimp on technical support and enjoy reliable computer services or computer security. Such support is very expensive, and likely to get more so.

Most of these technology-related problems could be solved with more money, and that raises the biggest issue of all: equity. Access to computers and the Internet in school is unfortunately correlated with socioeconomic status in the United States, and all the problems that are tied to lack of funds are worse in poor schools. Student-to-computer ratios are higher, teacher training is rare, software purchases are fewer, and technical support is in short supply.

In its 1997 report *Computers and Classrooms*, the Educational Testing Service (ETS) said bluntly, "The data show that students with the most need get the least access." As the percentage of Title I students or minority students goes up, so do the ratios of students to computers. Schools with minority populations of 25 percent or less had, in 1997 data, a ratio of 10 students to 1 computer, on average, while schools with minority populations of 90 percent or more had a ratio of 17.4 to 1.[21] The ETS study went on to say:

> Previous analyses have shown a positive relationship between the percentage of Title 1 students and computer availability. The general trend was more technology in poorer schools. This no longer appears to be the case. While Title 1 funding is designed to help poor schools, these targeted resources are apparently ineffective in getting these schools up to par technologically with other schools. Since much of the technology that currently resides in poor schools is probably due to Title 1 funds, it is hard to imagine what the technology level in these schools would be like without federal programs.[22]

These data follow similar patterns for Internet access. In the Department of Education's report of February 1999, 37 percent of schools with more than 50 percent minority enrollment were connected to the Internet, up from 3 percent in 1994, but this compared with 57 percent in 1998 for schools with less than 6 percent minority enrollment.[23]

Equally important, home ownership of computers, or home Internet access, is also below the national average in low-income households. About 37 percent of households with incomes below $35,000 per year had home computers in 1997, compared with more than 45 percent for households with incomes over $35,000. For households below $10,000 per year, the figure was just under 10 percent. An even greater concern is the relationship between ethnicity and computer ownership, according to the National Telecommunications and Information Administration (NTIA).

> Significantly, the digital divide between racial groups in PC-ownership has *increased* since 1994. In 1997, the difference in PC-ownership levels between white and black households was 21.5 percentage points, up from 16.8 percentage points in 1994. Similarly, the gap in PC-ownership rates between white and Hispanic households in 1997 has increased to 21.4 percentage points, up from 14.8 percentage points in 1994.[24]

This disparity appears to have expanded because of increasing computer purchases among more affluent households, with fewer computers purchased by African Americans and Hispanics. These data may be changing, however, now that PCs are approaching $500 for complete systems. The average income and education level of first-time buyers appears to be lower than in the past, and more first-time buyers are people who do not use a computer at work.[25] Nevertheless, there are huge disparities to overcome, especially in extreme poverty zones. Moreover, for poor schools, sustainability is an issue, because one-time grants or bond issues are not capable of keeping a school technologically current.

Students need ready and free access to computers outside of school hours to do homework, stay in touch with school, and keep up their skills and familiarity with the Internet. When a household cannot afford a computer or Internet access, its members need an alternative. In a 1997 study of racial differences in the use of the Internet conducted by Vanderbilt University professors Donna Hoffman and Thomas Novak, they reported that:

> Overall, white students are more likely than African Americans students to use the Web. But given a home computer, this race difference in Web use goes away. The important difference is among students who lack a home computer: here, whites are more likely to use the Web than African Americans. This may be due in part to the fact that white students, regardless of whether they have a home computer, are much more likely than their African American counterparts to use the Web at places other than home, work or school. This suggests the importance of not only creating access points for African Americans in libraries, community centers, and other non-traditional places where individuals may access the Internet, but also encouraging use at these locations.[26]

Many African American leaders are beginning to view community technology centers (CTCs) as an essential goal. CTCs are public places where people can use computers and access the Internet for free or a small fee. They may be in schools, churches, community centers, recreation centers, youth centers, or dedicated buildings. They are proliferating: CTC-Net, an umbrella organization of affiliated CTCs throughout the United States, lists more than 250 affiliated CTCs throughout the nation on its web site.[27] Break Away Technologies in Los Angeles has a program called 200 by 2000, through which the organization will start two hundred CTCs in Central and South Central Los Angeles by the year 2000; it celebrated its one hundredth center in April 1999.[28] The Clinton administration has proposed a $65 million line-item to support CTCs.

The role of CTCs illustrates an important lesson for schools. Large investments in technology, sometimes in the millions or even tens of millions of dollars, should not be locked up, out of reach, from three or four o'clock in the afternoon until early the next morning, not to mention two full days every week. Schools must explore new roles, new hours, and new programs outside of their traditional pedagogical models to get the most out of their technological investments, especially in communities with low home ownership of computers. Some schools are doing this by creating after-hours computer labs or classes, by cooperating with nonprofit organizations that run after-hours programs, or by venturing into adult education. With large investments in technology, the imperative is to use it as much as possible, in a wide variety of ways. Most schools have yet to make this transition because of staffing limitations, insurance requirements, funding problems, or other obstacles. But this is an opportunity for schools, as well as an example of practicing social responsibility.

In summary, the state of technology in U.S. schools depends on one's perspective. Much has been accomplished in the past few years, in terms of connectivity to the Internet, access to computers, and building of awareness on the part of teachers, administrators, and parents that this technology plays an important part in education today. Many schools are doing innovative things with computers, and studies show positive results on learning.

However, not enough attention has been paid to, or enough money spent on, teacher training, software quality, and equitable access. Most policymakers understand this—these are the priorities in most U.S. plans for technological investment. Much more could be done to break down the metaphorical "four walls" of schools and help them use their technologies for purposes other than traditional grade-based pedagogy, such as by collaborating with communities in CTC-like programs. All public sector institutions, and especially schools, should avoid the limitations of what experts call "stovepipe networking," which means that all the networking takes place inside the boundaries of the institution. Computer networking technology is expensive enough that it should be leveraged for a diversity of community activities and goals, and schools should be cooperating with other groups to maximize technology resources within their communities. Much work needs to be done before an understanding is reached of how to do this well. Unfortunately, schools are typically not great sources of innovation, so they will need help.

Internet-related technology is simply too new to come to any firm conclusions about its value to education, apart from simply learning how to use it. Most policymakers seem to understand this. A period of bandwagon enthusiasm seems to be ending, and a phase is beginning of some sober and rational reflection about whether computers and the Internet are valuable tools for learning, and in what ways. Private businesses have commonly seen their productivity go down after the introduction of computers and networks, or at least stay unchanged, before they figure out how to use these tools effectively. Until just recently, economists spoke of the "productivity paradox," the fact that U.S. productivity had not grown appreciably during the decade when the nation invested most heavily in new information technologies.[29] But this seems to be turning around, primarily because of new forms of commerce on the Internet.[30] Something similar may happen in K-12 education. But many mistakes will be made getting to the point of effective use of this technology, and some of these mistakes will be expensive. And doubters will think that getting computers and networks right may not be what young people need.

The Federal Role in Supporting Technology

President Clinton's Educational Technology Initiative has four goals:

1. All teachers in the nation will have the training and support they need to help students learn using computers and the information superhighway.

2. All teachers and students will have modern multimedia computers in their classrooms.

3. Every classroom will be connected to the information superhighway.

4. Effective software and on-line learning resources will be an integral part of every school's curriculum.[31]

These four goals have become parts of many federal agencies. The U.S. Department of Education's Office of Educational Technology, led by Linda Roberts, has developed several programs to help support K-12 technology programs in U.S. public schools, including these major initiatives: Preparing Tomorrow's Teachers to Use Technology, Technology Innovation Challenge Grants, the Technology Literacy Challenge Fund, the Star Schools Program, and Learning Anywhere Anytime Partnerships (LAAP).

The Technology Literacy Challenge Fund was launched in fiscal 1997 with funding of $200 million; this figure more than doubled the following year, to $425 million, then stayed the same for fiscal 1999. This fund provides grants to schools that are pursuing the president's four goals, based on Elementary and Secondary Education Act Title I criteria. The president requested a $25 million increase for this program in the proposed fiscal 2000 budget.

Preparing Tomorrow's Teachers to Use Technology is also a grant program, for supporting new teacher training. The program will award $75 million in grants in 1999. The grant program requires consortia of groups, such as institutions of higher education, to work with school districts or nonprofit organizations. The fiscal 2000 request keeps this program at $75 million.

The Technology Innovation Challenge Grants are meant to support innovative and effective uses of technology in classrooms in mostly low-income areas. The program was funded with $106 million in fiscal 1998, $115 million in fiscal 1999, and the fiscal 2000 request is for $110 million. These grants range from nearly $1 million per year for five years to $2 million per year for five years.[32]

The Star Schools Program was launched in 1988 during the Reagan administration and focuses on how to improve student learning in disadvantaged and underserved communities and settings through the use of telecommunications, primarily in the subjects of mathematics, science, and foreign languages. The program was funded at $34 million in fiscal 1998, $45 million in fiscal 1999, and the request for fiscal 2000 is the same as fiscal 1999.

Learning Anywhere Anytime Partnerships is aimed at postsecondary education. It provides federal matching grants to consortia exploring educational delivery modes that seek to eliminate barriers of time and space, such as asynchronous distance education. This program is managed by the Department of Education's Fund for the Improvement of Postsecondary Education.

The largest program for assisting schools in Internet access has also been the most controversial: the E-Rate. Also known as the Universal Service Fund, the E-Rate was part of the mammoth Telecommunications Act of 1996, the most significant reform of U.S. telecommunications regulation in nearly seventy years. The legislation provided for a fund that would support discounts of up to 90 percent for telecommunications access for schools and libraries. The fund's program was determined by a new bipartisan Federal-State Joint Board on Universal Service convened by the Federal Communications Commission (FCC). In 1997 the FCC ruled unanimously for a provision that would allow schools and libraries access to a fund of up to $2.25 billion for such discounts, supported by assessments on telecommunications carriers operating in the United States. By April 1998 the first round of grant applications included more than thirty thousand requests totaling $2.02 billion.[33] The program is administered by a nonprofit corporation, originally called the Schools and Libraries Corporation, which is now part of the Universal Service Administrative Corporation.[34]

The E-Rate came under fierce attack in 1998 from Republican legislators, who labeled it "the Gore tax," because of the program's association with Vice President Al Gore. Telecommunications companies announced that they would raise their rates to cover their payments into the fund, and this prompted opposition from some legislators as well as consumer and antitax organizations, including Consumers Union and Americans for Fair Taxation. The E-Rate's critics also objected to the imposition of an assessment by the FCC, which they labeled a tax without the constitutionally approved method of levying taxes.[35] Because of this dispute, the FCC lowered the E-Rate's total target fund to $1.275 billion in June 1998, a sum that was disbursed to applicants beginning in November 1998.[36] But the E-Rate is still under attack in Congress. In May 1999 FCC commissioner William Kennard said he wants the program funded at its previous, maximum level of $2.25 billion per year.[37]

Many other federal programs assist K-12 schools in technology and are found in agencies as diverse as the National Science Foundation, the Department of Energy, the National Aeronautics and Space Administration, the Department of Energy, and the Department of Commerce, among others.[38]

Federal grant programs are available for para-educational programs that offer alternative means of access to computers and the Internet. The Department of Commerce's Telecommunications and Information Infrastructure Application Program (TIIAP) awards matching grants to partnerships exploring innovative uses of telecommunications technology supporting education, cultural activities, health care, public information, public safety, and other social services. This program has helped fund community networks and community technology centers in the United

States. However, the program has seen its funding repeatedly cut from its original goals; in 1998 it awarded $18.5 million in grants, and $17 million was available in fiscal 1999.[39]

The Department of Education also has two programs for after-school learning and community technology education, its 21st Century Community Learning Centers program and a program to support community-based technology centers. The former program, with a huge increase in funding proposed for fiscal 2000, to $600 million, attempts to help schools stay open longer, develop after-school programs, and support after-school learning and homework. The program supporting community-based technology centers makes grants to public housing facilities, community centers, libraries, and other community facilities to make educational technology available to residents of low-income urban and rural communities. It is budgeted at $65 million in the president's fiscal 2000 request, an increase of $55 million over fiscal 1999. The increase is meant to support three hundred new grants, over the forty supported in 1999.[40]

The federal technology budget for K-12 education is immense and diverse, but only a small part of the picture, as the federal government has traditionally left most education funding to states. Federal spending for technology education is not as high as many people think it should be, but it is constrained by the budget caps negotiated in 1997. Nevertheless, the Clinton administration made technology education one of its highest priorities.

The largest deficit in federal spending for technology-based education is for research and development (R&D). The Department of Education's Technology Innovation Challenge Grants are budgeted at $110 million in the president's fiscal 2000 request, $5 million below the fiscal 1999 authorization. The National Science Foundation has programs for R&D in K-12 education, but its grant programs are relatively small and the agency is focused on math and science education.

By contrast, PCAST recommended annual R&D funding of $1.5 billion, or 0.5 percent of all national spending on elementary and secondary education.[41] Officials of the White House Office of Science and Technology Policy have also called for similar levels of funding for technology-related R&D for K-12 schools. Only the federal government could commit this level of funding to this kind of research. However, under current budget constraints, generous funding for educational technology R&D is not likely to happen.

Another recommendation for the federal government to consider is a national clearinghouse of high-quality software and courseware (software for teaching courses).[42] Accompanying evaluations could be done by a national network of educators and education specialists. This idea has yet to materialize.

Finally, the federal government is increasingly concerned about how young people use computers and the Internet, how young people can be exposed to objectionable material on the Internet, invasions of privacy, and so on. Some Web-based resources for educators exist on how students should use the Internet in a responsible way, but these resources are difficult to find and they are often sketchy, weak, and outdated. The Department of Education, perhaps in collaboration with the Department of Justice, should consider implementing a major new initiative on educating young Americans about the ethical and responsible use of computers and the Internet.

Computer-Based Instruction in K-12 Schools

Thousands of teachers in the United States are doing interesting things with computers in their classrooms. Perhaps millions of people are enthusiastic about the use of computers and the Internet in K-12 education. Probably millions—or so it seems—of books, reports, studies, news stories, magazine articles, monographs, and dissertations have been produced on this subject.

What follows is a list of the general arguments used by proponents of computer-assisted education. Not all advocates endorse every one of the points described; some proponents may even have doubts about one or more of them. But on the whole, a core set of beliefs among proponents encompasses most of the points described below.

Computers help young people learn. This is the most important and critical assertion for justifying large investments in computational technologies for K-12 education. Many studies support this assertion, including the commonly cited 1994 source of James A. Kulik:

At least a dozen meta-analyses involving over 500 individual studies have been carried out to answer questions about the effectiveness of computer-based instruction. The analyses were conducted independently by research teams at eight different research centers. The research teams focused on different uses of the computer with different populations, and they also differed in the methods they used to find studies and analyze study results. Nonetheless, each of the analyses yielded the conclusion that programs of computer-based instruction have a positive record in the evaluation literature.[43]

Kulik offered five conclusions from this work:

1. Students usually learn more in classes in which they receive computer-based instruction;
2. Students learn their lessons in less time with computer-based instruction;
3. Students also like their classes more when they receive computer help in them;
4. Students develop more positive attitudes toward computers when they receive help from them in school;
5. Computers do not, however, have positive effects in every area in which they were studied. The average effect of computer-based instruction in 34 studies of attitude toward subject matter was near zero.[44]

Some critics have pointed out that these data were limited to traditional computer-assisted instruction, such as "drill and practice" models; that the reports Kulik studied varied widely in quality; and that the data came from studies done before 1990.[45] The Software Publishers Association commissioned a more recent meta-analysis of 176 studies published between 1990 and 1994, and it concluded, "The use of technology as a learning tool can make a measurable difference in student achievement, attitudes, and interactions with teachers and other students."[46] Studies also suggest that computers help with students' writing and math skills.[47]

Most reviews of computer-based instruction note that evaluations of new models of teaching, such as "experiential" learning, are difficult to assess and that conventional tools for evaluation, such as test scores, may not be appropriate for new modes of instruction using information technologies. As such, reports on educational technology commonly call for more research on evaluation and assessment. A host of methodological problems are involved with evaluating computer-based instruction, not the least of which is that the subject is a moving target because of the rapid changes in the technology itself.[48]

Exposure to computers is a necessary and important element in contemporary education because of the critical role of this technology in today's economy and society. This argument usually motivates parents and business leaders, who are most likely to think of education's task as preparing young people for employment.

Unfamiliarity or incompetence with computer technology is a serious liability in the job market. The majority of jobs in the U.S. economy now require daily use of a computer or related device. Workers with computer skills make more money than people without such skills, they are more likely to be employed, and they often report higher job satisfaction.

A widespread feeling exists that early exposure to computers in school is an important part of young people's preparation for well-paying and high-skill employment. A general consensus is also found that the national aggregate of such skills will be an essential component of future U.S. economic competitiveness in a rapidly changing global economy.

Computers and the Internet are important new tools for promoting social and economic equity. Because of the new significance of computers and the Internet in the U.S. economy, concerns have arisen that new technologies could cause even bigger gaps between the "haves" and "have-nots," reinforcing traditional patterns of inequality by race or ethnicity. Improving computer-related skills in low-income and minority communities in the United States could help attenuate inequality, or at least prevent it from worsening. Herman Lessard, a national African American leader and president and chief executive officer of the Greater Austin Urban League, has called equalizing access to computers, the Internet, and computer training "the new frontier of civil rights."[49] Welfare reform has made it necessary to provide equal access to technology training.

The federal government has focused on low-income, Title I schools in nearly all its funding programs for educational technology and for community technology centers and infrastructure development. The private market seems to be doing a good job of providing technology and network access to most American consumers, but "market failures" are clearly evident in many communities and schools where the federal government has chosen to intervene. While it is too early to assess whether these efforts will help alleviate inequality in the new economy, without such public investments, low-income communities likely would have few alternatives for capital and skill development.

Computers, and especially the Internet, open the world for students and teachers, and they help equalize access to educational resources that might otherwise be unavailable. One feature of the education field that has changed dramatically in the past fifty years has been the proliferation of new subjects, new knowledge, and new specialties that may be relevant to the education of young people. As a result, many schools find it difficult to provide instructors in some foreign languages, for example, or advanced math and science, or specialized topics in literature or history.

New technologies supporting distance education and resource sharing, especially through the Internet, may be a solution for such deficits, many experts believe. In Texas, the most rural of the lower forty-eight states, technologies can support the delivery of courses to students in small rural communities that cannot afford teachers in foreign languages or advanced math and science. The Texas Telecommunications Infrastructure Fund is a ten-year, $1.5 billion public investment program to build Internet connections to all public schools in the state, as well as libraries and nonprofit medical facilities. The federal government is also supporting such efforts through its Star Schools program and its Learning Anywhere Anytime Partnerships.

For all schools, the Internet opens up a wealth of information available worldwide, as well as interactivity with people, both experts and peers, through e-mail or the World Wide Web. Many schools sponsor popular "key-pal" programs through which students communicate with their peers in other countries and learn about foreign places from real residents. Classes can network with each other, sharing experiences or collaborating with each other on projects such as environmental data analysis or tracking the migration of animals or comparing economic development. Students have even used e-mail to communicate with astronauts on the U.S. space shuttle, through which they learned about space travel, space physics, and experiments conducted on the shuttle. Many schools took advantage of the opportunity to learn about Mars when the Jet Propulsion Laboratory offered live pictures on the Internet from the Mars exploration vehicle. The National Science Foundation has sponsored educational

Internet video feeds from underwater exploration vehicles or from its research station at the South Pole.

New uses of the Internet in classrooms have helped "break down the walls" and eliminate the traditional isolation of classrooms, especially in low-income and remote communities. This is a new but no doubt permanent part of learning in K-12 schools, which will expand in the future as schools acquire higher bandwidth telecommunications links and new software applications. The federal government is supporting such innovation, both by encouraging new forms of collaboration and networking and by helping build the technical infrastructure required.

Computers help make learning more fun and stimulating for students, increasing their interest in learning and in subjects that they might otherwise find boring or difficult. Numerous studies on the impact of computer-assisted instruction report positive attitudinal changes in students, with computers helping students enjoy learning. Interactive and graphically rich software programs can engage students in ways that lectures or textbooks cannot. Some teachers and administrators believe that students expect this kind of engagement, given their saturation with television, movies, and computer games, although this belief engenders a good deal of controversy.

Educational software packages often employ visualization techniques, computer simulation, digital animation, music, and other features to offer an educational experience that cannot be matched by textbooks. Interactivity can supply what-if capabilities that allow imaginative explorations of a subject or experiments that contribute to both learning and problem-solving skills. Computer software, for example, allows chemistry students to see visual models of molecular structures and to experiment with different combinations of molecules.

Another commonly cited advantage of computer-based instruction is that "drill and practice" programs allow students to interact with an instructional program that is infinitely patient and that circumvents public embarrassment over mistakes.

The proper use of interactive technologies in the classroom can be the catalyst for comprehensive educational reform and innovation, a transformation essential for schools in the twenty-first century. This argument asserts that one important contribution of computers and the Internet to K-12 education is that these technologies help shift the role of the teacher from the "sage on the stage" to a "guide on the side," relocating the responsibility for learning to students and their peers. In academic circles this model of education is called "constructivist" learning, in which students "construct" their own learning instead of having it "dumped" inside their heads by a teacher. This model is viewed, by its advocates, as an essential reform of U.S. public education with the aim of fostering a lifelong desire for learning and problem-solving skills, rather than producing students with a corpus of received knowledge.

Constructivist education has its passionate proponents and its equally passionate critics. It is a restatement of progressive education. Most experts, advocates and critics alike, admit that it is difficult to evaluate at present, that its outcomes are uncertain, and that it is likely to be at odds with the most widespread methods of assessing student achievement.[50]

The technological application of constructivist models of education typically involves students using computers and the Internet as tools in a learning project whose parameters and content unfold as the students explore the subject themselves. This model is at least in part derived from changes in the way businesses pursue their goals in the knowledge economy, as workers are increasingly expected to be self-directed problem-solvers who know how to find answers using information technologies. It is also a response to the expanding universe of knowledge. Many educators believe that it is hopeless to try to inform students, through lectures or textbooks, about many subjects because the knowledge base has become too vast. The alternative is to help students learn how to find answers to their questions, with help from computers and the Internet. The constructivist model also attempts to foster collaboration and teamwork, additional features of the new workplace but also skills valuable in themselves. Ironically, the fact that most schools have multiple students per computer makes collaboration and teamwork imperative when the learning project requires computer use.

The benefits of constructivism combined with computer-assisted instruction are uncertain. Their realization may require significant changes in educational philosophy, in training, and in the preparation and quality of teachers. Proponents of constructivism tend to believe that such changes will, in part, be imposed by computers and the Internet, or at least accelerated. Their critics reply that changing educational philosophy and preparation at the same time that teachers are required to learn complex technologies may be asking too much and that the results will be mixed at best, chaotic at worst. Educators and specialists in pedagogy also doubt the claims and effectiveness of the constructivist approach altogether, seeing it as yet another rehash of failed progressive practices that work best in theory, not the classroom.

Critiques of Computer-Based Instruction

Critics of the current national program for getting computers and the Internet into K-12 schools run from mild objectors or people with reservations to full-blown rejectionists, such as Clifford Stoll in his 1996 book *Silicon Snake Oil: Second Thoughts on the Information Highway*.[51] Some of the nation's leading computer experts have questioned the current enthusiasm for getting computers into schools. Yale University computer scientist David Gerlernter has called the national campaign to get the Internet into every classroom "toxic quackery."[52] The cofounder and current head of Apple Computer, Steve Jobs, one of the icons of the computer age, told *Wired* magazine in 1996:

> I used to think that technology could help education. I've probably spearheaded giving away more computer equipment to schools than anybody else on the planet. But I've had to come to the inevitable conclusion that the problem is not one that technology can hope to solve. What's wrong with education cannot be fixed with technology. No amount of technology will make a dent.

Jobs added:

> Lincoln did not have a web site at the log cabin where his parents homeschooled him, and he turned out pretty interesting. Historical precedent shows that we can turn out amazing human beings without technology. Precedent also shows that we can turn out very uninteresting human beings with technology.[53]

Underlying nearly all the specific criticisms of the current national effort to get computers and the Internet into classrooms is the feeling, among nearly all critics, that an unbalanced emphasis favoring this particular technology is being created at the expense of more well-rounded education. Computers, say most critics, are good for some things but not for others, and giving too much emphasis to computers in K-12 education pulls educators closer to becoming "tools of their tools," rather than "masters of their tools." Most critics also point out that the evidence for improvements in learning among young people attributable to computers is simply too equivocal to justify large expenditures, especially when schools are having difficulty paying for other essential expenses such as improving teacher salaries and schools' physical plant.

What follows is a list of the basic criticisms of the campaign for putting computers and the Internet into schools. Not all these points will be consensual among all critics. Critics who publish are far less numerous than advocates who publish. Two critics who have stood out recently are William L. Rukeyser, founder and president of Learning in the Real World, and Jane M. Healy, author of the 1998 book *Failure to Connect: How Computers Affect Our Children's Minds—For Better and Worse*.[54] Even more controversial has been Todd Oppenheimer, who wrote a scathing critique of computers in schools in the *Atlantic Monthly* in July 1997, which became the subject of heated debates at several national conferences.[55]

Evidence that computers and the Internet help young people learn is equivocal, uncertain, and methodologically flawed. It remains unknown whether information technologies significantly improve learning among young people. Many research studies call into question the positive influence of computers on student learning.[56] The essential critique of studies finding a positive influence is focused on what social scientists call the "Hawthorne effect," named after a series of workplace studies conducted from 1927 to 1932 at the Western Electric Hawthorne Works in Chicago by Harvard Business School professor Elton Mayo. The Hawthorne effect is a kind of sociological version of Heisenberg's Uncertainty Principle: Mayo demonstrated that worker productivity was influenced more by the attention paid to the workers by researchers than by any changes in the technologies the workers used. This lesson has become one of the standard factors of consideration in studies involving work and human productivity, a lesson taught in every school of business and work organization.

The Hawthorne effect applies to studies of students using computers as well—to any study of students using any technology in the classroom. A combination of factors sets up the conditions for the Hawthorne effect: computers are typically in short supply in most schools, at least in ratios of multiple students per computer, and researchers are interested in student performance in computer-assisted instruction. Therefore, separating the positive contributions of the technology from the positive effects of giving students more attention is difficult. Students in small classes, supervised by trained and motivated teachers who provide a great deal of attention, is a model that improves student performance. How much computers add to this model, when they are part of a study, is unknown. Jane Healy says:

> In short, the research on software's effectiveness is still limited, vague, and open to question. Some computer use appears effective within a narrow set of educational objectives, and it appears to motivate children, at least to use the computer and at least temporarily. Can it actually improve learning? No one really knows. Even if it were possible to measure or equalize the quality of adult interaction, definitive "results" on complex cognitive variables are never easy to come by.[57]

Critics also note that, even though the U.S. educational system has employed more computers than any other country, educational performance among U.S. students has not shown great improvement over the past twenty years. U.S. students still lag behind their peers in many other industrialized nations, especially in mathematics and science, two fields that would appear to be natural and expected beneficiaries of computer-based instruction. Samuel G. Sava, executive director of the National Association of Elementary School Principals, wrote:

> In the U.S., 37 per cent of students use computers in at least some math lessons—nearly triple the international average. Yet this increased use seemed to make no difference to our math results. In sum, if computers make a difference, it has yet to show up in achievement.[58]

Sava pointed out in the *New York Times* in 1997 that:

> In the 26-country Third International Mathematics and Science Study earlier this year, fourth graders from seven other countries outscored American students on the math portion of the test. Teachers in five of the seven countries reported that they "never or almost never" have students use computers in class.[59]

Because of the widespread national concern about school performance, schools are trying a variety of approaches to improve student performance, and many of the promising approaches have nothing to do with computers: enhancing parental engagement; reducing class sizes; implementing tutoring and both peer and adult mentoring programs; exploring a "return to basics"; requiring student uniforms; reforming curricula; increasing discipline; and a host of other approaches. Computers may be a part of the solution, but, critics argue, they are not likely to have the return on investment attributed to them. Some schools, such as David S. D'Evelyn Junior/Senior High School in Golden, Colorado, deemphasize computer instruction and still produce high achieving students.[60]

In general, as Healy notes, educational success is the product of a complex combination of factors, and computers are likely to play only a small role in this nexus. Few critics argue that students should have no exposure to computers at all. Most insist that computers should have a proper, balanced place in a well-rounded curriculum that stresses basic skills, discipline, reading, critical inquiry, and a passion for learning, which are all primarily the product of good personal relationships between students and teachers.

Computers can be an expensive distraction from more important school requirements and a never-ending drain on school resources. Many critics of the computers-in-schools bandwagon have pointed out that this expensive national effort is coming at the same time that public officials have recognized huge deficits in schools' physical plants, in teachers' salaries, and in support for nontraditional sports, the arts, extracurricular activities, and other features of schools that were once the pride of the nation. Many stories are heard of schools cutting back electives, art and music classes, language classes, library hours, and after-school programs to pay for computers and networks.

For example, the Austin Independent School District budgeted $37.5 million for computers, networks, and electricity in a bond package approved by Austin, Texas, voters in November 1998. By December the district's expenses had increased $24 million, or 64 percent, because of cost overruns in the contract. Electricity for computers in 102 campuses was originally budgeted at $16.5 million less than what was required. Cabling was budgeted at $5 million less than the figure that eventually emerged. This $61 million budget is for equipment for only four years, and it does not include money for teacher training, curriculum reform, technical support, or other collateral expenses.[61] This 1998 bond package came after a $26 million bond package for technology was approved by Austin voters in April 1996.[62]

By contrast, teacher salaries in Texas are, on average, $6,000 (15 percent) below the national average of $39,385. In a 1999 poll, 63 percent of Texans reported their belief that teacher salaries are too low.[63] Texas ranks thirty-eighth in the nation for teacher salaries. The average teacher salary does not qualify for a home loan even at the bottom of the housing market in Austin.[64] Ironically, the Austin Independent School District is losing some teachers to the private high-technology sector once these teachers get technical training on computers.

This is just one example of what many people view as skewed priorities in public schools. If school districts cannot attract good teachers, no amount of technology will improve learning. The combination of expensive technology (which is often more difficult to learn and use) and low teacher pay often means that the technology itself is underutilized or never even used at all.

The same can be said of technical support expenses. Most schools cannot afford adequate tech support, which means that school computers are often broken, in repair shops, or simply unused. Patrick Welsh, a high school English teacher in Alexandria, Virginia, wrote in *USA Today*:

> The two computer specialists assigned to the school to provide training are so overwhelmed fixing glitches that many staff members are afraid to ask them for help. Early last year, I made the mistake of turning my laptop in for repairs. It has been over a year now, and I am still hearing promises that I will be getting it back soon. I am told that the company not only won't service them, but also has run out of spare parts.
>
> Perhaps half of the school's teachers don't have these problems. They simply never use their laptops.[65]

This story unfortunately is not uncommon. Tech support is a nightmare for well-funded companies, let alone cash-strapped schools. Large networks of computers are difficult to maintain, even when the users are experts. When the users are novice teachers and children, the task becomes manifestly more complicated and vexing. And the more a school becomes dependent on computers and the network for its teaching mission, the more important it is that the equipment operate reliably. Unfortunately, computers are among the least reliable technologies in everyday use.

Finally, this technology is obsolete by design and therefore must be replaced constantly and repeatedly. A kind of symbiotic relationship exists between computer hardware and software that makes upgrades imperative for those who want to stay current with new operating systems and software applications. Windows 98, for example, will not run on older PCs, and the current Macintosh operating system will not run on early Macs. Windows 2000, a promised replacement to Windows 98, will require a fast Pentium II or III machine. Again, an irony of these developments is that such machines are in all respects pure overkill for the kinds of applications schools need—a Pentium III computer could run a large hotel or a small hospital. But school boards will have to buy these machines if they expect students to learn the latest in technological features.

In short, computers are expensive. They may add up to only a small percentage of aggregate school expenditures. But they are still a significant expense when many schools have difficulty finding enough money to repair buildings or facilities, raise teacher salaries, offer professional development to teachers, or sponsor elective courses, after-school programs, and a diverse array of sports and arts. Critics point out that, when the magnitude of expenses for computers is added to the uncertain character of the evidence about whether computers improve learning, the wisdom of the investment is questionable.

Computers engender a certain style of learning, which can shorten attention spans and lead to deficits in other, perhaps more important, styles of learning. Computers are often touted by technology proponents as devices that support the development of imagination and critical inquiry because of their interactive capabilities.

But technology critics point out that instructional software is, because of the way computer programs are built, in reality tightly scripted. Computer programs impose boundaries on inquiry and on the information they offer, an inherent limitation of the technology. Massachusetts Institute of Technology sociologist Sherry Turkle discusses this phenomenon in her 1995 book *Life on the Screen: Identity in the Age of the Internet.*[66] She describes how students commonly view the assumptions built into computer simulations as givens, inaccessible to criticism, and now a tendency "to take things at 'interface' value."[67] Todd Oppenheimer wrote in his *Atlantic Monthly* article:

> Indeed, after mastering SimCity, a popular game about urban planning, a tenth-grade girl boasted to Turkle that she'd learned the following rule: "Raising taxes always leads to riots."[68]

Often, the way computers work is beyond the understanding of teachers. If a teacher is asked by a student, "How does a computer know how to alphabetize?," that teacher is unlikely to know the answer, because explaining sorting algorithms is nontrivial even for computer science students. When teachers cannot answer such questions, the impression left with young students is that the computer "just knows" how to do things, that it is a "black box" with near-magical powers, and that asking such questions is irrelevant to learning. This tends to close off critical inquiry rather than open it up.

Another concern is that the current paradigm of computer use may devalue books in the minds of students. Computer software is usually rich with graphics and interactivity, features that some technology advocates say appeal to students because of their exposure to television and computer games. But reading long passages of text on a computer is difficult, something that even adults are reluctant to do. Web publishers often report that the maximum length of text Web readers will read is about fifteen hundred words; consequently, most articles on the Web are tailored to this length, and novels or other book-length materials are rarely found on the Web. Book publishers attempted to enter the CD-ROM market, but the effort never took off because few people are willing to read book-length material on a computer screen. The fear is that, by asking young learners to regard the computer as their primary instructional device, their reading skills will be constrained to short lengths of text, which have limited value. Such students may in turn be reluctant to tackle long works of fiction, history, or other subjects, many of which are essential for a well-rounded education.

Critics are also concerned about an apparent preoccupation with the Internet's ability to deliver information to students, without an adequate evaluation of this information. A great deal of information on the Internet is of questionable value, inaccurate, or misleading. Sometimes such deficits may be subtle enough to escape a teacher's competence. Moreover, say some critics, no one can argue that a lack of information is a problem for most schoolchildren; most kids are saturated with information. What they need is information relevant to learning, and teachers, especially in colleges and universities, commonly express astonishment over how little young people know about basic facts and how much they know about popular culture. In other words, kids are learning, but they are not learning or remembering the right things for educational achievement. The Internet can make this problem worse because its growing commercial character tends to emphasize popular and ephemeral trivia.

Finally, educational software vendors usually enhance the appeal of their products by attempting to make them fun or entertaining, features that some teachers say students now expect from software. But, some critics argue, learning cannot always be made fun or entertaining, and it may suffer by comparison, leading to an erosion of important learning discipline. "Maybe I'm the weird one," said Clifford Stoll to the *New York Times*, "but I never thought learning was supposed to be fun. It requires discipline, responsibility and attention in class. Learning is work. Turning scholarship and class work into a game is to denigrate the most important thing we can do in life."[69]

A good deal of friction currently exists between people who believe that books will be a lasting and important part of learning for young people and technophiles who believe that books are a technology that will soon be superseded by computers, CD-ROMs, and "electronic books," a new technology only now appearing. This debate seems to be masking a much larger and deeper debate about what the content of education should be: whether education should be "classical," with attention paid to great works of literature and history found in books, or whether it should be oriented more toward "information" conveyed through the most efficient and appealing means. How this debate will be resolved will influence the penetration of computer technology in K-12 schools. In other words, some debates about the appropriateness of technology in schools are really debates about what education in general should look like.

Teaching kids how to use computers may be useful in preparing them for a job, but not in preparing them for being well-rounded citizens, the true goal of education. Neil Postman, a technology and education critic, has said that the mission of schools is to teach young people "how to make a life, which is quite different from how to make a living."[70] Some technology critics believe that an overemphasis on teaching computers and the Internet in K-12 schools will teach students how to "point and click," but not why these skills might be valuable to them or to their future.

Few schools, if any, teach students anything about the role of computers and the Internet in modern society, as opposed to the mere technical skills of how to use these technologies. If any "social" component exists to the technological education of students, it is typically about the "dos and don'ts" of computer use, limited to what can get students in trouble if they use a computer in a way not approved by the school or parents. This kind of education, as such, is too often limited to a documented list of approved activities, usually part of an Acceptable Use Policy (AUP) that students are given for their parents to sign and return to the school. AUPs are usually drafted by attorneys, not educators, and are designed principally to protect a school or district from liability should a student encounter a disagreeable experience using the Internet. AUPs rarely help educate students or parents about the social context of using information technologies.

However, this social context arguably is the most important thing students can learn about new information technologies. The basic technical skills required for using computers and the Internet, other than typing, can be learned in a day or two. Most students already have these skills because of the widespread presence of computers and the Internet in homes. What students typically lack is judgment about what they will experience using computers or the Internet, such as exposure to objectionable material; copyright laws; privacy violations; "netiquette"; and how computers and the Internet are reshaping the economy, jobs, politics, media, and society as a whole.

Computer-based instruction in public schools in the United States is often too focused on narrow technical skills or on using commercially produced educational software packages. What is currently neglected is helping students understand how the use of computers and the Internet is transforming society and shaping their future. Computer civics classes are needed, which should be regarded as equal in importance to the development of basic computer skills. And an expanded idea of computer literacy would be beneficial, one that ventures beyond mere technical skills to a grasp of how computers operate in society in general.

An Attempt at Synthesis

Computers in K-12 schools still have passionate advocates and equally passionate critics, but most educators and parents fall somewhere in between the two extremes, and this is a healthy sign. A new middle ground still needs articulation, however, especially by government officials. What follows is an abbreviated attempt at a synthesis of advocacy and critique.

Computers are an important part of modern education, and all children should be exposed to this technology because it is changing the economy, jobs, education, politics, and society. All high school graduates should know how to use a computer, how to type, how to use a mouse, how to drive an operating system, and how to use several basic software applications such as a word processor, a spreadsheet, a database program, e-mail, and Web applications. Ideally, graduates should know generally how a computer works and how new technological developments are integrated into the technologies used today. In addition, graduates should have some grasp of how computers are influencing the economy, education, politics, and society, and how people use information technologies at home and at work. They should be exposed to some of the more pressing public policy issues surrounding the technology, such as netiquette, copyright, privacy, censorship, and the equitable use of technology by those in poverty or those with physical handicaps.

High school graduates should know how to find information on the Internet and, equally important, how to evaluate the information that they find. They should know how to behave in cyberspace, such as by observing rules of netiquette or refraining from unauthorized break-ins of computer systems or copyright violations.

Students should be comfortable using this new and valuable tool for work, further education, entertainment, and enhancing the quality of their lives. Using computers and the Internet should be as natural as using the telephone or watching television.

Computers do not need to be a central or dominant part of students' education. Computers and the Internet should be regarded as means to an educational end, not as ends in themselves. The biggest deficits among U.S. public school students are in basic skills and knowledge, and in their motivation for learning, not in their technical skills or their access to information. A pressing need exists for educational reform to address these deficits, but that educational reform does not need to, and should not, focus on technology. The biggest obstacles to educating students have nothing to do with a dearth of technology. They include poor teacher pay and preparation, low parental engagement, low expectations, poverty, and the overwhelming influence of popular consumer culture. Computers should be viewed mainly as tools for implementing reform, not as the reform itself. A complex combination of reforms likely will be required before significant improvement becomes evident in educational outcomes, and technology likely will play only a small role.

The federal government's focus on getting computers and the Internet to low-income students is the right approach for the most important problem involving technology. However, no rational reason exists for the federal government to promote a computer and Internet connection in every classroom in the United States. The U.S. government is right to focus on where the private market cannot or will not provide technology to certain segments of the population, such as in low-income or remote and underserved communities. Low-income communities must have access to information technologies, especially the Internet, and the federal government's approach to helping solve this problem is admirable, although the effort could always use more money. It is especially encouraging to see federal support for community technology centers, because computer and Internet access outside of school hours and off-campus is just as important as access in school.

However, the benchmark set by President Clinton for getting a computer and an Internet connection into every classroom in the United States has no rational basis. It is mostly a political pledge, a slogan, and a tool for counting steps toward the goal itself. There is no reason to believe that a computer in every classroom should be a desired goal for schools. Computer labs, for example, available to teachers and students from all fields, may be a better way to organize technological resources. One computer in a classroom does little to enhance learning—that number is too small and mostly symbolic—while multiple computers in some classrooms can distract from proven models of learning. Putting a symbolic computer into each classroom may foster low use, or no use, of the technology, the opposite of the government's intentions.

Concentrating computers in a school can be a huge cost savings, too, while attempting to get a computer into each classroom can entail unnecessary expenses. In general, schools should feel free to experiment with how they introduce and use computers, with how many computers are appropriate, and with what they are used for. No single approach or configuration of computer networks is going to work for all schools. Schools with only a small number of computers, used well, can perform as well as schools with lots of technology. Conversely, schools with many computers may not see improvements in learning if the technology is used poorly.

The federal government is correct in its current focus on teacher training, although this task will be much larger than most people expect. The government should also implement ways for schools to afford technical support personnel. Also, the government should consider implementing a national clearinghouse for educational software, explore and promote new and nonmarket incentives for developing educational software, and foster far more professional expertise in evaluating software. The current paradigm for training teachers in technology is far too narrow. Most teachers are trained only in the basic skills required for using a computer and the Internet. Teachers are rarely taught how a computer works or exposed to the public policy controversies they are likely to encounter when their students use the Internet. Teachers need time for this training, which is expensive.

Not enough attention has been paid to the need for qualified technical support personnel. Insufficient tech support personnel is a factor that will quickly kill enthusiasm for computers in education or anywhere else. At the same time, many school officials either go faint when they contemplate how much it costs to hire sufficient and qualified personnel, or, in many school districts, they cannot even find such people. The federal government should work with states and school districts, as well as professional societies, to address this problem. Volunteer support is not an adequate solution. Nor is relying on student help.

The quality of educational software is somewhere between insufficient and horrendously bad. A school can have all the computers it can fit into its buildings and do a bad job using them if the software is poor. The federal government can and should explore ways to promote better educational software, such as developing a national clearinghouse for educational software programs, a new network of unbiased professionals qualified to assess software, and perhaps new nonmarket approaches that provide alternative incentives for experts, including teachers, to develop better software. One promising approach is the Open Source model of software development, which has recently taken the software industry by storm.

A pressing need exists for a computer civics approach to educating young people about the use of computers and the Internet in modern society, but this kind of education is rare. The federal government should consider implementing a major new initiative, perhaps involving cooperation across agencies, such as between the Department of Education and the Department of Justice. The April 20, 1999, tragedy in Littleton, Colorado, in which two high school students killed a dozen of their classmates and a teacher, raised the Internet as a possible negative influence in the lives of young people because the two perpetrators used the Internet to distribute a message of hate, anger, and threats. Few events in recent memory have had as much effect on the minds of Americans, and the Internet's part of the story has disturbed many parents and even some young people.

However, few examples are available of teaching kids responsible use of the Internet in a comprehensive and well-rounded fashion. Schools have tended to rely on AUPs.

The federal government should help teachers educate students about the sociological, political, and historical issues surrounding the most influential technology of the current time. Even apart from issues surrounding the development of norms in cyberspace, most kids have no idea where the Internet came from or how it works. This is true of many teachers, too. Teachers are not trained in this kind of thinking about technology, business leaders are not encouraging it, and parents are not demanding it, even though they are all worried about the results given the absence of such education.

Because most young people either already have well-developed or adequate computer skills or will pick them up in the course of their schooling, the most important missing element is a social context for how this technology will shape their future and that of the nation. The federal government could help foster a solution to this problem, possibly through interagency cooperation between the Department of Education and the Department of Justice, a collaboration that has produced guides for computer ethics in the past.[71] A much broader, deeper, and more effective national program is required now.

Conclusion

The federal government has, on the whole, done an excellent job, especially since 1996, in fostering the use of technology in K-12 public schools in the United States. The Department of Education's focus on getting computers and Internet access to low-income schools and communities is the right approach. This effort has struggled with budget constraints and with the traditional limitations of the federal government's influence on educational policy, but a great deal of progress has been made.

The federal government has also been somewhat responsible for overselling computers and the Internet to school officials, teachers, and parents, especially via the president's goal of getting a computer and network connection into every classroom. This almost certainly stems from the political requirements of selling a national program in an era of suspicion about federal spending, and to a somewhat hostile Congress. Nevertheless, teachers and parents should know that the effect of computers on achievement is uncertain. Federal officials have a tough balancing act: to do things they can do, such as promote technology through federal grants and other programs, while acknowledging that computers are only part of the solution, perhaps only a small part. Mostly for political reasons, federal officials have tended to overstate the case for technology.

Access to technology will be more or less ubiquitous within ten years, and most students will have the basic skills required to use computers and the Internet. Colleges and universities rarely run into students who are completely incompetent or even unfamiliar with computers. Unfortunately much less rare are students who cannot write well, cannot speak well in public, or have vast and alarming gaps in their basic knowledge about science, math, literature, history, or current events. This is the biggest educational problem facing the nation, and computers are unlikely to have a major impact on this problem.

It is time to redirect attention regarding education technology to the problems that schools face. Those include teacher training, technical support, equity, and a broader, more civics-oriented approach to educating students about information technologies. The federal government has recognized some, but not all, of these issues. Officials have tackled the training and equity issues, but not the tech support and civic education deficits.

While all students should know something about computers and technology issues, the most important challenges facing K-12 schools have little to do with technology. The best of all possible worlds would be for computers and the Internet to become part, and probably only a small part, of a thriving academy of motivated learners whose time in cyberspace is significantly exceeded by time spent reading, visiting interesting places and people, having fascinating conversations, helping their peers, developing their physical and artistic talents, and enjoying life.

Comment by Tom Loveless

I enjoyed Gary Chapman's paper on federal policy promoting technology in education. The paper summarizes the role of technology in the growth of the American economy, offers an exhaustive account of current federal programs, and presents, in a balanced fashion, the arguments for and against a larger role for technology in American schooling. Chapman concludes by splitting the difference between advocates and critics of technology, endorsing middle-ground proposals that include increased aid to low-income and rural areas, an emphasis on teacher training and technical support, a national clearinghouse for software, the establishment of community technology centers, and a "computer civics" program that would teach responsible use of technology and its historical and social context.

No one will argue that technology is a rapidly growing component of the economy. The dawn of the "new economy" is truly remarkable. In the spring of 1999, for example, the total market value of stock in America Online (AOL) reached $150 billion, three times that of General Motors. In June 1999 the contribution of Internet-related business to the nation's gross domestic product was estimated at more than $300 billion, roughly equivalent to the auto industry. Considering that it took the auto industry almost the entire twentieth century to grow to this size and that most Internet companies are only a few years old, the industry's rate of expansion is astounding.

Enter the policy problem. Chapman cites a Department of Commerce study that the United States will need ninety-five thousand technology workers annually through the year 2005. Studies of this sort were used by the Clinton administration to campaign for several technology programs in the 1990s. Essentially, the administration argued that a federal effort would help prepare children for employment in the twenty-first century. I am not an economist, but I am suspicious of using projected economic trends as a rationale for new education programs. After all, the founders of AOL, Microsoft, Cisco Systems, Amazon.com, and today's other high-tech companies seem to be doing well without the benefits of such an initiative when they were in grade school. Moreover, a recent study by the Labor Department estimates the greatest employment demand in the next several years will be not for technology workers but for home health aides, human service workers, and personal home-care aides. This study also estimates that, in sheer numbers, more sales clerks will be hired than any other occupation, about 700,000 of them between now and 2005. The point is that labor economists are not unanimous on what the labor market will look like two or three decades out. Technologically savvy workers will be in demand, but workers with other skills will also be needed.[72]

Paul Krugman of the Massachusetts Institute of Technology observes that technology can have the paradoxical effect of lessening demand for specialized skill. He notes that the value of an innovation typically increases when it makes complex tasks more simple. In the 1980s, for example, most skilled computer users possessed at least a cursory knowledge of computer operating systems. High school computer courses taught students DOS protocols and programming in BASIC. Not anymore. The Macintosh and Windows environments rendered this knowledge obsolete. And yet accurate and speedy keyboarding remains indispensable. In "Technology's Revenge," Krugman describes what this selective obsolescence may mean for future labor markets: "The time may come when most tax lawyers are replaced by expert systems software. But human beings are still needed—and well paid—for such truly difficult occupations as gardening, house cleaning, and the thousands of other services that will receive an ever-growing share of our expenditure."[73]

Chapman accurately points out that a federal technology program rekindles a long-running dispute over the purpose of education, whether schools should emphasize giving students marketable skills or disciplinary knowledge. The history of the school curriculum suggests that society should proceed with caution. Whenever vocational ends have assumed the same urgency as knowledge in mathematics, science, literature, and history, the intellectual underpinnings of the school have been undermined. In 1917 a landmark document, known as the *Cardinal Principles of Secondary Education*, elevated vocational training and satisfying students' personal interests to the same status as disciplinary knowledge. Educational progressives believed these pursuits would make schools more relevant and interesting to students. Historians David Angus and Jeffrey Mirel have shown how the widespread application of this idea precipitated a decline in the rigor of academic coursetaking extending over several decades. Not until the 1980s, when Americans awoke to the fact that students were leaving school without a basic grasp of academic subjects, was the trend reversed and disciplinary content recognized as important again.[74]

A fundamental principle of policy analysis is at work here. How policymakers define "the problem" technology is intended to solve will affect how it is used. Chapman takes the eminently reasonable position that computers and the Internet should be regarded as means to an educational end, not as ends in themselves. I would specifically apply this logic to the school curriculum. If schools use technology to improve the teaching of traditional knowledge, it may yield benefits for education, but to emphasize students' technological competence for the sake of future job preparation is a questionable enterprise.[75]

Even if a consensus is reached that schools need more technology, the question arises whether the federal government is the best vehicle for getting more of it into schools. During the 1980s, it did not take long for the percentage of schools with personal computers to skyrocket. This was accomplished without federal intervention, although Chapman is correct that Title I monies had much to do with the purchase of computers by schools serving poor children. Chapman offers an excellent summary of current federal efforts, but I wish he had cast a more critical eye on how these programs are administered within the federal bureaucracy. Take the issue of fragmentation. Ten federal programs are described, several housed within the Office of Educational Technology in the Department of Education. Programs are also run by the Department of Commerce, the Department of Energy, the Federal Communications Commission, and the National Science Foundation. Doesn't spreading programs over this many agencies make a coherent federal effort more difficult? How can officials be held accountable for producing concrete results when this degree of overlapping authority exists?

Questions pertaining to federalism are equally important. Why run a program involving schools and classrooms out of Washington? After all, states and localities finance 93 percent of K-12 education in the country; the federal government, only 7 percent. Simply identifying a good idea for educational funding is not enough to warrant federal action. More analytical thought is needed about the areas where federal involvement is justified and where it is not, not as an ideological exercise, but from the practical standpoint of finding out which level of government can deliver services most efficiently.

Chapman endorses federal intervention to ameliorate "market failures," when the private market cannot provide technology to certain segments of the population, such as low-income or rural communities. This is an argument for using policy to redistribute educational resources, a mainstay of federal policy since the 1965 passage of the Elementary and Secondary Education Act (ESEA)—in particular, Title I of that act. ESEA channels funds to communities lacking the resources to acquire technology on their own, which makes sense. As a simple matter of fairness, why should children in poor communities be left behind while middle-class and wealthy children experience the wonders of scientific discoveries and new inventions? A big federal technology program is not necessary for redistribution to occur, however. Augmentation of the Title I program would accomplish the same objective. Washington could also assist local governments in issuing bonds to build a technological infrastructure—laying cables and wires for broadband Internet access, upgrading the electrical wiring of buildings, installing the hardware needed for distance learning.

It is a different matter, however, for the federal government to get involved in deciding how schools use technology. I doubt that Washington is the best place to find answers to these questions. If I were looking for the nation's top experts on technology, I would look in Silicon Valley, Austin, Boston, or the D.C. suburbs, not in the Department of Education. If I wanted to find experts on teaching, I would talk to successful classroom teachers. So I do not agree with Chapman's call for teacher training and technical support, a national clearinghouse on software, community technology centers, and a computer civics course—or, at least, I have not seen compelling evidence that the federal government should be the one to initiate these projects. These programs might be appropriate in some local districts, but each district should be left to decide the relative need for each reform. Some might need hardware, some might need technical support, and others might decide that they have more pressing concerns than technology. Many high schools do not offer a civics course, let alone a computer civics course.

There is a deeper problem. Micromanaging instruction through policy has never worked, no matter what level of government has tried it. Teachers respond to the practical—and particular—circumstances of their classrooms, including the characteristics of students and curricula, the demands of parents and administrators, and the reality of local resource constraints. By necessity, policy is based on generalities, what happens to most people most of the time. It also reflects an idealization of what should happen if everything is just right, instead of the messy circumstances in which teaching and learning typically occur. These gaps are evident anytime policymakers attempt to regulate classroom instruction. When the regulation comes from Washington, and is based on the latest fads instead of careful science, the policies are not only intrusive, they are also unhelpful.

Unfortunately, the camel's nose has already slipped under the tent. Federal reports on technology in education show a propensity for condemning "traditional" forms of teaching and endorsing "progressive" pedagogy. The basic tenets of progressive education have been around for a long time, but every generation of educational thinkers puts its own spin on four or five key planks. Frowned upon are basic skills, learning through memorization and practice, and curriculum organized by separate disciplines. For example, the *Report to the President on the Use of Technology to Strengthen K-12 Education in the United States*, issued by the President's Committee of Advisors on Science and Technology (PCAST) in 1997, laments that teachers use computers for "individual instruction in isolated basic skills, most often in a 'drill and practice' mode" and that lessons are "focused on a single content area rather than on the integration of a wide range of skills to solve complex problems."[76] The irony is that PCAST goes on to cite research showing that computers are effective when used in the same way that it condemns—providing basic skills instruction, often through drill and practice, in discrete disciplinary subjects.

Today's progressive education is known as constructivism, the guiding philosophy of the PCAST report. Constructivists believe that students construct their own knowledge, instead of that knowledge exists in an objective form, independent from the learner. If PCAST had its way, technology would be used to completely revolutionize classrooms, with student-centered instruction, cooperative group work, and multidisciplinary projects assuming prominence. The report admits that constructivism's ideas are largely untested. And Chapman is right that constructivism is extremely controversial, questioned especially by parents and teachers who value traditional forms of education. Although it is not appropriate to debate the merits of constructivism here, a critique of the science cited by advocates of constructivism was offered by John R. Anderson and other Carnegie Mellon researchers in *Brookings Papers on Education Policy 1998*. It offers an important lesson for technology policy. Federal pronouncements on how technology should be used in classrooms is an iffy proposition to begin with, but PCAST has compounded the error by endorsing a set of practices that are dubious at best and potentially even counterproductive to academic achievement.

Comment by Linda G. Roberts

My perspective on Gary Chapman's paper comes from more than a decade of policy analysis on technology and learning for the U.S. Congress Office of Technology Assessment (OTA), coupled with many years of experience as a teacher and university professor and now as director of the Office of Educational Technology and senior adviser to Secretary of Education Richard W. Riley. I have played a key role in initiating and developing the U.S. Department of Education's educational technology policies and programs.

Chapman raises critical questions about how technology is used in American classrooms and its impact on teaching and learning. Programs and policies must be focused on the end result. But attention must also be paid to access, because without access, or even with limited access, much of the promise of technology falls short. The question at all levels of policymaking is not whether technology should be used but how full advantage can be taken of these new tools and resources to provide benefit to all learners. Therefore, policymakers must be concerned about disparities in access as well as disparities in teacher training and operational support. All schools have some computers, and more than three quarters already have some Internet access. But school access cannot be the goal; computers and on-line resources have to come directly to the classroom, just as curricular reform and new teaching materials matter little if they fail to reach students.

In examining technology access, the gap between rich and poor schools has decreased, but the digital divide in classrooms is still real (see figures 1 and 2). The recent Department of Commerce report *Falling through the Net* makes clear why students in poor schools have the most to gain by federal policies and programs that address classroom needs. Those same students are the least likely to have access to technology at home or in their communities.[77] An impact has already been seen of the first round of the E-Rate telecommunications, in which the greatest discounts were targeted to the schools and libraries with the highest concentrations of poverty. In addition, almost 60 percent or $1 billion of the total amount of the E-Rate funds went to the neediest applicants.[78] Moreover, new data confirm that federal technology programs, such as the five-year, $2 billion Technology Literacy Challenge Fund and other programs targeted to disadvantaged students, have helped reduce the technology disparity that would have been far greater without them. For example, while all schools have continually added and upgraded their base of computers, half of the new computers purchased by high-poverty schools were purchased with federal funds.[79]

In addition to building the infrastructure and keeping it up-to-date and operational, no technology strategy would be successful without focusing on effective and compelling use of these resources. Here is where teachers and the quality of the content and applications are

Figure 1. Internet Access: Low-Poverty versus High-Poverty Schools

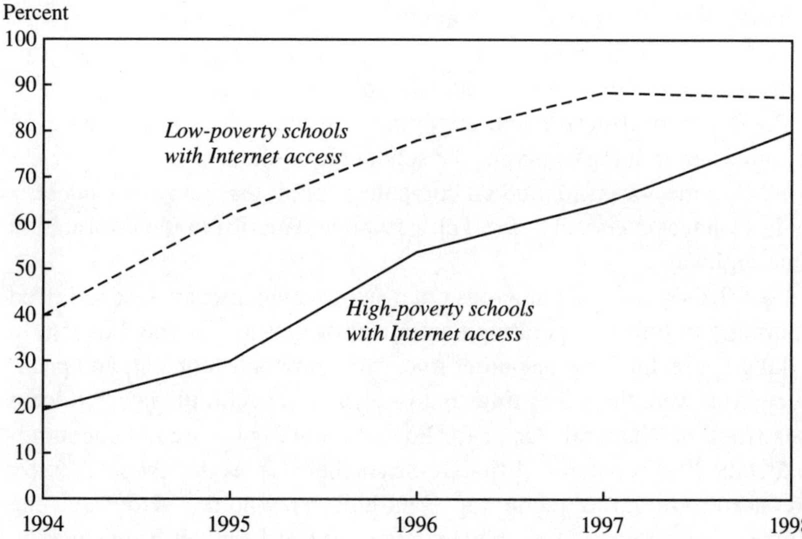

Source: Department of Education, National Center for Education Statistics, *Internet Access in Public Schools and Classrooms: 1995–1998* (Washington, February 1999).

Figure 2. Internet Access: Low-Poverty versus High-Poverty Classrooms

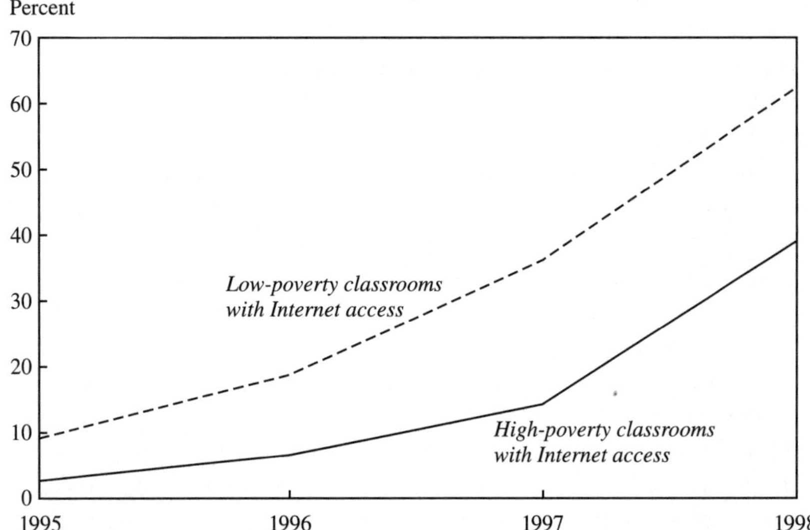

Source: Department of Education, National Center for Education Statistics, *Internet Access in Public Schools and Classrooms: 1995–1998* (Washington, February 1999).

absolutely key. Four equally important goals are part of the National Educational Technology Plan. They are:[80]

1. Provide all teachers the training and support they need to help students learn through computers and the information superhighway.

2. Develop effective and engaging software and on-line learning resources as an integral part of the school curriculum.

3. Provide access to modern computers for all teachers and students.

4. Connect every school and classroom in America to the information superhighway.

As OTA's study and numerous other studies demonstrate, teachers need training, not only in operating equipment or getting on-line, but also in linking the technology resources to curriculum goals, content, and pedagogy. And, yes, this takes time and is not easily accomplished.[81] Recent data from the National Center for Education Statistics are not encouraging. Only 20 percent of full-time K-12 teachers report that they are "fully prepared to integrate technology" in their classrooms.[82] However, the 1998 survey conducted by the University of California at Irvine and the University of Minnesota indicates teachers who use technology have moved well beyond drill and practice, and an increasing number are using computers and the Internet for complex, curriculum-based tasks.[83]

The substantial funding in technology and more recently the investment of both dollars and time for teacher development require evidence that they make a difference. It is time to move beyond the evaluations and analyses that were completed more than a decade ago, because their data and the designs are outdated, given today's technology and new capabilities for teaching and learning.

In the past year, a number of studies have offered new evidence of impact or lack of impact, and they raise important questions. The recent analysis conducted by researchers at Columbia University's Teachers College on West Virginia's grade-by-grade introduction of computers for reading and math shows gains in student achievement, especially for the lowest performing students.[84] Furthermore, these gains are cumulative over time. However, a recent analysis of the National Assessment of Educational Progress mathematics achievement among fourth and eighth graders raises questions about the value of drill and practice, especially for eighth graders, but show positive impacts for problem-solving and math simulation applications.[85]

OTA's 1988 report *Power On!: New Tools for Teaching and Learning* called on Congress to invest in educational research and development (R&D), with levels comparable to the Manhattan Project.[86] More recently, the *Report to the President on the Use of Technology to Strengthen K-12 Education in the United States* called for concentrated broad-scale initiative.[87] Up until now these calls have had little influence. What factors contribute to a concerted effort now? Given the large and growing base of technology, and the significant level of investment at all levels, local educators, state leaders, members of Congress, and the research community are demanding results, and there is so much more to analyze.[88]

I have five recommendations that would advance the nation's use of computers, new interactive tools, and on-line resources and telecommunications in powerful and beneficial ways. These recommendations underlie the Department of Education's proposed Title III, Technology for Education, in the reauthorization of the Elementary and Secondary Education Act (ESEA).

1. Close the digital divide. With full funding for the E-Rate ($2.25 billion annually), all schools and libraries can have affordable access to telecommunications services, the Internet, and internal connections to the

classrooms. The Department of Education proposes to target funding to the poorest and low-performing schools in the Technology Literacy Challenge Fund and other related programs.

2. Focus on teaching and quality teachers. While technology must be a component of teacher training and teacher preparation, the quality and preparation overall is critical. Increased emphasis on professional development that incorporates technology can help reach more teachers in the field. The opportunity to reach the next generation of teachers must not be missed. As programs prepare teachers in their content areas and provide prospective candidates with field experiences, technology applications must be integrated. Preparing Tomorrow's Teachers to Use Technology is a new program that needs to continue.

3. Raise the standards for content and high-quality software and Web-based learning resources. Technology development is largely the responsibility of the commercial sector, and software publishers look to the education community for guidance. An increasing number have begun to build products around state and national content standards, especially in areas where broad consensus and agreement exist over the standards. Research studies, such as the recent National Research Council report *Preventing Reading Difficulties in Young Children*, can have broad influence, especially if the states and districts bring these findings to the attention of developers and provide clear signals about market demand.[89] The federal government can help bring the parties together. Reading instruction is one of the most promising areas for new development, not only because of the substantial knowledge base about reading and its acquisition, but also because new technological capabilities, such as speech recognition, are coming into development. Now is the time to merge insights from research with the creative minds in the software industry.

The federal role can also encourage much broader development of content, from teachers and students in classrooms to faculty on campuses in research centers, with tools that enable collaborative and shared development. Several efforts already highlight teachers' lesson plans, and many federally funded projects share their content development on-line, but much more can be accomplished.

4. Help the education community look to the future; invest in research and development. All projections of technology suggest that costs will decline while power and capability will increase. Education ought to be at the front line, involved in new development, with schools serving as test

beds for new technology and applications. As the federal government invests in information technology R&D, learning applications have to be part of the mix of the R&D portfolio. The Next Generation Innovation Awards Program in Title III of the ESEA reauthorization proposal could help accomplish that goal.

5. Fund evaluation. The time has come to ask hard questions, gather serious data, improve the tools for assessment and evaluation, and conduct serious evaluations.[90] Student achievement must be determined, using both traditional measures and tools that capture new skills and new ways of learning. The imperative now is to develop better diagnostics, better tools for student and teacher self-assessment, multiple-site classroom evaluation protocols, and other new tools, many of which can be imbedded in the technology applications.

Notes

1. Department of Commerce, *America's New Deficit: The Shortage of Information Technology Workers* (Government Printing Office, October 1997).

2. Department of Commerce, *America's New Deficit*, p. 1.

3. American Electronics Association, *Cybereducation: U.S. Education and the High Technology Workforce, A National and State-by-State Perspective* (Washington, April 1999).

4. President Bill Clinton, State of the Union address, January 23, 1996, available at http://www.whitehouse.gov/WH/New/other/sotu.html/.

5. President's Committee of Advisors on Science and Technology, *Report to the President on the Use of Technology to Strengthen K-12 Education in the United States* (Washington, March 1997).

6. Educational Testing Service, Policy Information Center, *Computers and Classrooms: The Status of Technology in U.S. Schools* (Princeton, N.J.: Educational Testing Service, 19997), p. 10.

7. Tom Zeller, "Amid Clamor for Computer in Every Classroom, Some Dissenting Voices," *New York Times*, March 17, 1999, p. 9.

8. Quality Education Data, *Schools with Online Access: School Survey* (Denver, Colo., 1999).

9. Department of Education, National Center for Education Statistics, *Internet Access in Public Schools and Classrooms: 1994–96* (Washington, February 1999). See also Jeri Clausing, "Clinton Says All Classrooms Will Be Wired by 2000," *New York Times*, March 2, 1999.

10. Educational Testing Service, *Computers and Classrooms,* p. 11; and Department of Education, National Center for Education Statistics, "Internet Access in Public Schools and Classrooms," p. 2.

11. Zeller, "Amid Clamor for Computer in Every Classroom."

12. President's Committee of Advisors on Science and Technology, *Report to the President on the Use of Technology to Strengthen K-12 Education in the United States.*

13. Quality Education Data, *Schools with Online Access.*

14. Educational Testing Service, *Computers and Classrooms,* p. 13.

15. President's Committee of Advisors on Science and Technology, *Report to the President on the Use of Technology to Strengthen K-12 Education in the United States.*

16. Jane M. Healy, *Failure to Connect: How Computers Affect Our Children's Minds—For Better and Worse* (Simon and Schuster, 1998), p. 64.

17. Department of Education, *Getting America's Students Ready for the Twenty-First Century: Meeting the Technology Literacy Challenge* (Government Printing Office, June 1996).

18. President's Committee of Advisors on Science and Technology, *Report to the President on the Use of Technology to Strengthen K-12 Education in the United States.*

19. National Engineering Search, *Salary Survey* (Buffalo, N.Y., 1998).

20. American Federation of Teachers, *Teacher Salaries in the One Hundred Largest Cities, 1996–97* (Washington, 1998).

21. Educational Testing Service, *Computers and Classrooms,* p. 11.

22. Educational Testing Service, *Computers and Classrooms,* p. 12.

23. Department of Education, National Center for Education Statistics, "Internet Access in Public Schools and Classrooms," p. 17.

24. Department of Commerce, National Telecommunications and Information Administration, *Falling through the Net II: New Data on the Digital Divide* (Washington, 1998).

25. Tom Dunlap, "Low-Income Folks Buying PCs," c/Net Newscom, September 4, 1998, http://www.news.com/News/Item/0,4,0-26076,00.html?st.ne.ni.rel.

26. Donna Hoffman and Thomas Novak, "Bridging the Digital Divide: The Impact of Race on Computer Access and Internet Use," Vanderbilt University Project 2000, April 1997.

27. CTC-Net, http://www.ctcnet.org.

28. Gary Chapman, "Reaching Out to Bring Low-Income Blacks across the 'Digital Divide,'" *Los Angeles Times*, April 12, 1999, p. C1.

29. See Thomas K. Landauer, *The Trouble with Computers: Usefulness, Usability, and Productivity* (MIT Press, 1996).

30. Steve Lohr, "Computer Age Gains Respect of Economists," *New York Times*, April 14, 1999, p. 1.

31. Educational Testing Service, *Computers and Classrooms,* p. 8. See also Department of Education, Office of Educational Technology, http://www.ed.gov/Technology/inititiv.html.

32. Department of Education, "Technology Innovation Challenge Grants," http://www.ed.gov/Technology/challenge/.

33. Department of Education, *Discounted Telecommunications Services for Schools and Libraries: E-Rate Fact Sheet* (Washington, June 9, 1998).

34. Universal Service Administrative Corporation web site, http://www.universalservice.org/sl/sldesc.html.

35. Courtney Macavinta, "Net Subsidy Fight in Congress," c/net Newscom, June 8, 1998, http://www.news.com/News/Item/0,4,22833,00.html.

36. Courtney Macavinta, "FCC Cuts E-Rate Funding," c/net Newscom, June 12, 1998, http://www.news.com/News/Item/0,4,23127,00.html.

37. Associated Press, "FCC Chief Wants Web-Hookup Funding," May 5, 1999, http://www.nytimes.com/aponline/w/AP-Internet-Subsidies.html.

38. Department of Education, Office of Educational Technology, *Resource Guide to Federal Funding for Technology in Education* (Washington, June 1998).

39. Department of Commerce, National Telecommunications and Information Administration, "The Telecommunications and Information Infrastructure Assistance Program (TIIAP)," http://www.ntia.doc.gov/otiahome/tiiap/index.html.

40. Department of Education, *FY 2000 Budget Summary* (Washington, February 1999).

41. President's Committee of Advisors on Science and Technology, *Report to the President on the Use of Technology to Strengthen K-12 Education in the United States.*

42. Educational Testing Service, *Computers and Classrooms,* p. 55.

43. Quoted in Thomas K. Glennan and Arthur Melmed, *Fostering the Use of Educational Technology: Elements of a National Strategy*, RAND Corporation report MR–682–OSTP (Santa Monica, Calif.: RAND Corporation, 1995). The original article is James A. Kulik, "Meta-Analytic Studies of Findings on Computer-Based Instruction," in E. L. Baker and H. F. O'Neil Jr., eds., *Technology Assessment in Education and Training* (Hillsdale, N.J.: Lawrence Erlbaum, 1994).

44. Kulik, "Meta-Analytic Studies of Findings on Computer-Based Instruction."

45. Healy, *Failure to Connect,* p. 63; and Educational Testing Service, *Computers and Classrooms,* p. 35.

46. Jay Sivin-Kachala and Ellen R. Bialo, *Report on the Effectiveness of Technology in Schools, 1990–94* (Washington: Software Publishers Association, 1994).

47. Department of Education, *Getting America's Students Ready for the Twenty-First Century.*

48. Educational Testing Service, *Computers and Classrooms*, p. 38.

49. Gary Chapman, "Reaching Out to Bring Low-Income Blacks across the 'Digital Divide.' "

50. President's Committee of Advisors on Science and Technology, *Report to the President on the Use of Technology to Strengthen K-12 Education in the United States,* section 4.1.

51. Clifford Stoll, *Silicon Snake Oil: Second Thoughts on the Information Highway* (New York: Anchor Books, 1996).

52. Stannie Holt, "Wiring the Classroom," CNN Online, November 5, 1998, http://www.cnn.com/TECH/computing/9811/05/classroom.idg/index.html.

53. Gary Wolf, "Steve Jobs: The Next Insanely Great Thing," *Wired*, February 1996.

54. Learning in the Real World web site, http://www.realworld.org/; and Healy, *Failure to Connect.*

55. Todd Oppenheimer, "The Computer Delusion," *Atlantic Monthly*, July 1997, pp. 45–62.

56. See Healy, *Failure to Connect*, pp. 63–67.

57. Healy, *Failure to Connect,* pp. 63–64.

58. Ethan Bronner, "High-Tech Teaching Is Losing Its Gloss," *New York Times*, November 30, 1997.

59. Samuel G. Sava, "Maybe Computers Aren't Schools' Salvation," *New York Times*, September 6, 1997.

60. Mary Ann Zehr, " 'Alternative' School Sits Out Computer Craze," *Education Week*, vol. 18, no. 30 (April 7, 1999).

61. Laylan Copelin, "School Computer Plan Runs $24 Million Over," *Austin American-Statesman*, December 9, 1998

62. Scott S. Greenberger, "Schools Embracing High-Tech Cautiously," *Austin American-Statesman*, February 6, 1997.

63. A. Phillips Brooks, "Texans: Teacher Salaries Too Low," *Austin American-Statesman*, May 2, 1999.

64. Ben Wear, "As City Tries to Manage Growth, Housing Costs Go through Roof," *Austin American-Statesman*, April 22, 1999.

65. Patrick Welsh, "Hooking Up Kids to Computers Won't Make Them Smart," *USA Today*, May 4, 1999, p. 13A.

66. Sherry Turkle, *Life on the Screen: Identity in the Age of the Internet* (New York: Touchstone Books, 1997).

67. Oppenheimer, "The Computer Delusion," p. 56.

68. Oppenheimer, "The Computer Delusion."

69. Bronner, "High-Tech Teaching Is Losing Its Gloss."

70. Bronner, "High-Tech Teaching Is Losing Its Gloss."

71. Jay P. Sivin and Ellen R. Bialo, *Ethical Use of Information Technologies in Education: Important Issues for America's Schools* (Department of Justice, May 1992).

72. Paul Krugman, *Pop Internationalism* (MIT Press, 1996), p. 196, table 12.1.

73. Paul Krugman, "Technology's Revenge," in *Pop Internationalism* (MIT Press, 1996), p. 202 (originally published in *Wilson Quarterly* (Autumn 1994), pp. 56–64).

74. David L. Angus and Jeffrey E. Mirel, *The Failed Promise of the American High School, 1890–1995* (Columbia University, Teachers College Press, 1999).

75. David A. Rochefort and Roger W. Cobb, *The Politics of Problem Definition* (University of Kansas Press, 1994).

76. President's Committee of Advisors on Science and Technology, *Report to the President on the Use of Technology to Strengthen K-12 Education in the United States*, quotes from section 4.1.

77. Department of Commerce, National Telecommunications and Information Administration, *Falling through the Net: Defining the 'Digital Divide'* (Washington, July 1999).

78. Schools and Libraries Division of the Universal Service Administrative Company web site, http://www.sl.universalservice.org.

79. Department of Education, unpublished tables from *Study of Educational Resources and Federal Funding*, January 22, 1999, table 43.

80. Department of Education, *Getting America's Students Ready for the Twenty-First Century.*

81. U.S. Congress, Office of Technology Assessment, *Teachers and Technology: Making the Connection* (Washington, April 1995).

82. National Center for Education Statistics, *Teacher Quality: A Report on the Preparation and Qualifications of Public School Teachers* (Washington, January 1999).

83. Ronald E. Anderson and Amy Ronnkvist, *The Presence of Computers in American Schools: Teaching, Learning, and Computing, A 1998 National Survey* (University of California at Irvine and University of Minnesota, Center for Research on Information Technology and Organizations, June 1999).

84. Dale Mann and others, *West Virginia Story: Achievement Gains from a Statewide Comprehensive Instructional Technology Program* (Santa Monica, Calif.: Milken Foundation, Milken Learning Exchange, March 1998).

85. Harold Wenglinsky, *Does It Compute?: The Relationship between Educational Technology and Student Achievement in Mathematics* (Princeton, N.J.: Educational Testing Service Policy Information Center, September 1998).

86. U.S. Congress, Office of Technology Assessment, *Power On!: New Tools for Teaching and Learning* (Washington, September 1998).

87. President's Committee of Advisors on Science and Technology, *Report to the President on the Use of Technology to Strengthen K-12 Education in the United States.*

88. Department of Education, National Conference on Evaluating the Effectiveness of Technology web site, http://www.ed.gov/Technology/TechConf/1999/indx.html.

89. National Research Council, *Preventing Reading Difficulties in Young Children* (Washington, 1998).

90. See, for example, the discussion and papers prepared for the Secretary's Conference on Educational Technology, "Evaluating the Effectiveness of Technology," July 12–13, 1999, Washington, D.C., http://www.ed.gov/TechConf/1999.

The Federal Role in Educational Research and Development

MARIS A. VINOVSKIS

THE FEDERAL GOVERNMENT has been collecting, analyzing, and disseminating educational statistics for more than 130 years. Over time the focus has shifted from data gathering to research and development (R&D) to find more effective ways of educating children. Educational research and development, however, has not been held in high esteem by most academics and policymakers in the twentieth century.[1]

Policymakers have usually downplayed the value of supporting long-term research and development compared with providing immediate and direct assistance to local schools. When the sciences and social sciences were called upon to increase their contributions during World War II, the U.S. Office of Education (USOE) scaled back its support of educational research and development.[2] However, as it became increasingly evident in the mid-1960s that adequate knowledge was lacking about how to improve the schooling of poor children, the Johnson administration and Congress supported larger investments in long-term educational research and development.[3]

The need for federal involvement in educational research, development, and statistics has increased today. Analysts and policymakers are slowly and reluctantly acknowledging that many of the basic federal compensatory education programs established in the 1960s are not as effective as originally hoped. Large-scale, popular federal educational initiatives such as Title I and Head Start probably do offer assistance for some disadvantaged students. But these programs have not provided the same educational opportunities for at-risk children as their more fortunate counterparts enjoy. Many of these federal initiatives are only general funding mechanisms rather than specific programs proven to be particularly effective for helping children who live in impoverished homes and neighborhoods. Nor is there enough detailed and reliable statistical information about schools to help educators formulate better policy alternatives. As a result, a growing need exists for better educational research, development, and statistics to improve education and schooling for everyone.[4]

Both the Bush and the Clinton administrations have emphasized standards-based reform. The Clinton administration and the 103rd Congress enacted the Improving America's School Act (IASA), which called for the close coordination of high academic standards, assessment measures, and the curriculum. While the concept of the new systemic reform approach in IASA was plausible, it was not an empirically tested approach and critics have raised some serious questions about its efficacy. Although definitive evaluations of the systemic reform approach are still to come, a standards-based or systemic reform approach by itself probably will not be enough to close the achievement gap between at-risk children and their more fortunate peers.[5]

Unfortunately, the federal government in the 1980s and 1990s has not devoted much attention and resources to supporting rigorous development and evaluation of alternative ways of providing better opportunities for disadvantaged children at the school or classroom level. As Robert E. Slavin has aptly stated:

> For decades, policymakers have complained that the federal education research and development enterprise has had too little impact on the practice of education. With a few notable exceptions, this perception is, I believe, largely correct. Federally funded educational R&D has done a good job of producing information to inform educational practice, but has created few well-validated programs or practices that have entered widespread use.[6]

Therefore, consideration should be given to how the current Office of Educational Research and Improvement (OERI) structure and practices could be altered to facilitate the support of more high-quality research and development.

A short essay such as this one cannot hope to explore all of the important matters related to the current, ongoing reauthorization of OERI.

Therefore this paper will briefly address seven issues: (1) the relative independence of OERI, (2) the quality and quantity of the research staff, (3) the funding and flexibility in the allocation of resources, (4) the fragmentation of the research and development efforts, (5) the quality of the research and development produced, (6) the intellectual leadership at OERI, and (7) the role of politics in the agency.

The Relative Independence of OERI

Although widespread agreement exists on the need for federal involvement in educational research and statistics, less consensus is found on where that effort should be located organizationally. Mid-nineteenth century educational reformers wanted a separate cabinet-level department of education to signal the importance of a federal role in schooling. Congress did establish a separate Department of Education in 1867 (almost immediately reorganized and renamed as the Bureau of Education) but deliberately confined its responsibilities in practice to gathering, analyzing, and distributing data on schooling—thereby emphasizing the importance and autonomy of the federal government's statistical and research activities.[7]

As the Bureau of Education acquired new responsibilities in the early twentieth century, its statistical and research activities gradually received less internal attention and support. Calls for enhancing federal involvement in education often justified themselves by emphasizing the importance of gathering educational data. But once the broader federal involvement was attained, the statistical activities in practice usually were downplayed.[8]

The Bureau of Education was reconstituted as the U.S. Office of Education in 1930. As the agency grew rapidly in the 1960s, fear arose that the statistical and research functions of USOE had been neglected and mismanaged.[9] As a result, a separate National Institute of Education (NIE) was created to provide more visibility and coherence for educational research in the 1970s. Unfortunately, strong congressional hostility to NIE initially prevented the agency from fully capitalizing on the benefits of its new independent status.[10]

When the Department of Education was created in the late 1970s, NIE was transferred into a new Office of Educational Research and Improvement and eventually lost much of its autonomy and visibility. The incoming Reagan administration tended to be suspicious of social science research or program evaluations and tried to curb educational research and development.[11] The OERI reorganization in 1985 further diminished the role of researchers and scholars within the agency as the remnants of NIE became further submerged within the larger organization.[12]

Starting in fiscal 1989, the transfer of many new, but less research-oriented, programs to OERI meant that the overall budget and focus of the agency shifted still further away from the original NIE concentration on research and development. In fiscal 1989 funding for the National Center for Education Statistics (NCES), the regional laboratories and research centers, field-initiated research, and the Educational Resources Information Clearinghouses (ERIC) made up 98.7 percent of the OERI budget. But by fiscal 1993 these more traditional OERI activities were only 52.8 percent of the overall budget; by fiscal 1997 they had shrunk to 47.6 percent.[13]

Given OERI's current limited research and development capabilities and disappointing past achievements, perhaps the time has come to reconsider the organizational location of the agency. Should OERI and its rapidly increasing number of programs be maintained as they currently exist or should the research and development components within that unit be separated from its other growing responsibilities? Congress has strongly recommended that the Department of Education consolidate even more of its research and evaluation functions into OERI. This may be a useful step—depending on which programs and activities are designated as research-oriented and transferred to OERI.[14] At the same time, perhaps OERI should also focus more of its attention on research, development, and statistics by shedding some of its recently acquired, but less research-related, program activities. In a surprising, but refreshing, move by the head of any federal agency, Assistant Secretary Kent McGuire recently stated in testimony before the Senate that he believed that OERI's service-oriented programs should be transferred to elsewhere in the Department of Education.[15] The ultimate decision will be made by Congress, but McGuire's efforts should be applauded as a first step toward reorienting OERI in the direction of research and development.[16]

Another consideration might be restructuring some of the more important analytic functions in the Department of Education such as program evaluation. Currently the Planning and Evaluation Service (PES) has the primary responsibility for conducting program evaluations. But given its limited funding and preoccupation with numerous short-term assignments, PES has not been able to produce many scientifically sound program evaluations.[17] Perhaps the department should work with both OERI and PES to develop a unit that plans and monitors more rigorous, large-scale evaluations of education programs. The program evaluation unit might be overseen by an independent, objective group of experts who would not only provide technical assistance, but also ensure that the design, implementation, and interpretation of the evaluations are statistically reliable as well as useful to educators and policymakers.[18]

Some analysts have suggested that the existing OERI program should be abolished. The more research-oriented components of the current OERI could then be merged with some other federal agency such as the National Science Foundation (NSF) while its more statistically oriented activities might be incorporated into another unit such as the Bureau of the Census. This is certainly a plausible alternative that should be explored. The suggestion is attractive because educational research and development would be attached to another more scientifically rigorous and accomplished federal agency. Yet a danger exists that overall the focus on educational research might be diminished in another federal agency. Moreover, the links between practitioners and researchers may be stretched too far if the direction and control of educational research are to be removed from the Department of Education.

Another recent and thoughtful suggestion has been to create a separate, but independent, educational research agency. Christopher T. Cross, a former OERI assistant secretary, called for taking the research and data collection out of the current OERI organization and creating a new Agency for Learning—somewhat similar to the National Science Foundation or the National Aeronautics and Space Administration. Similarly, Diane Ravitch, another former OERI assistant secretary, has also advocated a separate, independent educational research agency. While locating the educational research agency outside the Department of Education has some drawbacks, they are outweighed by the benefits of having the research unit be relatively free from political interference and able to institute more rigorous and scientifically sound research practices.

Naturally, no easy or ideal answer can be found to the difficult but fundamental question of where federal educational research and development should be located. NIE and OERI have experienced repeated reorganizations in the past—many of which involved considerable time and effort but yielded few real improvements. Therefore, one should be wary of yet another call for reorganization. What is needed is less moving the existing organizational boxes around than creating a situation in which knowledgeable researchers can have more influence on how the goals of the agency are formulated and implemented. Thus, it is more a question of power and influence than just how the agency is structured, though the two issues are by no means unrelated. While any major reorganization by itself will not solve the many difficulties besetting OERI today, such organizational alternatives should at least be explored because research and development has not fared well within the current OERI structure and practices.[19]

The OERI Research Staff

One major problem within OERI has been the lack of adequate staff to implement and oversee the operations of the agency. This deficiency is not a problem unique to OERI as the recent efforts to "reinvent" the federal government have led to significant staff reductions at the same time that aggregate federal expenditures continue to increase. The reinvention program has been helpful in reorganizing federal agencies and improving their customer services. But while some of the staff reductions can be justified by improved efficiency, the cuts may have been too deep in some areas such as educational research and development. At the same time that OERI's budget mushroomed in the 1990s, the agency lost 25 percent of its staff, including some of its most experienced and capable individuals (who were eligible for the new early retirement buyouts).[20] As a result, recent expectations for higher quality work at OERI are making even greater and perhaps somewhat unrealistic demands on a significantly reduced and less-experienced staff.

The challenges of doing high-quality work in the Department of Education are particularly difficult because the general field of educational research and development is not as methodologically sophisticated or scientifically rigorous as in other social and behavioral sciences.[21] Therefore, the OERI staff initiating and implementing federal initiatives in educational research and development need to be particularly well trained and knowledgeable to ensure that the work supported meets high-quality standards. At the end of the Bush administration, outgoing OERI assistant secretary Diane Ravitch correctly pointed out the lack of first-rate researchers in the agency—a situation that appears to have deteriorated even further after she left in early 1993.[22]

There are several explanations for the absence of a distinguished research staff at OERI. First, most of the OERI assistant secretaries have not been experienced or productive scholars themselves and therefore have not always appreciated the need for hiring well-established researchers. Most of the top-level OERI positions have been staffed not by distinguished or active researchers but by civil servants, making it nearly impossible to operate a first-rate federal research agency or to recruit well-trained academics.[23]

Second, the relative overall weakness of the field of educational research has created difficulties in identifying and hiring a well-trained and methodologically sophisticated OERI professional staff. The agency has not been particularly interested in recruiting the often better-trained scholars from the other social science and behavioral disciplines. And given the more activist and less research-oriented focus of the American Educational Research Association compared with many of the other social science professional associations, less peer pressure has been exerted on OERI to hire outstanding researchers.[24]

Third, the wholesale dismissal of many competent professionals during the early Reagan years significantly weakened the agency. And claims of subsequent periodic abuses of "excepted service" led to the more recent congressional and union opposition to this appointment process.[25] Instead of providing a way to attract distinguished scholars to serve in the federal government for a few years, excepted service has all but disappeared. This is unfortunate because the ability to recruit temporarily some of the more capable and knowledgeable researchers might be an important source for staffing OERI's changing educational research and development needs.

Finally, instead of trying to recruit and retain the best-trained and most-talented researchers, OERI often has promoted individuals within the agency who lack the necessary research skills or experience. The agency has not provided adequate incentives or opportunities for the professional staff to upgrade their research skills and knowledge; nor has OERI allowed them to continue doing much of their own professional work. Questionable hiring practices also have sometimes denied opportunities for professional advancement for career employees and contributed to the relatively low staff morale during much of the 1980s and 1990s. One result of these and other problems is that OERI has not been viewed by distinguished researchers as an attractive place to work.[26]

Thus, while not everyone in a federal research and development agency needs to be an expert in those areas, a substantial proportion of the professional staff should have those skills. And for those who are not well versed in research and development, opportunities and encouragement should be available to receive additional training. Unfortunately, in recent years OERI has failed to attract and hire the high quality of research and development experts necessary for the agency to fulfill its internal goals as well as its congressional mandates.

Funding and Flexibility in Allocation of Resources

Educators and researchers have repeatedly pointed out the lack of adequate federal support for research, development, and statistics. Given the unusually broad and ambitious agenda expected of NIE and OERI, this is a legitimate complaint. Much more money has been available for research and development in medicine and science than in education. Even compared with other behavioral and social sciences, funding for educational research and development has trailed badly.[27]

The National Educational Research Policy and Priorities Board (NERPPB), which was created in 1994 to advise OERI, has recommended that:

> Funding for education research must be increased dramatically. An interim target should be to reach the level proposed by the President's Committee of Advisors on Science and Technology of 1/2% of our nation's expenditures for elementary and secondary education—about $1.5 billion annually. This would be a feasible target to reach over a five year period.[28]

Similarly, the Independent Review Panel on the Evaluation of Federal Education Legislation has criticized the lack of knowledge about which programs and practices are most effective in helping disadvantaged children:

> We find it unacceptable that as a nation we spend hundreds of billions on education, but do not fund the research and evaluation necessary to assess the effects of that investment. Title I illustrates this problem. The nation spends several billion dollars each year on the Title I program, but since reauthorization the budget for evaluation has averaged only $5 million a year.
>
> During the next reauthorization, we recommend a set-aside of 0.5 percent of program funds, half of which should be allotted for evaluation and the other half for research and development. In evaluation, we believe it will be imperative for the Department of Education to support studies that assess more definitively the achievement of students participating in Title I. . . .
>
> Paired with the set-aside for evaluation, an equal sum for research and development is needed to identify effective practices in the field, to build on theory, and to refine model programs for wider implementation. The demand for "best practices" is increasing, and the knowledge base needs to keep pace. A significant investment in research and development is the best foundation for the dramatic improvements in education that all the nation's children need and deserve.[29]

Part of the explanation for the lack of support is that most educators and policymakers do not have a high regard for educational research and development. Many of them think that what needs to be done to improve schooling is already known. If anything, they feel that the dissemination of the results from the "treasure chest" of earlier work should simply be expanded.[30] Others, who are more supportive of the need for additional research and development, have a low opinion of the quality and relevance of much of the previous work. This lack of enthusiasm for research and development is compounded by the fact that even many sympathetic educators and policymakers have considerable difficulty in citing examples of past successes despite three decades of sizable federal expenditures in this area.[31]

The problem of limited funding is compounded by a lack of focus and long-term commitment to supporting research and development.[32] Members of Congress and educators attacked NIE and OERI for the lack of relevance of educational research and development and forced the agency to devote a relatively large percentage of its scarce resources to dissemination compared with NIH or NSF so that little was left for research and development. As a result, research and development expenditures were particularly devastated in the mid-1980s.[33] Yet the increasing attention and monies spent on dissemination in the late 1970s and early 1980s were not sufficient, compared with other federal research and statistical agencies, to protect NIE and OERI from the unusually severe reductions in overall funding during the Reagan years.[34]

While monies available for research, development, and statistics have been limited, the ability of NIE or OERI to spend those existing funds efficiently and effectively has been hampered by Congress. Rather than allowing the agency to decide how to distribute its own resources to achieve the general goals set forth by the legislators, a few members of Congress since the mid-1970s have allied themselves with some of the largest beneficiaries of those federal contracts and mandated how the federal educational research and development funds must be spent. While Congress certainly has the responsibility and power to set the general policy goals for federal research and development activities, its specific and detailed efforts to micromanage NIE and OERI have been counterproductive for the nation as a whole—especially given that Congress has not been able to devote the type or quality of oversight of these activities necessary to ascertain the full impact of its legislative interventions. Particularly problematic is the frequent practice of inserting in congressional report language at the last moment major policy directives that have not been adequately considered through the regular authorization and appropriations process.[35]

As Congress and OERI look to the future, perhaps it would be useful to review the distribution of monies allocated for research, development, statistics, dissemination, and other activities. How much money is needed to achieve the projected needs and priorities of the office for the next five or ten years? Does the optimal division of expenditures in OERI exist given those future objectives? And within each of these subcategories of expenditures, are the best mechanisms being used for achieving stated objectives? For instance, how much of the dissemination monies should be spent on ERIC compared with alternative ways of reaching educators and policymakers? What proportion of the expenditure of NIE and OERI monies has been congressionally mandated and what have been the advantages and disadvantages of that approach? For example, has congressional earmarking of funds for labs and centers during the past two decades been the best way of distributing those monies? Should such earmarking continue in the future or are there more flexible and less intrusive ways of achieving the same overall congressional goals more effectively?

Fragmentation of the Research and Development

One of the persistent complaints about educational research and development is that it has been fragmented and too oriented toward short-term projects. Educators and policymakers usually have wanted to address more topics than could be reasonably expected given the limited funding. Rapid changes in leadership at NIE and OERI have contributed to the episodic and impermanent nature of much of the work of the agency. While numerous long-term research and development plans have been drawn up, few have survived more than one or two years and even those have not provided adequate guidance and direction. During its first twenty-five years, NIE and OERI were not willing or able to create a short list of research and development priorities and then stick to them for any length of time. And the recent OERI research priorities do not provide the detailed and focused direction that is essential for guiding future work in this field.[36]

OERI's research priorities, issued in 1997, are already being supplemented by more detailed and more focused suggestions from other groups. The National Research Council has issued a fifteen-year strategy for improving the usefulness of education research.[37] The NERPPB commissioned the National Academy of Education (NAE) to provide research priority recommendations.[38] And NERPPB issued a set of new recommendations stating that "the priority for research in education must be *high achievement for all students* and, within that domain, the initial emphasis should be on *reading and mathematics* achievement."[39] As the new, often competing sets of research priorities are debated and resolved, it will be interesting to see how (and whether) OERI changes its funding of the existing labs and centers to reflect the new directions in research and development, and whether Congress permits the agency to have any discretion over research funds.[40]

The centers and the labs established in the mid-1960s were intended to focus on a small set of long-term educational research and development problems. Unfortunately, neither the labs nor centers fulfilled that initial vision. Educators and policymakers often gambled by creating a larger number of small centers and labs in the mistaken belief that additional monies soon would be provided so that these institutions could be properly enlarged. Efforts to fund long-term, large-scale curriculum development projects were discouraged in the mid-1970s first by Congress and then by NIE. Responding to internal and external pressures, each of the labs and centers usually funded twenty to thirty small, short-term projects that did not necessarily fit together into a coherent and sustained research and development program.[41] A conference of leaders from more than a dozen of the better education research and development initiatives was convened by OERI and NERPPB in July 1998; they candidly acknowledged that "OERI's centers and labs are not preeminent in the field, partly because they have lacked the resources."[42]

Given the continued fragmentation and funding of numerous small projects, Congress and OERI should reexamine their strategies for encouraging long-term research and development. How much has the fragmentation of research and development in NIE and OERI hindered the ability of those agencies to make a more lasting impact on educational practice? What proportion of the lab and center activities should focus on larger and more long-term research and development projects? Why does there often seem to be a disconnect between calls for more integrated, long-term projects in the labs and centers during reauthorizations and the more fragmented, small-scale projects funded? Are there ways of improving the coordination and long-term planning in other areas such as field-initiated grants?

OERI is certainly a logical agency to sponsor and oversee high-quality, systematic development; and its recent assistant secretaries have expressed support for this type of work on many occasions. So why hasn't more been accomplished? After three decades of frustration and mutual recriminations, the time has come to acknowledge that many of the R&D centers and regional educational laboratories have not been producing much high-quality, systematic development.[43]

A separate program should be set up for soliciting and implementing large-scale, systematic development. Initially this program might focus its energies on three to five long-term projects in areas such as developing reading improvement programs or helping at-risk children make a successful transition from early childhood programs into the regular classroom. A distinguished board of experts might oversee the progress of these development projects and ensure the scientific soundness of the work as well as its usefulness for educators and policymakers. Anyone, including the existing centers or laboratories, could compete for these demonstration projects. The open competition would not only spur existing educational research and development providers to draw up better proposals, but it might also attract interest from other major social science research organizations such as the Manpower Demonstration Research Corporation, RAND, or the Urban Institute.[44]

Because much of the existing work of the laboratories is providing research-based technical assistance to their regional clients, the labs and the department's Comprehensive Regional Assistance Centers should be merged. As five of the ten labs are already operating one of the fifteen comprehensive centers, this merger would eliminate wasteful duplication and provide more efficient and effective services. To provide more flexibility at the state and local levels, some of the monies saved by the merger could be redistributed directly to the states and local school districts so that they could acquire whatever particular technical assistance they need (including purchasing additional services from the newly merged labs and comprehensive centers). In the distribution of technical assistance monies to the states and local districts, those funds perhaps should be targeted to schools that lack the resources necessary to improve their operations and that also serve the most economically disadvantaged children.[45]

The five-year R&D centers should continue to play an important role in educational research, but they should be much larger and their work should be more focused. Instead of supporting some centers at an annual budget of only $1.5 million or $2 million, the minimum size of an R&D center should be at least $4 million or $5 million annually. Moreover, these centers should develop a coherent, focused five-year research program; centers should not have twenty to thirty different small-scale, uncoordinated projects scattered among a half-dozen different institutions throughout the nation.[46]

Congress in 1994 increased the amount of monies for field-initiated research in OERI. This was a good idea, and field-initiated research should be expanded in the next reauthorization. At the same time, however, OERI should target some of its field-initiated research competitions on particular educational problems by developing more focused, mission-oriented initiatives. Perhaps a useful model to consider would be the research and evaluation work that was done in the mid-1970s and 1980s on the issue of adolescent pregnancy and early childbearing by the National Institute for Child Health and Human Development. The targeted competitions for educational research sometimes might be most appropriately staffed by distinguished outside experts who join OERI temporarily as members of the excepted service staff.[47]

Quality of the Research and Development

A few questions also have been raised about the types of educational research and development funded by the federal government. A major shift has occurred from historical and philosophical studies in the late nineteenth century to behavioral and social science investigations in the twentieth century. While most educators and policymakers welcomed this change, some individuals in the early 1980s challenged the increasingly exclusive use of the behavioral and social sciences. The debate today focuses more on the relative use of quantitative or qualitative methods as well as on the benefits of doing case studies instead of large-scale and more systematic investigations.

Much of the quality of research and development produced by education researchers is regarded by academics in other behavioral and social science disciplines as second-rate methodologically and conceptually. The low opinion of the quality of much of educational research and development is frequently shared by policymakers who consider the work sponsored by NSF or the National Institutes of Health (NIH) generally to be more rigorous and scientifically sound than that produced by OERI.

Despite recurrent questions about the quality of educational research and development, NIE and OERI have done little to assess the work of their grantees and contractors. The groups and panels looking at the labs and centers in the 1970s, for example, did not investigate the quality of their contributions.[48] Nor did the recent National Academy of Sciences (NAS) study of OERI consider the quality of the products produced by the agency or its funding recipients.[49] A review of the statistical work done by NCES in the mid-1980s raised serious questions about its quality—though later evaluations of the subsequent work done by NCES have provided a much more reassuring picture of its products.[50] The one recent evaluation of the quality of the research and development produced by the centers and the labs painted a mixed, but overall disappointing, picture of the conceptual and technical soundness of much of their work.[51] More attention needs to be paid to the types and quality of studies being supported by OERI to ensure that federal research and development monies are being well spent. Has the focus been too much on contemporary problems using a behavioral and social science approach without adequate attention to historical and philosophical analyses? How should quantitative and qualitative methods be used in educational research and development? Should educational evaluations employ more randomized-controlled experiments? What is the proper role of case studies and large-scale investigations? How good are the OERI-funded studies conceptually and technically? What can be done to enhance the quality of the work in educational research, development, and statistics?

Although concerns about the quality of research and development usually have not been prominent features at NIE and OERI, the 1994 legislation took an important step forward by calling for OERI, in consultation with NERPPB, to establish "standards for the conduct and evaluation of research."[52] OERI and NERPPB have risen to that challenge and issued strict quality assurance standards.[53] The agency and NERPPB also commissioned a thoughtful and useful analysis of the peer review system.[54] Moreover, the Department of Education and OERI have been involved in an ongoing third-year review of the centers and labs, which, one hopes, will consider the quality of their research and development products.[55] It is too early to know how effective OERI has been in improving the quality of its research and development work, but the agency now is addressing this important issue.

Intellectual Leadership at OERI

Federal involvement in educational research, development, and statistics has often suffered from unstable and weak intellectual leadership. Some outstanding and distinguished leaders served in NIE and OERI. But some appointees had credentials that were based more on their political experience than on their distinguished educational and research achievements. Moreover, the rapid turnover of NIE directors and OERI assistant secretaries has not provided the much-needed continuity or stability for the agency. During just the four years of the Bush administration, there were five assistant secretaries. And recently OERI has had four assistant secretaries in less than one year. Particularly lacking during much of the past three decades has been the type of intellectual leadership needed in a major federal research and development agency.[56]

OERI has also lacked strong intellectual leadership in its middle management research positions. While the Office of Research in OERI used to have a director who oversaw the operation of all of the centers, today the five National Research Institutes created in the 1994 legislation are operating independently of each other and without adequate intellectual coordination. Moreover, three of the five institute directors recently have decided to leave OERI—raising some questions about the attractiveness of those key positions for the agency's research leaders as well as further diminishing the already depleted number of researchers in the institutes. Finally, while recent OERI assistant secretaries announced plans to appoint a distinguished research adviser for the agency, that post has remained vacant throughout the Clinton administration.

OERI and Congress should examine some of the questions raised about the leadership and staff of the agency. Why has such a rapid turnover occurred in leadership in NIE and OERI, and what can be done to provide more stability and continuity? How well have NIE and OERI handled the repeated interruptions in leadership, and what might be done in the future to make such transitions not only less frequent, but also less disruptive when they do occur? What should be some of the essential attributes of any assistant secretary at OERI, and how often has this been achieved in practice? What should be some of the most important characteristics of a professional staff at any distinguished federal research, development, and statistics operation, and how well has this been reflected in the ever-changing composition of employees at NIE and OERI? Given the labor-intensive nature of work expected at agencies such as NIE and OERI, what should be the size of the professional staff and how does this match what has been available over time? Why have NIE and OERI offered inadequate intellectual leadership in educational research, development, and statistics? And what must be done to improve the quality of intellectual leadership in the future?

Role of Politics in OERI

One of the more important and troubling issues that has not received much analysis is the charge that NIE and OERI have been too political. Compared with much of the work in medicine or science, school reforms and improvements to some extent are by their nature controversial and political. The education and socialization of children involve highly sensitive decisions not only about how students should be educated, but also about what they should be taught. Given the historic charge to the Bureau of Education to help improve state and local schooling as well as NIE's commitment to promote excellence and equity in education, it was not entirely surprising that a conservative reaction occurred in the early 1980s against the seemingly liberal and activist federal research and development agenda—though many of the proposed revisions were just as political and ideological as the earlier policies that the new appointees were criticizing.

Many observers have condemned the more blatant and transparent political controversies of the early 1980s.[57] But an even more fundamental and subtle issue is how much and what kind of separation should exist between the immediate policy interests of any administration or Congress and the independence and integrity of NIE or OERI. While almost everyone agrees that OERI should critically investigate and evaluate the strengths and weaknesses of alternative educational policies and procedures, how much of its research and development agenda should be focused on short-term policy-related questions? Because NIE and OERI have always had a strong educational reform component in their mission statements, how should the leaders and staff of that agency interpret their responsibility to support any particular set of current reforms advocated by policymakers in the executive or legislative branches—especially when little bipartisan agreement is found on what educational reforms or improvements are needed?

A tendency in recent years exists to accuse OERI of engaging in politics. Diane Ravitch, an OERI assistant secretary in the Bush administration, rejected that accusation during her tenure and continues to reject it today, but she acknowledges that the perception remains and continues to hurt the agency:

> The overriding weakness of federal education research is a lack of trust, on the Hill, in the press corps, and among the public. When I was at OERI, I was told repeatedly by Congressional staff and members that the agency lacked any credibility, that it was thoroughly politicized. This reputation made it hard to recruit top-flight researchers. Based on my own experience, I did not believe this to be true, and I do not believe it is true today. But certainly this perception is commonplace. Today, there is still a widespread perception that the federal research agenda reflects the political needs of the party in power or the interests of professional educators and researchers.[58]

While all federal agencies engaged in research and development are involved in the political process, some members of Congress have been particularly intrusive in the area of education. For example, Chester E. Finn Jr., one of the original supporters of NIE, complained about the inappropriate and inordinate involvement of Congress in educational research and development:

> Congressional people have no business setting research agendas. They create research agencies. They fund research agencies. They don't tell it what to do. They can tell it how much money to spend, yes. They don't tell the director of the National Cancer Institute which drug to test on which forms of tumor. They have not told the director of the National Science Foundation, to my knowledge, how much money to spend on particle physics versus solid state metallurgy.... Congress is far more intrusive in the management of federal education programs than it is in the management of federal science research programs. But NIE, because it is overseen by the education committees and subcommittees, and so on, is stuck with the same mind set, the same political culture if you will, as Title I, where in fact it should be treated the same as NSF or NIH.[59]

An open and candid discussion also is needed of the proper role of interest groups in guiding the operations of a federal research agency. In other federal agencies such as NIH and NSF, academic and other outside interest groups have often tried to influence the general goals and lobbied to help secure the necessary federal funds.[60] Some institutions of higher education in the last two decades have sought congressional earmarking of funds for special projects.[61] But most outside involvement seems to have been focused on providing support for a particular NIH division or for trying to cure a specific disease (such as acquired immune deficiency syndrome [AIDS], cancer, or heart disease). Much less frequently have any of these outside groups and their congressional allies attempted to mandate the details of how research monies should be spent or which specific institutions should receive federal assistance once they have been allocated to an agency. And when outside attempts to interfere in the ongoing day-to-day operations of other federal research agencies have been made, strong protests usually have arisen from those agencies, the academic community, and members of Congress committed to protecting research objectivity and integrity.[62]

The troubled history of NIE and OERI with influential outside interest groups such as the former Council on Educational Development and Research (CEDaR), which lobbied on behalf of the regional laboratories, suggests the need to explore this topic openly and in more depth. While inevitably in any federal research and development operation there will be some politics, the extent and nature of that political involvement needs to be carefully monitored and contained lest it compromise the ability of the agency to do scientifically objective and efficient work. The periodic congressional micromanagement of NIE and OERI, often at the instigation of CEDaR, seems excessive and inappropriate in the setting and implementing of a scientifically sound and educationally effective research and development program.

Congress and outside interest groups have not been the only potential threat to the relative political independence of OERI. Efforts were made during the Reagan administration to replace many of the existing OERI staff who were viewed as too liberal ideologically.[63] More recently concerns have been raised about the Clinton administration's efforts to further its educational agenda by using OERI staff and discretionary funds to develop and oversee the proposed voluntary individual national tests in fourth-grade reading and eighth-grade math. Fortunately, that issue now appears to have been resolved as the administration and Congress have reached at least a temporary compromise on the national testing issue, which has removed OERI from the direct development and supervision of that highly controversial undertaking.[64]

Similarly, questions have been raised about the Clinton administration's decision not to renominate Pascal "Pat" Forgione Jr. to a six-year term as the commissioner of education statistics to oversee the operation of the National Center for Education Statistics in OERI. Forgione was widely regarded as a conscientious and effective leader of NCES, and the agency's Advisory Council on Education Statistics had urged Secretary Richard W. Riley to reappoint him.[65] The reason given for not reappointing Forgione was that he had been late in filing his income taxes.[66] But some Washington insiders suspect that it may have been Forgione's public protesting of Vice President Al Gore's inappropriate intrusion during the release of the National Assessment of Educational Progress reading scores that doomed his candidacy—something the administration strongly denies.[67] Whatever happened, the entire unfortunate episode has raised additional questions about the relative political independence of NCES and OERI and reinforced those calling for additional protection of those agencies from political interference.[68]

Conclusion

Since the mid-nineteenth century, a general consensus has emerged that the federal government should play a key role in collecting, analyzing, and disseminating educational data as well as exert some responsibility for supporting educational research and development. Today awareness is growing among the public and policymakers of the need for better research and development to help improve schools.

For more than three decades the federal government has intermittently tried to create more rigorous and systematic educational research and development. The R&D centers were developed in 1964, and the following year Congress authorized the regional educational laboratories. Although these institutions periodically have experienced changes in their focus and operations, they have been among the major recipients of federal research and development expenditures during these years. While the monies allocated to research and development have never been adequate, substantial funds (in constant 1996 dollars) were spent on the centers and labs from fiscal 1964 through fiscal 1998: $1.16 billion for the centers and $1.59 billion for the labs. While the reasons for the shortcomings in these and other federal educational research and development programs are complex, the bottom line is that the public and policymakers still have not received the adequate and reliable information needed to ensure that all children have a real chance of succeeding in school.

As one follows the history of federal educational research and development during the past three decades, one is struck by the thoughtful but often repetitive suggestions for making improvements. Almost everyone involved in these discussions seems to call for more research funding; better trained researchers; more permanent and distinguished NIE or OERI leaders; more strategic planning to meet the needs of classroom teachers and students; more long-term, coherent research and development projects; scientifically sound research and development that is useful to practitioners; and preservation of the intellectual and political independence of the agency. Most of these recommendations have found their way into the legislative language of the agency's periodic congressional reauthorizations.

Yet looking back to what has been accomplished at the end of each reauthorization, the results seldom match the earlier stated expectations and promises. Structural weaknesses in the design of the agency, inadequate funding, and excessive congressional micromanagement partly explain the deficiencies. But some of the responsibility for the agency's shortcomings must also rest with its own leadership over the past twenty-five years. NIE or OERI directors have not always tried to recruit distinguished researchers or been committed to insisting upon high-quality work from all of the agency's grantees and contractors. Nor have all members of the educational research community been sufficiently committed to making NIE or OERI a distinguished agency—especially if it has meant sacrificing their own short-term interests by subjecting their own federally sponsored work to more rigorous evaluations or facing more frequent competitions for their funding.

Thus, the issue during the current reauthorization of OERI is not just how to restructure the agency, but also how to ensure that the ideas put forth in the legislation will be carried out. In many ways the legislation that reauthorized OERI in 1994 was good and reasonable, and many of the shortcomings that have appeared subsequently might have been corrected administratively. Perhaps a large part of the problem rests with how the legislative suggestions and directives have been implemented in practice. As a result, some policymakers are becoming impatient with listening to the same, familiar promises of improving research and development in the near future when not enough has been done during the previous four or five years. Unless educational policymakers as well as researchers are prepared to make the necessary and often difficult decisions and sacrifices needed to make OERI into a first-rate, high-quality research and development operation, some policymakers might consider shifting some of the monies and responsibilities currently allocated to OERI to other research and statistical agencies outside the Department of Education.

The Senate Budget Committee Task Force on Education, for example, seems to have limited confidence in the ability of OERI to produce the high-quality research and development needed:

> Unfortunately, it is often difficult to discern good research from bad. The precursor to OERI was the National Institute of Education (NIE). Mod-

eled after the National Institute of Health, which is widely respected, the NIE never realized the same success as its role model. The Task Force heard that OERI does not seem to be closing the gap either. Inadequate peer-review processes and a lack of good quality control measures stymies progress. Even the PCAST [President's Committee of Advisors on Science and Technology] group recommends that additional research on education and the use of technology in education be undertaken by "a distinguished independent board of outside experts." There seems to be little faith in our current education infrastructure to produce the needed research on policies and programs that work.[69]

Finally, while a review of past and present federal strategies for educational research, development, and statistics serves as a reminder of the difficulties of making significant and lasting improvement, it also provides occasional examples of outstanding success stories. The National Academy of Sciences in the mid-1980s was so disappointed with the statistical work of NCES that it recommended the dissolution of that entity if immediate corrective measures were not taken.[70] Faced with that harsh reality, a few dedicated and talented individuals emerged who accepted the challenge. Working closely with the appropriate OERI staff as well as with several influential members of Congress, they managed within the space of only a few years to create an organization that is now acknowledged as a distinguished and effective federal statistical agency.[71] Given the challenges and opportunities facing OERI today, much more has to be done to make OERI a first-class federal agency. While the task of reforming and improving OERI will be difficult, it can be done if both Congress and the executive branch are willing to work together in a bipartisan fashion to restructure the agency into one capable of providing the high-quality research, development, and statistics needed to help all American children thrive educationally in the twenty-first century.

Comment by Carl F. Kaestle

Maris A. Vinovskis and I were colleagues at the University of Wisconsin many years ago, and we collaborated on a book and some articles back in the 1970s. We have different political instincts but agree on many things about the history of American education and about educational research. We have also had some similar relationships to the Office of

Educational Research and Improvement (OERI), the subject of Vinovskis's paper. We both have written about the history of the agency, and we both have spent some time around it. But Vinovskis on both of these counts—knowing the history of the agency and hanging around its hallways—has gone far beyond anything I have done, so my remarks on his paper are given with some modesty and as a friend. Still, worrying about the fate of the National Institute of Education (NIE) and OERI has been a Division I sport since 1972, so I am not unusual in having opinions on the matter.

Vinovskis begins his paper with an argument that policymakers need better federally sponsored research to evaluate federal programs designed to help disadvantaged youth and to create alternative approaches to educating these kids. This policy emphasis is understandable, not only because Vinovskis has been steeped in the literature on these programs for the past few years, but also because the education of disadvantaged children is an important and legitimate focus of federally funded research.

However, pinnng the justification for better federally funded education research principally on its potential usefulness in assisting federal education policy may be unrealistic. This may overestimate its potential, on the one hand, and give too narrow a view of the functions and audiences of federally funded education research, on the other. I do not think that solid educational research evidence will ever be a litmus test for the establishment of new federal policies, and I think its application to ongoing programs will always be controversial, even with more and better evaluation research. Nonetheless, the aim should be for more and better evaluation. To do so will require policymakers and researchers to collaborate in building a new cohort of better trained researchers, making strong provisions for evaluation in policies and legislation, and perhaps experimenting with ideas such as that proposed by Chester E. Finn Jr. to run state trials followed by tough evaluations, in advance of launching national policies in a given area.

Nonetheless, policymakers are not likely to achieve consensus about the effectiveness of education programs in advance of their launch or in their first few years of operation. Politicians have to decide whether to establish programs on the basis of necessarily fragmentary, preliminary evidence, often from analogous programs that are not the same or from pilot programs, the results of which can be argued either way. Whether the program is about compensatory education to fight poverty, inclusion in special education, block grants for more responsive decisionmaking, systemic reform for higher academic achievement, or vouchers for generally more effective schooling, the problems are the same. A tidy, attractive model sometimes invoked from research and development (R&D) in business or the military begins with laboratory-scale production followed by evaluation, then moves to pilot-scale production and evaluation, and finally to larger-scale production and evaluation. However, this model will probably not save educational research and development. It does not always work well in other sectors, and it rarely pertains to education (although I would not mind seeing it attempted more often and more rigorously). The variables in education are not as controllable and the process is more complicated. Because the activity is important, public, and political, education R&D is not allowed the insulation and time that careful, research-based development and evaluation enjoys in other more protected spheres.

Policymakers should be given the best, toughest evaluations possible, as promptly as possible, and their limitations and usefulness should be made clear. But education researchers should not be expected to make quick summary judgments about complex educational processes and outcomes. They are better, in the short run, at assessing the importance of context, the ambiguity of program labels, the appearance and impact of unintended consequences, and other complexities. Over the longer haul, they may reach some consensus about trends in educational outcomes. Even when the drift of judgment about effectiveness seems to be going in one direction, there will always be diverse studies and results, and policymakers can select the research that supports their own policy instincts and interests.

Major compensatory programs are always moving targets. Good policymakers are interested not only in short-term learning measures but also in long-term outcomes, the persistence of academic gains, and nonacademic goals in late youth or early adulthood. Thus, the research has to be long term. In the meantime, while multiyear longitudinal research is progressing, the program is changed, presumably for the better. So when results arrive from Ypsilanti, the *Prospects* study, or some other source, researchers are evaluating data from a program as it existed some years before. The results are relevant, but not conclusive.

Again I am not arguing that tough-minded evaluations of federally funded education programs are not needed but that the launching and the early adjustment of programs will often have to continue without thorough, credible evaluation of outcomes—whether it is big federal programs, Chicago decentralization, Milwaukee choice, or Success for All. It is the nature of the beast. A program's effectiveness cannot be fully evaluated until a substantial investment has been made in it. Even then, if it is tinkered with along the way (as it should be), the evaluations will always be a little out-of-date.

If I seem to be more skeptical than Vinovskis about education research in the service of federal policy, I am also reminded of other, more diffuse purposes of education research. In educational federalism (a complicated American invention), the tilt in educational governance is toward the state and district levels. Only a small portion of policy and practice is determined at the federal level. But education research sponsored by the federal government can have an influence on policy and practice determined at the state level, by the district, in the school building, in the classroom, or for an individual student. Federally sponsored research can serve all of these actors, and agencies such as OERI must keep all of them in mind. The school finance research of the 1970s was largely relevant at the state level; the recent work on reading is relevant to states, school districts, and individual teachers, as is work on cognitively guided instruction in math or the work on domain-specific knowledge conducted at the Learning and Research Development Center in Pittsburgh. So, while I agree with Vinovskis that the main agency charged with conducting educational research should be doing a more impressive job evaluating large federal initiatives and exploring alternatives, I would keep in mind the many nonfederal uses of federally funded education research.

Vinovskis considers possible areas for improvement in the structure, personnel, and purposes of OERI. I will select only a few for discussion: changing the structure of OERI, restoring its capacity for high-quality research, and bringing focus to its fragmented research mission.

One recurring issue in the twenty-eight-year history of OERI has been the desire to insulate it from politics and give it stability through some structural design. The same thing was heard in 1999, from various quarters. Vinovskis seems properly skeptical about this, though he says that the performance of the agency is so problematic that thoughts about restructuring should be entertained. I believe that the quest for a haven from politics is quixotic. It did not work with NIE (witness the treatment on Capitol Hill of Tom Glennan, NIE's first director, or the Reagan administration's summary dismissal of the independent NIE research board chaired by Harold "Doc" Howe). And after the National Center for Education Statistics (NCES) had developed a remarkable reputation for independence and impartiality, it was thrust overnight into the Clinton administration's education program as the main developer and advocate of the president's Voluntary National Test. Politics can scale any walls in Washington, especially if the walls were built with federal dollars.

The costs of restructuring are fearsome and should not be taken lightly. When people look back on the creation of the Department of Education, the creation of OERI, even the more modest restructuring of NIE under Patricia Graham, they uniformly tell tales of paralysis, deep decline of morale, and preoccupation with bureaucratic adjustments in jobs and functions that last months and months. The authors of such changes later expressed doubts that structural changes matter much. In the oral histories I did for the National Research Council's committee on the previous OERI reauthorization, the following remarks were made about reorganizations that had taken place from the mid-1970s to the mid-1980s: Virginia Richardson, head of research on teaching at NIE, said there was "more cost than benefit"; Sally Kilgore, director of the Office of Research, said it was an "incredible distraction"; Chester Finn, assistant secretary of OERI, said, "The more I've been here, the less I think that you cause change by moving boxes around"; and Ernest Boyer, commissioner of education, said, "Structure is almost totally inconsequential."[72] Isn't that some sort of bipartisan consensus? Before politicians undertake to save OERI by abolishing it and starting over, recall that one never "starts over" in Washington bureaucracies. New structures will not change ongoing obligations, existing staff, and—more important—existing attitudes. What is wrong is something deeper than structure and harder to change.

I agree with Vinovskis's central emphasis on the gradual, regrettable dilution of the research orientation and research capacity of OERI, a woeful, vicious circle. I join him in applauding Kent McGuire's emphasis on repairing this capacity. I agree with his well-phrased statement that there is no easy or ideal answer. I agree that the main problems are research capacity, stability, leadership, and focus. Repairing these does not preclude some structural changes within the framework of OERI. The notion that something like the success of NCES could be replicated on the research side of OERI lingers. Some have urged a fixed term for the head of OERI. I do not know what kind of animal a fixed-term assistant secretary is. It sounds like a mythical animal, like Doctor Doolittle's Push-me-Pull-you, with two heads. But perhaps there could be a commissioner of education research parallel to the commissioner of education statistics, in charge of a Center for Education Research.

These changes might facilitate a renewed dedication to quality research, with the assistant secretary still in charge of the office as a whole, with a reduced portfolio of improvement activities, plus two centers with fixed-term commissioners. The twin demand would be to reduce the fragmentation of the research agenda itself. Vinovskis rightly points out that this will necessitate hard thinking about the role of the labs and centers, and, I would add, the five institutes within OERI, which are diverse in their coverage and have not fulfilled their potential following that structural change within OERI. They were not funded as amply as some had hoped. Their directorships were too long filled with acting appointments, and then permanently with agency staff, not the visible outsiders who would bring new energy and prominence to the agency's research mission. Apart from these considerations, if OERI adopts the proposal of the National Education Research Planning and Priorities Board for a more focused research agenda, it will mean that the structure and activities of the institutes need to be reevaluated.

These commitments—to revitalize the central research mission of OERI and to focus its research agenda on a shorter list of priorities—might mean internal structural changes of some magnitude. But they would remain within the structure of OERI. Abolishing the agency to keep it from politics is, I think, wishful thinking. Abolishing it to escape its reputation and its diminished capacity avoids the issues that have led to its low reputation and its diminished capacity, issues that will not go away with a new acronym and a new address. What is needed is a new consensus; a consensus spanning Congress, the secretary of education's office, the agency itself, the research community, and the leaders of policy and practice groups; a consensus that OERI must define, sponsor, evaluate, synthesize, and use high-quality research around a focused agenda of long-term, practical importance. It would follow from such a consensus that OERI must recruit a small cadre of research leaders. It needs to have in place shortly after the new administration takes office an energetic assistant secretary with first-rate credentials in research leadership and the uses of research. It will have to redirect the existing staff to a new priority on quality—quality peer review, quality monitoring, and new opportunities for professional development directly related to research. To survive, the agency will have to dedicate itself to the proposition that better work on a smaller agenda is mandatory.

The agency desperately needs to reverse the downward spiral of low performance, low respect, low expectation, and low resources. The agency should not be cast aside, and in my opinion, its salvation does not depend mainly upon restructuring. Instead, OERI needs a change of will, a sense of urgency that the work must be done better, and a newfound confidence that it can be done better. Perhaps this will not happen until (in the words of the 1960s rock song) "the moon is in the Seventh House and Jupiter aligns with Mars," but it is, nonetheless, what the agency needs.

Comment by Thomas K. Glennan Jr.

Maris A. Vinovskis has provided a comprehensive analysis of the problems that the U.S. Department of Education (and previously, the Department of Health, Education, and Welfare) has faced in creating an effective research and development (R&D) program. Basing his analysis on his deep knowledge of the history of the Office of Educational Research and Improvement (OERI) and its predecessor, the National Institute of Education (NIE), he sets forth seven problems that have inhibited the conduct and sponsorship of educational R&D in the department:

1. The lack of sufficient autonomy, independence, and prominence of the organizational locations of the departmental R&D enterprise.
2. The limited numbers and low quality of staff, particularly in recent years.
3. Limited resources to support R&D.
4. The fragmented, episodic, and short-term nature of the individual R&D efforts.
5. Low quality in the research and development itself.
6. Turnover in top agency leadership and uneven quality in the middle-level management leaders.
7. Overly strong emphasis of politics (as opposed to science merit) in the development of the agency's agenda.

As the first director of NIE, I had intimate familiarity with many of the problems Vinovskis cites in the early years of federal support for education R&D. I know little of the activities of the 1980s and early 1990s. Recently I have been working on issues of research quality with the current OERI leadership. On the basis of this incomplete experience, I find little quarrel with the facts he presents and the picture that he paints. However, the fairly even-handed painting of his picture may provide a potpourri of suggested reforms when a narrower and more focused effort is required.

In my view, much of the situation that OERI faces today can be traced to the pattern of funding for educational research since the early 1970s when NIE was created. NIE was established in response to many of the same concerns that Vinovskis outlines; for example, poor-quality and fragmented research, inadequate funding, too many politically motivated projects, a lack of organizational independence, and inadequate staff talent. NIE was provided independence, the opportunity to hire new staff, and, by today's standards, fairly substantial funding. NIE's first-year budget was nearly $500 million in today's dollars, and the Nixon administration asked for a substantial increase for its second year.[73]

In fiscal 1973 NIE's proposed budget contained nearly the only request for increased funding in the entire federal educational budget, a fact that did not endear it to the legions of lobbyists for various education causes. NIE (and its intended mission) began life with the unenviable role of being the Nixon administration's excuse for not spending more on education. Moreover, the mere establishment of a new agency did not increase Congress's dim view of the quality of educational research. The leadership of NIE clearly failed to build the needed support in Congress and with important elements of the education community. The result was not only a failure to obtain the hoped-for increases in funding but also a 50 percent cut in the appropriations for research from nearly $500 million in fiscal 1973 to just over $200 million in fiscal 1974 (1999 dollars).

It is hard to overstate the negative consequences the cut had for the agency. It had been successful in attracting capable new staff, but many were quickly thrown into scaling back existing programs rather than building the new ones that NIE had been intended to create. While little doubt exists that, from a scientific perspective, many of the programs that NIE tried to eliminate had little value, the need to make the cuts further exacerbated the divisive political wrangling that has so frequently characterized the NIE and OERI reauthorizations and appropriations over the years.

From fiscal 1974 through 1980, NIE continued with funding at a little less than $200 million a year (1999 dollars). Some important planning was done and research supported. However, beginning with the Reagan administration, funding steadily fell, reaching levels as low as $65 million (1999 dollars) around 1990.[74] Since that time, educational research funding in OERI has begun to rise and in fiscal 1999 stands at about $160 million, still only a small fraction of what was contemplated at NIE's founding.[75]

From my perspective then, the key problems of federal education research stem from its low funding and dysfunctional political battles over dividing up that limited funding. The key to future success of federal support for educational R&D is obtaining more funds and resisting the temptation to spread them among many potential claimants. The best hope for more funds is to clearly demonstrate the value of educational R&D and the capacity of OERI to manage that R&D. While I do not doubt that many or all of the changes that Vinovskis proposes are desirable, I think that the time they require and the political energy that is likely to be needed to achieve many of them will detract from this important task.

To demonstrate the usefulness of effective and focused education R&D, I would avoid devoting limited managerial resources to immediate restructuring of the existing research programs. Instead, I would focus on the effective use of the limited increases in funding now being provided by Congress in this time of high national concern about education and economic prosperity. I would emphasize a small number of problem areas of unquestioned national importance such as literacy and numeracy, and I would frame the research program in a way that sets that program on a (perhaps ten-year) course to making major contributions to solving those problems.

In the near term, OERI probably lacks the ability to recruit first-rate intellectual leadership to its regular staff. But this does not seem to be the most important near-term goal. What seems far more important is to engage some of the best minds in the field in the planning, conduct, and assessment of the performance of the programs. Perhaps leading members of the research and practice community can be brought together in study groups, panels, or networks to perform these functions. In doing this, OERI should draw upon the managerial experience of more credible research agencies such as the National Institutes of Health and the National Science Foundation (NSF), which rely heavily on members of the research community to plan research and evaluate proposals and progress.

While the full value of such an effort will be known only some time in the future, let me propose some indicators by which Congress, the public, and the educational community can judge the conduct of the program:

—It attracts solid research performers and creates an active and exciting research community.

—It engages practitioners both as performers and users; the work is continually tested against the needs of users.

—It actively promotes the accumulation of understanding, providing regular reflection on what has been learned and what new work is needed.

—It discards unproductive lines of inquiry.

—The work of the program involves development—it produces programs, embodying the findings of research that can be demonstrated to be effective.

Most important, perhaps, such programs lead to a critical mass of individuals and institutions that are engaged in sustained inquiry and development.

Program elements needed to carry out such problem-centered program efforts are already in place. OERI, NSF, and the National Institute for Child and Human Development (NICHD) have joined to carry out an Interagency Educational Research Initiative in fiscal 1999 and the Clinton administration has asked for increased funding for fiscal 2000. Parts of the field-initiated studies program might be focused on these priorities, and several of the National Research Centers and Regional Laboratories have important and relevant work under way or planned. The problem is to bring direction, coherence, and cumulativeness to the effort.

However, one factor emphasized by Vinovskis cannot be ignored. Limiting OERI's focus to a few key problems, engaging the best of the nation's research community in dealing with those problems, and selling the effort to Congress is critical. Without leadership capable and willing to do this, I fear federal support for education R&D will continue to have the features Vinovskis has laid out.

Notes

1. On the federal role in education statistics and research after the Civil War, see Harry Kursch, *The United States Office of Education: A Century of Service* (Philadelphia, Pa.: Chilton Books, 1965); Manuel J. Justiz and Lars G. Bjork, eds., *Higher Education: Research and Public Policy* (New York: MacMillan, 1988); and Donald R. Warren, *To Enforce Education: A History of the Founding Years of the United States Office of Education* (Wayne State University Press, 1974). On the more general developments in educational research in the twentieth century, see Ellen Condliffe Lagemann, "Contested Terrain: A History of Education Research in the United States, 1890–1990," *Educational Researcher*, vol. 26, no. 9 (December 1997), pp. 5–17.

2. David Featherman and Maris A. Vinovskis, "Growth and Use of Social and Behavioral Science in the Federal Government since World War II," in David Featherman and Maris A. Vinovskis, eds., *The Social Sciences and Policy Making* (University of Michigan Press, forthcoming).

3. Julie Roy Jeffrey, *Education for Children of the Poor: A Study of the Origins and Implementation of the Elementary and Secondary Education Act of 1965* (Ohio State University Press, 1978); and Charles Philip Kearney, "The 1964 Presidential Task Force on Education and the Elementary and Secondary Education Act of 1965," Ph.D. dissertation, University of Chicago, 1964.

4. On the effectiveness of federal compensatory education programs, see Steven Barnett and Sarane Spence Boocock, eds., *Early Care and Education for Children in Poverty: Promises, Programs, and Long-Term Results* (Albany, N.Y.: State University of New York Press, 1998); Ron Haskins, "Beyond Metaphor: The Efficacy of Early Childhood Education," *American Psychologist*, vol. 44 (1989), pp. 274–82; Robert E. Slavin and others, *Effective Programs for Students at Risk* (Boston: Allyn and Bacon, 1994); and Maris A. Vinovskis, "Do Federal Compensatory Education Programs Really Work?: A Brief Historical Analysis of Title I and Head Start," *American Journal of Education*, vol. 107, no. 3 (May 1999), pp. 187–209.

5. For discussions of the new reforms, see Michael G. Fullan, "Turning Systemic Thinking on Its Head," *Phi Delta Kappan*, vol. 77, no. 6 (February 1996), pp. 400–07; John F. Jennings, ed., *National Issues in Education: Elementary and Secondary Act* (Bloomington, Ind.: Phi Delta Kappa International, 1995); John F. Jennings, *Why National Standards and Tests?: Politics and the Quest for Better Schools* (Thousand Oaks, Calif.: Sage Publications, 1998); Stanley Pogrow, "Reforming the Wannabe Reformers: Why Education Reforms Almost Always End Up Making Things Worse," *Phi Delta Kappan*, vol. 77, no. 10 (June 1996), pp. 656–63; Diane Ravitch, ed., *Debating the Future of American Education: Do We Need National Standards and Assessments?* (Brookings, 1995); Diane Ravitch, *National Standards in American Education: A Citizen's Guide* (Brookings, 1995); Robert Rothman, *Measuring Up: Standards, Assessment, and School Reform* (San Francisco: Jossey-Bass, 1995); Mary Jean Le Tendre, "Supporting School Reform through Title I," *Journal of Education for Students Placed at Risk*, vol. 1, no. 3 (1996), pp. 207–08; and Maris A. Vinovskis, "An Analysis of the Concept and Uses of Systemic Educational Reform," *American Educational Research Journal*, vol. 33, no. 1 (Spring 1996), pp. 53–85.

6. Robert E. Slavin, "Design Competitions: A Proposal for a New Federal Role in Educational Research and Development," *Educational Researcher*, vol. 26, no. 1 (January/February 1997), p. 22.

7. Kursch, *The United States Office of Education*; Warren, *To Enforce Education*.

8. For example, see Victor W. Hennigsen III, "Reading, Writing, and Reindeer: The

Development of Federal Education in Alaska, 1877–1920," Ed.D. dissertation, Harvard University, 1987; Paul C. Pickett, "Contributions of John Ward Studebacker to American Education," Ph.D. dissertation, University of Iowa, 1967; Darrell H. Smith, *The Bureau of Education: Its History, Activities, and Organization* (Johns Hopkins University Press, 1923); and Stephen J. Sniegoski, "John Eaton, U.S. Commissioner of Education, 1870–1886," December 1994.

9. For discussions of the state of educational research in this period, see Benjamin S. Bloom, "Twenty-Five Years of Educational Research," *American Educational Research Journal*, vol. 3, no. 3 (May 1966), pp. 211–21; Orville Brim Jr., *Sociology and the Field of Education* (New York: Russell Sage Foundation, 1965); John B. Carroll, "Neglected Areas in Educational Research," *Phi Delta Kappa*, vol. 42, no. 8 (May 1961), pp. 339–46; Arthur P. Coladarci, "More Rigorous Educational Research," *Harvard Educational Review*, vol. 30, no. 1 (Winter 1960), pp. 3–11; Lee J. Cronbach and Patrick Suppes, eds., *Research for Tomorrow's Schools: Disciplinary Inquiry for Education* (New York: MacMillan, 1969); and Carter V. Good, "Educational Research after Fifty Years," *Phi Delta Kappan*, vol. 37, no. 4 (January 1956), pp. 145–52.

10. Richard A. Dershimer, *The Federal Government and Educational R&D* (Lexington, Mass.: Lexington Books, 1976); and Lee Sproull, Stephen Weiner, and David Wolf, *Organizing an Anarchy: Belief, Bureaucracy, and Politics in the National Institute of Education* (University of Chicago Press, 1978).

11. Robert Glaser, ed., *Improving Education: Perspectives on Educational Research* (Pittsburgh, Pa.: National Academy of Education, 1984); and Philip Zodhiates, "Bureaucrats and Politicians: The National Institute of Education and Educational Research under Reagan," Ed.D. dissertation, Harvard University, 1988.

12. Some policymakers such as former representative John Brademas and former secretary of education Terrel Bell would have preferred that the Office of Educational Research and Improvement (OERI) be abolished and all of the research and development (R&D) activities placed in the National Institute of Education (NIE). John Brademas, *The Politics of Education: Conflict and Consensus on Capitol Hill* (University of Oklahoma Press, 1987), p. 76.

13. Maris A. Vinovskis, *Changing Federal Strategies for Supporting Educational Research, Development, and Statistics* (Washington: National Educational Research Policy and Priorities Board, 1998), pp. 25–26, 34–35. The budgets for OERI have been reconstructed from OERI documents and the House and Senate appropriation committee reports. I am indebted to Thomas Brown of OERI in particular for his assistance in assembling the recent budgets. For analytic purposes, OERI budget funds for the library programs were excluded as the unit was run separately from the other operations.

14. While Congress has pushed for the transfer of other research-related programs in the Department of Education to OERI, so far little has been accomplished. While the Department of Education has said that OERI is now coordinating and overseeing much of the other research-related activities, in practice OERI has not increased its involvement significantly.

15. Remarks made at *Education Research*, hearings before the Senate Committee on Health, Education, Labor, and Pensions, April 14, 1999.

16. Some individuals in OERI expressed surprise and strong disappointment with Assistant Secretary Kent McGuire's proposal to transfer some of the nonresearch functions elsewhere. They felt that there is no reason that an agency such as OERI should not handle both research and more direct reform-oriented activities. While these critics may be correct in principle, in practice OERI has become so bereft of researchers that it may be necessary

to shed these more service-oriented activities to refocus the energies of the agency on research and development. If as the more service-oriented programs are transferred elsewhere the full-time equivalents (FTEs) of the individuals who administered them are also shifted out of OERI, the overall benefits to the agency would be considerably diminished.

17. On the difficulties of doing systematic program evaluations in the Department of Education, see Maris A. Vinovskis, "Missing in Practice?: Systematic Development and Rigorous Program Evaluation at the U.S. Department of Education," paper presented at the Conference on Evaluation of Educational Policies, American Academy of Arts and Sciences, Cambridge, Mass., May 13–14, 1999.

18. The nature of the program evaluations would vary according to the types of information needed. For the most rigorous and statistically reliable studies, the use of randomized-assignment control groups should be considered—though the much higher costs of these efforts will limit the number of studies that can be expected to employ this approach. Planned variation projects, building upon the work of the early 1970s in educational evaluation, can be profitably used in many other instances. And more limited and less costly information might be routinely gathered in most projects to provide guidance and feedback to local areas to help them make any necessary improvements. Testimony of Maris A. Vinovskis, "Improving Federal Educational Research, Development, and Evaluation," *Overview of Federal Education Research and Evaluation Efforts*, joint hearings before the House Committee on Education and the Workforce and Senate Committee on Health, Education, Labor, and Pensions, June 17, 1999.

19. On the problems of reorganization, see Carl F. Kaestle, "The Awful Reputation of Education Research," *Educational Researcher*, vol. 22, no. 7 (January/February 1993), pp. 23–31; and Grady McGonagill, "Reorganization—Faith and Skepticism: A Case Study of the 1977–78 Reorganization of the National Institute of Education," M.A. thesis, Harvard University, 1981.

20. The figures on changes in staff FTEs were provided by Sharon Taylor of the Department of Education, Budget Services, May 1997.

21. Robert Boruch, "The Importance of Randomized Field Trials in Education and Elsewhere," paper presented at the Conference on Evaluation of Educational Policies, American Academy of Arts and Sciences, Cambridge, Mass., May 13–14, 1999; and Thomas Cook, "Considering the Major Arguments against Random Assignment: An Analysis of the Intellectual Culture Surrounding Evaluation in American Schools of Education," paper presented at the Conference on Evaluation of Educational Policies, American Academy of Arts and Sciences, Cambridge, Mass., May 13–14, 1999.

22. Diane Ravitch, "The State of the Agency," *OERI Bulletin*, no. 1 (Winter 1992–93), p. 2.

23. One does not necessarily have to be a trained and experienced researcher to be a good OERI assistant secretary—and several of the better assistant secretaries were not distinguished researchers themselves. However, they do have to have an understanding and appreciation of the strengths and weaknesses of the fields of research and development. Moreover, they should have at least some capable researchers on their staff and in leadership positions to help them develop and implement appropriate research and development strategies.

24. On the general weakness of the field of education research and development as well as the poor reputation of its scholars, see Alexander W. Astin, "The Decline in Public Faith in Education Research," in Manuel J. Justiz and Lars B. Bjork, eds., *Higher Education Research and Public Policy* (New York: MacMillan, 1988), pp. 147–56; Kaestle, "The Awful Reputation of Education Research"; Lagemann, "Contested Terrain"; Gerald

E. Sroufe, "Improving the 'Awful Reputation' of Education Research," *Educational Researcher*, vol. 26, no. 7 (October 1997), pp. 26–28.

25. Zodhiates, "Bureaucrats and Politicians."

26. See Vinovskis, *Changing Federal Strategies for Supporting Educational Research, Development, and Statistics.*

27. For example, see Richard C. Atkinson and Gregg B. Jackson, *Research and Education Reform: Roles for the Office of Educational Research and Improvement* (Washington: National Academy Press, 1992).

28. National Educational Research Policy and Priorities Board, *Investing in Learning: A Policy Statement on Research in Education* (Department of Education, April 5, 1999), p. vii.

29. Independent Review Panel on the Evaluation of Federal Education Legislation, *Measured Progress: An Evaluation of the Impact of Federal Legislation Enacted in 1994* (Department of Education, April 1999), p. 20. I was one of twenty-three members on the panel.

30. For a summary of this position as well as a refutation of it, see the testimony of Diane Ravitch at *Education Research*, hearing before the Senate Committee on Health, Education, Labor, and Pensions, April 14, 1999.

31. Astin, "The Decline in Public Faith in Education Research"; and Kaestle, "The Awful Reputation of Education Research."

32. On the lack of interest in long-term educational research and development, see Brademas, *The Politics of Education,* pp. 14–48.

33. General Accounting Office, *Education Information: Changes in Funds and Priorities Have Affected Production and Quality*, GAO/PEMD–88–4 (Washington, 1987).

34. Justiz and Bjork, *Higher Education Research and Public Policy.*

35. See Vinovskis, *Changing Federal Strategies for Supporting Educational Research, Development, and Statistics.*

36. The recent OERI research priorities plan is not adequate and was not available to be used in the allocation of funds for most of the current R&D centers. For example, see Maris A. Vinovskis, *History and Educational Policymaking* (Yale University Press, 1999), chapter 8.

37. Lynn Olson, "NRC Seeks New Agenda for Research: Proposal Calls for Year-Long Dialogue," *Education Week*, vol. 18, no. 31 (April 14, 1999), pp. 1, 27.

38. National Academy of Education, *Recommendations Regarding Research Priorities* (New York, March 1999).

39. National Educational Research Policy and Priorities Board, *Investing in Learning*, p. iv, emphasis in original.

40. The Senate Budget Committee Task Force on Education has raised questions about the structure and effectiveness of the National Educational Research Policy and Priorities Board (NERPPB). It recommends that the model of the National Assessment Governing Board (NAGB) be used instead. Senate Budget Committee Task Force on Education, *Prospects for Reform: The State of American Education and the Federal Role,* interim report (Washington, 1998). For a discussion of the strengths and weaknesses of NAGB, see Maris A. Vinovskis, *Overseeing the Nation's Report Card: The Creation and Evolution of the National Assessment Governing Board* (Washington: National Assessment Governing Board, November 1998).

41. Maris A. Vinovskis, "Analysis of the Quality of Research and Development at the OERI Research and Development Centers and the OERI Regional Educational Laboratories," OERI, June 1993.

42. Michael Timpane, *National Directions in Education Research Planning* (National Educational Research Policy and Priorities Board, December 1998), p. 8.

43. Vinovskis, "Missing in Practice?"

44. Vinovskis, "Improving Federal Educational Research, Development, and Evaluation."

45. For discussion of the Comprehensive Regional Assistance Centers, see Katrina G. Laguarda and others, *A Conceptual Framework for an Evaluation of the Comprehensive Regional Assistance Centers* (Washington: Policy Studies Associates, December 1997).

46. Vinovskis, "Improving Federal Educational Research, Development, and Evaluation."

47. On the uses of research in the area of adolescent pregnancy, see Maris A. Vinovskis, "The Use and Misuse of Social Science Analysis in Federal Adolescent Pregnancy Policy," Distinguished Lectures in the Social Sciences, Northern Illinois University, DeKalb, Ill., November 1989.

48. Roald F. Campbell and others, *R&D Funding Policies of the National Institute of Education: Review and Recommendations, National Institute of Education* (Department of Health, Education, and Welfare, 1975).

49. Atkinson and Jackson, *Research and Education Reform.*

50. Daniel B. Levine, ed., *Creating a Center for Education Statistics: A Time for Action* (Washington: National Academy Press, 1986).

51. Vinovskis, "Analysis of the Quality of Research and Development at the OERI Research and Development Centers and the OERI Regional Educational Laboratories."

52. P.L. 103–227, Title IX, Section 941 (h) (7).

53. National Educational Research Policy and Priorities Board, *Attaining Excellence: A Handbook on the Standards for the Conduct and Evaluation of Research Carried Out by the Office of Educational Research and Improvement* (Department of Education, April 1999).

54. Diane August and Lana D. Muraskin, "Strengthening the Standards: Recommendations for OERI Peer Review," Summary Report Draft, National Educational Research Policy and Priorities Board, January 30, 1999.

55. For a discussion of the difficult issues involved in ascertaining the quality of the work in these areas, see Maris A. Vinovskis, "An Analysis of the Proposed Phase Three Standards for the Conduct and Evaluation of OERI Activities," background paper prepared for OERI, March 26, 1997; and Maris A. Vinovskis, "Measuring the Interim Performance of the Regional Educational Laboratory's Educational Research and Development Activities," background paper prepared for the U.S. Department of Education, October 4, 1998.

56. See Vinovskis, *Changing Federal Strategies for Supporting Educational Research, Development, and Statistics.*

57. For example, see Paul E. Resta, "The Depoliticization of Educational Research," in Manuel J. Justiz and Lars G. Bjork, eds., *Higher Education Research and Public Policy* (New York: MacMillan, 1988), pp. 157–73.

58. Testimony of Diane Ravitch at *Education Research*, hearing before the Senate Committee on Health, Education, Labor, and Pension, April 14, 1999.

59. Personal communication of Chester E. Finn Jr. to Carolyn Breedlove, July 23, 1981. Quoted in Carolyn Jean Breedlove, "Origins of a Conflict: The National Institute of Education, the Laboratories and Centers, and the Congress, 1972–1976," Ed.D. dissertation, University of Illinois, 1996, p. 163.

60. For a useful summary of the developments in the sciences, see Joseph P. Martino, *Science Funding: Politics and Porkbarrel* (New Brunswick, N.J.: Transaction Publishers, 1992).

61. Constance Ewing Cook, *Lobbying for Higher Education: How Colleges and Universities Influence Federal Policy* (University of Michigan Press, 1998).

62. On the abuses in the use of federal funds to support political activities of the nonprofit groups in science-related activities, see James T. Bennett and Thomas J. DiLorenzo, *Cancer Scam: Diversion of Federal Cancer Funds to Politics* (New Brunswick, N.J.: Transaction Publishers, 1998).

63. Zodhiates, "Bureaucrats and Politicians."

64. Carol Innerst, "Goodling Plans Effort to Stop National Tests: Critics Fear Rise of National Curriculum," *Washington Times*, July 31, 1997, p. A7; Millicent Lawson, "House Blocks, While Panel Settles On, New Tests," *Education Week*, vol. 17, no. 13 (November 19, 1997), pp. 1, 20; and Millicent Lawson, "Test Proposal to be Tested by Experts," *Education Week*, vol. 17, no. 13 (November 19, 1997), pp. 1, 20.

65. "Pat Forgione is a strong and energetic leader of the National Center for Education Statistics [NCES]. In his brief time in that post, he has accomplished a great deal. He has ensured the quality and timeliness of publications, vigorously pursued the use of the World Wide Web to make NCES statistics more widely and readily available, and reorganized his staff in ways that connect their talents and interests more effectively with the work to which NCES is committed. All the while he has managed to have the agency respond successfully to an ever-increasing scope of work without increases in staff available to perform that work," wrote Andrew C. Porter, chair of Advisory Council of Education Statistics, to Richard W. Riley, secretary of education, November 3, 1998.

66. "For the past eight years, Mr. Forgione said, he has applied for an extension before the April 15 filing deadline for federal income-tax returns. But each of the years until this one, he missed the Aug. 15 deadline granted under those extensions. He has not paid penalties or been subjected to criminal charges, he said, because each year he has been due a refund. But the pattern has created an ethical cloud that administration officials did not want, he said. Mr. Forgione decided to withdraw his name from consideration last week so he can pursue others jobs." David J. Hoff, "Renomination Blocked, Forgione to Depart," *Education Week*, vol. 18, no. 37 (May 26, 1999), p. 3.

67. Considerable controversy arose over the appropriateness of Vice President Al Gore, instead of the commissioner of education statistics, releasing the 1998 National Assessment of Educational Progress report card. Mark Musick, chair of the National Assessment Governing Board, was among those protesting that Gore's actions violated established guidelines and procedures. Mark D. Musick, chair of NAGB, letter to Pascal D. Forgione Jr., commissioner of education statistics, February 18, 1999.

68. For discussions of this episode, see Jonathan Fox, "Forgione Resigns Post as Top ED Statistician," *Education Daily (*May 20, 1999), pp. 1–2; Jonathan Fox, "Politics Blamed for Ouster of NCES Commissioner," *Education Daily* (May 27, 1999), pp. 1–2; Hoff, "Renomination Blocked"; and David J. Hoff, "Republicans Vow to Free NCES from Political Meddling," *Education Week*, vol. 18, no. 38 (June 2, 1999), p. 18.

69. Senate Budget Committee Task Force on Education, *Prospects for Reform*, p. 25.

70. Levine, *Creating a Center for Education Statistics.*

71. Atkinson and Jackson, *Research and Education Reform.*

72. Carl F. Kaestle, *Everybody's Been to Fourth Grade: An Oral History of Federal R&D in Education*, report prepared for the National Research Council, Committee on the Federal Role in Education Research (Madison, Wis.: Wisconsin Center for Education Research, April 1992), p. 31.

73. While counted as research in the historical data, important parts of the programming that the National Institute of Education (NIE) inherited from the Office of Education and

the Office of Economic Opportunity were demonstration programs of limited research merit, which NIE's leaders expected to complete and replace with more research-oriented activities.

74. In interpreting these figures as research, it is important to understand that NIE and the Office of Educational Research and Improvement (OERI) have always carried dissemination activities such as the Educational Resources Information Clearinghouses in their research category. In fiscal 1990, 13 percent of the research budget was devoted to these efforts, and significant proportions of the activities of the Regional Educational Laboratories and Educational Research Centers were devoted to dissemination and technical assistance.

75. As Maris A. Vinovskis points out, Congress in the mid-1980s began to increase the funding for educational statistics and the National Assessment of Educational Progress as well as to add significant demonstration and limited service programs to OERI's portfolio. OERI today is responsible for nearly $800 million in programs.